D1565801

Moral Minorities
and the
Making of American Democracy

Moral Minorities and the Making of American Democracy

KYLE G. VOLK

OXFORD
UNIVERSITY PRESS

OXFORD
UNIVERSITY PRESS

Oxford University Press is a department of the University of
Oxford. It furthers the University's objective of excellence in research,
scholarship, and education by publishing worldwide.

Oxford   New York
Auckland   Cape Town   Dar es Salaam   Hong Kong   Karachi
Kuala Lumpur   Madrid   Melbourne   Mexico City   Nairobi
New Delhi   Shanghai   Taipei   Toronto

With offices in
Argentina   Austria   Brazil   Chile   Czech Republic   France   Greece
Guatemala   Hungary   Italy   Japan   Poland   Portugal   Singapore
South Korea   Switzerland   Thailand   Turkey   Ukraine   Vietnam

Oxford is a registered trademark of Oxford University Press
in the UK and certain other countries.

Published in the United States of America by
Oxford University Press
198 Madison Avenue, New York, NY 10016

© Oxford University Press 2014

An earlier version of Chapter 3 was published as "The Perils of 'Pure Democracy': Minority
Rights, Liquor Politics, and Popular Sovereignty in Antebellum America," *Journal of the Early
Republic* 29 (2009), 641–679.

Library of Congress Cataloging-in-Publication Data
Volk, Kyle G.
Moral minorities and the making of American democracy / Kyle G. Volk.
pages cm
Includes bibliographical references and index.
ISBN 978-0-19-937191-4 (hardback : acid-free paper)   1. Minorities—Civil rights—United
States—History—19th century.   2. Minorities—Political activity—United States—History—19th
century.   3. United States—Politics and government—1845–1861.   4. Democracy—United
States—History—19th century.   5. Political participation—United States—History—19th
century.   6. Dissenters—United States—History—19th century.   7. United States—
Moral conditions—History—19th century.   8. United States—Social conditions—19th
century.   9. United States—Ethnic relations—History—19th century.   I. Title.
E184.A1V73 2014
305.800973—dc23
2013050576

3 5 7 9 8 6 4 2
Printed in the United States of America
on acid-free paper

親愛的 許秀祺

Whenever you find yourself on the side of the majority, it is time to pause and reflect.

—MARK TWAIN

Contents

Acknowledgments

IN MY YOUTH, a trusted mentor known to everyone as "Cal" told my friends and me that it takes an entire community to educate one person. Since then I have discovered that education is a way of life that requires multiple communities. After working many years on this project, it is my pleasure to thank those who have helped along the way. At home, I thank George and Char for constant support and total love. They have always been on my team, a team that they routinely sponsored. Chris, Janice, Mikaela, and Brady rooted me on and provided the best escapes.

At Boston College, I was fortunate enough to walk into Alan Rogers's class as a freshman. He told the best stories, convinced me to become a history major, and later sent me off to get lost in the sources. I've never recovered. Lynn Lyerly inspired confidence and brought me to think critically about America's paradox of slavery and freedom. That she guided my senior research project while on leave is only the easiest way for me to convey her immense commitment to students. A model mentor, she has never stopped being a font of wisdom and a rock of support.

At the University of Chicago, where this project began, I was privileged to find several true teachers of graduate students among the faculty. Ted Cook, Kathy Conzen, Mae Ngai, and Jim Sparrow provided critical assistance at pivotal moments. With his characteristic enthusiasm, Bill Novak shared his vast knowledge of American law and government and breathed new life into political history. Amy Stanley understood this project from the beginning and did so many things along the way. My debt is immense. In addition to those faculty members, the chief benefit of studying at Chicago was the diverse group of fellow travelers that happened to be there at the dawn of the twenty-first century. For ideas and support, laughs and distractions, I thank Cathleen Cahill, Beth Cooper, Mike Czaplicki, Joanna Grisinger, Allyson Hobbs, Roman Hoyos, Michelle Huie, Jon Levy, Scott Lien, Matt Millikan, Steve Porter, Gautham Rao,

Andrew Sandoval-Strausz, Laurel Spindel, Tracy Steffes, and Ellen Wu. Thanks also to David Goodwine, Joanne Berens, and especially Diane Brady for making all of our lives easier.

The research for this book took me many places. Along the way, friends put me up and put up with me generally. Thanks to Wayne Harman, Jodi Pukl, Roshni Desai, Janice O'Campo, Kristine Marshall, Matt Towers, Tom Dunn, Matt Majewski, Emily Stanback, Anne Buckman, Paula Huie, Kin Lui, Chris Volk, Steve O'Reilly, Ernie Volkmann, Greg "Gene" Chludzinski, Mike O'Reilly, Erik Schneider, Krissy Frazao, and Mike Czaplicki. Numerous librarians and archivists opened doors to the past. Thanks to the staff at the University of Chicago's Regenstein Library; the University of Chicago Law Library; the University of Montana's Mansfield Library; the Massachusetts Historical Society; Houghton Library and the Divinity School Library at Harvard University; the Library Company of Philadelphia; the Historical Society of Pennsylvania; the Presbyterian Historical Society; Juniata College Special Collections; Chambersburg Public Library; Alexander Library at Rutgers University; Carnegie Library of Pittsburgh; University of Delaware's Morris Library; New York Public Library; Boston Public Library; the Nantucket Historical Society; Massachusetts State Archives; the American Jewish Archives in Cincinnati; the Cincinnati Historical Society; and the American Antiquarian Society. Special thanks to Jim Green, Wendy Woolson, and Nicole Joniec at the Library Company; Elizabeth Pope and Jackie Penny at the American Antiquarian Society; Nick Kersten at the Seventh Day Baptist Historical Society; and Donna McCrea at the Mansfield Library. For financial support, I thank the University of Chicago, the Dolores Zohrab Liebmann Fund, the Institute for Humane Studies, the Andrew W. Mellon Foundation, the University of Montana, the William Nelson Cromwell Foundation, the American Society for Legal History, the National Endowment for the Humanities, and the American Antiquarian Society.

As this project developed, I have greatly benefited from thoughtful commentary from scholars who were under no real obligation to provide it. Thanks to Michael Willrich, Barbara Welke, Richard John, Robin Einhorn, Bill Rorabaugh, Reeve Huston, Johann Neem, Harry Watson, Nancy Isenberg, Doug Bradburn, Bob Gordon, Manisha Sinha, Melissa Johnson, Steve Porter, Judy Giesberg, and Tracy Steffes. Special thanks also to the participants of the 2005 J. Willard Hurst Legal History Summer Seminar and to the members of the Upstate Early American History Workshop at SUNY Binghamton. I was fortunate to spend the better part of a year at the American Antiquarian Society, where this project started to become a book. Exchanging ideas with Elizabeth Dillon, Sean Harvey, Dan Rood, Lisa Wilson, Lois Horton, Jim Horton, Allison Stagg, Chris Pastore, and Steve Bullock made it stronger. Paul Erickson made sure we had what we needed and made our year at the AAS successful and enjoyable. Reeve Huston and several anonymous reviewers provided excellent suggestions that improved the manuscript.

In Missoula, my colleagues graciously commented on draft chapters and helped in many other ways. Thanks to Richard Drake, Linda Frey, Gillian Glaes, Robert Greene, Michelle Huie, Anya Jabour, Paul Lauren, Ken Lockridge, Mike Mayer, Pat O'Connor, Jody Pavilack, Rob Saldin, Tobin Shearer, Jeff Wiltse, and Erica Woodahl. Ken played with the entire manuscript and provided a world of insight. Jeff has heard more about this project than perhaps anyone else. His sage advice and incisive readings made this book better, while his discriminating palate made life better. A final thanks to Lisa, Erica, and Jeff for pulling me to the finish line.

The most thanks, of course, go to Waka for love and understanding.

Moral Minorities
and the
Making of American Democracy

Introduction

All, too, will bear in mind this sacred principle, that though the will of the majority is in all cases to prevail, that will, to be rightful, must be reasonable; that the minority possess their equal rights, which equal laws must protect, and to violate which would be oppression.

—THOMAS JEFFERSON, First Inaugural
Address (1801)

ON A SEPTEMBER evening in 1859, several thousand New Yorkers, most of them immigrants and many of them freethinkers or Catholics, made their way to a popular German beer garden in Manhattan's Bowery district. Dancing, singing, and lager were the typical attractions, but not this night. Two associations—the American Society for Promoting Civil and Religious Liberty and the German Association for Resisting All Arbitrary Sunday and Prohibitory Laws—had gathered "without distinction of sect or party" to oppose attempts by Protestant moralists "to revive and enforce the old Sunday laws." When local businessman Henry Garbanati ascended the stage, he echoed other speakers who had scorned prohibitions against work, play, and the sale of alcohol on the so-called Christian Sabbath as an affront to religious freedom. He challenged, in particular, the political justification of these measures. "The pretension of those who defended the Sunday laws," he observed, "was that they were formed in compliance with the will of the majority." Garbanati retorted that "the minority has its rights also, and...those rights as guaranteed by the Constitution, could not be invaded even by the majority." Sunday laws, he concluded, unconstitutionally infringed upon the rights of religious and cultural minorities. People in the audience agreed, for they pledged themselves "to resist to the utmost, now and forever, every attempt to interfere with our national and inalienable right to freedom of opinion and worship."[1]

That same year, black men and women in Providence, Rhode Island, protested local policies preventing their children from attending public schools with white children. A committee headed by businessman and abolitionist George T. Downing petitioned the state legislature to end school segregation, claiming it denied black children their constitutional rights to "equal school privileges." Supporters of separate schools had dismissed their pleas as irrelevant because "the large majority" of the community viewed race mixing as a grave immorality. To Downing and the other protesters, this argument was an abhorrent political "doctrine" because it suggested that "men or at least colored men have no rights which majorities may not dispose of." Downing and his friends responded with their own theory of democracy: "the majority" had no "right to do anything which violates the principle of the entire social equality" of the minority. Until the state ended segregation, these activists promised to advocate forcefully for their rights as a racial minority.[2]

In a democracy, should the majority always rule? If not, how should the rights of minorities be protected? Amid the rising majoritarianism, nativism, and racism of the mid-nineteenth century, a motley array of Americans tackled these recurrent questions anew. The New Yorkers combating Sunday laws and the Rhode Islanders challenging school segregation joined thousands of other Americans—black and white, native and foreign born, male and female—who challenged the received wisdom that majorities should rule absolutely. Told that such policies were appropriate because they embodied the majority's moral sensibilities, immigrants, entrepreneurs, drinkers, Jews, Catholics, Seventh Day Baptists, freethinkers, abolitionists, northern blacks, and others articulated an alternate vision of democracy. They rejected unbridled majority rule as the unquestioned source of political authority, identified fear of majority tyranny as a valid democratic concern, and included the protection of minority rights as a critical obligation of democratic government. Told that minorities like themselves should dutifully submit to the majority's wishes, they forged a new, popular minority-rights politics to defend their interests within America's emerging political order. In the process, they made vital contributions to the theory and practice of democracy that have shaped America's political culture down to the present.

This book tells the story of these self-understood minorities. It begins in the turbulent early nineteenth century when two concurrent forces transformed public life and set the stage for their encounter with majority rule. On the one hand, the rise of mass democracy—characterized by an expanding electorate, high voter turnout, and vigorous two-party politics— revolutionized American political life and produced new reverence for "majority rule." Whereas many republican statesmen of the late eighteenth century had sought to contain the influence of the people and the power of popular majorities in government, a new generation of democratic polit- icos following Andrew Jackson and Martin Van Buren emphasized the opposite. To them and their many followers, the political empowerment of white men and the rule of "the people" through their agent, the major- ity, defined the rising democracy. On the other hand, Protestant evangeli- cal ministers and lay men and women, in part because they feared these monumental political changes, spurred a different revolution in public life. Beginning in the 1820s and 1830s, these self-described moral reform- ers began grass-roots movements to ensure that a Christian moral major- ity ruled America's ascendant democracy. Their efforts were controversial and consequential. As moralists active in three of the most divisive cru- sades—the Sabbath reform, the temperance movement, and radical aboli- tionism—pressured policymakers and the public to embrace their agenda, they sparked dissent and initiated the nation's lasting practice of popular moral politics. The ensuing conflicts exposed competing conceptions of democracy, spawned popular minority-rights activism, and ignited broad reassessments of the era's hallowed promise of majority rule.

Temperance reformers and Sabbath reformers seeking, respectively, to end alcohol consumption and to preserve the sanctity of the Christian Sabbath spurred these developments unintentionally. They strategically followed the majoritarian currents of the age, particularly as they sought to impose moral order through restrictive liquor and Sunday regulations. Most Americans, they said, were Christians who worshipped on Sundays; therefore, state laws and local ordinances preventing work and play on the Christian Sabbath were legitimate. Similarly, temperance reformers by the 1840s boldly insisted that a majority of Americans opposed drinking and favored new laws restricting and even prohibiting the sale of alcohol. Thus, such measures were entirely appropriate and perfectly democratic. But not everyone agreed. A diverse group of antireformers resisted the temperance and Sabbath crusades' punitive measures and offered a dif- ferent notion of democracy. Among them were Jews and Seventh Day Baptists, both religious groups that worshipped on Saturdays; European immigrants who recreated on Sundays and drank alcohol; and business owners who made a living selling alcohol. To these groups and their allies, majority rule in the hands of intrusive Protestant moralists became not the postulate of a free democracy but rather a despotic one. Majority rule, then, needed to be circumscribed so the rights of minorities could be protected.

Unlike temperance and Sabbath reformers who embraced majority rule to justify their efforts, the third set of moral reformers—black and white radical abolitionists—deliberately battled for minority rights. Abolitionists tackled a somewhat different moral problem—racial prejudice—as they struggled to eradicate northern policies mandating racial segregation in marriage, public schools, and public transportation. To abolitionists and their supporters, these policies demeaned black men, women, and children and bolstered the prejudice that undergirded slavery and poisoned the nation, north and south. They needed to be purged. Antiabolitionists and other defenders, however, countered that these race regulations preserved moral order by preventing amalgamation—the ungodly and licentious mixture of blacks and whites—which would degrade the white race and destroy the American republic if not curbed. Advocates further insisted that because an overwhelming majority of Americans abhorred amalgamation, segregation was entirely democratic. Black and white racial egalitarians disagreed. While combating segregation, they advanced a theory of democracy that checked the power of majorities and protected minorities, especially the racialized minority of black Americans.

In what might seem a case of strange bedfellows, abolitionists challenging segregation joined opponents of liquor and Sabbath regulations as vocal champions of minority rights during the age of majoritarian democracy's ascendance. Perhaps unsurprisingly, these groups did not always support each other's campaigns. Most abolitionists, for example, advocated temperance and rejected the pleas of immigrants and liquor dealers for the protection of minority rights in response to liquor regulations. Alternatively, most opponents of liquor regulation had little sympathy for the rights of black men and women. This, then, is not a story of ideological consistency or of a coherent movement for minority rights over majority rule. Few if any of the minority-rights defenders described in these pages thought the majority should *never* rule. Rather, each advocated particular circumstances in which the power of majorities should be limited, and predictably, each articulated boundaries consistent with their specific goals and interests. What they shared was, first, finding themselves on the wrong side of a purported moral norm enshrined in public policy and defended with the powerful concept of majority rule; and second, publicly resisting those norms and employing the equally powerful political discourse of majority tyranny and minority rights to challenge the supposed rule of majorities. Though acting separately and even inconsistently, these assorted moral minorities collectively countered the trajectory of a political era that celebrated majority rule. Beginning in the 1840s and expanding in the 1850s, their struggles with three of the great moral questions of the age—Sabbath observance, alcohol consumption, and racial prejudice—raised ethical dilemmas of America's democratic political order. Their activism pushed a generation to consider the manifold tyrannies that might accompany an unproblematic celebration of majority rule.

These moral minorities were not the first to raise questions about majority rule, nor were they alone in doing so in mid-nineteenth-century America. They built upon a well-established tradition dating back to the ancient world and continued by constitution-makers—James Madison most famously—during the era of the American Revolution. They sometimes expressed arguments similar to those used by nineteenth-century elites to limit popular participation in government and by slaveholders to safeguard slavery. Foes of Sabbath, liquor, and race regulations, however, transformed this tradition by making the struggle to protect the rights of minorities a thoroughly popular, democratic affair. Formerly, statesmen, intellectuals, and constitution-makers had dominated discussion of majority tyranny and sought to remedy it in learned treatises, through well-balanced constitutions of republican government, and in high politics. By contrast, the moral minorities championed a model of democratic political engagement that worked at the grass roots and targeted both public opinion and public policy. They mobilized elite and ordinary people—often across boundaries of class, religion, race, ethnicity, gender, and party affiliation—to form networks of dissent and associations dedicated to the protection of minority rights. They publicized their concerns widely through pamphlets, petitions, editorials, acts of civil disobedience, and public protests. They sought to overturn obnoxious policies by lobbying town meetings, school boards, and state legislatures and by using state constitutions and the common law to initiate "test cases" before local and appellate courts. In short, they pioneered a tradition of political participation and minority-rights advocacy that subsequent generations of activists would adopt.

If these antebellum moral minorities democratized minority-rights advocacy and developed new modes for asserting rights, they also altered the substance of minority-rights claims. Before the mid-nineteenth century, the predominant apprehension about majority rule concerned elite

property rights and the threat of the redistribution of wealth. James
Madison mustered this long-standing argument to justify the ratification
of the US Constitution. As he famously argued in *Federalist* 10, differences of opinion on religion and on government had divided societies, but
the leading cause of tyrannical majorities was the "various and unequal
distribution of property" and the tendency of propertyless majorities to
threaten the rights of the wealthy minority. Nineteenth-century conservatives would return to this argument to repel the expansion of voting rights
and other democratic reforms. And in the decades before the Civil War,
John Calhoun and other slaveholders added a southern flavor to the existing minority-rights thinking in order to defend the slaveholding minority
from local and national majorities that held no slave property. This tradition informed the opponents of Sabbath, liquor, and race regulations. At
times, they and their allies openly appropriated it in ways that reveal, if
somewhat ironically, the close connections between antidemocratic, conservative, and even proslavery ideas about minority rights and the vital
concepts of civil rights and civil liberties that continue to stir democratic
politics.[3]

Nonetheless, these mid-nineteenth-century moral minorities raised
different concerns that made countermajoritarianism newly relevant to
a wide array of Americans. These democratic theorists-in-action displayed to the nation how majority tyranny could stem not only from a
propertyless majority striking at the property rights of the few. It could
also come from moral regulations that transcended boundaries of class
and involved troubling issues of religious, racial, and ethno-cultural
discrimination. Property rights and other socioeconomic interests
regularly shaped their concerns, but these groups were not defending
themselves from a needy multitude seeking a redistribution of wealth.
Nor were they guarding the peculiar rights of slaveholders. If anything
they were protecting themselves from moral majorities, whether actual
or rhetorically conjured by influential elites and organizations that
mobilized public support for policies demanding moral conformity.
Classic fears about property redistribution would continue to animate
minority-rights thinking, but after the mid-nineteenth century they
operated alongside a more modern brand of social and cultural countermajoritarianism popularized by those challenging Sabbath, liquor,
and race regulations.[4]

Indeed, these moral minorities propagated a pluralistic conception of
democracy in which the protection of minority rights was essential to the

preservation of moral freedom, cultural diversity, and social equality. They protested against a democratic political order that enabled majorities to infringe upon a range of rights: rights to education, religion, travel, commerce, leisure, and consumption. Many of these "rights" had acquired particular social and economic value in the dynamic age of nineteenth-century market capitalism, thus making interference with them particularly objectionable. Moral minorities, however, also found such interference harmful to their communities and personally invasive. Majorities, they protested, invaded such cherished spaces as the home, the tavern and beer garden, the small business, and the schoolhouse, as well as the individual conscience. They dictated deeply personal decisions: whom to befriend and marry; when to work and worship; what to drink and how to structure one's leisure. With so much at stake—their interests, identities, cultures, social standing, and their very freedom within American democracy—it is little wonder that they resisted.

In developing these broadened defenses of minority rights, opponents of Sabbath, liquor, and race regulations grappled, at times explicitly, with the insights of French intellectuals Alexis de Tocqueville and Gustave de Beaumont. After visiting the United States in 1831, Tocqueville and Beaumont each crafted lengthy appraisals of American democracy. Their treatises highlighted the threat they believed the "tyranny of the majority" posed to popular liberty. In *Democracy in America*, Tocqueville saw majority tyranny manifesting not in the classic peril of the redistribution of wealth. Instead, he identified cultural constraints on "thought" and emphasized how the pressures of conformity brought by the "moral authority" of the majority were as coercive and as dangerous as formal governmental authority. "I know of no country," he famously declared, "in which there is less independence of mind and true freedom of discussion than in America." Tellingly, his prime examples were religious and moral in nature: the lack of organized atheism and the dearth of "licentious books." His often overlooked colleague, Beaumont, similarly lamented how the "irresistible" power of the majority "crushes, breaks, [and] annihilates everything which opposes its power and impedes its passions." Beaumont, however, focused on the incongruence of slavery and racism within America's supposedly free and equal democracy. His novel *Marie or, Slavery in the United States* exposed the rampant racial prejudice within the "free" northern states. He concentrated especially on the tyrannical moral taboo against interracial marriage decreed, he explained, by the majority. To both Tocqueville and Beaumont, moral freedom in various guises seemed decidedly and dangerously absent in American democracy. True liberty for those who disagreed with the moral authority of the majority seemed a doubtful prospect.[5]

During the several decades after Tocqueville's and Beaumont's visits, an explosion of grass-roots moral reform would bring Americans to debate the appropriate limits to majority rule and to implement the tactics needed to challenge moral majoritarianism. Those resisting Sabbath, liquor, and race regulations would play essential roles. They built upon Tocqueville's and Beaumont's observations as they turned the battle for minority rights into an organized, popular endeavor. In so doing, they shaped policy and public culture in their own time and left an enduring mark on American democracy.

THIS HISTORY OF grass-roots minority-rights activism recasts the political history of the United States during the antebellum period. Until now, most scholars have viewed and often celebrated the struggle for majority rule as the ideological essence of nineteenth-century democracy, so much so that some have simply overlooked claims for minority rights in this era. "Minority rights," a prominent political historian suggests, "had little room in a majoritarian heaven." Meanwhile, others recognizing minority-rights concerns have focused almost uniformly on opponents of democracy and defenders of slavery. This leaves the impression that concerns about majority rule and for minority rights in the nineteenth century mattered very little or were, at most, anachronistic and antidemocratic views held by aging Federalists, propertied elites, and southern slaveholders. This history tells a different story. In shifting focus to the competing conceptions of democracy emanating from key conflicts over moral reform, it shows that minority rights were a major concern for many Americans. Foes of Sabbath, liquor, and race regulations loosened the tradition of questioning majority rule from its elitist and antidemocratic moorings. They made the protection of minority rights a popular, democratic concern and played foundational roles in making the tension between majority rule and minority rights a hallmark of nineteenth-century democracy.[6]

This history also illustrates that battles over moral reform and the minority-rights politics they engendered were other highly participatory parts of nineteenth-century political practice beyond voting and two-party politics.[7] This grass-roots action transpired within, yet independently of, the partisan political environment, often began at the local level, and occurred, with notable exceptions, in northern states where reformers most successfully influenced public policy. But when engaging with the seats of governmental authority and publicized by the expanding news media, even the most local of struggles achieved national prominence. They enlivened the public sphere by bringing thousands upon thousands of Americans to read, write, and rally about questions of public policy and minority rights. Not just lawyers, policymakers, and jurists but ordinary Americans were forced to consider issues of policy, law, and constitutionalism largely because of moral minorities' increasingly organized resistance. This political activism did not take place outside the normal parameters of nineteenth-century democratic engagement but became an ongoing component of a capacious democratic political culture.[8]

The political conflicts presented here also reveal underexplored aspects of the meaning of freedom and the nature of rights-consciousness in nineteenth-century America. Previous scholars have emphasized that the axis of freedom and unfreedom in this era was shaped by battles over voting rights, slavery, women's rights, and the changing socioeconomic conditions tied to the rise of market and industrial capitalism. In their histories, abolitionists fighting slavery, disgruntled laborers, and those battling for formal inclusion in the polity—especially slaves and women—led the way in articulating rights and shaping what it meant to be free.[9] Although workers, former slaves, women, and abolitionists certainly play important roles in the pages that follow, this history shows that nineteenth-century Americans' conceptions of freedom were also informed by competing visions of the power of majoritarian democracy and of the proper relationship between morals and government.[10] For the moral minorities in particular, the enshrinement of purported moral norms in policy laid bare how varying minority statuses—religious, racial, and ethno-cultural—could foster unfreedom and threaten their rights within democracy, even if they could vote. For both the proponents and opponents of Sabbath, liquor, and race regulations, theirs was a political freedom defined by law and by public culture.[11] Unsurprisingly, it was in these arenas that they organized for combat and where a tremendously important democratic political tradition—popular minority-rights activism—was born.

The emergence of grass-roots minority-rights activism is often regarded as a more recent development of the so-called rights revolution of the twentieth century, when popular struggles for the civil liberties and civil rights of minorities combined with the activism of the US Supreme Court.[12] By detailing a much longer and more complex history of minority-rights politics, this history highlights an important continuity in American history. Developed in the mid-nineteenth century amid conflicts over Sabbath-keeping, alcohol, and racial prejudice, minority-rights activism would continue to expand in the late nineteenth and twentieth centuries and remain a powerful mode of popular political engagement.[13] At the same time, this history emphasizes significant ruptures in the long history of minority-rights politics. Nowhere is this more apparent than in considering the types of people who explicitly thought of themselves as oppressed minorities. In addition to such familiar minorities as black northerners, this history recovers other groups—such as liquor dealers and Seventh Day Baptists—whose past status as influential minorities has been largely forgotten. In no way were these varied minorities, whether black northerners, German immigrants, or others, and their respective situations equivalent. Yet their sheer diversity and collective importance in the mid-nineteenth century are reminders that minority status and identity can be situational and change over time. To write the history of minorities and to understand the long tradition of minority-rights activism means rediscovering those in the past who found themselves in the minority and took action.[14]

Unfortunately for the moral minorities at the heart of this history, they often did not rule the day. The New Yorkers challenging Sunday laws and the Rhode Islanders challenging segregated schools in 1859 had a long way to go to achieve their ultimate goals of religious freedom and racial equality. Their fundamental significance is not built on their immediate victories—whether they won in court, in public opinion, or elsewhere. They enjoyed successes but also suffered many disappointments. More than a story of winners and losers, this history demonstrates how opponents of Sabbath, liquor, and race regulations chose to resist and developed long-lasting techniques to battle for rights. As they realized, the preservation of free democracy was neither a given nor an individualistic enterprise. It required cooperation, organization, and unity as well as persistence and vigilance in the face of both triumphs and setbacks. Antebellum America's moral minorities would bequeath these fundamental values to later civil-liberties and civil-rights activists who would ensure that the tension between majority rule and minority rights remained at the heart of modern democracy.

I

Making America's First Moral Majority

"WILL OUR BLESSINGS be perpetuated, or shall ours be added to the ruined republics that have been?" More than fifty years after America declared independence from Great Britain, Lyman Beecher posed this question to an audience that had assembled in Plymouth, Massachusetts to commemorate "the Landing of the Pilgrims." One of the most renowned Protestant ministers of the day, a concerned Beecher seized the moment to consider the nation's future. In his assessment, American prosperity had not been accompanied by the elevation of the "moral condition of the multitude." Americans regularly desecrated the Sabbath, they consumed alcohol to extreme excess, and men "in high places" settled disputes through deadly duels. Such behavior offended the legacy of their Puritan "models of moral excellence." More dangerously, it threatened "the permanence of [their] republican institutions." For America's unique political system to endure, "the work of moral renovation" needed to commence.[1]

And in fact it had. As Beecher spoke in 1827, a grand reform movement promising a pathway to national and even global deliverance was well underway. Spurred by the vast socioeconomic transformations of the early nineteenth century and fueled by the religious fires of the Second Great Awakening, evangelical Protestant clergymen and lay men and women reinvigorated Christianity and roused, as Beecher described, the "voluntary energies" of the people to emancipate the nation from sin. As leading reformers made sense of their participation and sought to involve others, they, like Beecher, repeatedly turned to the political point of their efforts. They spoke a language of moral nationalism and insisted that the survival of America's "great political experiment" depended on the "extensive prevalence and diffusion of *moral and religious principles.*" Just as the republican political world of the founding generation was giving way to a new age of mass democracy, moralists disseminated these concerns widely. Would the majorities that were to rule America's rising democracy, they trepidatiously asked, be Christian and moral enough to guarantee good government? Or would an immoral majority pave the way for despotism and extinguish "the last hope of the world" for popular self-government?[2]

With these weighty apprehensions, reformers joined an age-old debate about the viability of democracy. Like others suspicious of democracy, they might have decried majority rule and sought formal ways to limit the power of the people in American government. Instead, they set out to ensure that decidedly moral majorities ruled America's young democracy. Riding the democratic currents of the age, reformers competed for the hearts and minds of the people by organizing the first widespread grass-roots sociopolitical movement in American history. They targeted the people's everyday behavior. But reformers also aimed to alter public opinion on such vexed questions as alcohol consumption and slavery, encouraged the converted to vote with Christian morals in mind, and lobbied federal, state, and local governments to purge practices that sanctioned immorality and embarrassed the nation. Their efforts brought millions of Americans to take an active interest in public questions, public policy, and electoral politics, contributing mightily to the democratization of nineteenth-century American public life.[3]

This process continued as reformers' early attempts to ensure moral majorities incited dissent from those who feared the power of organized reform and who clung to alternate religious and moral values. In particular, the movements to protect the Christian Sabbath, to limit alcohol consumption, and to abolish slavery sparked foundational controversies in the 1820s and 1830s that revealed the divisiveness of moral questions in American political life. These early controversies would foreshadow the conflicts of the 1840s and 1850s that would spur reassessments of foundational premises of popular sovereignty—not least that the majority should rule—and would catalyze sustained political action on behalf of minority rights. To understand why the influential tradition of popular minority-rights activism emerged as it did in the mid-nineteenth century means exploring how a rising coalition of moral activists made sense of mass democracy and how they made their own interventions in public life to guarantee that the United States would be a Christian and moral democracy.

LEADING MORALISTS IN the early nineteenth century insisted that the United States was a distinctive nation that provided an otherwise dubious world with a shining example of popular sovereignty's viability. "Our country," proclaimed renowned Baptist preacher Francis Wayland in 1825, "has given to the world the first ocular demonstration, not only of the practicability, but also of the unrivalled superiority of a popular form of government." This was a remarkable development. "It was not long since fashionable," Wayland reminded his audience, "to ridicule the idea, that a people could govern themselves.... The people were treated like a ferocious monster, whose keepers could only be secure while its dungeon was dark, and its chain massive." No more. The American example was changing minds and making the global spread of popular sovereignty a possibility. For many, this was a product of divine intervention. "God himself," Dutch Reformed minister and Sunday School champion George Bethune announced, "has placed our country on the mount of his favour." The world was watching.[4]

Despite this providential favor, ministers and their followers saw "dark clouds skirting our political horizon" precisely because the people seemed to be out of control. In the often chaotic climate of vast territorial expansion and migration, transportation and communications revolutions, economic transformation, urbanization, and population boom, early nineteenth-century reformers stood at the forefront of those who perceived a pending apocalypse. Mob violence and gang warfare; poverty and crime; disorderly wage workers in new canal towns; young single men and women in bustling cities lacking traditional family guidance; adultery and rampant prostitution; irreligion and organized infidelity; lawlessness on the western frontier; alien Catholic immigrants overwhelming Protestant America; a growing population of black slaves that could foment rebellion at any moment—all were evidence of a pending destruction that would beset America.[5]

Within this perceived atmosphere of decay, reformers complained that their countrymen and women were extraordinarily vice-ridden. One of the most widespread grievances was that Americans drank too much, and by historians' estimates, they just might have. Helped by the abundance of cheap grain that made whiskey the national spirit, Americans fifteen years of age and older downed an average of seven gallons of alcohol per year in 1825. When compared to the early twenty-first-century average intake of less than two gallons, it is perhaps understandable why the "spectacular binge" of the early nineteenth century elicited such concern. In 1826 a graphic broadside—*The Drunkard's Progress*—revealed temperance reformers' view of alcohol's destructive tendencies (fig. 1.1). The commonplace ritual of the morning dram would lead men to shirk familial responsibilities by seeking rowdy, male conviviality in grog shops. These moral cesspools facilitated a downward spiral, leading the drunkard's family to suffer emotionally and financially until finally all was lost. The only home the once respectable middle-class family would know would be the poorhouse, and liquor was to blame. Complete abstinence, a position that rose to prominence in the 1830s, was the only remedy.[6]

Beyond the bottle, other trailheads to vice abounded. Opponents of lotteries, for instance, complained that gambling's unrealistic expectation of gain without labor destroyed the work ethic and promoted idleness. They also protested that lotteries were often held on Sundays, desecrating the Sabbath, and that perpetual losers drowned their bad luck in drink. As Philadelphia lawyer Job R. Tyson explained in 1833, lotteries could pave the way for female depravity. In recounting the tale of a "respectable" married woman who gambled in the lottery without informing her hard-working husband, Tyson explained how one vice led to others. Having "lost a large sum" of money that she stole from her husband's desk, the woman "submitted to prostitution" in order to replace the missing funds. "The facts were subsequently developed, and the family, in consequence, 'were ruined and broken up.'" As these didactic tales multiplied and circulated throughout the nation, it seemed that immorality almost uniformly threatened the fundamental bases of social order. Religion, the home and family, the trust between man and wife, feminine virtue and sexual purity, and masculine industriousness could only be preserved by embracing the moral life.[7]

More than just personal failings, such vices, to the reform-minded, were "national sins" that needed eradication lest the nation incur "the wrath of God." The same held true for America's thorniest moral ill— slavery. Antislavery activists sharply disagreed about the proper way to eradicate slavery. Colonizationists allied with the American Colonization Society (ACS) preached slavery's gradual abatement and insisted that freed men and women be expatriated to Africa, particularly the colony of Liberia, which the ACS helped found in the early 1820s. Black and white radical abolitionists, by contrast, rejected colonization and called for the

FIGURE 1.1 *The Drunkard's Progress, or the Direct Road to Poverty, Wretchedness & Ruin* (1826). Courtesy of the Library of Congress.

immediate, uncompensated abolition of slavery without expatriation. Despite these extremes, many if not most activists across the antislavery spectrum would have agreed with Joseph R. Underwood, a Whig congressman and colonizationist from Kentucky, that slavery was "a great moral, political and national evil." Among other problems, it exposed America's hypocrisy to the world. There was little worse, New Jersey reform champion Theodore Frelinghuysen declared, than hearing "the grateful shouts of American Freemen and the heart-sickening groans of subjugated slaves." To ensure national honor and national survival, America's hideous paradox of slavery and freedom must be destroyed.[8]

Leading reformers repeatedly spoke of "the inevitable dependence of our political on our moral prosperity" and regularly insisted that a distinctly *virtuous and intelligent people* must govern America. Beneath these demands was a recognition that political life was changing.[9] First, Lyman Beecher and other New England clergymen were suffering a loss of formal power, coupled no doubt with substantial status anxiety, as Congregational churches in Connecticut (1818), New Hampshire (1819), and Massachusetts (1833) lost the explicit state support they had enjoyed since colonial times. Beecher at first greeted this end to the so-called Standing Order with horror, yet within a decade, he viewed disestablishment as a critical foundation for the era's religious and moral ferment. Second, many leading reformers had been Federalist partisans and in the years after the War of 1812 and the Hartford Convention found themselves without a party and in search of new outlets for their public energies. Before becoming the most important white radical abolitionist in the 1830s, William Lloyd Garrison, for example, absorbed the teachings of such iconic arch-Federalists as Timothy Pickering and Fisher Ames. He embraced Lyman Beecher's brand of evangelical reform in the 1820s, edited a temperance newspaper, and protested lotteries and Sabbath-breaking. Turning to antislavery, Garrison first advocated the American Colonization Society's gradualist program before championing immediate abolition. This one-time Federalist had found a new calling.[10]

In an even broader sense, however, reformers trembled as American politics became a far more popular affair in the early nineteenth century. Spurred from below by disgruntled urban wage earners and rural farmers and from above by ambitious politicos seeking to oust entrenched statesmen, so-called democratic reformers sought to enshrine equality in the political system through a variety of structural changes. New western states entered the Union without property requirements for voting and office-holding. Soon eastern states revised their state constitutions to expand voting rights for adult white men, to reapportion state legislatures to better mirror shifting populations, and to provide for the election of a wider range of previously appointed government officers, including judges. For proponents, popular political empowerment (at least for white men) would help ensure that popular government remained responsive to the people and the majority that should rule. Was this not the genius of popular sovereignty?[11]

Perhaps no series of events did more to bolster the predominance of majority rule as the essence of the ascendant democratic political culture than the presidential elections of 1824 and 1828 that pitted John Quincy Adams against Andrew Jackson. Multiple regional candidates ran in 1824, and when the balloting concluded, no candidate was left with a majority in the Electoral College. Jackson had ninety-nine votes, Adams eighty-four, and Henry Clay, the next closest, had thirty-seven. Infamously (and allegedly), Adams and Clay brokered a smoke-filled-room deal that sent Clay's votes to Adams. Adams won the presidency, and in return Clay was promised the position of secretary of state within Adams's cabinet. The "corrupt bargain" was struck. With the presidency stolen from him, the irate Jackson set his sights on 1828 with the goal of returning American government to "the will of the people." When he defeated Adams and finally entered the White House in 1829, Jackson had little in the way of a policy platform, but he did have what he announced as "the first principle of our system—that the majority is to govern."[12]

Already by 1829 such leading statesmen as Martin Van Buren were founding new styles of political parties to mobilize the expanding mass of voters and to secure electoral majorities. Gone were the deferential republican politics of the early nineteenth century in which gentleman insiders controlled an intensely personal political environment and only a small percentage of voters went to the polls. Politicians of this earlier era had viewed parties at best as a necessary evil. By the 1830s, an intense partisanship nurtured by professional politicians, relentless campaigning, vigorous newspaper wars, and political spectacle—rallies, processions, torchlight parades, caucuses, conventions, meetings, and electioneering—became the order of the day. The Democratic Party that formed around Andrew Jackson took the lead in pushing forward this new political culture, and, by the mid-1830s, the anti-Jackson coalition calling itself the Whig Party joined the partisan wrangling. The 1840 presidential election—the highpoint of voter turnout in this "golden age" of American democracy—proved that two could play at the game of mass politics, as the Whigs' "Log Cabin and Cider" campaign scored a victory for William Henry Harrison. The dynamic culture of unapologetic two-party politics and high voter turnout that developed during this so-called Second Party System would remain a leading feature of political life until the end of the nineteenth century.[13]

Leading divines and moralists feared that majoritarianism in the form of the new democratic politics would destroy "the moral tone of our country" and, ultimately, the American republic itself.[14] To them, parties shamelessly hurried the people "along without any object." In lieu of "cool discussion...addressed to the rational and moral nature of man," party principals and "artful demagogue[s]" sought "the ephemeral applause of the multitude" by appealing to man's animal nature with passion and prejudice. How horrid that presidential campaigns were filled, Presbyterian minister Samuel T. Spear complained, with "rum, political songs, mass meetings, inflammatory rage, newspaper slanders, forgery, and an extensive system of bribery and betting." Adding insult to injury, parties even enlisted the participation of women. Though some moralists hoped a female presence might "preserve order and decorum" in politics, others feared that women would become "mere female men" and unable to play their "most precious" role as keepers of "quiet" homes that sheltered families from the competitive public world of commerce and politics. These dubious developments led Congregationalist clergyman Horace Bushnell and others to lament, "Our politics are now our greatest immorality."[15]

At the most basic level, evangelical reformers encountering mass democracy felt outnumbered and recognized that the political world had become a game of numbers as never before. Going back to the presidential election of 1828, most reformers preferred Adams to Jackson, and many would eventually be drawn into the Whig Party. But beyond partisan considerations, they objected that the masses of western frontiersmen, propertyless workingmen, infidels, and recent immigrants, especially the Catholics among them, exercised the same political influence as the educated and pious—themselves—did. This uncouth social segment not only rejected many of the standards of moral respectability that reformers and other members of the rising Protestant middle class actively advanced. They also held "the balance of power" in American politics. "The number of those in our country who deny the divine authority of Christianity," the Baptist Missionary Society's *Christian Watchman* agonized in 1834, "is supposed to be the majority of our male inhabitants." Unless reformed, this irreligious and immoral majority—what reformers referred to variously as the "debased populace," the "mass of ignorance," the "miserable multitude," the "army of intemperance," and the "unprincipled mob"— would corrupt the ballot box, elect unrefined office-seekers and unprincipled demagogues, and demand irresponsible legislation.[16] At that point, champions of reform ominously predicted, the righteous minority would abandon popular self-government to ensure their own self-preservation. As Francis Wayland explained, "Should our people become ignorant and vicious…that moment are our liberties at an end; and, glad to escape from the despotism of millions, we shall flee for shelter to the despotism of one." Such events would extinguish "the world's last hope" for popular sovereignty and leave "the whole human race" in "darkness."[17]

IN FEARING IMMORAL majorities, antebellum reformers appeared to join a long-standing tradition of doubting democracy. Reaching back to antiquity, Aristotle set the terms of debate in *The Politics* while contemplating the merits of different schemes of government. To him, democracy was a dirty word. It was a government in which the many worked to benefit only themselves at the expense of the few. Aristotle established what would become the standard class-based indictment of democracy. Despite flirting with the possibility of a wealthy majority and a "needy" minority, Aristotle found it a "fact" that "everywhere the well-off are few and the needy many." When the "needy have control," they would, "because they are the majority, divide up the property of the wealthy." To Aristotle, this was an act of "ultimate injustice," and he labored to balance the three types of governance—of the one, the few, and the many—to create a stable republic and prevent this great bane of democracy. Finding the right mixture and protecting the rights of the propertied minority would trouble classical republican theorists and statesmen for centuries.[18]

Aristotle's fears for the elite classes and the propertied minority had informed much political thinking in the age of the American Revolution. For some, especially frontier farmers, urban workers, and debtors, the Revolution provided an opportunity to establish a new political order that recognized the equality of all citizens regardless of wealth or social standing. Some plebeians followed the Enlightenment faith in the popular will articulated by such thinkers as Jean-Jacques Rousseau, but many more were mobilized by recent difficulties with Great Britain and a long history of nonresponsive colonial governments. To ensure that new state governments obeyed the people, they supported simple blueprints of government, like those offered by Thomas Paine, which kept state governments close to the people through unicameral legislatures elected annually by wide suffrage.[19]

For others, especially those eager to prevent the Revolution from fostering a full-scale social revolution, these plans were, in the words of John Adams, "too democratical." Revolutionary conservatives countered proposals like Paine's with constitutional schemes grounded in popular sovereignty yet steeped in the tradition of mixed government.[20] In defending these early state constitutions, particularly those with bicameral legislatures whose upper houses represented property, John Adams returned to the threat tyrannical majorities posed to property rights. He situated the American state constitutions within the long-standing tradition of balancing the competing social orders and emphasized their ability to protect "the minority...from the tyranny of the majority." In true Aristotelian fashion, Adams pointed to the protection of property rights and the inevitable existence of a wealthy minority. There would always be "rich and poor, high and low." "A great majority of every nation," he argued, "is wholly destitute of property, except a small quantity of clothes, and a few trifles of other movables." If not properly checked, this majority, either through legislation or by electing demagogues promising a redistribution of wealth, would imperil property rights and thereby the entire sociopolitical order. Young America, he explained, remedied this perennial problem of simple democracy by dividing sovereignty among different branches of state government, some representing education and property.[21]

In the meantime, other statesmen—most famously James Madison—were finding that even balanced state constitutions were not up to the task of protecting property rights from hostile majorities. In the context of framing the US Constitution, Madison emerged as the founder of American countermajoritarianism. For him, a stronger national government was the answer not only to the weaknesses of the Articles of Confederation but also to the unruly behavior of state governments, whose democratic lower houses were dominating these new states and threatening confiscatory taxes on the rich. In the economically turbulent 1780s many state governments had responded to popular clamor by passing laws favoring debtors over creditors. To Madison, these actions called "into question the fundamental principle of republican Government, that the majority who rule in such governments are the safest Guardians both of public Good and private rights."[22] Madison's "republican remedy" for the sins of these largely rural majorities was twofold. First, he advocated limiting the power of state governments, and Article 1, Section 10 of the Constitution would contain key restrictions on the states. Second, Madison famously argued for crucial powers to be placed in the hands of an extended federal republic whose large electoral districts would prevent majority factions from forming and allow virtuous elites to come to the helm of the new national state. As Madison defended this constitutional handiwork in *Federalist* 10, he returned to the threat majorities posed to property rights. Though noting that majority factions resulted from "different opinions" on government and on religion (something he had witnessed in Virginia), he nevertheless stressed that "the most common and durable source of factions has been the various and unequal distribution of property." The majorities to be most guarded against were those that would strike at property rights with laws affecting creditors and debtors, tax legislation, and tariff policies. Though Madison and other like-minded constitution-makers responded to the explicit circumstances of the 1780s, their identification of hostile needy majorities nonetheless echoed Aristotle. A substantial revision of Aristotle's concerns with majority tyranny—a revision that looked beyond the bugaboo of property redistribution—would come later.[23]

Concerns about the tyrannical potential of propertyless majorities would persist well into the nineteenth century. In the various populist uprisings, especially those exploding during times of economic strife— the Kentucky Relief Wars, the Anti-Rent Wars, and the Dorr War—critics responded to calls for majority rule with classic concerns for the fate of property rights. These issues also surfaced at the state constitutional conventions in which statesmen considered expanding suffrage rights to propertyless white men among other democratic reforms. Supporters insisted that such changes reflected the "fundamental maxim in all free governments"—that "the majority should govern." Opponents, however, responded with traditional countermajoritarian language. "There is a constant tendency in human society," aging Federalist James Kent declared, "in the poor to covet and to share the plunder of the rich; in the debtor to relax or avoid the obligation of contracts; in the majority to tyrannize over the minority, and trample down their rights." Similarly, at the Massachusetts Constitutional Convention of 1820, John Adams emerged from retirement to insist that democratic reforms would allow "those who have no property" to "vote us out of our houses." Had not the French Revolution provided glaring evidence of the apocalypse that would follow excessive democracy? There "the utility and excellence of universal suffrage" brought social leveling, the guillotine, and the "colossal despotism of Napoleon" that "desolated France and all the rest of Europe." In no way, Adams argued, should Massachusetts turn down this ominous path. Kent and Adams, however, were fighting a losing battle.[24]

Leading moral reformers of the 1820s and 1830s, many of them recovering Federalists, in many ways echoed Kent and Adams, pointing to the haunting specter of the French Revolution and advancing the sanctity of property rights. In his influential *Six Sermons on Intemperance*, Lyman Beecher, for example, warned that "the laboring classes," which constitute "an immense majority" in America, were liable to use "the power of taxation" and to enact laws "subservient to the debtor and less efficacious to protecting the rights of property." If these predictions rang true, Beecher insisted, violence and revolution were sure to follow. Similarly, foremost education reformer Horace Mann lauded public schooling—another critical reform enterprise of the age—as a tool "to mold democracy and simultaneously fend off the dangers of excessive democracy," which to him included legislation confiscating property. As Mann announced, "should besotting vices and false knowledge bear sway, then will every wealthy, and every educated, and every refined individual and family, stand in the same relation to society, in which game stands to the sportsman!" Sunday School advocate George Bethune, amid condemning labor strikes for wages and hours, also dreaded "the physical and numerical force of the many in the laboring classes" that might one day "combine against the rich."[25]

Yet reform leaders subtly began to depart from this older countermajoritarian tradition by embracing the burgeoning exceptionalist vision of American class relations. Instead of suggesting that the struggle between a rich minority and poor majority was inevitable, they maintained that the relatively equal distribution of property freed the United States from the worst dangers that propertyless majorities traditionally posed. This position had been circulating since the Revolution, but it received a meaningful boost at the 1820 Massachusetts Constitutional Convention. Amid debates over suffrage reform and legislative reapportionment, Federalist statesman Daniel Webster advised his fellow delegates to remember "how great a portion of the people of this State possess property." Disagreeing with old-line Federalists, Webster saw no poor majority that might threaten property rights. Unlike Europe, Massachusetts had no feudalistic heritage, and its colonial founders had divided lands widely. Most importantly, the "fundamental laws respecting property"—the abolition of the "right of primogeniture" and entail and the dominance of freehold property—had ensured a wide distribution of property. The result, Webster glowed, was "a great subdivision of the soil, and a great equality of condition; the true basis, most certainly, of a popular government." Even with other delegates fearing the creation of a class of permanent wage laborers in Massachusetts's rising factory towns, Webster thought it would take "a great revolution in regard to property" for a needy majority to emerge in their state.[26]

Webster's American exceptionalism would prove highly influential in antebellum political life, swaying more conservative statesmen to embrace popular democracy, especially those who would move into the Whig Party in the 1830s. Famously, Alexis de Tocqueville would also adopt it. In *Democracy in America*, Tocqueville described the traditional dangers posed by the power of the numerical majority, yet joined Webster in finding no imminent threat in America because of widespread property ownership. America's "equality of conditions," which Tocqueville, like Webster, attributed to the patterns of colonial settlement, the absence of feudalism, and the abolition of primogeniture and entail, made it less likely for the needy to take property from the rich. "Universal suffrage," Tocqueville maintained, "really does hand the government of society over to the poor." But since "the great majority of American citizens possess something," it was unlikely that political power would be controlled by "the needy" and property rights threatened. Tocqueville's legendary trepidation with "the tyranny of the majority" would be rooted in rather different concerns—the tyranny of public opinion linked, in part, to the cultural power of a largely middle-class society.[27]

Leading reformers, many of whom would become Whig partisans, embraced this exceptionalist vision of safe popular majorities but insisted that it was vice and immorality that most threatened America's special social order. For Lyman Beecher, it was the "unrighteous monopoly of the earth" in other societies that had given rise to the chief "political evils which have afflicted mankind," including those brought about by the empowerment of needy majorities. America had thankfully avoided such a monopoly. Presbyterian divine and temperance champion Albert Barnes similarly lauded America's socioeconomic egalitarianism and "the right of the people to fee simple in the soil." To him, these conditions allowed a responsible "republican freedom" to flourish in tandem with "the fundamental principle of this republic"—that "the will of the majority is to govern." Widespread property ownership, he explained, provided "the conscious independence which swells the bosom of the American people." Barnes worried, however, that rampant intemperance bred dependence by forcing sinful men into the growing ranks of the property-less. Intemperance, then, would create a new propertyless class not to be trusted with political power.[28]

Alcohol was only one concern among many. Lotteries, one Philadelphian declared, also sapped the main foundation of republican-ism—"equality." Certainly lotteries allowed some to get rich quick, but "many more" were "ruined" as the prospect of easy wealth sapped the work ethic. The "bankruptcy and ruin" that followed sowed "the seeds of anarchy and despotism" by contributing to the "unequal distribution of wealth." Sabbath reformers echoed these concerns, particularly in pro-testing Sunday work. The Pennsylvania branch of the General Union for Promoting the Observance of the Christian Sabbath imagined that Sunday work would upset class relations by giving rise to "a monied aristocracy" and by "dooming" Sunday laborers to the status of permanent and depen-dent wage workers. This had political consequences. "If you continue to violate the Sabbath," reformers explained to Sabbath-breaking workers, "you may wear the livery of freemen, but it will be in the house of bond-age—you may go through the mockery of voting for your rulers, but it will be done under the powerful dictation of masters." In reformers' view, immorality bred economic dependence; dependence undercut America's relatively equal distribution of property; inequality would doom popular self-government by dangerously creating a propertyless majority.[29]

In light of these grave concerns about the narrowing distribution of property—blamed, significantly, not on the rich but on sin among ordinary citizens—it is not surprising that reformers' declensionist tales of vice and immorality often concluded with the loss of the home and a journey to the poorhouse. Certainly, "the home" took on new cultural significance in the ascendant nineteenth-century world of the market-oriented middle class. In an exceptionalist vision of America predicated upon widespread property ownership, the loss of the home symbolized a political problem—the threat of a property imbalance and the growth of an impoverished majority that might use its political power to destroy the republic. The root causes of the danger, however, remained moral ones. Preventing intemperance, gambling, Sabbath-breaking, slaveholding, and other sinful behavior would ensure the wide distribu-tion of property vital to the prevention of majority tyranny. In fearing the immoral majority, reformers suggested that the dangers of major-ity rule stemmed not from inevitable class conflict but from otherwise avoidable class conflict brought about by immorality. To maintain their exceptional property relations, a prerequisite for democratic viability, Americans had to become morally exceptional as well. And who better to lead the majority back to virtue than the new reformers.[30]

This linkage of morals, property relations, and democracy, of course, gave reformers an opportunistic justification for imposing their religious, moral, and cultural values on potentially unwilling Americans. It also allowed reformers and their middle-class converts to blame poverty, the growing inequality of wealth, and the rising permanence of wage labor not on the uncertain, uncontrollable, and often invisible forces of market capitalism but on the moral failings of the middle and lower classes. Advancing this perspective, moralists helped to legitimate and to link the rising economic regime of market and industrial capitalism (in which many of them were profiting) with the rising political regime of majoritarian democracy, even while cautiously embracing democracy. Like earlier countermajoritarians who rejected democracy, leading moralists still privileged "the right of property." But where the older generation depended on constitutions, laws, deferential politics, and limitations on suffrage to secure property rights, reformers emphasized the vitality of "moral and religious principles." "A free constitution is of no value," Francis Wayland wrote in his widely distributed *Elements of Political Economy*, "unless the moral and intellectual character of a people be sufficiently elevated to avail itself of the advantages which it offers. It is merely an *instrument* of good, which will accomplish nothing, unless there exist the moral disposition to use it aright." Without coincidence, Wayland also reminded his readers that "moral and religious nations grow wealthy so much more rapidly than vicious and irreligious nations." All in all, Christian morals would facilitate democracy, protect property rights, and produce wealth, all of which would foster national greatness.[31]

"WHEN THE MAJORITY of the people are fast tending to viciousness, or are already confirmed in a course of error and wickedness, how are they to be brought back?" Evangelical ministers and lay reformers thought long and hard about this question in the first third of the nineteenth century. Their answers reflected a growing recognition, no doubt grudging for many, that the ascendant democratic political culture was not going anywhere. Gone were the days when local elites and patriarchs could mandate standards of behavior and when the strong arm of the law could reliably coerce morality. "When we were colonies," Lyman Beecher observed in 1827, "the law could make provision for the creation and application of moral powers." Times, however, had changed. In the rising democratic era, reformers realized they would need techniques targeting America's political deity, its arbiter of morals, and its basis of legal legitimacy—public opinion. The people, it seemed, needed to be reformed from the bottom up.[32]

In the early nineteenth century Protestant evangelicals would spur a massive grass-roots movement to reform public morals. The nation was ripe for it in no small part because the religious fires of the Second Great Awakening had already began scorching the nation. On the western frontier, in cities, in the "burned-over" districts of upstate New York and Ohio, and later in New England and elsewhere, itinerant preachers like Charles Finney and Lyman Beecher incited mass religious revivals and camp meetings. Thousands of men and women attended and embraced new personal relationships with God, which evangelicals claimed could redeem their sinful lives and ensure their salvation. This explosion of popular religiosity was reflected in the era's skyrocketing church membership, especially among Methodists, Baptists, Presbyterians, and Congregationalists, as well as in the widespread organization of Sunday schools, Bible classes, and missions.[33]

Preaching a public religiosity and armed with the spirits of Christian perfectionism and Protestant millennialism, evangelicals also convinced their followers that they must remedy the sins of society. In the aftermath of revivals, the converted crossed denominational boundaries to join societies targeting Sabbath-breaking, swearing, intemperance, slavery, and other vices. These "local voluntary associations"—what Beecher referred to as "a sort of disciplined moral militia"—served as the backbone for a broader crusade that would infiltrate all regions of the country. Soon prominent clerics and influential laymen helped coordinate local activism with well-financed national institutions like the American Bible Society (founded in 1816), the American Colonization Society (1817), the American Tract Society (1823), the American Sunday School Union (1824), the American Home Missionary Society (1826), and the American Temperance Society (1826). "Such an array of moral influence," Beecher announced in 1827, "was never before brought to bear upon the nation." It would continue as membership in this "benevolent empire" swelled. By 1835 some 1.5 million men and women, for example, were participating in eight thousand local affiliates of the American Temperance Society, while some 2 million Americans had pledged to abstain from drinking hard alcohol. Even the most controversial of the major reform crusades—abolitionism—expanded significantly. Founded in 1833 by black and white radicals, the American Anti-Slavery Society by 1838 counted thirteen hundred local branches and 250,000 members. By then reform was an undeniably powerful force in American public life.[34]

By involving millions of predominantly middle-class men, women, and children, reform associations emerged alongside political parties as a major force of democratization. To inspire public spiritedness, some reform leaders, in fact, took their cues from the age's politicos. As Charles Finney asked, "What do the politicians do?"

> They get up meetings, circulate handbills and pamphlets, blaze away in the newspapers, send their ships about the streets on wheels with flags and sailors, send coaches all over town, with handbills, to bring people up to the polls, all to gain attention to their cause and elect their candidate. All these are their "measures," and for their *end* they are wisely calculated. The object is to get up an excitement, and bring the people out.

Reformers proceeded similarly, but instead of rallying the people behind candidates and parties, they used what to them were pressing public issues of religion and morals. They held countless local meetings, organized state and national conventions, sponsored public lectures, and employed traveling agents who raised funds and established auxiliaries to national societies. Reformers also put steam-powered printing presses and the postal system to work, flooding the nation with tracts, pamphlets, journals, newspapers, annual reports, circular addresses, and other reform propaganda. Typically lauding self-control and self-discipline, these materials embodied the moral suasion approach that reformers adopted to persuade (and not compel) men and women to embrace the moral life and to convince others to do the same.[35]

The embrace of grass-roots voluntarism and moral suasion did not mean that reformers were uninterested in law or politics, nor did it suggest that their movements were somehow apolitical. Moralists drew no stark lines between the people they sought to reform and the government. "The American people," Presbyterian clergyman Gardiner Spring declared, "in a high sense, constitute the American government." Leading black abolitionist William Wells Brown would agree. "When I speak of the character of the American people," he wrote, "I look at the nation. I place all together, and draw no mark between the people and the government. The government is the people, and the people are the government." This viewpoint made reform a highly political undertaking: a Christian and moral people would mean a Christian and moral government. This was especially the case because the people, at least white men, voted. Though William Lloyd Garrison's small camp of radical abolitionists would eventually reject voting in order to protest democracy's sanction of slavery, to most reformers voting was not only a right but a duty. In the dominant view, citizens needed to vote with morals in mind and "independent of the trammels of party."[36] Reformers looked to the behavior of public officials as examples for the masses and urged "all Christians and all patriots" to investigate the moral qualifications of candidates. Whether a candidate was a dueler, a drinker, a Sabbath-breaker, or, for some, a slaveholder should be among voters' preeminent concerns. The "moral effect" of barring such debased men from office, Lyman Beecher proclaimed, "will be great." The strongest formulation of this perspective came from Presbyterian minister Ezra Stiles Ely, who in 1828 called for "a Christian party in politics." Far from demanding a formal party predicated upon Christian principles, Ely, like other evangelicals, urged the great mass of Christians to cast ballots only for moral candidates and regardless of party affiliation. A properly reformed majority—a Christian moral majority—ruling American democracy would guarantee the survival of the republic. Indeed, in the burgeoning reform movement, there was only a two-party system of right and wrong. Only the right should rule.[37]

Not everyone welcomed the rise of grass-roots reform or its broad political objectives. Beginning in the 1820s, Old School Baptists, antievangelicals, deists, free enquirers, Unitarians, and others accused reformers of ultraism, bigotry, priestcraft, and attempting to unite church and state. Outspoken radical Frances Wright indicted the clergy for stymieing free inquiry. Another Scottish-born freethinker named Robert L. Jennings agreed, warning that reformers "saturated" the country with "vile pernicious tracts...to prepare the minds of our now politically free citizens, for that passive submission to the expounders of the holy oracles." To Unitarian clergyman William Ellery Channing, evangelicals' associational politics was one of the "most remarkable" yet troubling features of the age. The "evil," he explained in 1829, was their inordinate "power" in the democratic public sphere. To Channing, "a few hands" were unduly shaping the minds of the many, promoting conformity, and imperiling free society. Through "an artful multiplication of societies," Channing warned, powerful reformers constituted an "irregular government" that depended on the "sway of numbers" and threatened to turn "public opinion" into "a steady, unrelenting tyrant, brow-beating the timid, proscribing the resolute, silencing free speech, and virtually denying the dearest religious and civil rights." While "great associations" were "sometimes useful," they needed to "be watched closely." Should reformers and their associations attempt "to bear down a respectable man or set of men, or to force on the community measures about which wise and good men differ," Americans needed to announce their disapproval.[38]

Condemnations increased when moralists initiated campaigns to reform the American state that they saw obstructing their various reform crusades. How, reformers asked, could they convince the people to act morally when government sanctioned the very behavior they hoped to eradicate? As Theodore Frelinghuysen announced, "We must reform our political administrations in the all-important point of their moral principles." To do this, moralists initiated an issue-oriented political style, lobbying national, state, and local governments to change a variety of policies. One of the earliest and most momentous efforts of this kind concerned the federal mails. In 1810, Congress had passed an act compelling post offices to remain open on Sundays if they received mail that day. Ministers were already appalled that Americans were choosing commerce and pleasure instead of worship, spiritual contemplation, and rest on Sundays, but they were horrified that the federal government encouraged such behavior. There was no way, Lyman Beecher argued, "to resist the floods of worldliness and pleasure which are rolling over the Sabbath, while they are sustained and led on by the omnipresent example of government— under the high sanction and command of *national law*." Even worse, it seemed that the United States was following the atheistical path of the revolutionary French National Assembly, which in 1793 had abolished the traditional Sabbath by instituting a rationalized calendar that established ten-day weekly cycles with a rest day on the tenth day—"Décadi." To avoid France's dreadful fate, Americans needed to take back the Sabbath from the federal government.[39]

In two separate periods—1810–1817 and 1828–1833—reformers mounted campaigns to change federal policy. In the second epoch Josiah Bissell Jr., a Presbyterian merchant from Rochester, New York, followed the trend of grass-roots reform and organized the General Union for Promoting the Observance of the Christian Sabbath (GUPCS) with the help of Lyman Beecher and Lewis Tappan, a successful New York merchant. The GUPCS

insisted that it only intended to change public opinion on Sabbath observance and did not wish to enforce the old laws prohibiting almost everything but worship on Sundays that remained on the books in nearly every
state. It did want, however, Congress to repeal the law requiring post offices
to stay open on Sundays. As the GUPCS initiated an immense lobbying
effort, complete with public meetings, propaganda, and a huge grass-roots
petition campaign, to bring pressure on the federal government, thousands of Americans objected. Mounting a counterpetition campaign, they
protested that evangelicals sought to compel Sabbath observance with
federal law in violation of civil and religious liberty. Some saw an even
broader conspiracy to promote "priestly despotism" at work. Evangelical
reformers, one petition suggested, "are introducing this measure, in part,
for the purpose of ascertaining whether Congress will legislate on the subjects touching religion." If Congress sanctioned Sabbath observance by
heeding the calls of reformers to end the Sunday mails, a union of church
and state would soon follow (fig. 1.2).

Much of this popular sentiment opposing the Sabbath reform found
its way into two reports produced by Colonel Richard M. Johnson, a
Democrat from Kentucky and the chair of the Senate Committee on the
Post Office in 1829. Johnson defended the Sunday mails and repudiated
Sabbath reformers. "Extensive religious combinations to effect a political object are," he wrote, "always dangerous." His reports, which were
reprinted as pamphlets and distributed widely, quickly became sacrosanct
texts for defenders of religious liberty and the separation of church and
state. A sour Lyman Beecher predicted that the "most lax in morals will
be loudest in its praise." Sabbath reformers had lost and sparked organized resistance, but they had also organized on a grand scale. They would
return.[40]

In the meantime, other reformers inflamed the nation as they too
flooded Congress with petitions. Since the 1790s, antislavery activists
had politely lobbied national leaders to address the precarious problem
of slavery, but as an insistence on immediate abolition came to define
radical abolitionism in the 1830s, the extent, tone, and demands of abolitionist petitions intensified.[41] Members of the American Anti-Slavery
Society sent petitions to Congress bearing the names of hundreds of
thousands of men and women, black and white, and making a variety of
demands. The chief target of their "Great Petition Strategy" was slavery
in the District of Columbia. Surrounded by the slave states of Maryland
and Virginia, Washington, DC, had become a bustling slave-trading depot.

FIGURE I.2 *The "Holy Alliance" or Satan's Legion at Sabbath Pranks* (1830). Courtesy of the American Antiquarian Society. To many Americans, evangelical reformers' attempt to halt Sunday mail delivery threatened to establish a priestly despotism and a national religion. The preservation of religious freedom and American liberty, they insisted, necessitated the continuance of the Sunday mails.

The Constitution empowered Congress to regulate the capital city, and abolitionists demanded an end to slavery there. To them, it was a matter of embarrassing hypocrisy. "We are ashamed," William Lloyd Garrison instructed Congress, "when we know that the manacled slave is driven to market by the doors of our Capitol, and sold like a beast in the very place where are assembled the representatives of a free and Christian people" (fig. 1.3). Congress should, in the words of abolitionist leader William Jay, "purge the capital of the Republic of its loathsome plague, and restore the Federal Government to its legitimate functions, of establishing justice and securing the blessings of liberty." Ending slavery in the District would be a major step in the reformation of the American state.[42]

By the mid-1830s, radical abolitionists had already incited an uproar by inundating the South with incendiary antislavery propaganda, and leading southern statesmen took a stand against their expanding petition

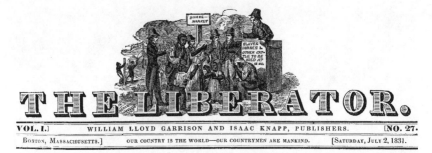

FIGURE 1.3 Masthead of *The Liberator* from July 2, 1831. Courtesy of The Library Company of Philadelphia. The masthead of William Lloyd Garrison's *Liberator* protested the hypocrisy of slavery and the slave market under the shadow of America's symbol of freedom and democracy—the Capitol Building in Washington, DC.

campaign. Representative James Henry Hammond and Senator John Calhoun, South Carolinians who viewed abolitionists' demands as an affront to the South, boldly urged Congress to discard the petitions. "I cannot see the rights of the Southern people," Hammond announced, "assaulted day after day, by the ignorant fanatics from whom these memorials proceed." When the smoke cleared, both houses of Congress, with substantial backing from northerners, enacted a "gag rule," which tabled abolitionist petitions and remained in place until 1844 in the House of Representatives and until 1850 in the Senate. Abolitionists responded with ever more petitions. With the help of former president turned congressman John Quincy Adams, abolitionists exploited the gag rule to show how white southerners would limit the civil liberties of white northerners, including the right to petition, to protect their peculiar institution. Though slavery would remain in Washington, DC, until the Civil War, their effort succeeded in growing antislavery sentiment and revealing the influence of the "Slave Power" over the federal government.[43]

Temperance reformers also entered the fray. At the federal level, they spurred the creation of the Congressional Temperance Society so congressmen could model temperance for the nation. They also succeeded in ending the military's policy of supplying whiskey to soldiers.[44] But far more central to their policy agenda were state laws licensing the sale of alcohol. Temperance men and women had mounted an assault on liquor dealers—the owners and operators of taverns, grog shops, and other "manufactories of drunkards"—and blamed them for tempting others to sin and for the litany of social problems attributed to intemperance. Reformers lamented when local governments failed to enforce laws against the illegal sale of liquor, but they increasingly became dissatisfied with the system of licensing that structured the legal sale of alcohol. Reformers long condemned the inadequacy of this system, but by the early 1830s many moved to demand an end to licensing. To them, it lent legal sanction and respectability to the sale and consumption of liquor, counteracting reformers' efforts and standing in the way of temperance's triumph.[45]

Reformers experimented with different methods to defeat licensing. In the early 1830s, local temperance associations in New England and elsewhere began urging authorities not to issue licenses. No-license advocates formed local majorities at annual town meetings and instructed their selectmen not to recommend anyone for licensing. Although instructions were not binding on selectmen, their annual election usually kept them in line with the local majority. When county officials followed the recommendations of selectmen, which they often did, these grass-roots efforts brought an end of licensing in numerous towns and counties. This method of prohibiting the sale of alcohol had its problems. Officials could ignore antilicense sentiment and issue licenses. Moreover, consistent success required temperance forces to mobilize annually for each new local election. By the late 1830s, reformers seeking more permanent solutions began lobbying state legislatures to replace existing license laws with more stringent measures. Their most widely broadcast victory occurred in Massachusetts, where the legislature prohibited the sale of ardent spirits in quantities of less than fifteen gallons. Reformers, who viewed small-quantity consumption in taverns and grog shops to be the most detrimental to society, applauded. Workers, immigrants, and other drinkers who congregated in those establishments and could not afford to buy liquor in large quantities found the law less than appealing.[46]

The fifteen-gallon law turned the Bay State into "the seat of war." Drinkers and dealers held meetings and published their own propaganda condemning intrusive reformers and state legislators. They also engaged in acts of civil disobedience, openly shirking the law. Most infamously, dealers employed the tactic of offering customers a look at a striped pig (a pig with zebra-like stripes painted on it) and providing complimentary grog (fig. 1.4). Thus, liquor was not sold but given away, and the law was not broken. Authorities did their best to close down establishments that attempted to evade the law, but the striped pig became a powerful symbol of dissent for those in the Bay State and beyond who resisted coercive temperance measures.[47] In addition, popular dissatisfaction turned, in the

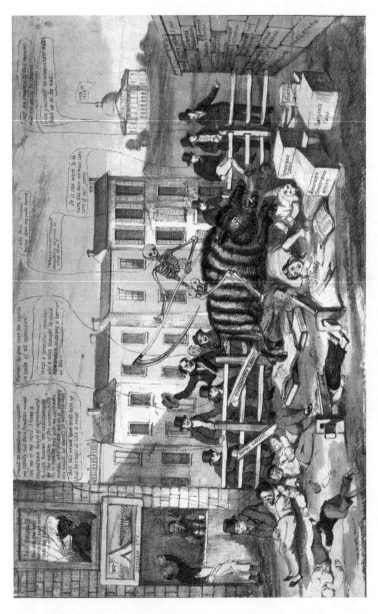

FIGURE 1.4 *Death on the Striped Pig* (1839). Courtesy of the American Antiquarian Society. For temperance activists, the "striped pig" evasion of the fifteen-gallon law was further proof that alcohol and the liquor business threatened to destroy American democracy.

words of John Quincy Adams, "into a political engine against the administration of the state." Angry voters blamed the Whig Party for the law and promptly installed Democrat Marcus Morton as governor in 1840. One historian of Massachusetts's politics suggests that though a number of factors contributed to the Whig defeat, "among Whig politicos it rapidly became accepted as gospel that the temperance law had caused their party's defeat." With a Democrat in the governor's seat and an anti-fifteen-gallon-law coalition of Democrats and Whigs controlling the legislature, the law was speedily repealed and licensing was reinstated. In the aftermath, politicos of both parties avoided the touchy issue of temperance, which, they discovered, could pose a serious threat to their tenure in office. Reformers would go looking for a new approach to end the license system.[48]

BY THE LATE 1830s, grass-roots moral reform had assumed a central place in American public life and given rise to the nation's first era of popular moral politics. The efforts of clergymen and lay reformers had utterly transformed the public sphere, bringing millions of men and women to join associations, take stands on public issues, lobby formal authorities, and mobilize others to do the same. Their controversial mission to promote Christianity and to improve the morals of the people, the state, and the nation, and the grass-roots tactics they employed, brought elite condemnation and popular backlash and exposed some of the challenges reformers faced in the age of mass democracy. Nevertheless, Protestant moralists would persevere and continue to organize varied crusades to ensure the survival of the republic. As they did this over the course of the next two decades, they would continue to spark dissent. This was especially true in the persistent struggles of Sabbath reformers, temperance reformers, and radical abolitionists, who despite earlier setbacks pressed policymakers in the 1840s and 1850s to embrace their moral agenda. Their exertions would continue to transform public life in the nineteenth century, not least by giving rise to popular debates about American democracy's central postulate—that the majority should rule—and by rousing a range of new grass-roots political action on behalf of minority rights.

Indeed, by the dawn of the Civil War, moral reformers—many of whom had joined reform crusades out of a fear of the emergent democratic order that worshipped majority rule—would succeed, often unwittingly, in bringing large segments of American society to question the virtues of such majoritarian genuflection. The fears of majority rule raised as a result of reform activism in the 1840s and 1850s differed markedly from the long-standing fears of elites who worried about protecting property rights from the propertyless masses. For black and white radical abolitionists who would launch an assault on racial prejudice in tandem with their attack on slavery, this was quite intentional. They were eager to secure the equal rights of the black minority regardless of the wishes of white majorities. For Sabbath and temperance reformers who would turn to majority rule to justify their preferred measures, however, the articulate resistance of minorities to their efforts was very much an unforeseen development.

2

Sunday Laws and the Problem of the Christian Republic

ON A SUNDAY in June 1844, Alderman Horatio Mott entered Daniel Hawley's porterhouse on New York City's West Side and "told him to close his place or be fined." Hawley refused. For purveyors of drink, Sunday was the day of the week bringing the best profits. On their one day free of labor, workingmen in cities and towns poured into establishments like Hawley's to find refuge and refreshment. No doubt Hawley felt he performed a valuable service to his patrons, and no doubt he gained his clientele's gratitude in addition to their business. Mott's attempt to halt the flow of libation not only threatened this businessman's bottom line and his manly ability to provide for his family but also endangered his standing within the local working-class and immigrant community. Perhaps this helps explain why when threatened with closing early or being fined, Hawley seized the alderman "by the throat, chocked [sic] him, and ejected him from the premises." Another official later arrested Hawley for assaulting the alderman and "violating the Sabbath day."[1]

Hawley was not the first American told to close his shop on a Sunday. Since colonial times, legislatures and local governments had criminalized work, travel, and other activities on the Lord's day. Some of the earliest laws mandated church attendance and even called for the death penalty. These provisions faded, but states and localities re-enacted Sunday laws following the Revolution despite the disestablishment of state-sponsored churches in most states. These measures spread westward and remained subject to spotty enforcement that was dependent upon local circumstances. But in the 1840s, Sabbath enforcers in New York and elsewhere had gained energy from the emergence of a new epoch for Sunday legislation.

Having failed in their earlier effort to halt Sunday mail delivery, Protestant clergymen and middle-class lay reformers had turned to state and local battles to reinvigorate their movement to protect the Christian Sabbath. Especially when combined with the mid-1840s burst of political nativism, this reform revival facilitated a surge of Sunday surveillance in numerous cities and towns. To Sabbath reformers and their often anti-immigrant allies, the legal protection of the Sabbath symbolized America's identity as a Christian republic, and it also reflected America's rising embrace of majoritarian democracy. Advocates insisted that the broad religious character of the American people—the majority of them—was rightly reflected in public policy. Since an overwhelming majority worshipped on Sundays, government properly shielded the day from desecration and protected the majority's ability to worship undisturbed. Majority rule, then, would promote Protestant Christianity and protect American democracy from enemies foreign and domestic.[2]

Not all Americans greeted these developments with enthusiasm. Many no doubt wanted to follow Daniel Hawley's lead in seizing intrusive officers by the throat, but resistance came in many forms. Numerous shopkeepers and tavern-owners registered their discontent by blatantly staying open; others more clandestinely kept back doors ajar, inviting knowing customers to enter and find their own style of Sunday salvation. Still others mounted more formal challenges that targeted public opinion and represented a commitment to a democratic public sphere in which dissent and resistance on behalf of rights and liberties were essential features. A diverse coalition emerged. Freethinkers, radical abolitionists, Catholics, labor advocates, and immigrants attempted to strangle reform efforts and enforcement binges in print. Sunday laws, they charged, violated America's commitment to separating church and state and frustrated the promise of religious pluralism that they saw at the core of the American nation.

But the even more influential dissenters were Jews and Seventh Day Baptists, who believed their God commanded them to worship on Saturdays and to work the rest of the week. Especially after authorities prosecuted members of these groups for Sabbath-breaking, Jews and Seventh Day Baptists forged a network of dissent and grass-roots political style focused on the protection of their rights as religious, cultural, and ultimately, moral minorities. Challenging Sunday laws in public, before local and state governments, and in court, they called attention to the potential pitfalls of America's deification of majority rule. Their organized resistance helped lay a cornerstone in the larger cultural reckoning with the place of minority rights in American democracy.[3]

IN NOVEMBER 1844, delegates to the National Lord's Day Convention assembled in Baltimore and chose John Quincy Adams as their presiding officer. Making the trip from Washington, the aging Massachusetts Whig congressman joined an elite group of seventeen hundred clergymen, lawyers, statesmen, doctors, and businessmen from nine states representing various Protestant denominations. They gathered to promote the Christian Sabbath's "sanctification," and to Adams, few causes were as important. Americans had a "duty," he believed, to adhere to God's law, and it was the duty of the convention to convince them. As if the delegates needed reminding, Adams invoked the Fourth Commandment—"Remember the Sabbath day to keep it holy."[4]

Unable to end mail delivery on Sundays the previous decade, Sabbath reformers re-emerged in the 1840s and continued the process of bringing more and more Americans to take an active interest in public life. The National Lord's Day Convention was one of many events that signaled the revival of the Sabbath reform. From Vermont to Alabama to Indiana, reformers formed new associations at the local and state levels. In 1843, committed temperance reformer Justin Edwards took the torch of leadership from Lyman Beecher and organized the American and Foreign Sabbath Union to bring national unity to the burgeoning movement. These associations, composed of prominent preachers and elite and middle-class laymen, spread the reform message at numerous meetings and conventions, by publishing their proceedings widely, and by bombarding the nation with pro-Sabbath literature. Priding themselves on their ability to look past sectarian differences, leaders enlisted the support of various local pulpits and religious presses, with Presbyterians, Congregationalists, Methodists, and Baptists taking the lead. Continuing the message of moral nationalism that guided other reform efforts, Sabbath reformers insisted that the survival of American democracy required widespread Sabbath observance, and thus, their unyielding grass-roots activism in the democratic public sphere.[5]

Moving away from postal policy, these reformers focused on new demons. Most readily, they faced the practical results of market capitalism's continued expansion, which much to their chagrin brought the widespread movement of both goods and people on Sundays. To them, commercial activity and pleasure travel aboard steamboats, canals, railroads, and the "cheap and public modes of conveyance" in cities "perverted" the Sabbath and allured "the population from the sanctuary to scenes of mirth and sin." There was some irony, for the reform movement counted among its ranks prominent businessmen and champions of the very internal improvements that caused Sabbath disruptions. Nonetheless, they still advocated limits to growth and saw the rhythm and moral force of the Sabbath as vital to social stability. Only closing businesses and the arteries of transportation would ensure that "the rights of the people" disturbed in their rest and worship were protected.[6]

Particular segments of society raised concern, none more than wage workers and immigrants. Sunday trade and travel, reformers protested, necessitated labor that fell particularly hard on the antebellum service sector, particularly those "people on our numerous steamers and canal boats, lock tenders, stage drivers, keepers of toll gates, at bridges and on our turn pikes, cooks, waiters, and chamber maids in taverns." As the Sabbath Association of Pittsburgh and Allegheny protested, these men and women were "cruelly deprived of their Sabbath day rights" to worship and rest. More than choosing between God and Mammon, these workers, reformers realized, often had little choice but to work Sundays or seek alternate employment. At least one Sabbath convention was moved to describe this situation as "a slavery more intolerable than that at the South." The employers—state governments, corporations, and the "wealthy or employing portion of the community"—were to blame. If workers were to regain their status as free laborers, and if employers were to shed their disgraceful status as slave masters, the latter groups needed to end their "bad policy of promoting Sabbath desecration."[7]

The European immigrants who arrived in great numbers during the 1840s with Sabbath traditions differing from the Protestant mainstream elicited far fewer sympathies. The question facing the nation, declared O. S. Powell of the Philadelphia Sabbath Association, was whether "the sentiments which our honored forefathers held on this subject, or those which are held on Continental Europe [are to] prevail throughout our beloved country."[8] The "thousands of foreigners—French, Germans, Italians, and English," the New York Evangelist lamented, treated the Sabbath "as a holiday" devoted to "recreation" and "excursions of pleasure." To make matters worse, alcohol figured prominently in their festivities. Joining temperance reformers, Sabbath reformers urged that liquor dealers' "pest houses and dens of iniquity" be shut on Sundays. They also allied with nativists who feared the particular influx of

Catholics, especially those of Irish and German origin. For Cleveland merchant Harmon Kingsbury, Sabbath desecration combined with continued Catholic immigration would foster "a phalanx, headed by a Nero or a Robespierre, [that would] vote away our Sabbaths and our religion; pillage our dwellings; ravish our wives and our daughters; and butcher every man, woman, and child who embraced the Protestant religion." Nativist organs echoed these apocalyptic concerns. "Reader, do you love the Sabbath?" the *Protestant Vindicator* pointedly asked. "Then detest Popery!"[9]

Underlying reformers' concerns, then, was a vision of American democracy predicated on religious and cultural homogeneity and particular ideas about political economy, class relations, and sociopolitical order. First, the type of Sabbath reformers countenanced—religious, restful, quiet, home-centered, contemplative, free of recreation and alcohol—reaffirmed the values of the Protestant middle class while negating the traditions of immigrants and workers. Their efforts also continued to legitimate the rising regimes of market and industrial capitalism. Even while seeking to reduce the days of labor, reformers reaffirmed a discipline of six days of work and one day of rest, and they often did so under the guise of greater profit. Like labor activists in the contemporary ten-hour movement, they mustered the testimony of doctors to prove that more work could be done in six days with Sabbath rest than in seven days without.[10] They even championed Sabbath observance as a way to overcome the widening class divisions of the era. As reformers meeting in Rochester maintained, "The Sabbath brings together all classes of the people: all distinctions are thus broken down; the rich and the poor, the learned and the unlearned, are all brought into the presence, and under the control, of the same infinite God." When combined with its moral force, the Sabbath's equalizing function might help remove "a great political evil"—the power of the "foreign population" and propertyless men "at the ballot box." It would temper the "immediate will" of "the heterogeneous mass" by teaching the hoi polloi to vote with "the highest public good" in mind. To endure, America's democracy, in their appraisal, needed the purifying power of the Protestant Sunday Sabbath.[11]

While some southerners echoed these concerns, many feared the power of a different social segment: slaves and free blacks. Slaves often worked Sundays, but by law and custom the day differed from others. On plantations and in cities slaves were set free from their masters' work demands, and many worked in their own garden plots, gathered socially, and traveled to other plantations to visit kin. Those living in or near towns and cities took the opportunity to purchase goods. Sabbath champions reminded white masters that the Fourth Commandment extended "to all the varied domestic relations," including "master and servant." But beyond the physical well-being and spiritual salvation of their slaves, white southerners desperately feared the risk disorderly slaves posed, particularly in the form of a slave rebellion, and considered Sunday the most dangerous day. In cities where free blacks mingled with slaves, many whites worried that disruption might turn deadly, especially if slaves and free blacks had illegally obtained alcohol from white shopkeepers. In response, some towns and cities organized Sabbath patrols to monitor the black population so that white men and women could attend church without dreading that black men and women might be plotting to kill them.[12]

South and North, as reformers considered how to protect the Sabbath, they contemplated the prospect of legal coercion, including the enforcement of existing bans on Sunday business, industry, and travel. Reformers protested that employers (including state governments) compelled travel and work on Sundays "in direct violation of the laws," and they petitioned canal boards and state legislatures to close canals and government-owned railroad lines. When it came to demanding the enforcement of existing Sunday laws, many hesitated. Some suggested that enforcing these "dead letter[s]" would prompt legal evasion and "create more immorality than it would suppress." Better to use the tactics of moral suasion to influence public behavior. The Pennsylvania Sabbath Convention agreed but also shed light on the perspective held by many professed moral suasionists. "As citizens, we approve the laws which protect the Sabbath" but "ask, as a Convention, no aid from human legislation." With the lessons of the previous Sunday mails campaign and "the Massachusetts Fifteen-Gallon Law" in mind, many reformers felt an overt call for legal coercion would damage their cause.[13]

Others, however, saw great possibilities in using law to achieve reform. Before the National Lord's Day Convention, Delaware jurist Willard Hall, for example, celebrated officials in Delaware and Philadelphia who had restricted Sunday travel with Sunday laws. Despite initial "opposition," he explained, adversaries ultimately "yielded to the firmness of the magistrates; and public opinion has sustained them." So why not use the old Sunday laws elsewhere? Some reformers went as far to insist that government officers were under a "sacred obligation to enforce" Sunday measures, and as authorities in various hamlets, towns, and cities did so in the

1840s, support mounted. As the *New York Evangelist* announced, "This is right. If the laws are just, they ought to be executed; and that they are—that an institution that involves so completely the moral, physical, and political welfare of a people should be protected from violation, no thinking man can doubt."[14]

IN FACT, PLENTY of thinking men and women had other ideas. Immigrants, particularly the much-maligned Catholics, rejected efforts to interfere with their Sunday recreations and deplored the organized movement among Protestant divines. The Baltimore-based *United States Catholic Magazine*, for example, chastised the National Lord's Day Convention for arrogantly taking "the title of *national* convention" and presuming to speak for the entire nation. Sabbath observance, the organ insisted, was "one of those points upon which every one is free to follow his own views." Legal coercion, the magazine rightly predicted, would follow the surge of Sabbath reform, but regardless, it asked, was not the entire Sabbath movement clear evidence of Protestant hypocrisy in the celebrated "land of civil and religious liberty"?[15]

Catholics already had their hands full negotiating the broader nativist outbreak of the 1840s, which they linked to the Sabbath reform and several of the decade's Sunday law enforcement sprees. In New York City, for example, the brouhaha at Daniel Hawley's porterhouse was tied to a fleeting but fundamental shift in the city's political winds that brought the election of a nativist mayor, James Harper, in 1844. In defeating both Whig and Democratic candidates, Harper of the American Republican Party promised to reclaim city government from corrupt foreign influence, sustain the King James (Protestant) version of the Bible in public schools, and bring about tougher naturalization laws. Along with resistance to public funding for Catholic schools, these issues were the heart and soul of political nativism in the 1840s. Harper, however, also pledged to enforce Sunday laws, particularly the long-neglected ordinance banning the Sunday sale of alcohol. Not only were the "multitudes of drinking shops" open for business on the Sabbath, they were, he lamented, "thronged with customers" of the worst kind.[16]

Two key strains of dissent followed Harper's Sunday-closing crackdown. First, critics denounced Sunday laws as an assault on working-class and immigrant culture. In the pages of his *Workingman's Advocate*, labor leader George Henry Evans asked why it was that "the new city government shut up the *small* rum shops in this city" and entirely forgot "the *larger* ones." The answer was obvious. Immigrants typically ran small shops and served the rabble; large establishments, bearing the names "Astor House" and "Marion House," attracted the affluent. Should not attempts to prevent Sunday drinking at least apply equally?[17] A writer for the respectable New York literary magazine *The Knickerbocker* echoed Evans and defended the city's often-targeted German population. To this author, German familial gatherings in beer gardens on Sundays—the bane of many a reformer's existence—explained their communal strength and "superior social manners." Reformers and their "*Special Sabbath Legislation*," by contrast, produced "little else than moroseness and hypocrisy."[18]

Other opponents protested that Sunday laws violated religious liberty and the separation of church and state. The notorious Spartan Band led by Irish immigrant and Democratic politician Mike Walsh, for example, resolved that Sunday laws countered "the spirit of our institutions" by attempting "to unite Church and State." Expanding on this position, the *Knickerbocker*'s critic affirmed that America's democratic commitment to equality, including religious equality, required that all issues of religion be "disconnected from the political power." Because America was home to "a great many different [religious] sects," none should be favored by government. Sunday laws improperly established a "government religion"— Protestant, Sunday-Sabbatizing Christianity—which "in a free republic" was "as absurd as a national costume." Government should stay out of such private matters. Elsewhere, freethinkers and self-described "infidels" reiterated these concerns amid other enforcement binges. Like others, the *Boston Investigator*, the free-thought paper originally founded by Abner Kneeland, urged reformers to return to moral suasion. There was great value in Sunday rest and "religious worship," but local governments had no right "to indicate in what manner an individual shall perform those devotions, or take that rest." To them, such efforts to enforce Sunday laws as Boston Mayor Swift's in 1841 had no genuine religious or moral objectives anyway. They were political tricks designed "to gather in a few votes from the bigoted or unwary."[19]

Countering Sabbath reformers and other advocates of Sunday legislation, these critics advanced cultural pluralism and religious liberty as cornerstones of American democracy. In their view, governmental protection of religious worship would ruin the republican experiment. The implications of their position reflected not only the diversifying ethno-religious order but also the everyday changes accompanying the ascension of market capitalism. During a time when wage work was rising and the divide between work and leisure sharpened, the anti-Sunday law position afforded citizens, especially members of the working class, greater freedom to choose when to work and how to rest. Like Sabbath reformers, critics of Sunday laws no doubt lamented that Americans were increasingly called to work on Sundays. But unlike reformers, they were not about to empower state and local governments to regulate their work and leisure time with punitive measures that impinged upon citizens' ability to determine for themselves how to spend their leisure time. Notably, their position was not merely a laissez-faire, antistatism that detested all government power. To some, government had a far more positive role to play. According to *The Knickerbocker*, local authorities should fund museums, reading rooms, and libraries and keep them open on Sundays for use by all classes. Such government-supported "innocent recreations" would improve the character of the people and Sundays far more than measures criminalizing Sabbath-breaking.[20]

Implicit in many of the anti-Sunday law arguments was the existence of groups whose religious practices differed not only from the Protestant mainstream but also from the mainstream that worshipped on Sundays. As one correspondent to the *United States Catholic Magazine* asked, how was it that "the Jew, the Seventh day Baptist, the Mahometan, the Indian and the infidel are prevented from working on Sunday?" While opponents of Sunday laws pointed to all of these groups, Jews and Seventh Day Baptists were most often cited. The very existence of these respectable God-fearing religious groups with long histories in America mounted a standing challenge to a vision of the United States as a homogeneous Christian nation bound by the usual Christian Sabbath. They ensured that the debate over the Sabbath would not center only on how Sunday should be kept but whether Sunday should be kept at all.[21]

Reformers saw the propensity of critics to rely on these miniscule populations as all too convenient. The *Syracuse Religious Recorder*, for one, found it "curious and instructive" that the New York legislators who refused to close canal locks on Sundays were so sympathetic to the "civil rights" and "consciences" of Jews and Seventh Day Baptists. Could not "a *Christian* government" of an overwhelmingly Christian people prevent violations of "the *Christian* Sabbath"? These few should not stand in the way of a government of the people. Like other evangelical reformers, Sabbath reformers exalted the idea that the United States was a Christian nation to justify their crusade, but when responding to concerns for the rights of seventh-day Sabbath keepers, they amplified this position and applied it to

the character of American government. The United States was undoubtedly a Christian republic, and history, tradition, and the original intent of
the "founders of our republican institutions," who "wisely enacted laws"
protecting the Sabbath, proved it. Though the nation at the outset repudiated "the favouring of one sect more than another," this commitment did
not change the fact that "we were a Christian people, in contradistinc-
tion from Pagan or Mahomedan." Nor did it prohibit the American people
from protecting "the fundamental institutions of Christianity" by law.
Because Sunday laws broadly sanctioned Christianity and favored no particular religious sect, there "was no approximation to a union of Church
and State." Sunday laws were entirely appropriate.[22]

The other side of their defense was linked to the "great canon of
our popular politics"—the democratic dictum that the majority should
rule. "The rules of the social order," as prominent New Jersey Whig
politician and leading reformer Theodore Frelinghuysen put it, must be
suited to "the great mass of citizens." Sunday legislation was no exception. "There may be jews, there may be mussulmen, among a generally christian population," he wrote, "but the law of the majority must
govern." Supporters of enforcement binges concurred. As a backer of
Cincinnati's 1845 Sunday-closing crusade contended, "the government"
could compel the "temporal observance" of the Sabbath and ought to do
so "whenever a majority of the people will support them in its exercise."
The *Syracuse Religious Recorder* put it another way: no self-governing "community of Christians" should have "to accommodate a handful of Jews
and Sabbatarians!" The majority should rule, and their rule was Sunday
Sabbath observance.[23]

More than symbolic pawns in the chess match of Sabbath reform
and Sunday laws, Jews and Seventh Day Baptists emerged in the 1840s
as leading opponents and cemented their place as foundational participants in lasting debates over the nation's religious identity and the rights
of religious and moral minorities within American democracy. Seventh
Day Baptists unwittingly helped spur the Sabbath reform by audaciously
questioning the divinity of the first day of the week as the true "Christian
Sabbath." Since the mid-seventeenth century, Seventh Day Baptists in
England and America had stood apart from other Christians in advancing
the seventh day of the week, Saturday, as the proper Sabbath of God. They
attributed the switch in days from Saturday to Sunday to Roman emperor
Constantine, who first mandated the pagan celebration of Sunday, and the
decision of Catholic authorities to follow this tradition. To Seventh Day

Baptists, the Protestant Reformation was incomplete without the return of the biblical Sabbath first ordained in the Old Testament. Sabbath reformers countered that Christ's resurrection on a Sunday transferred the Sabbath from the seventh day to the first day of the week, but to Seventh Day Baptists this was mere "religious *humbug*."[24]

In the 1840s Seventh Day Baptists remained a small but united religious community, counting sixty-four churches and over six thousand communicants from Rhode Island to Virginia to Iowa. Regional associations and an annual General Conference tied together these local communities. They remained committed to growing their church and disseminating their religious views, especially their perspective on the seventh-day Sabbath, and as Sabbath reformers resurfaced, they sprang to action to combat their "absurd and false" equation of Sunday and the Sabbath. At conferences, meetings, and in the pages of their New York City–based *Sabbath Recorder*, they publicized the opinions of other dissenters and kept tabs on reformers' activities. To them, laws sanctioning Sunday observance were the chief "obstacles" to the growth of their religious group, and as reformers sought "legal enactments in their favor," Seventh Day Baptists cried "despotism" and urged all religious dissenters not to "sleep over the present crisis."[25]

Unlike the Seventh Day Baptists, Jewish Americans in the 1840s were less united by formal institutional mechanisms. Local communities and congregations served as the locus of American Judaism, leaving local groups to defend their own religious liberty. Sunday laws were not the only threat. In 1844, for example, over one hundred Jews in Charleston, South Carolina, challenged the Christian bias of Governor James Henry Hammond's proclamation of a day of thanksgiving. Finding themselves "excluded" and pointing to the South Carolina Constitution's guarantees of religious freedom, they asked Hammond to apologize. Unwilling, Hammond defended his proclamation, reiterated his belief that South Carolina was a "Christian community," and argued that no better evidence of the broad relationship of Christianity to the state than the "laws recognizing the Christian Sabbath." If they "do not violate the Constitution," he asked, "how can my Proclamation?" "If both are unconstitutional, why have not the Israelites commenced by attacking these long-standing laws, and purifying our legislation?" Soon enough, Jews in Charleston and elsewhere would heed Hammond's challenge.[26]

Throughout the developing struggle, efforts to enforce Sunday laws were motivated not just by rising reform sentiment and political nativism but by other decidedly local circumstances. In Charleston, for example, the local Society for the Due Observance of the Lord's Day pushed the city council for a new ordinance to end "Sunday Markets." The common council of Richmond, Virginia, aimed to police the "vicious population of slaves and free Negroes" who illegally purchased goods and alcohol from white merchants on Sundays by raising the existing fine. The city council in Cincinnati, Ohio, also created "considerable excitement" in the summer of 1845 with a new ordinance targeting Sunday businesses, especially those selling liquor. Here, though local reformers applauded this moral advance, the far more skeptical *Cincinnati Daily Times* suggested that the city's financial needs constituted the real impetus behind the new measure. The five-dollar fine brought " 'Fat' times…for the City Treasury," especially because there were "lots of Jews in our city, and plenty of persons to be 'picked up,' for violating the Sabbath." Indeed, in each of these cities, Jews were among those prosecuted and fined for keeping their shops open on Sundays, and several objected.[27]

Seventh Day Baptists also became entangled with Sunday laws. The most important incident developed in rural south-central Pennsylvania, where a group of German Seventh Day Baptists resided together at a commune known as Snow Hill. The Snow Hill Society was linked to the nearby Ephrata Cloister, begun by Conrad Beissel, a German Pietist (or Dunker) believing in the seventh-day Sabbath, in the eighteenth century. Ephrata flourished, becoming renowned for its music, and by the late eighteenth century, some members sought to expand Beissel's teachings by founding the Snow Hill Society not far from Gettysburg and Chambersburg. In the mid-1840s Snow Hill comprised about thirty members who lived, worshipped, and worked a 165-acre farm together. Despite the fact that the members observed the Saturday Sabbath and worked the other six days of the week, they had never been prosecuted for violating Pennsylvania's Sunday law.[28]

For several years, young men and boys from neighboring towns made uninvited and disruptive visits to the Snow Hill Society's annual meetings. The peaceful Snow Hill brethren, as one commentator remembered, "being entirely averse to litigation or contention of any kind…patiently bore with all." In 1845, however, the annual disruption turned riotous as intoxicated, foul-mouthed youths ran wildly through the buildings, cut property with knives, broke windows, and smeared butter on the kitchen floor and walls. In the aftermath, authorities threatened to lock up the "meetinghouse if such disorderly gatherings were continued" and pushed members to disclose the identities of the miscreants. Eleven youths received thirty-day prison sentences; others were fined. In the aftermath, the Sunday law became a tool of retribution. As three Snow Hill members recounted, "The defendants were sentenced on Saturday. Within ten days afterwards, prosecutions were commenced against several members of the congregation for working on Sunday, and fines collected from them." Snow Hill's Seventh Day Baptists became victims of repeated prosecutions, as they saw it, only out of "malice and revenge."[29]

Sunday laws were that type of regulation. They could be "dead letters" for years, only to be suddenly deployed to harass the unpopular and to reap retribution. The reigning method of private prosecution, by which any citizen could file a complaint before a justice of the peace and gain a portion of any fine collected, compounded this. "Any blind bigot or designing hypocrite," a Seventh Day Baptist critic objected, could "wreak his vengeance upon the man who may have offended him, and *that* under the cloak of religion." The accused also were at the mercy of local justices of the peace who might have their own interest in targeted enforcement. The magistrate who fined the Snow Hill Baptists was reportedly the father of "one of the young men imprisoned for riotous conduct." Understating the situation, one commentator suggested that the justice "may have been biased in his decision." Like their Jewish compatriots, Seventh Day Baptists were not about to allow these miscarriages of justice to stand.[30]

"HOWEVER PERFECT ANY system of government may originally be…there will always occur in the process of time, something to warn one that no man can sit down quietly under the assumed security which the laws give him; but that, on the contrary, it is his business to watch carefully the executors of the law, if he wishes to have his liberties preserved, untouched, so that they be not taken from him little by little." In 1846, American Jewish leader Isaac Leeser called for vigilance. The spirit of religious freedom, cherished by the "sages of the American Revolution" and enshrined in the federal and state constitutions they established, was under assault by measures threatening the rights of Jews and others who did not worship on Sundays. The "worst feature in all this," Leeser protested, was "that the whole agitation is presupposed to rest upon the will of the majority." Even if majorities did support Sunday laws, it was of no consequence. There were some issues in which the majority could not rule; religion was one of them. For American democracy to survive, dissenting minorities needed to defend their rights by taking a stand against Sunday laws.[31]

As Jews and Seventh Day Baptists protested the thickening web of Sunday surveillance in the 1840s, key leaders, such as Isaac Leeser, stepped forward to provide intellectual sustenance and coordination between local theaters (fig. 2.1). Born in Germany in 1806, Leeser immigrated to the United States in 1824 and at a young age established himself as an advocate for American Jews and a vocal defender of Judaism internationally. In 1829 he relocated from Richmond to Philadelphia to become the religious leader (*hazzan*) of the Michveh Israel congregation and in that post became the most prominent Jewish leader in America. Amid the vast increase in Jewish (mostly German) immigration in the mid-1840s, Leeser founded the first successful American Jewish periodical, the *Occident and American Jewish Advocate*, to unite this widely dispersed community.[32]

Even before the mid-1840s, Leeser identified Sunday laws as evidence that Jews in America were second-class citizens. Leeser followed Moses Mendelssohn, a late eighteenth-century German-Jewish enlightenment thinker who surpassed John Locke's theory of religious toleration, which

FIGURE 2.1   Isaac Leeser. Courtesy of the Library of Congress. Jewish leader Isaac Leeser coordinated dissent and spearheaded resistance to Sunday laws in the 1840s.

limited the toleration afforded to Catholics and atheists, by insisting on full equality for all religious sects through the complete separation of church and state. In a touchstone pamphlet published in 1840 entitled *The Claims of the Jews to an Equality of Rights*, Leeser echoed Mendelssohn and demanded that American Christians "not merely *tolerate* the sons of Israel as a special act of grace, but do more, and declare us your equals." Critically, Leeser adapted Mendelssohn's ideas to America's rising faith in majority rule. "The majority no matter how large," he maintained, "have no right to claim any merit for leaving the minority undisturbed in the enjoyment of equal right." It was not for the Christian majority to tolerate the Jewish minority altruistically, nor could they violate the rights of religious minorities. To Leeser, America's democratic order required the protection of religious minorities and the abrogation of Sunday laws. Only then would Judaism have an equal opportunity to flourish in American society.[33]

Leeser used the *Occident* to alert Jews to the rising threats of Sunday legislation and, in fact, dedicated more space to their discussion than any other measure of public policy in the 1840s and 1850s. To Leeser, the general forces of Protestant conformity already endangered the Jewish Saturday Sabbath—"the soul of our religious polity"—and Sunday laws would only exacerbate an already trying situation. Jews would perceive two days of rest, one by religious law and the other by Sunday law, to place them at a serious economic disadvantage to most Americans, who worked six days a week. When forced to choose between observing their Sabbath and working Saturdays, many Jews, Leeser feared, would choose to work. This would be a major blow to Judaism in the United States.[34]

Leeser's position was not that of all Jewish Americans. Prominent diplomat and journalist Mordecai Noah, for example, never thought Jews should abandon their own Sabbath, but he nevertheless counseled respect for the Christian majority's tradition of Sunday Sabbatizing. Such deference would allow American Jews to gain social acceptance and maintain harmony between Christians and Jews. Noah's vision of religious liberty was far more tolerationist than Leeser's. "Freedom of religion," Noah explained, "means a mere abolition of all religious disabilities. You are free to worship God in any manner you please; and this liberty of conscience cannot be violated." According to Noah, Sunday laws were merely minor prohibitions that did not prevent Jews from worshipping on Saturday. Agreeing with those who insisted that America was a Christian nation, Noah contended that if Jews "possessed a government of their own, they would assuredly prohibit labor on the Sabbath day." So why should Jewish Americans seek to "prohibit Christians from enforcing" their Sabbath? In no way should Jews "question" the Sunday laws. "Respect to the laws of the land we live in, is the first duty of good citizens of all denominations." To him, Leeser's call for minority-rights activism would only damage American Jews.[35]

Leading Seventh Day Baptists sided with Leeser. As they echoed his call for resistance and the protection of minority rights, Samuel Davison, William M. Fahnestock, Eli S. Bailey, George B. Utter, and others began to transform from mere religious leaders into new types of grass-roots minority-rights activists (fig. 2.2). They recognized that defeating Sunday laws would require alliances beyond their small religious group, so they joined with Leeser and others to create a network of dissent. Their goals: to combat criminal prosecutions of Sabbath-breaking and to create "a revolution in public sentiment" about Sunday laws and the rights of religious minorities. Implementing a democratic politics of dissent predicated upon the uninhibited expression of ideas, they used their presses

FIGURE 2.2   George B. Utter. From the archives of the Seventh Day Baptist Historical Society, Janesville, WI. Seventh Day Baptist leader George B. Utter edited the *Sabbath Recorder*, which staunchly opposed Sunday laws and alerted readers to the growing threat to religious liberty.

to publicize the mounting threat and to persuade all Americans that "the religious rights of every minor sect in the country" were at risk. They highlighted the local tribulations of seventh-day observers and printed scores of articles and petitions addressed to local and state authorities asking for the repeal of Sunday laws or, at the very least, exemptions for seventh-day observers. In 1846, the Seventh Day Baptist General Conference capped the public-opinion campaign with an influential pamphlet—*Religious Liberty Endangered by Legislative Enactments*—that their American Tract Society circulated widely. This was all foundational activism in the era's emerging popular minority-rights politics.[36]

These dissenters found support in a variety of circles. The freethinking *Boston Investigator*, for example, bolstered the emerging network of dissent by publicizing Sunday-law conflicts and reprinting articles from the Seventh Day Baptists' *Sabbath Recorder*.[37] Arguably their most controversial support, however, came from the radical abolitionists allied with William Lloyd Garrison. Garrison had broken with Sabbath reformers amid his growing disillusionment with northern churches that refused to support abolitionists' call for immediate emancipation. The turning point came in 1836 when Garrison lashed out at Lyman Beecher, who at a Pittsburgh Sabbath meeting uttered the catchphrase that the Sabbath was the "great sun of the moral world." Miffed that Beecher refused to embrace abolitionism, Garrison accused him of privileging the Fourth Commandment above the nine others, which the institution of slavery so obviously violated. Garrison ridiculed Beecher's position, maintaining that every day should be spent in the service of Christ, not merely the first. Garrison made few friends among more orthodox clergymen, several of whom denounced him as an infidel. Nonetheless, several leading abolitionists, especially Quakers James and Lucretia Mott, joined him in opposing the Sabbath reform and Sunday laws.[38]

Garrison had long used the *Liberator* to advance the cause of radical abolition, and in the 1840s he used its pages to criticize Sabbath reformers, but the apotheosis of Garrisonian efforts came at an Anti-Sabbath Convention held in Boston in 1848. For two days radical abolitionists deplored Sabbath reformers, Sunday legislation, and the quandary of Jews, Seventh Day Baptists, and other victims of Sunday laws. This last group included abolitionists, who had themselves fallen victim to malevolent prosecutions. The most notorious incident involved Philadelphian Charles C. Burleigh, who was arrested for violating the Sunday law after besting an elder of the Presbyterian Church named James McKissick in a public antislavery debate. Burleigh regularly sold abolitionist tracts after meetings, even on Sundays, and McKissick contended that this was work that violated Pennsylvania's Sunday law and had Burleigh fined four dollars. Burleigh refused to pay and spent time in prison before friends secured his release. This highly public incident further incensed Garrisonians, bringing them to join Jews and Seventh Day Baptists as leaders of the anti-Sunday law network.[39]

The heart of their collective resistance was the wide dissemination of a political and constitutional critique of Sunday laws, which they hoped would counter Sabbath reformers' activism and sway the public. First, they repudiated the notion that the United States was "a Christian country" with a Christian government. Though the bulk of Americans were Christians, their broad religious persuasion did not transfer to the government. This did not make the United States "an atheistical country," as many advocates of Sunday laws claimed it would. It merely meant that there was no "state religion." To Isaac Leeser, for Christianity to be the "religion of the state," the US Constitution and the constitutions of the several states would have to say as much. Except for a handful of state constitutions, these documents remained "absolutely silent." Rather than enshrining Christianity in American government, the "sages of the American Revolution" intended that "all religions" should stand "alike on one platform" and be "left at perfect liberty to extend themselves by persuasion or by the strength of their principles." This was the brilliant "voluntary principle" under which religious pluralism flourished in the United States. It meant that Sunday Sabbatizers were "no more entitled to protection from the annoyance of worldly occupations in their holy time, than the Jew and the Seventh day Baptists in theirs."[40]

More concretely, opponents pointed to constitutional protections of religious liberty. Looking to the national Constitution, they targeted the First Amendment's establishment clause, assumed its provisions applied to the actions of state governments, and argued that it restricted their ability to support one religion or religious practice over another. They treated Johnson's Sunday Mail Report, which had repudiated reformers' campaign against the Sunday mails, as sacrosanct. They insisted its dictum that Congress could not "legislate in favor of the first day of the week" applied to state governments that acted "under similar Constitutions." Most state constitutions and bills of rights denied "the right of the legislature to enact laws which shall give preferences to any form of religion." These restrictions mandated religious equality and prevented state and local governments from "assigning to Sunday-keeping Christians more legal protection than is accorded to Jews and the Seventh-Day Baptists." Sunday laws violated these provisions.[41]

Jews, Seventh Day Baptists, and Garrisonian abolitionists also suggested that Sunday laws violated natural rights, particularly the "perfect liberty for every inhabitant to worship God according to the dictates of his own conscience." Some state constitutions, like the national Constitution's First Amendment, protected the "free exercise" of religion, and nearly all declared, as did Pennsylvania's, that government could not "interfere with the rights of conscience." But what exactly were the rights of conscience? According to the anti-Sunday law network, the rights of conscience guaranteed, at the very least, "the right of private judgment in matters of religion" without state interference. Much like "Jewish circumcision, infant baptism of the Episcopal and Presbyterian Churches, the immersion of adults of the Baptists, or the confession and extreme unction of the Roman Catholic body," government had no power to control the day of Sabbath observance.[42] Defenders maintained that Sunday laws did not infringe on seventh-day sabbatizers' ability to worship on Saturdays and, thus, presented no limitation on conscience. But Jews and Seventh Day Baptists retorted that it was "a matter of conscience both to work six days and to rest the seventh." By requiring seventh-day observers to stop working a second day in the week, Sunday laws amounted to a "tax upon conscience." As one critic described, "the opinion of a majority" was robbing "a conscientious minority . . . *of the privilege of transacting business on fifty-two days of the year.*" Only the eradication of Sunday laws would allow seventh-day observers to "worship God *on his* own sanctified day . . . and *give the remainder of the week* to [their] own wonted, unostentatious industry." Especially because the laws prevented them from fulfilling their God's command to work six days and rest one, Jews and Seventh Day Baptists argued that Sunday laws were unconstitutional.[43]

In conjunction with these constitutional objections, Jews, Seventh Day Baptists, and abolitionists tackled the majoritarian rationales that supporters had offered to legitimate Sunday laws. Here these groups began the process by which antebellum moral minorities broadcast a conception of democracy that included the protection of the rights of social and cultural minorities. We are "commonly urged," Seventh Day Baptist leader Eli S. Bailey bemoaned, "that we are the minority, and therefore must submit to the dictation of the majority." This, he thought, was "not only illogical

but untrue" because America's commitment to democracy did not authorize "an absolute Religious Despotism in the Majority." In its widely circulated pamphlet, the Seventh Day Baptist General Conference expanded
on Bailey's position. "Might is not right," the pamphlet declared; "neither does the accident of being a *majority* give any claim to trample on
the rights of the minority." While majorities could rule in purely "civil
affairs," when dealing with religion and "the laws of God," they could not
"oppress the minority, or set at naught their indefeasible rights." In violating the constitutionally protected rights of minorities, Sunday laws violated American democracy.[44]

Opponents insisted that authorizing legislatures to "legalize and
enforce the religious opinions of the majority" established a dangerous
precedent that would not end with Sunday legislation. Leading critics
conjured slippery-slope scenarios to illustrate the potentially frightful consequences of absolute religious majoritarianism. In their petition to the
city government, Richmond Jews invited readers to imagine a majority
composed of "Israelites and Seventh-Day Baptists" compelling "Catholics,
Episcopalians, and Methodists, to close their places of business and retire
from the field and workshops" on Saturdays. A Roman Catholic majority might compel Protestants to observe all "holy days of their church";
a non-Sabbatizing majority might forbid "the observance of any day as
the Sabbath." Some of these imagined majorities and their hypothetical
measures pushed the limits of rational plausibility, but the dissenters'
broader point remained. If legislatures supported by popular majorities
could legitimately "appoint days of religious worship, and enforce their
observance," nothing would stop them from extending their power over
other religious subjects.[45]

These challenges built upon the arguments of others who worried
about majoritarian democracy's tyrannical potential, especially those who
sensed early dangers posed by religious majorities and Sunday legislation. In 1838, for example, the mercurial intellectual Orestes Brownson, in
addition to bewailing moral reformers' tendency toward "ultraism," repudiated evangelicals who turned to majority rule to establish the United
States as a "Christian nation" and to support measures like Sunday laws.
Though Brownson remained committed to Andrew Jackson's Democratic
Party, which strongly championed majority rule, by the late 1830s he was
increasingly drawn to John C. Calhoun's warnings about the hazards
democracy posed to minority rights. Calhoun's concerns were linked
to the defense of the slaveholding minority, but like other antebellum

Americans, Brownson saw the fruits of Calhoun's apprehensions manifesting in other policies too. To Brownson, religious belief was "an individual concernment," which majoritarian democracy could not interfere. "Are the rights of man," he asked, "matters dependent on the will of the majority? Does one's rights as a man vary as he chances to be in the majority or in the minority?" Brownson thought not. Though Christianity undoubtedly formed the "moral sense" of an overwhelming majority of the community, it did not justify "legal and political sanctions" supporting "the dogmas or discipline of Christianity." Certainly, those questioning Sunday laws during the following decade agreed.[46]

While amplifying Brownson's assessment and showing how Sunday laws actually impinged upon religious minorities, dissenters in the 1840s added new depth and flavor to earlier warnings. Many, for example, peppered their indictments with suggestions that Sunday laws represented "a union of Church and State" but implied that the "church" of concern was a new church of the Christian majority. Supporters retorted that Sunday laws created no union of church and state because they were sanctioned by a nonsectarian Christian majority, not a particular sect, religious denomination, or church. Critics, however, suggested that the movement among several united denominations for Sunday laws necessitated a rethinking of the idea of the "church" because in the question of Sunday observance, nearly all sects "united in one." "We are presented," one commentator in the *Sabbath Recorder* lamented, "with the alarming spectacle of several different orders amalgamated in one entire denomination, having a creed which contains but one single article"—"the sacredness of Sunday." What would stop them from becoming "united on other points" to the extent that they might "apply to have their tenets enforced by law"? Would this not constitute "a union of Church and State"? Sunday laws required immediate abatement lest the amalgamated church of the Christian majority point to these measures "as precedent for farther enactments."[47]

In recognizing this problem, opponents of Sunday laws were returning in some ways to James Madison's thinking on religious freedom. Working with Thomas Jefferson to disestablish the Anglican Church in Virginia in the 1780s, Madison argued in his *Memorial and Remonstrance Against Religious Assessments* for the religious rights of minorities. "Religion," he maintained, "must be left to the conviction and conscience of every man; and it is the right of every man to exercise it as these may dictate." Precisely because "the majority may trespass on the rights of the minority," Madison declared, religion needed to "be exempt from the authority of the Society at large" and especially "the Legislative Body." But beyond offering constitutional limitations to protect religious minorities from overbearing majorities, Madison argued that religious liberty would best be protected through the continual competition among religious sects. Religious pluralism would prevent one church or a group of churches from forming a majority and seeking the aid of public policy. Antebellum opponents of Sunday laws were witnessing a breakdown in Madison's theory as a powerful interdenominational coalition—the Sabbath reformers—united to enshrine the protection of the majority's ability to worship on Sunday in law. This breakdown had led dissenters to do what even Madison might not have foreseen: form their own grass-roots coalition—a minority group—that transcended sectarian boundaries. It also brought them to embrace the constitutions and bills of rights that Madison himself had doubted could adequately protect the rights of minorities.[48]

Some detractors pushed the analysis of majoritarian democracy even further by questioning if the amalgamated church of the Christian majority actually supported Sunday laws. Advocates had often assumed as much, and many opponents failed to question the veracity of this assumption. Others, however, reminded the public that an influential cadre of reformers had sparked controversy by "manufacturing public opinion." Absent their well-financed and influential media campaign, Sunday laws, some suggested, would find little support. As Isaac Leeser argued, "Were the vote taken throughout the country and each man were to answer without the fear of his neighbours upon him, it would be 'Let those keep Sunday who will, and let others do as they like.'" Majorities did not really support the oppressive regime of Sunday legislation. Their tacit support came only because reformers had fostered "an artificial state of public opinion, for the purpose of crushing those who differ from them." Echoing Alexis de Tocqueville, Leeser maintained that this ordeal illustrated "the potent arm of legislative enactments," and worse, "the still more powerful one of 'Public Opinion,'" which was "a tyrant greater in power over the mind of men in a free country, than is the will of the Czar in his dominions." To Leeser, the will of the majority could and should be determined in a purer way, certainly without inordinate influence of the moralists. Regardless, whether majorities were constituted by "numbers, or physical power, or dominant influence," they should be powerless on the question of Sunday observance. To make this point, the anti-Sunday law minority embraced the tactics of their adversaries—associationalism and public-opinion crusades. Only by meeting the enemy in the democratic public sphere could they hope to protect their rights.[49]

THE FINAL ESSENTIAL tactic employed by the anti-Sunday law minority—and one not used by their adversaries—was a turn to the judicial system. As authorities prosecuted them for Sabbath-breaking, Jews and Seventh Day Baptists hired attorneys and tested the constitutionality of Sunday laws. To them, the court system and judicial review posed no counter-majoritarian difficulty. The protection of minority rights was part of the normal workings of American democracy, and courts, in their view, were properly charged with that responsibility. Beyond the decisions, court action also served a public-opinion function. Their test cases before three state supreme courts gave the anti-Sunday law network yet another prominent place to put their critique of the Christian republic, Sunday legislation, and absolute majority rule on display.

Two so-called Jew Cases grew out of arrests of Jewish residents of Charleston, South Carolina, and Cincinnati, Ohio, for keeping open shops on Sunday in violation of city ordinances. The cases yielded somewhat opposite conclusions. In *City Council v. Benjamin*, the South Carolina Supreme Court ruled that Charleston's Sunday ordinance did not violate the state constitution's protections of the "liberty of conscience" and the "free exercise and enjoyment of religious profession and worship, without discrimination or preference." Judge John Belton O'Neall, a leader in South Carolina's Sabbath reform drive, fashioned himself as a religious expert. Not only did he insist that Christianity was the only "standard of good morals," but in rejecting the plea that the Sunday ordinance interfered with Jewish citizens' ability to labor six days in keeping with their religious views, he examined the Old Testament and denied that Jews were under any such obligation. Because the "Hebrew" could freely observe the seventh day "at his peril," the Sunday ordinance did not interfere with the "free exercise" of religion or violate the liberty of conscience. O'Neall also rejected arguments that the Sunday ordinance gave "preference" to any religious tradition by secularizing the Sunday ordinance. It was, "in a political and social point of view, a mere day of rest." The law was "general, operating upon all" and did not "give a Christian a preference over an Israelite," nor did it divide citizens "into Christians and Hebrews." Everyone equally had to "cease from business on Sunday." Any difficulties Jews encountered were not "the effect of our law" but the result of their religion. If Jews wanted to continue enjoying their religion's "cherished benefits" while "living in a community who have appointed a different day of rest," they needed to refrain from Sunday work.[50]

In the other leading case involving a Jewish litigant, the Ohio Supreme Court agreed with the ruling of a lower court that exempted seventh-day observers from Cincinnati's Sunday ordinance. The ordinance's first section restricted a range of Sunday activities, yet a second section stipulated that nothing in the first section "shall be construed to extend to those who conscientiously" observed the Sabbath on the seventh day of the week. While Jacob Rice's counsel suggested that the ordinance itself violated the Ohio Constitution's protections of religious freedom, the case ultimately turned on whether Rice's activities as a merchant were exempted from prosecution because he was Jewish and conscientiously celebrated the Saturday Sabbath. Sidestepping the larger constitutional question, the Court ruled that Rice's activities and those of other "Jewish merchants" were exempted from the Sunday ordinance. Rice's conviction was void. Some opponents of Sunday laws misread the relative narrowness of the decision and hoped, as did one Seventh Day Baptist commentator, that the Pennsylvania Supreme Court would follow it and "extend the same rights and immunities" to the German Seventh Day Baptists of Snow Hill. He would be disappointed.[51]

Having failed to secure any relief from the state legislature or from local courts, the Snow Hill Society, with the support of the larger Seventh Day Baptist network, appealed the case of one of their Sabbath-breaking farmers, Jacob Specht, to the Pennsylvania Supreme Court. They gained the assistance of a lawyer named Thaddeus Stevens (fig. 2.3). In the mid-1840s Stevens was practicing law in nearby Gettysburg, and he had already established credentials that made him a fitting advocate for the Seventh Day Baptists. Though a Whig partisan, Stevens had a reputation for independent-mindedness and a history of embracing controversial causes. He staunchly advocated free public education, criticized capital punishment, defended fugitive slaves, supported black suffrage rights, and opposed slavery's westward expansion. His defense of the Snow Hill Baptists, which involved, in the words of the critics of Sunday laws, principles of equality, civil rights, human rights, minority rights, and democracy, provided another site in which Stevens cemented lifelong commitments to social equality and the defense of oppressed minorities.[52]

When *Specht v. Commonwealth* came to court in 1848, Stevens's argument provided a capstone to the many arguments previously made against Sunday laws. Most centrally, Stevens maintained that Pennsylvania's

FIGURE 2.3   Thaddeus Stevens. Courtesy of the Library of Congress.

Sunday law violated the state constitution's protection of religious free-dom and "the rights of conscience." To him, the rights of conscience were a key part of "the inalienable rights of man." Despite arguments to the contrary, Stevens insisted that the Sunday law was more than a secular civil regulation. It treated Sunday as a "*holy*, and a *sacred* day" and prohib-ited labor, not to give "rest to man," but because labor "*profanes* the Lord's day." For those like his clients who believed that Sunday was "not a holy day" and not the "true Sabbath of the Lord," to prevent them from working was "an 'interference' with and a constraint of their rights of conscience" and akin to ordering them to "kneel before the altar, or the images of the Saints." If the Court did not take the opportunity to prevent the legislature from enforcing "the *religious* observance of the day," it would set a dan-gerous precedent that would authorize potentially limitless "power over religious subjects" and facilitate "a perfect union of Church and state" that would "inevitably lead to religious persecutions, and finally to civil and religious tyranny."[53]

Stevens concluded with a full endorsement of the "independent Judiciary" and its most important role in America's constitutional democ-racy: to "protect *minorities* against the will of majorities." The Court needed to "stand by the constitution, and interpose their protecting shield between the *many* and the *few*" by defending religious minorities from the majority's oppressive Sunday law. If the Court failed "to do this out of respect to a majority, that sovereign of Republics, history" would rank them with the lowliest of judges. Not to put too fine a point on it, Stevens reminded the Court that "It was the same influence—the voice of the PEOPLE, crying 'crucify him! crucify him!' that bore down the judgment of Pilate, and made him the judicial murderer of HIM, who suffered for conscience's sake." Unlike Pilate, the Court needed to ignore the "majorities forgetful of the true principles of our government" and defend the "civil and religious liberty" of minorities.[54]

In defending the Sunday law, opposing counsel, Democrat James Nill, echoed those who emphasized the restful benefits brought by the Sunday law. Not a religious regulation, the Sunday law was a highly beneficial "political regulation" that restricted "worldly employments" and furnished "repose to the weary" and "opportunities for reading, study, and reflection." To Nill, majorities could control rest, and as the "vast majority" rested on Sundays, why, he asked, would "it be pretended that the legislature cannot protect them in so doing?" Nill also addressed the rights of conscience. To him, the Sunday law prevented no one "from worshipping God as he chooses, or as his conscience dictates" and therefore, posed no threat to "the rights of conscience." Claims of "conscience" like those advanced by Seventh Day Baptists, he maintained, presented serious problems for a society trying to regulate itself. What were the limits of the rights of conscience? How could a society pass laws if an individual or a minority group could claim they were unconstitutional because they had some sort of conscientious objection? He explained:

> If laws could be made to conform to all the religious caprices that frenzied fanaticism would suggest, there would not be days enough in the week to accommodate such conscientious scruples. Mohammedans would want Friday, another sect another day, &c., &c. The laws against bigamy would have to be declared unconstitutional, because of the consciences of those who would desire a plurality of wives.

Positions like these already had "been assumed," and if the Court allowed the consciences of the Seventh Day Baptists to quash the Sunday law, there was no telling what immoral practices would be out of the reach of the laws.[55]

In *Specht v. Commonwealth* the Pennsylvania Supreme Court unanimously upheld the constitutionality of the Sunday law but offered two very different opinions that signaled a growing divergence in how Sunday laws were justified. Unswayed by Stevens's "ingenious argument," Judge Thomas S. Bell agreed with James Nill that the Sunday law was "a civil regulation" mandating a day of rest and not a religious regulation that might interfere with religious freedom. "All agree," he wrote, "that to the well-being of society, periods of rest are absolutely necessary," and the legislature had the power to "fix the time" of rest and to "enforce obedience." One day needed to be chosen, and "in a Christian community, where a very large majority of the people celebrate the first day of the week as their chosen period of rest from labour, it is not surprising that that day should have received the legislative sanction." That a "large majority" devoted the day to "religious observances" did not change the secular "character of the enactment."[56]

Judge Bell agreed that the state constitution secured "freedom of conscience and equality of religious right," but heeding Nill's warnings, he limited the scope of those guarantees. In his understanding, freedom of conscience meant that "no man, living under the protection of our institutions, can be coerced to profess any form of religious belief, or to practise any peculiar mode of worship, in preference to another." There was no such coercion in the Sunday law. It did not command "the performance of religious rites" or "infringe upon the Sabbath of any sect, or curtail their freedom of worship." It compelled no one "to attend, erect, or support any place of worship, or to maintain any ministry against his consent." Neither did it treat any "religious doctrine as paramount in the state" or give "preference to any religious establishment or mode of worship." All were free to exercise "their distinctive religious tenets" without interference. The "inconvenience" that "the Jew and the Seventh-day Christian" suffer from having "two successive days of withdrawal from worldly affairs" was merely "an incidental worldly disadvantage" that did not interfere with their rights of conscience. In addition, Bell rejected the "supposed article of" the Seventh Day Baptist faith that required them to work six days. Like South Carolina's Judge O'Neall, Bell assumed the role of biblical interpreter and maintained that the Seventh Day Baptists had gotten their own religious interpretation wrong. The Fourth Commandment did not require six days of labor and one day of rest, and therefore, Sunday laws presented no violation of conscience and thus, were perfectly constitutional.[57]

From the other end of the bench Judge Richard Coulter agreed that the Sunday law was constitutional but for very different reasons. Not a secular labor regulation, the law functioned quite properly to "guard the Christian Sabbath from profanation." Repeating the arguments of Sabbath reformers, Coulter observed, "We are a Christian people and State; we are part and parcel of a great Christian nation. All over the length and breadth of this great nation, the Christian Sabbath is recognised, and guarded by the law as a day of sacred rest." Pointing to William Penn and "the pilgrims in the Mayflower," Coulter asserted that America was born with Sabbath observance. All social order depended on it. Clearly bothered by the implications of Bell's secularized defense of Sunday law, Coulter asked why the Court did "not regard it as our forefathers regarded it, and as the statute declares it to be—the Lord's day?" The Sunday law should stand on its proper religious foundations and as an emblem of the Christian republic.[58]

To those moral minorities who had worked to defeat Sunday laws, the decision was a setback that distorted their vision of an American democracy committed to religious equality and the protection of minority rights. Faithful *Sabbath Recorder* correspondent William M. Fahnestock surmised that the Court's decision would inflict "a deeper, more indelible infamy...on the institutions of our Republic" in the "eyes of the world" than America's reprehensible treatment of Native Americans and its "unrighteous and unjustifiable war with Mexico, to extend the area of *slavery*." For Isaac Leeser, it was a sign of things to come. "Religious and political equality," he wrote, "have been the day-dreams of the philanthropist for many centuries; and it was ardently hoped that this country was the place where man could meet man upon a uniform level...But, alas! The dream was but a dream." Should the views of the Court prevail, all semblance of religious and political equality was destined to disappear.[59]

The decision brought extensive commentary and allowed the public yet another opportunity to consider Sunday laws' political and constitutional legitimacy. Seventh-day observers and other dissenters continued their opposition and exposed the great "inconsistencies" between the "two sets of...arguments" offered by the Pennsylvania Supreme Court.[60] For others, *Specht v. Commonwealth* seemed to generate confusion and concern. Noting that many presses remained curiously silent about the decision, the *Sabbath Recorder* surmised that the "Sunday sticklers" who cherished "its sacred character" could not approve of Bell's secularized Sunday law. Even though Coulter's opinion confirmed Sunday laws' religious sanctity, it too brought concerns. For example, the *Christian Chronicle*, a Philadelphia-based Baptist paper, worried that Coulter's broad Christian defense of the Sunday law might obligate the state "to see that all men obey the laws which emanate from the founder of Christianity" and lead it to legislate "the proper mode of baptism." All in all, the *Sabbath Recorder* perceptively noted that the Court's decision did not satisfy either "the Court itself or the people." Rather, "its effect" was "to unsettle the whole question."[61]

The Pennsylvania case also brought new voices into the discussion, most critically the *United States Democratic Review*, which served as the national mouthpiece for the Democratic Party. Though baffled that Bell and Coulter legitimated the Sunday law "on diametrically opposite grounds," the *Review* maintained that it was irrelevant whether the Sunday law was "regarded as a civil, or as a religious establishment." Either way, it was "a flagrant violation of political right." The *Review* saw other threatening implications of the decision, notably Bell's assertion that "since a 'large *majority* of the people celebrate the first day of the week... it is not surprising that that day should have received the legislative sanction.'" This spoke to a dangerous tendency with majoritarian democracy. Echoing partisan foe Thaddeus Stevens and finding a rare moment of implicit agreement with Garrisonian abolitionists, the *Review* explained:

It certainly is not good law that a majority, because "very large," can of right do what the established constitution of their government expressly prohibits them from doing. One great pride and glory in this fundamental contract of the people is, that it was designed to secure the "natural and indefeasible rights" of the minority, however small, from the violations and encroachments of the majority: and to deny that the sacredness of conscience shall be measured by its popularity.

Like other opponents of Sunday laws, the *Review* was not about to concede that legislatures acting on behalf of popular majorities could violate national or state constitutions. As other critics had proclaimed, American democracy had to be more than majority rule. If democracy were to establish a truly free society, it had to ensure the rights of even the smallest minorities.[62]

Not everyone agreed. Though doubting that enforcing Sunday laws would prevent Sabbath-breaking, the *Methodist Quarterly Review*, for example, still rejected "the fanatical crusade that Infidelity is now waging against" them. Whether the laws worked or not, "the majority of every political community, be it Christian, Pagan, Mussulman, or Jewish, have a right to enact laws for the protection of their lawful privileges; and a minority have no right to disturb them in its peaceful exercise." Religious majorities could in fact rule, and no motley mishmash of Jews, abolitionists, freethinkers, Catholics, and Seventh Day Baptists was going to tell America's Sunday-Sabbatizing, Protestant majority otherwise.[63]

NOT LONG AFTER the German Seventh Day Baptists of Snow Hill lost their case, the local sheriff came to collect fines and court costs. He took and sold property of Jacob Specht and Peter Fyock, and since Andrew Monn, David Monn, and John Burger had no property worth taking, the bail they had posted during their drawn out case was not returned. All in all, about $100 was wrested from them. As if to add insult to injury, the "persecution" continued. During the fall harvest of 1848, members of the society were again "informed against" for immoral behavior: first for harvesting wheat and then for picking apples on Sunday. At least three offenders spent time in jail. Looking on, Isaac Leeser deemed this to be the picture of "the Christian Sabbath, as Sanctioned by the Supreme Court of Pennsylvania." What exactly, he implicitly asked, was so Christian about this penal veneration of the Sabbath? Rather, it was the picture of "tyranny," and it was "a tyranny the more galling as there is no redress, the majority not likely being willing to repeal a law, which, though evidently against the spirit of the constitution, has been sanctioned by the Supreme Bench in deference to popular clamour." A tyrannical majority reigned in Pennsylvania.[64]

With the persecution continuing, the Snow Hill brethren turned again to the state legislature, hoping this time to secure an exemption from the Sunday law like the one that had protected Jews in Cincinnati. Twice they would be rejected, but not without comment. In 1850, a House committee headed by John B. Meek, a Democrat, concluded the Snow Hill Baptists were probing fundamental questions about dissent and difference within American democracy that needed to be addressed. Even "under the most liberal forms of government," the committee declared, "it must be the condition of some—often a large minority—to submit to laws to which they are sincerely and strongly opposed." Echoing James Nill's arguments before the Pennsylvania Supreme Court, Meek's committee suggested that "if no law can be enacted and enforced against which a minority may conscientiously protest, there can be no government. One class may object to one law, and another class to another law, until all great public interests are abandoned to utter insecurity." There were times when a minority's conscience had to yield to what the majority advanced for the public good, and the situation of the Seventh Day Baptists was a prime example. The Snow Hill Society "must inevitably endure the inconvenience of having formed conscientious convictions which conflict with the conscience of the mass." Conscientious minorities, it seemed, were destined to be inconvenienced.

The committee also showed their decision to be informed by other social and political anxieties of the age, such as rampant immigration and westward expansion. Suppose "a party of Pagans from Asia, whose system of religion requires the offering of human beings in sacrifice," came to the "gold mines...of California." Would governments be unable to interfere because of constitutional provisions protecting the "rights of conscience"? To these legislators, the conception of freedom of conscience offered by critics of Sunday laws would restrict their ability to prohibit such "horrid rites of this bloody superstition." On the other hand, the committee pointed to the mounting sectional crisis and those abolitionist "fanatics" who interfered "with the execution" of the Fugitive Slave Law. Should citizens who conscientiously opposed slavery, the legislators asked, be exempted from the "legal penalties" incurred by violating the laws of states and the nation? Certainly not. Such a practice would force "the dissolution of the union of these States." Though equating the introverted Snow Hill Baptists with radical abolitionists and their practice of Saturday Sabbatizing with human sacrifice, the committee insisted that it meant not to "attach odium to the memorialists." It only intended to show that at times even "the most liberal and equitable government must of necessity come into conflict with the religious convictions of some of its subjects." The laws protecting the Sunday Sabbath were one such area. If they were repealed or made obsolete by granting exemptions, the harm done to the "the community at large"—"the many"—would be "greater than the benefit resulting to the few."[65]

For the Snow Hill Baptists and no doubt for many others who combated Sunday laws in the 1840s, their ordeal brought a "severe trial of their faith." But as Azore Estee, a Seventh Day Baptist elder, recounted, "The persecution and reproach...have not shaken their faith or inclined them to turn away from the commandment of the Lord." In fact, they remained committed to their beliefs and felt their resolve had had an effect on "their enemies," who ceased their persecution in 1850. Despite their long battle, Estee also reported that the farmers at Snow Hill rejoiced that their tribulations had brought "thousands" to investigate "the Sabbath question," including many "who otherwise might not have had their attention called to it at all." Indeed, Seventh Day Baptists and Jews, by challenging Sunday laws in the court of public opinion and before state legislatures and high courts, led many Americans to consider the democratic limits to majority rule.[66]

Subsequent conflicts over Sunday laws would continue to play that role. Especially in cities teeming with European immigrants, Protestant reformers in the 1850s would again look to enforce punitive Sunday measures. Even more than they had in the 1840s, immigrants, workers, and liquor dealers would join Jews and Seventh Day Baptists and expand upon their pioneering minority-rights activism to defend themselves.

3

The License Question and the Perils
of "Pure Democracy"

IN APRIL 1845 the citizens of Ann Arbor had something new to determine at the ballot box. A month earlier, the Michigan legislature passed a law asking voters to decide whether or not liquor licenses would be issued in their towns. Previously, a body of government administrators held discretionary authority to make this determination, but the new law empowered voters to do so in a referendum-like fashion. At a special license election, citizens would cast ballots for either "License" or "No License." A "License" victory authorized government officials to issue licenses and approved the sale of liquor by license holders. A "No License" victory prohibited licenses from being issued and rendered the sale of liquor illegal. There was no space for compromise. Simple majorities ruled. In Ann Arbor, a majority of 125 voters supported "No License," forcing "the dealers in Ardent Spirits...to stop selling" or to "sell in defiance of the Law." As state legislatures from Rhode Island to Iowa similarly empowered local voters to decide "the license question" in the latter half of the 1840s, majorities throughout the North, as in Ann Arbor, voted their communities dry.[1]

The new local option laws (as they would eventually be known) emerged as temperance reformers continued to rail against the system of liquor licensing that to them sanctioned drinking, legitimated the "drunkard-making business" of liquor dealing, and obstructed their mission to emancipate the nation from booze. Since most state legislators were reluctant to end licensing explicitly, these reformers turned to the people. Like those who sought to punish Sabbath-breakers with Sunday laws, temperance crusaders drew inspiration from the ascendant ethos of majority rule. But where Sabbath reformers had conjured a Christian majority to legitimate their favored measures, temperance reformers directly embraced the age's equally powerful call for popular political empowerment. Eager to prove the existence of a temperate majority and to have it flex its moral muscle, they demanded that actual majorities be allowed to put licensed dealers out of business at the ballot box. What could be more "purely democratic"? The local option approach to licensing, advocates insisted, ensured that public policy was rooted in "public sentiment," authorized "the will of the majority" to "control" the sale of intoxicating liquors, and recognized that "the people...are the legitimate source of power—the sovereigns of the land." Local option was American popular sovereignty incarnate.[2]

But was this democracy? As local option laws took effect and voters returned "no license" decisions, some began to rethink exactly what their commitment to popular sovereignty entailed. A consortium of liquor-dealing entrepreneurs and their allies joined together to challenge local option laws in multiple states and locales, giving rise to debates beyond the wisdom of advancing temperance with legal coercion. Some also questioned if the ballot box mechanism at the heart of local option was a legitimate mode of democratic decision-making. The license question was not the only instance in which legislators called upon the antebellum electorate to decide policy at the local ballot box. They asked voters to decide isolated local issues, like the division of a county, and in some states, to approve internal improvement projects, state debts, and taxation for common schools. Some of these measures helped legitimate the local option call, while others brought important early questions about the propriety of ballot box legislation. But because local option was enacted widely and suddenly in twelve states and territories, because it advanced the divisive moral objectives of temperance reformers, and because it sparked immediate coordinated and highly publicized resistance, local option became the premier site where Americans began grappling with direct democracy.[3]

In the process, local option laws joined Sunday laws in stimulating important debates about limits to majority rule and in prompting grass-roots modes of dissent focused on the protection of minority rights. Here liquor-peddling businessmen began to emerge as another of the era's influential, nonelite minorities. The opposition of Jews, Seventh Day Baptists, and others to Sunday laws had given rise to questions about American democracy's religious identity and the rights of religious minorities. Liquor dealers' concurrent resistance to local option raised the vital question of whether the United States was a democracy (or to some, a republic) where elected officials and government officers made policy decisions or a nation where the people acting through their agent—the majority—would directly decide public policy at the ballot box. In considering their positions, a wide array of participants returned to essential themes basic to popular sovereignty, questioning the obligations of elected officials and government officers to "the people" and simultaneously asking whether public policy should always reflect public opinion. These debates also addressed the implications of early nineteenth-century democratization, especially the rights of minorities and their proper place in policymaking and posing the question of whether "the people" could ever be too involved in popular self-government. Though these issues found few permanent resolutions, the ideas of direct democracy's opponents—ideas steeped in the protection of minority rights—did mature and gain legitimacy as liquor dealers challenged local option in public, in court, and before legislatures. Subsequent groups would refine their entwined defenses of minority rights and representative democracy to challenge future attempts at ballot-box legislation. On its own, however, the local option episode proved another critical spur to bringing the problem of minority rights to bear on everyday Americans like the alcohol-selling entrepreneurs and imbibers who sought to repel powerful antialcohol, moral majorities throughout the North.

THE TURN TO direct democracy to resolve the license question resulted from the protracted struggle of temperance reformers, whose movement became more radical in the 1840s. State and national organizations bolstered by countless local societies proliferated across the nation with their members taking the teetotal pledge and stridently condemning the liquor business, especially dealers who sold alcohol in small quantities to workingmen and immigrants in taverns and grog shops. These "unworthy members of society" and "agents...of evil," reformers argued, were responsible for intemperance and the crime, poverty, sexual impropriety, abuse of wives and children, and related ills that followed in its wake. Exhibiting some of the same nativist tendencies that helped fuel the Sabbath reform's resurgence, temperance activists complained that "the rumselling business has fallen very much into the hands" of immigrants, especially the whiskey-drinking Irish and beer-drinking Germans, and particularly the Catholics among them. In 1845 the *Journal of the American Temperance Union (JATU)*, the leading national temperance periodical, protested that "every foreigner, whether he be naturalized or not, whether he can read, or even speak our language, is permitted...to open a groggery, and perhaps with his own countrymen, fill up our prisons and almshouses." Even worse, they promoted social decay courtesy of the government, whose system of licensing, reformers continued to argue, lent legal sanction and respectability to dealers' destructive business.[4]

As temperance men and women came to advance local option as their preferred method to end licensing, they resisted forming their own "distinct political party." Instead, they implemented a mode of democratic practice that worked outside of party structures, mobilized public support at the grass roots, and targeted public policy. Like the Sabbath reformers of the 1840s with whom they often allied, their practice revealed a vision of democracy in which organized associational life in the public sphere was essential to the nation's vitality. An elite core of reformers spearheaded the effort. In New York State, for example, a cadre of evangelical Protestant clergymen, businessmen, lawyers, doctors, and others of the burgeoning white middle class lobbied legislatures, waged public opinion campaigns, and mobilized the "no license" vote. They held numerous conventions and turned local temperance societies into political infrastructure; used them as hubs of organization and communication; and spurred members to launch petition drives, circulate propaganda, and hold rallies of their own. Prominent leaders included Reverend John Marsh, secretary of the American Temperance Union (ATU); Horace Greeley, the well-known Whig editor of the *New York Tribune*; and Abigail Powers Fillmore, wife of Whig senator, future president, and local option supporter Millard Fillmore.[5]

At the helm of this select group was one of the Empire State's wealthiest citizens, Edward C. Delavan. After successfully speculating in real estate during the Erie Canal boom years, Delavan discontinued his wine business and devoted his time and money to the temperance cause. When the New York State Temperance Society, which Delavan helped found, refused to adopt teetotalism as an organizational principle, he seceded and donated $10,000 to launch the ATU under total abstinence principles. Through the ATU, he would oversee New York's local option movement, help coordinate efforts outside the state, and publicize their efforts internationally. Delavan was so committed to the antilicense cause that he created a special newspaper, *The Balance, or "License," or "No License," Examiner*, to unite temperance forces. He also personally funded the distribution of an antilicense appeal to every household in New York on the

eve of the state's first license elections in 1846. Like other leading moralists, Delavan stopped at nothing to ensure that the age's reform activism
worked on the grandest of scales.[6]

Reformers' experiences in the public policy arena and within the
existing party system drove local option's ascendance as their chief policy goal. Acting locally, temperance reformers in the 1830s and early
1840s had used existing laws and town meetings to persuade authorities
not to issue licenses, a tactic that brought virtual prohibition in some
areas. Yet reformers also learned that obtaining a statewide law ending licensing and prohibiting alcohol was extremely difficult. Nothing
shaped their education more than the Massachusetts fifteen-gallon
law of 1838. The unrest and striped pig shenanigans that followed the
measure had injured their cause's public standing. Perhaps even more
damning, the effort left state legislators—Democrat and Whig alike—
skittish about ending licensing with "direct legislative action" for fear
of electoral backlash.[7]

Temperance leaders needed a policy that they could market as agreeable
to the public and safe for legislators to enact; local option was their answer.
In returning to the local arena where they had some success restricting
licensing, reformers assured legislators and others opposed to coercing
temperance by law, including the anticoercionist Washingtonian wing of
the temperance movement, that local option was unlike the "compulsory"
fifteen-gallon law. Because local option only operated with the explicit
"consent of the people," the public would "cheerfully yield" to the outcome
of license elections. Moreover, reformers praised local option's ability to
separate the thorny license question from party politics. Governor William
Slade of Vermont was one of many politicos to take the bait. As he publicly
explained in 1845:

> I have been opposed to any attempt by the Legislature to enact a
> sweeping prohibition of the traffic, from the certainty that such
> an attempt would sweep the whole temperance question into the
> vortex of party politics, where it would be decided upon any other
> ground than that of its own merits.

But local option was different. To Slade and many other governors and
legislators, it allowed them neutrally to place a "great moral question"
before the voters without bearing any responsibility for the outcome and

leaving voters only themselves to blame. Here was a policy everyone could
agree on.[8]

Advocates' most powerful rationale for local option was that it was the
"*Democratic, Republican*" (terms they used interchangeably) remedy to a
license system that no longer harmonized with "the great Democratic doctrine, that the majority should govern." Reformers co-opted the populist
and conspiratorial rhetoric of Jacksonian democracy, deifying the people,
public opinion, majority rule, and local self-government while protesting
special privilege, monopoly power, and the aristocratic governance of the
few over the many. In the 1830s, Democrats had drawn on these concepts
to lampoon the "Money Power" and the Second Bank of the United States.
Temperance reformers applied them to the "Rum Power"—the many
liquor dealers who, they claimed, conspired with government officials to
gain the monopolistic power of license even in the face of strong antilicense public sentiment. Local option would return to the people their
"right, on pure democratic principles, to decide . . . for themselves" whether
licenses would be issued. It would give "the majority," insisted the *Ohio
Washingtonian Organ*, "the liberty to say whether they will have grog-shops
in their neighborhood." Ideally, local majorities would free themselves
from "the tyranny of a contemptible minority"—the Rum Power.[9]

This rationale was as political as it was principled, and it was designed
to push each political party, as one pundit observed, "to illustrate its
pre-eminent 'democracy.'" The general call for majority rule began to
shed its Democratic partisan affiliation by the early 1840s, particularly as
Whigs embraced two-party democratic politics. Temperance reformers,
many with strong ties to the Whig Party, expected a sympathetic hearing from Whig legislators and voters. They also counted on support from
nativist politicos who similarly linked intemperance, liquor dealing, and
immigrants. Democrats were another story. Not only were they more suspicious of moral regulations than their partisan foes, but they also sought
political support from the growing numbers of Irish and German immigrants. With local option, temperance reformers tested each party's commitment to majoritarian democracy and popular political empowerment
but especially the Democrats' commitment to the central axioms that had
guided the party's ascension in the 1830s.[10]

In such leading states as New York, the push for local option even
forced Democrats to wrestle with their own turn to ballot-box legislation.
In states where legislatures aggressively funded public projects through
state debts, the prolonged financial crisis after the Panic of 1837 left their

credit impaired, driving some to reassess state involvement in internal improvements. Along with other policy prescriptions, radical New York Democrats proposed state constitutional amendments requiring voters to approve at the ballot box any law creating a state debt. Their purpose in this was to provide voters with another check on elected officials. The so-called People's Resolutions would not become a part of the state constitution until 1846, after New York's 1845 local option law, but temperance reformers no doubt saw the opportunity to bring Democrats into their fold by similarly involving the electorate in public policy. Not surprisingly, supporters framed local option on liquor as another solution to state economic woes and a measure of taxpayer relief (fig. 3.1). "The License question" was not only "one of morals, but of taxation" because licensing promoted intemperance, which bred poverty and crime, the most costly sources of taxation. "In Republican Governments," champions of local option insisted, "the majority ought to decide all questions of taxation." Local option would ensure this.[11]

FIGURE 3.1 *The Farmer Groaning Under His Rum Taxes* from the *Journal of the American Temperance Union* (April 1846). Courtesy of the Library of Congress. Temperance reformers insisted that alcohol-induced poverty and crime were the main reasons for taxation. Voting "no license" and ending the licensed liquor trade, they maintained, would provide tax relief for hard-working Americans.

With local option, reformers and their supporters implicitly weighed in on two broad and interrelated questions that had been confronting the Anglo-American world since the rise of popular sovereignty. First, how was "the knowledge of public sentiment" obtained in self-governing societies; and second, were elected representatives and government officials obliged to adhere to majority will when implementing public policy? Prior to local option, these questions were most readily addressed in debates over the "right of instruction": the right of constituents to instruct their elected representatives on how to act and vote and the duty of representatives to follow those instructions. These debates centered on whether representatives were extensions of their constituents, obligated to conform to their demands and represent their specific needs, or if they were chosen to deliberate on policy issues, keep the general interest as well as their constituents' needs in mind, and ultimately use their "own judgement" when voting on legislation or administering law.[12]

Local option presented an alternate position on the relationship of public opinion, elected officials, and government administrative bodies as well as a particular view of what "public opinion" was and how it was best ascertained. Representatives offered a policy choice, asked voters to register their views at the ballot box, and bound government administrators to implement the majority will, in this case by either issuing licenses or withholding them. Local option fused the public opinion-finding function to the creation and execution of public policy, removing any intermediary between law and voters and guaranteeing, supporters argued, that public policy explicitly mirrored public opinion. "Public opinion fairly expressed," resolved the Albany County Temperance Society, "should govern in this as well as in all other matters regulating the government of a democracy." Reformers assumed that local option constituted fair expression and praised its poll-like ability to provide "tangible, reliable evidences, as to public sentiment." They conflated public opinion with the will of voting majorities, which in most states included only white men, and also implied that public opinion was best discovered when issues were placed in isolation and voters were given only two choices. Voters could only select between license and no license; there was no third or fourth ballot option, such as the ability to vote for fewer licenses or to support, for example, licenses for hotels but not for taverns. Complexity and compromises were shunned. Such expressions of voting majorities were purportedly the purest embodiment of public opinion and democracy's truest agent.[13]

These constructions of public opinion were calculated as well. Local optioners were eager to divest state legislators and other government officials of their traditional ability to gauge public opinion independently and to weigh it in the context of other short-term and long-term community or minority needs. Legislators had ignored temperance reformers' use of the more established methods of ascertaining antilicense opinion through petition and memorial, and local administrators often had foiled their efforts to control local licensing. Furthermore, the traditional place of frequent elections in keeping lawmakers responsive to public opinion failed temperance reformers as state legislators backpedaled after the Massachusetts fifteen-gallon fiasco. Local option would authorize voters to circumvent nonresponsive legislatures and obstructionist government officials, and by acting locally, they could ensure pockets of success without having to await a statewide transformation.

As never before, temperance reformers placed popular political empowerment at the center of their agenda; "the power of free suffrage" would, they argued, "exterminate the monster Alcohol." Twenty years earlier such leading reformers as Lyman Beecher advocated temperance in part to ensure that the expanding voting population, which many feared, possessed the moral qualities republican self-government required. By the early 1840s, however, leading reformers echoed other democratizers by routinely complimenting the "virtue and intelligence" of the people, and some even referenced contemporary democratic reforms. "If in the selection of Judges the people could be trusted," asked attorney John Van Cott, "how was it that they could not be trusted in the matter of establishing grogshops in the corners of the streets?" Truth be told, local option supporters went beyond arguing that white men were wise enough to vote for a wider range of public officials. Instead, they suggested that the electorate was moral enough to decide directly public policy and implied that bare majorities were morally superior to corruptible government officials. Responding to a critic, one supporter signaled the transformation in temperance thinking. "Our correspondent thinks the people are not to be trusted.... They might not have been, in old rum-drinking times, but in these cold-water days, when the judgment is cool and men begin to think about their own best interests and the interests of their children, it might be found to be quite otherwise." As Ann Arbor, Michigan's *Signal of Liberty* concluded, the work of the temperance reform had allowed "public opinion" to mature "in regard to the extent of the evil" of drink and now legitimated the empowerment

The Glorious Rising of the Sun of Temperance, on the 19th of May. Gathering of the Temperance Host.
Despairing Retreat under a broken Banner. Grog-shop to Let.

FIGURE 3.2 *The Glorious Rising of the Sun of Temperance* from the *Journal of the American Temperance Union* (May 1846). Courtesy of the Library of Congress. Temperance men and women celebrated when no-license majorities defeated the proliquor minority and put licensed liquor dealers out of business.

of men who would protect their families by drying up the Rum Power at the ballot box (fig. 3.2).[14]

Temperance women were fully cognizant that local option made them reliant upon male voters, and many, like those attending the Delaware Ladies' Temperance Convention, made it their mission to beseech their "male friends" to vote against licensing. The rise of local option also brought some women to reconsider their own lack of suffrage. Writing in 1846 on the heels of New York's first local option election, during the state constitutional convention, and shortly before the Seneca Falls Convention, an unnamed author, musing about the "Rights of Woman" in a New York women's temperance magazine, *The Pearl*, queried:

If all the women in New York were voters, how long would it be before their rights would be respected, in the making and the administration of the laws? How long would they permit the exis-tence of three thousand tippling shops in which females never enter, but which are yearly making thousands of drunkards of their brothers and sons?

For those thinking about woman suffrage in the mid-1840s, local option provided a critical context. Participation in this temperance battle catalyzed female politicization, no doubt exposing the limitations of their political agency but, at the same time, revealing that the vote itself was transforming. No longer merely used to elect government officials, the ballot was becoming a tool to enact social and moral change directly, and for some women (and perhaps members of other disfranchised groups) this burgeoning power more acutely underscored their exclusion.[15]

Temperance reformers, however, conveniently ignored any governmental transformation. They declared local option "in perfect harmony with the spirit and genius of our government" and demonized opposition not only as immoral enemies of temperance but also as adversaries of democratic self-rule. "They are false to Popular Government," announced Horace Greeley's *Tribune*, "who refuse the People the right to speak on this question." Supportive state legislators also got into the act. "To say that the people are not qualified to control this matter," an Illinois Senate committee argued, "is to doubt their ability for self-government, and to distrust the essential principle upon which our government is founded." One group of Maryland legislators put it even more strongly. Any one "who fears or objects to trust the people in any matters pertaining to general or national questions," they declared, "should have written on his forehead *anti-American*." According to this thinking, the only way to question local option, then, was by defying democracy and undermining the nation.[16]

In spite of the lofty, moralistic rhetoric, the numerous license campaigns and elections brought by local option opened the door for Americans to contemplate the workings of their political system and to consider if local option fit. This was particularly the case for those specially called to the polls in the twelve New England, Midwestern, and mid-Atlantic states that enacted some type of local option measure. While organizing "the temperance ballot box," often with the pomp and circumstance of partisan political campaigns, reformers bombarded the public with their democratic-republican rationale. And as voters brought no-license victories in countless towns and counties in numerous states, temperance odes to local option as the embodiment of popular sovereignty only became more strident. For some, temperance triumphs at the polls were evidence of their locales' high moral stature. If "New-England and the Middle States" knew the high number of towns in Wisconsin Territory that voted against license, a correspondent to the *Milwaukee Sentinel* surmised, "thousands" would emigrate to the clearly moral American West. For others, like former Ohio jurist Frederick Grimke, the framework was not transregional but transatlantic. No-license victories provided irrefutable evidence that America's peculiar political system worked. "Let no European after this," Grimke declared, "indulge in the fanciful notion that the people are incapable of self-government." American majorities, like those in 80 percent of New York's 813 towns in 1846, had voted themselves dry. Reformers set out to validate American democracy by seeing no-license decisions enforced. But with resistance brewing, this dream of a pure and temperate democracy would prove difficult to sustain.[17]

WHEN A NEW YORK legislative committee sponsoring an early local option proposal suggested that the law presented "no aspect of coercion, except that to which all cheerfully submit, the expressed will of the majority," Democratic state assemblyman and prominent editor of the *Democratic Review* John O'Sullivan no doubt shook his head in disbelief. The law, he retorted in 1841, was loaded with "legal physical compulsion" directed "against the minority." If license elections produced proliquor minorities, it would matter little that the law was "imposed upon them by the local majority" and not the state legislature. Proliquor groups would view local option as another "tyrannical...interference with the private liberty of drinking or selling what they should please" and would resist.[18]

Four years earlier, in his "Introduction" to the *Democratic Review*, O'Sullivan announced the creed of the Democratic Party: majority rule and, as he put it, bringing "public opinion...to bear more directly upon the action of delegated powers." Local option seemed the perfect fit. Yet even as he had rebuked opponents of majoritarian democracy in 1837, O'Sullivan had proclaimed "strong sympathy" for minority rights, cautioned democratizers "not to go too fast," and declared "the best government is that which governs least." By 1841, he was persuaded that local optioners had missed these caveats. They took the "democratic principle" too far, threatened minorities, and in attempting to prohibit the sale of alcohol, exceeded the legitimate bounds of government authority. The better approach, he posited, would be to abolish licensing and create a free market in liquor: to make "the whole matter open, and leave it to the undisturbed operation of public opinion, and the moral sense of men and communities." As the legislature again debated local option in 1845,

O'Sullivan announced his continued opposition and urged reformers to return to their proven techniques of "moral suasion" before this foray into legal coercion tore apart every "town, village, and ward in the State."[19]

Though temperance reformers gained the support and votes of many Democratic legislators, Democrats like O'Sullivan provided some of the most stinging public denunciations of local option. Many accused reformers of being overwhelmed by a "foolish and ultra spirit," and some overtly appealed to immigrant voters, jibing that reformers next would make "possession of a temperance certificate…an indispensable qualification for citizenship." Democrats also expanded O'Sullivan's position on limited government, holding local option particularly problematic because it sought to restrict personal freedom in "the field of morals" in which democratic government power, the *Albany Atlas* claimed, was rightly "limited." Notably, the *Atlas*, one of New York's leading Radical Democratic newspapers, had earlier supported the People's Resolutions that required statewide voting majorities to approve debt legislation at the ballot box. This did not, however, inspire them to support local option on liquor. To the *Atlas*, the two measures were worlds apart. Where the People's Resolutions aimed to circumscribe government power to "safeguard…liberty," local option sought to enhance government power to restrict personal freedom by controlling the "moral conduct of the minority." Like efforts to coerce Sabbath observance by law, added the *Brooklyn Eagle*, "There are some things which even a majority cannot rightfully do." This included stipulating "what the minority should be permitted to eat and to drink." The *Eagle* concluded, "The *minority* have rights, as well as the majority; and it is the duty of a republican government to respect those of the former." Unlike advocates who viewed local option and its strict majoritarianism as a logical expression of popular self-government, some Democrats saw it as a tyrannical perversion.[20]

Local option brought the ire of some Washingtonian temperance reformers who continued to oppose "legal force" and countenance only "moral suasion." Labor spokesmen, land reformers, and antirenters took the occasion to complain that temperance champions too narrowly focused on liquor as the root of all evil instead of the more treacherous "inequality of condition." But as O'Sullivan and others anticipated, the most prolific dissenters were those most directly threatened by no-license decisions: liquor dealers, tavern owners, hotel keepers, grocers, brewers, distillers, landlords renting property to liquor-based establishments, their families, friends, and loyal patrons. They might have yielded (as reformers had hoped) to no-license majorities, and no doubt some decided to close their shops or seek libation in jurisdictions where the sale of alcohol remained legal. Others chose differently. Entrepreneurs viewed local option as an unjust and unconstitutional assault on their long-standing legal businesses and livelihoods. They would defend "the liquor-seller's rights." Their customers, particularly workingmen and immigrants who gathered socially in taverns and grog shops, protested the invasion of their cherished masculine spaces and cultural traditions. They refused to "be governed, as to what they shall eat and drink, by a popular vote." This most basic decision—the decision to resist—constituted an important moment in the era's burgeoning minority rights politics—a politics in which liquor-selling entrepreneurs, drinkers, and other antiprohibitionists would figure prominently.[21]

The heart of their emergent political style was, like their adversaries', an embrace of civil society, especially the organization of voluntary associations and public-opinion campaigns. Acting on a conception of democracy that privileged the protection of "natural and constitutional rights," dealers and their allies contributed to the expansion of the democratic public sphere by implementing an array of extrapartisan, grass-roots political tactics. They built unity, registered discontent, and changed minds by holding public meetings, publishing resolutions, and circulating propaganda. Presenting themselves as a united bloc, they sent petitions, sometimes with "thousands of signers," to state legislatures and pushed for the election of state legislators sympathetic to their cause. Dealers' associational response to local option in the 1840s proved rather ad hoc and relatively short-lived. A significant exception to this trend emerged in New York City, the nation's most populous and socially diverse city that likely contained America's largest concentration of alcohol-sellers and drinkers. There dealers led by successful hotelier Richard French established the Tradesmen's Mutual Benefit Society in 1846 to combat, as they put it, the "fanatical and bigoted" reformers who "vainly attempt to promote the temperance cause by coercive laws, and political organization." A more formal association, members hoped, would help "open the eyes" of all dealers to the threat of local option while illustrating the strength of their opposition.[22]

For most proliquor groups, the critical aspect of their fight came after local majorities turned them into an unmistakably targeted minority by outlawing alcohol-based businesses with no-license decisions. Some dealers revived the "striped pig" technique. One tavern owner, for example, was glad to treat guests who made donations to the supposed "widow and orphan fund of the village." Another charged customers a lofty fee for hay and shelter for their horses before courteously providing them whiskey. Most, however, wasted no time with such trickery and blatantly shirked the law by selling liquor without a license. For some, this probably amounted to little more than business as usual, but for others, it was an intentional act of civil disobedience pregnant with a political vision that rejected local option as an inappropriate use of democratic state power and that countenanced the breaking of an unjust law. Proliquor groups often organized these protests, and participants expected to be arrested, hoping for the opportunity to challenge local option in court. Trials became public spectacles in which crowds heard attorneys deploy a range of arguments against local option, the most common of which was that local option was unconstitutional. A month after 80 percent of New York's towns returned "No-License" majorities in 1846, the *Journal of the American Temperance Union* lamented, "In every town and village the great question is raised, 'Is the License Law constitutional?'"[23]

Most asking this question were latching on to speculation that all license laws, of which local option was a type, violated the commerce clause of the US Constitution that empowered Congress to regulate foreign and interstate commerce. To combat reformer-led restrictive licensing efforts, dealers and their attorneys had argued that this clause prohibited state governments from interfering with the sale of liquor—an interstate and international commodity—through licensing. Their resistance made this question a fixture of public debate in the 1840s and ultimately resulted in a series of cases before the US Supreme Court. Indeed, just as local option laws were being put into practice, the *License Cases* brought a star-studded cast of lawyers to weigh in on whether the license laws of three New England states violated the commerce clause. In a telling moment in which political conservatives allied with some of antebellum America's moral minorities, conservative statesmen Daniel Webster and Rufus Choate eagerly took up the liquor dealers' position. Harboring traditional concerns about the excesses of democracy and the fate of property rights, it was no stretch for them to make constitutional arguments that would protect not only dealers' property rights but potentially others threatened by activist state governments. At stake in the *License Cases*, however, was also the general police power of state governments vis-à-vis the national government, which within the antebellum politics of slavery and antislavery had implications that threatened the Union. Temperance reformers monitoring the *License Cases* momentarily echoed states' rights advocates, apocalyptically warning that if licensing power was declared unconstitutional, the power to regulate liquor (and seemingly myriad other areas of commerce, including slaves) would be stripped from states, opening the door for a much more active federal regulatory role that could spark sectional controversy.[24]

When the Supreme Court in March 1847 ultimately affirmed states' licensing power, even suggesting that states could prohibit liquor, temperance forces celebrated it as an authorization of their agenda. "All doubt as to the '*Constitutionality* of the License Laws,'" proclaimed the American Temperance Union, was "swept away" alongside "the pretended '*rights* of the rumseller.'" Along with newspaper editors, both Whig and Democrat, they were sure that this validation of general licensing power applied as well to local option statutes. What effect, asked Greeley's *Tribune*, would it have on those who resisted no-license decisions "on the assumption that they were invalid because unconstitutional"? "On what pretext can they longer persist in their daily violations of the laws of the land?" Commentators presumed that those who intended to challenge local option's constitutionality would "abandon the idea," but with a new political and constitutional critique flowering in Delaware, they would be proven wrong.[25]

DELAWARE TEMPERANCE FORCES followed reformers in other states and spurred the passage of a local option law in 1847. As elsewhere, liquor dealers emerged to lead a group of dissenters who ridiculed temperance men and women as "fanatical" zealots, argued that moral suasion was the only effective temperance technique, and maintained that no-license decisions would infringe upon individual rights. The stakes of resistance were raised even higher as Delaware's dealers enlisted the critical input of two prominent citizens, Amos H. Wickersham and James A. Bayard, who by March 1847 had publicized a critique of local option that reached beyond police power and the commerce clause while also raising issues of minority rights. When proliquor forces organized the then largest public meeting ever held at Wilmington City Hall to protest Delaware's local option law, it came as no surprise that Wickersham presided over the meeting and Bayard served as the headline speaker. Their involvement would have monumental implications extending well beyond the small state and the license question.[26]

A locally influential Democrat, Wickersham had a reputation as a "ready debater" and for wielding "a sarcastic pen when fully aroused," on display when he ran for state legislature in 1846. Copying the pressure tactics of reformers in other states, the members of the Wilmington-based New Castle County Temperance Society (NCCTS) pledged to "vote for no man" unwilling to enact local option and formed a committee to ascertain candidates' views. Chairman John McClung, a Wilmington merchant, corresponded with each of the candidates, and when Wickersham, a Democratic candidate, came out against local option, reformers dubbed him a political opportunist seeking to curry favor with drinkers and an intemperate aristocrat not *"to be trusted by the people."* His stance on local option, like that of others, became the litmus test of both his temperance principles and his democratic commitments. Much to the dismay of reformers, their censure, as well as his loss in the legislative election, only drove Wickersham to further develop and disseminate his critique of local option. Wickersham amplified and enhanced the arguments made by other Democrats, pleading for limited government and challenging local option's strict majoritarianism. Pointing to the natural rights guarantees of life, liberty, and happiness in the Declaration of Independence and the Delaware Constitution, Wickersham contended these key statements on the promise of democracy established boundaries "limiting the exercise of power even by majorities." By forgetting that in *"a free government the minority has rights* which must be respected" local option was "anti-republican, and directly opposed to the spirit and principles of Democracy."[27]

Wickersham deepened standard Democratic criticism by connecting concerns about minority rights to long-standing arguments about legislators' roles and responsibilities. Here he echoed opponents of the "doctrine of instruction"—the idea that elected representatives were bound to adhere strictly to the expressed will of their constituents. Like them, Wickersham argued that legislators were not mere mouthpieces of popular sentiment nor strictly beholden to every shift in public opinion. Rather, legislators had broader obligations to the "general welfare" as well to the state constitution, which often required them to stand independent from the people. Wickersham, however, pushed the standard anti-instruction argument about the nature of representation by offering a conception of the general welfare that explicitly privileged the protection of minority rights. Indeed, legislators, in his view, were bound to listen to the wants of majorities, but they were also obliged to guard the rights of minorities. By allowing only the majority to dictate public policy directly, local option, he protested, removed legislators' ability to fulfill their vital responsibility to minorities.[28]

The root of the problem, Wickersham asserted, was the skewed logic offered by temperance reformers, which held that local option was a logical manifestation of the American tradition of popular sovereignty. To demonstrate the dangers posed by this distortion, Wickersham illustrated the effects if local option was used in scenarios other than licensing. Carefully selecting examples that would have horrified all good Protestants and that emphasized the hazards of strict majoritarianism in a culturally pluralistic democracy, Wickersham wrote:

> *Swine's flesh* is an abomination to the believers in Judaism. Now if the State of Delaware should contain a majority of Jews, and they should...ask the Legislature to pass a law referring the question of *eating pork* to the people; and prohibiting its traffic and use, wherever there was a majority of Jews, the man who should have independence enough to go the *"whole-hog"* in opposition to the law, would be unfit for a legislator and to vote for him, would be to *"vote away the right of self government."*

Within the realm of imaginable possibility, Wickersham also envisioned many Catholic immigrants who increasingly arrived in northern Delaware falling victim to local option. "The *people*" might want to vote to demolish the churches of "certain religious societies among us, whose doctrines and tenets, are considered...inimical to the safety and permanency of our institutions." The commitment to self-government as temperance reformers would have it, Wickersham quipped, would prevent legislators from standing in the way of laws empowering nativist and religiously intolerant majorities to oppress religious and cultural minorities. Clearly something was wrong with the local option principle.[29]

The import of Wickersham's position emerged as it fused with the arguments of prominent Wilmington attorney James A. Bayard, who hailed from one of Delaware's most prominent families (fig. 3.3). His father, James A. Bayard Sr., was a Federalist congressman and senator through the War of 1812, and his older brother, Richard, served as a US senator as well. James Jr. had followed this path of public service as a US district attorney in Delaware from 1838 to 1843. He also inherited his family's political conservatism, particularly their suspicion of popular rule and the extension of voting rights. Bayard remained wedded to the deferential political culture that had dominated his father's era and still held significance in Delaware politics during the 1840s. For those who

FIGURE 3.3   Prominent Delaware attorney James A. Bayard. Courtesy of the Library of Congress.

knew his politics, it probably came as no surprise that he led Delaware dealers' fight against a law that, to him, dangerously authorized ordinary citizens to decide public policy. Like Daniel Webster's and Rufus Choate's representations of liquor interests before the US Supreme Court, Bayard's involvement constituted a touchstone moment in which elitist political sensibilities fruitfully aligned with the interests of some of antebellum America's nonelite moral minorities.[30]

It was a natural alliance of strange bedfellows. The strongly immigrant and working-class community of dealers and drinkers needed stellar representation and fresh ideas if they were to defeat local option. For the patrician Bayard, this was an opportunity to put the brakes on the growing penchant for popular political empowerment. Notably and not coincidentally, this was not his first attempt. Indeed, Bayard brought rare practical experience challenging laws like local option in court to the dealers' cause. Six years earlier he had challenged the constitutionality of the Delaware school law, which gave localities the option of taxing themselves to fund common schools by majority vote. Bayard's client Steward voted against the tax but was in the minority, and when the tax collector seized his cow for the nonpayment of taxes, Steward sued the tax collector.

Before the Delaware Court of Appeals, Bayard claimed that the legislature unconstitutionally delegated its taxing power—"a power of high discretion"—to a "majority of voters" in school districts. Bayard likely took this argument from John Locke's discussion of the limitations of legislative power in his *Second Treatise of Government* in which he proclaimed, "The *legislative cannot transfer the power of making laws* to any other hands: for it being but a delegated power from the people, they who have it cannot pass it over to others." For Bayard, this included returning power to the people. Unfortunately for Steward, the Court held the law constitutional without opinion. Likely eager for another opportunity to voice his perspective, Bayard found one in the contentious liquor politics surrounding Delaware's local option law.[31]

The popular association of Delaware's proliquor forces that united in early 1847 to fight local option facilitated the synthesis, elaboration, and circulation of the Wickersham-Bayard position. At public meetings and in the pages of the Democratic *Delaware Gazette* participants and readers were exposed to their arguments and asked to reconsider local option within the American political system. Was local option an "unconstitutional abandonment" of the "discretionary power entrusted to Legislators"? Did the minority viewpoint have a place in policymaking? Did local option allow "the imperious will of the *majority*" to threaten "*human rights*," "*freedom*," and "the sacredness of our liberal institutions"? Most centrally, did local option violate core characteristics of America's type of democracy?[32]

This interconnected plea for minority rights and representative republican government (or representative democracy) was hardly without pedigree. In *Federalist* 10, James Madison had extolled the virtues of the new national Constitution and the large republic it created by contrasting it with a "pure democracy" in which a "small number of citizens...assemble and administer the government in person" without electing representatives. To Madison, pure democracies were breeding grounds for the factious majorities he so feared. They were "spectacles of turbulence and contention" and were "incompatible with personal security [and] the rights of property." Such democracies, he warned, most threatened the survival of popular self-government. More recently, American political theorist George Camp, in his 1841 treatise *Democracy*, refuted Alexis de Tocqueville's famous charge in *Democracy in America* that America's political system facilitated the "tyranny of the majority" by pointing to "the representative system" Americans had adopted. According to Camp, America's representative institutions not only harnessed the majority

viewpoint but also made "great provision for the sentiments and opinions of the minority" to be included in the policymaking process. This
fostered consensus, produced policy rooted in the "aggregate sense of [the]
community" rather than the whims of majorities, and ultimately freed the
United States from the dangers Tocqueville identified.[33]

Regardless of any tradition Wickersham, Bayard, and Delaware's proliquor forces were joining, temperance reformers scoffed at their position and dismissed their ideas as the product of unbridled self-interest.
They ridiculed the notion that local option was antirepublican, reaffirmed
majority rule as the "very foundation" of American government, and
mocked claims of "unconstitutional Legislation" and "Individual Rights"
as "false issues." As far as the Delaware Ladies' Temperance Convention
was concerned, only the "rights of property" of a few dealers were at issue,
and they dwindled "into insignificance when compared with the rights
of life and liberty" that local option could protect. Once the US Supreme
Court decided the *License Cases* in March 1847 and a no-license majority triumphed in New Castle County's April election, Delaware temperance forces no doubt concluded that the Wickersham-Bayard critique
was meaningless and mattered little to the majority. The local proliquor
minority's fight against local option, however, would continue.[34]

As Delawareans continued to spar over local option, the situation in
New York became increasingly volatile. Prolicense New Yorkers flooded
the legislature with petitions for repeal, and a second round of license
elections in 1847 yielded disastrous results for temperance forces, with
town after town returning "license" majorities. Not surprised by the reversal, the *New York Evening Post* suggested that it was caused by lax enforcement, the spirit of defiance surrounding the law, and the "bitter feuds"
that had erupted "between the license and the no license party." While
some thought local option should stand, all in all, the reversal of public
sentiment made it easy for New York's state legislators, both Democrat
and Whig, to vote for repeal.[35]

Before the reversal, however, a bipartisan New York legislative committee considering petitions for repeal of local option showed the distinct
influence of the Wickersham-Bayard concern for representative democracy and minority rights. "All other public majorities," they declared, "elect
delegates or representatives to form organic bodies, in which measures
or laws are discussed and adopted, and in which minorities can be heard;
or they elect public officers who are equally the servants of the minorities." Without representative structures there was no way for the minority

voice to be included in policymaking and there was nothing "to mitigate and restrain the delegated power of the several majorities over the minorities." Local option violated New York's state constitution and, the committee concluded, established a "new and anti-American kind of democracy" that facilitated majoritarian "despotism." Only by repealing the measure would democracy and freedom be reclaimed. As this committee's rationale illustrated, the Delaware anti-local-option position had gained currency elsewhere.[36]

If popular resistance, petitioning, and the legislative process proved essential to the successful minority-rights politics employed by New York's proliquor forces, their counterparts in Delaware, like the Jews and Seventh Day Baptists who contested Sunday laws, ultimately turned to the courtroom and judicial review. To challenge local option before Delaware's highest court, the Court of Errors and Appeals, they employed Bayard to contrive a fictional test case—*Rice* v. *Foster*—which their opponents ridiculed as "the Tavern-keepers *vs.* the People." Delaware's dealers also secured the assistance of Bayard's longtime friend John M. Clayton (fig. 3.4). Clayton was the leader of the state's Whig Party, the former chief justice of Delaware's highest court, and in 1847, one of Delaware's US senators—as well as a notorious drinker. His participation alongside Bayard, a Democrat, created a bipartisan team comprising two of the state's most respected legal minds, nearly guaranteeing that the case would garner widespread attention and that their arguments would be taken seriously regardless of party affiliation. Indeed, Clayton's remarks before the Court became the substance of the Court's opinion.[37]

The key argument Bayard and Clayton advanced would have been familiar to anyone following the Delaware debate: with local option the legislature violated the state constitution and "the limitations of legislative power necessarily involved in a representative republican form of government" by improperly delegating its legislative power "to a majority of the people of a county." The central question presented in the case was "whether the power of making laws shall continue in the legislature, where the Constitution placed it, or shall be transferred to the people to be settled by popular vote." To Bayard and Clayton, calling on voters to decide on a law amounted to lawmaking, and though they endorsed the "ultimate sovereignty" of the people, they insisted that it was "never to be exercised" by the people "collectively." In forming a constitution, the people had set limits to their own power. In particular, they had "surrendered" all lawmaking power to elected representatives "for their own good," and barring

FIGURE 3.4   Senator John Clayton of Delaware from *Harper's Magazine* (1879). Courtesy of The Library Company of Philadelphia.

constitutional change, they could never reclaim and the legislature could never return such power.[38]

Bayard and Clayton schooled the Court and onlookers in the significant advantages of "representative Democracy" over "pure democracy." First, they broadcast that representative government made for better policymaking because representatives could calmly meet, separated from the passions of the people, for "deliberation, consultation and judgment" to balance the competing needs of society, while acting "under oath" to protect and uphold the constitution. Direct democracies, by contrast, were not deliberative and involved the masses acting "not under oath" and "not in consultation, but assembled under all circumstances of excitement; swayed by every wave of passion or prejudice; misled by every demagogue, and subjected to every influence but those which should attend calm and sound legislation." This was in many ways classic antidemocratic language that conservatives used to defend deferential politics and to repel suffrage expansion, the doctrine of instruction, and other democratic reforms. Bayard and Clayton, however, appropriated it to condemn a new "democratic" reform—ballot-box legislation—that gave ordinary citizens, perhaps more radically, direct influence over policy. Political conservatives and all property owners, they implied, had as much to fear from local option as the liquor dealers.

Second, Bayard and Clayton argued that representative democracy allowed for greater protections of individual and minority rights from the potential injustices and oppression of shifting public opinion and majorities. Repeating Wickersham's position, they maintained that legislators were bound to consider the interests of minorities when enacting law. "The representatives of the people in the legislature, though, in general, bound to respect the will of their constituents, are also bound to exercise their own judgment, and to oppose that will, when it invades individual rights, or violates the principles of the social compact." Representative democracy, they concluded, was "a right of minorities," and Delaware's constitution was designed to secure it. Local option perilously and unconstitutionally removed the ability of legislators to protect minorities. Indeed, there was "no greater tyranny," they concluded, than local option's "mode of making or administering law," and the victims in this case were liquor dealers, drinkers, and other opponents of temperance legislation.[39]

This case was about more than alcohol, however, because local option, Clayton threatened, would not stop at liquor licensing. Whenever legislators "would seek to throw off the responsibility of a doubtful" or controversial law, they would "leave it to the people" to decide. These "experiments...would overthrow the Constitution itself." In 1847 there was no shortage of contentious issues that legislators hoped to avoid, and Clayton made telling choices, strategically designed to bolster the appeal of his indictment of local option. With capital punishment controversially under assault in the 1840s, Clayton warned that the local option approach might be taken such that "murder may be punished with death in one County, and by imprisonment or some milder penalty in the others." Imagine the chaos. Did not such fundamental issues of criminal justice, he implicitly asked, require a coherent, statewide policy? Clayton also turned to classic conservative arguments about how excessively democratic governments governed by needy majorities would infringe upon the rights of propertied minorities, referencing such contemporary events as the Anti-Rent Wars of upstate New York and labor reformers' calls for property redistribution. Quoting George Henry Evans's land-reform circular of 1845, Clayton asked, "How long will a majority refuse to 'vote themselves farms,' when the poll is opened for that purpose?" Most assuredly, he warned, direct democracy would allow the "wild doctrines of Agrarianism" to threaten "the permanency and stability of property titles" in the future. Property rights and the survival of social order, then, required Delaware's high court to quash local option before more radical causes co-opted the approach to advance their pet measures.[40]

There was another form of property Clayton suggested would be soon brought to the ballot box—slave property. Just as Delaware's legislators enacted local option, they also considered a bill to gradually abolish slavery in their state. The measure passed the lower house but was postponed indefinitely by one vote in the senate. If "the question of slavery" was put to local referenda, Delaware's three counties, Clayton insisted, would return different results, and "the State, instead of presenting one rule of conduct...may present as many rules as there are Counties." To Clayton, "general subjects" like licensing and slavery required centralized policy at the state level. With the legal difficulties slave masters encountered when sojourning with their slaves to free states widely known in the late 1840s, Clayton asked the Court to imagine the problems that would ensue if slavery were legal in one of Delaware's counties yet illegal in another. "Yet who will say," he maintained, "that the question of slavery is not as proper to be submitted to the people's decision in this form of legislation as the question of retailing liquor?"[41]

Delaware probably was not the only house dividing that concerned Clayton. Nationally, the Mexican War and the prospect of slavery's westward expansion had already sparked major controversy, and local option on slavery had appeared as a possible solution. The 1846 Wilmot Proviso, which proposed that slavery be excluded from any territory acquired from Mexico, catalyzed discussions about congressional power over slavery in the territories. By early 1847, some congressmen suggested that territorial residents decide for themselves whether to permit slavery. And by late 1847, before his 1848 presidential run, Democrat Lewis Cass—a temperance champion from Michigan—would publicize such a "popular sovereignty" proposal. He declared, "Leave to the people who will be affected by this question, to adjust it upon their own responsibility and in their own manner, and we shall render another tribute to the original principles of our Government, and furnish another guarantee for its permanence and prosperity." These words easily could have been mustered to support local option, but instead Cass applied them to the problem of slavery in the territories.

Clayton, as a senator, would have been privy to early proposals for territorial self-determination on slavery, proposals that could result in slavery's extension. But in 1847, Delaware's state legislature, led by Whigs and representatives from New Castle County, where slavery was in serious decline, advised Clayton to oppose the extension of slavery. It is possible that he sought to expose the contradiction of those who supported the local option approach to the license question yet would oppose the popular sovereignty solution to the slavery question (or perhaps vice versa). Regardless, Clayton saw legislators in both scenarios dodging responsibility by requiring voters to decide on highly contentious questions at the ballot box.[42]

Still, there were other connections to slavery. Just days before Clayton and Bayard argued *Rice v. Foster*, the *Delaware Gazette* offered further intellectual support for the anti-local-option position. The *Gazette* published an article entitled "Popular Government" containing an extract of a letter penned by the great defender of slavery John Calhoun in which he explained his opposition to the idea that the "'numerical majority...has the inherent and absolute right to govern, a sort of right divine like that claimed by Sir Robert Filmer for Kings.'" The editors urged readers, who no doubt included the jurists of Delaware's high court, to consider Calhoun's position as they pondered "the true character of government, the proper extent of popular power, the nature and objects of constitutions, and the possession of natural or reserved rights"—all themes presented by local option and particularly by dissenters. Calhoun, of course, combated absolute majority rule first and foremost to defend the right of white southerners to hold black slaves as property from the potential threat of an antislavery majority in the nation as a whole. Some challenging local option no doubt saw an explicit connection between Calhoun's proslavery political thought and the prospect of using direct democracy to decide the question of slavery either in Delaware or in western territories. Others, however, had different concerns and perhaps made no linkage to slavery. As dealers and drinkers came to terms with their own minority status amid the local option fight, Calhoun's concerns no doubt registered with many of them, perhaps in ways they previously had not. Ultimately, their decision to contest local option in court put these fundamental issues of the rights of the minority within American democracy before the nation anew.[43]

Despite the efforts of the opposing attorney in *Rice v. Foster*, the Delaware Court of Errors and Appeals held with Clayton. The Court unanimously declared local option a delegation of legislative power that unconstitutionally created a "pure democracy." Chief Justice James Booth, himself a Whig, crafted his own paean to representative government and attempted to reclaim the distinction between democratic and republican governments that local option's supporters and other antebellum Americans had conflated. He insisted that the United States and the state of Delaware were not democracies but republics, and unlike democracies, the very nature of republics demanded representative institutions. Though Booth rooted the Court's decision in the "principles, spirit, and true intent and meaning of the [Delaware] constitution," he also pointed to Article 4, Section 4 of the national Constitution, likely to preempt any future changes to the state constitution that might authorize local-option-style policymaking. According to Booth, the "guarantee clause," which commands, "The United States shall guarantee to every State in this Union a Republican Form of Government," prevented "the people" from altering the state constitution to "establish a democracy, or any other than a republican form of government." Barring a change to the national Constitution, hc implied, states could never subvert "representative republican" government by authorizing voters to decide directly policy at the ballot box.[44]

Standing out in Booth's lengthy opinion was his alarm with the disingenuous deification of the people that facilitated local option and blinded the populace to the dangerous transformation in governance it initiated. He derided temperance reformers' use of the unassailable rhetoric of democratization and insinuated that their laudable attempt to protect the nation's moral foundations actually steered a path toward political instability and demoralization. Booth had even less tolerance for legislators who had declined their constitutional responsibilities as lawmakers. Looking to Edmund Burke's conservative position on the value of the independent representative, he proclaimed, "*The representative owes to his constituents, not only his industry, but his judgment; and he betrays, instead of serving them, if he sacrifices it to their opinions.*" Legislators rightly were separated from the people and needed to balance momentary public opinion with a broad range of concerns. If legislators continued to pass difficult questions to the voters, Booth warned:

All barriers so carefully erected by the constitution around civil liberty, to guard it against legislative encroachments, and against the assaults of vindictive, arbitrary, and excited majorities, will be thrown down; and a pure democracy, "the worst of all political evils," will hold its sway under the hollow and lifeless form of a republican government.

With a nod toward the importance of judicial review, Booth concluded that the "independent and upright judiciary" must be the bulwark of representative government and minority rights by exorcising laws like local option from the statute book.[45]

Booth also justified his position with the words of James Madison: an expansive representative republic would prevent the "vices of democracy" that plagued "ancient and modern republics," not least "the majority trampling on the rights of the minority." Though Madison articulated this position in defense of the new national constitution back in 1787, nearly sixty years later, Booth brought it to bear on state-level lawmaking and constitutionalism. In the process, he ensured the continuing relevance of Madisonian countermajoritarian political thought in antebellum debates over the limits of democratization and in future considerations of direct democracy and minority rights.[46]

The context of Booth's turn to Madison—antebellum reform and liquor politics—signaled a subtle and important shift in the application of American thinking about the dangers of majority rule. In the political climate of the 1780s, Madison, like many other founding elites, most feared overly democratic state governments because they were too responsive to poor and indebted majorities, threatened the property rights of creditors, and imperiled the young nation's financial future. As Madison famously observed in *Federalist* 10, the inevitable "unequal distribution of property" produced propertyless majorities hostile to propertied minorities. John Clayton's contention that local option would be used to promote property redistribution indicated that these Madisonian apprehensions persisted in antebellum America. Nevertheless, as it had turned out by 1847, the tyrannical majorities and oppressed minorities that actually emerged as a result of local option (as was the case with Sunday laws) were not the impoverished agrarian masses pitted against the few propertied elites. Rather, moral majorities, brought to the ballot box by middle-class reformers with the support of wealthy elites and evangelicals alike, had threatened the property rights and cultural traditions of middle- and working-class, alcohol-friendly moral minorities. As they applauded the Delaware Court's decision, proliquor groups buttressed a tradition of political thought that predominantly had been mustered to defend the property rights of elite minorities. At the

same time, their embrace of countermajoritarianism, born of their conscious decision to counter local option, altered its significance, not least by
helping to democratize the tradition for future use by other nonelite minorities in battles against hostile public policies sanctioned by majority rule.[47]

RICE V. FOSTER QUICKLY became the paradigmatic local option case.
Temperance reformers unsurprisingly assailed the ruling and took shots
both at the "soulless" dealers whose organized resistance spurred the das-
tardly decision and at John Clayton and the members of Delaware's high
court. To the *Philadelphia Standard*, the decision was evidence of Clayton's
undue influence in his home state and of the court members' apparent
fondness for the bottle. How else could they have come to such a decision? The *Journal of the American Temperance Union (JATU)* helped make
Rice v. Foster national news even as it mocked the "frightful consequences"
Clayton and the Delaware Court alleged would follow the local option principle. "The permanency and stability of all property titles, the security of
slavery and of life were all considered at stake, and men were already seen
voting themselves farms out of the possessions of the rich." "The masses
in Delaware," the *JATU* laughed, "were viewed about as dangerous as the
serfs of Russia, or the down-trodden population of Ireland." All ridicule
aside, temperance leaders recognized the decision's importance and the
significance of the ideas raised by the anti-local-option minority. As they
put it, the decision in *Rice v. Foster* could end "all further reference of the
license question to the people."[48]

For others, the events in Delaware forced not just a rethinking of their
earlier stances on local option but a reassessment of the nature and structure of American government. Philadelphia's *North American*, which like
many Whig organs previously supported local option, now saw it not simply
as a question of liquor licensing but as "a question of Elective Legislation
or Representative Legislation—a question whether laws should be made at
the ballot box or in a legislative chamber." Such a fundamental issue, the
North American predicted, would "attract attention…all over the Union."
Indeed, it urged every "patriot" to read Clayton's argument to better inform
his thinking on whether America's brand of popular sovereignty was representative or pure democracy. Meanwhile, those who opposed local option
from the start gained a new way to condemn a policy they abhorred and a
nuanced perspective on American democracy. The Harrisburg *Democratic
Union*, for example, praised the efforts of partisan enemy John Clayton
and maintained that his nondelegation of legislative power argument was

"a Conservative Principle upon which the stability of the Government and the inviolability of the Constitution depended." If Clayton and the Delaware Court were correct, Pennsylvania's law "must be also unconstitutional."[49]

Liquor dealers and their attorneys outside of Delaware agreed. Armed with the Delaware precedent and arguments for representative democracy and minority rights, they joined forces "to test" the constitutionality of local option before other state courts and to demand that legislatures reinstate old laws giving discretionary licensing power to government officers. In the process they kept debates about ballot-box legislation and the character of American democracy on the front page. When allied liquor dealers in Pittsburgh pushed the Pennsylvania Supreme Court to rule against local option, for example, the *Pittsburgh Gazette* responded to the "general demand" for the Court's opinion by forgoing the usual litany of advertisements on the first page and publishing the "very long" opinion instead. *Parker v. Commonwealth* (1847) joined *Rice v. Foster* as another landmark ruling against local option and direct democracy. After New Jersey's first license elections yielded no-license decisions in a majority of towns in late 1847, newspapers reported that "many" Garden Staters deemed the law "unconstitutional, on the same grounds as the Pennsylvania law was decided to be." Shortly thereafter a New Jersey legislative committee borrowed from *Rice v. Foster* to legitimate repeal of their state's local option law. Even Bermuda's legislature rejected local option, arguing that it "was tantamount to the delegating back of the power of the Legislature." Important constitutional precedents were set, but equally important, a particular vision of freedom within democratic political society was authenticated and disseminated, one requiring representative political structures, the separation of popular majorities from formal lawmaking power, and the inclusion of minority interests in policymaking.[50]

For temperance reformers, adverse court decisions, repeals of local option laws, and the reinstatement of old licensing statutes signaled not only the passing of an era of temperance action but also the existence of a conspiracy to undermine what was to them the basis of American freedom—"the great democratic doctrine that the majority should govern." As the ATU explained in 1848, this "great republican principle"

has been the foundation of our freedom, the security of our rights, and the stimulus in all our efforts to make this an enlightened and virtuous republic.... But since we have come to matters of moral reform, ... it is not what the majority say, but what will gratify these panderers to wickedness, and enrich the men who are filling poor houses and jails with miserable tenants.

Once again, they bellowed, "the rum power rules the nation." The only solution was to fill state governments with incorruptible temperance men who would adhere to public opinion and end the license system once and for all. Over the next decade, they would set their sights on statewide prohibitory laws and spark yet another critical reassessment of majoritarian democracy as liquor dealers and other antiprohibitionists would expand their developing minority-rights politics to defend their interests, traditions, rights, and vision of freedom within democratic society.[51]

Though prohibitionists and antiprohibitionists would continue to battle over majoritarian democracy elsewhere, the local option episode remained significant as ballot-box legislation took on a life of its own. Those seeking to make government more responsive to the people built upon the tactics of temperance reformers who had pioneered an extrapartisan, single-issue grass-roots politics that successfully brought direct democracy to bear on the divisive license question in nearly half the states of the Union. Following their temperance predecessors, they would invoke the democratic creeds of majority rule and popular political empowerment to justify their proposals. Skittish politicians, fearful of shouldering the blame for controversial and politically dangerous measures, often happily obliged. Included in this general trend was the "popular sovereignty" approach to the question of slavery in the West. With the Kansas-Nebraska Act of 1854, Congress authorized the local majority to decide the free or slave status of the Kansas Territory. Infamously, Senator Stephen Douglas's "democratic" solution sparked a bloody territorial civil war known as "Bleeding Kansas," destabilized national politics, and pushed the nation further toward civil war. Local majority rule, it seemed, wasn't always the answer.[52]

Typically without bloodshed, opponents of ballot-box legislation turned to the arguments cultivated and constitutionalized in Delaware. Whether confronting measures asking voters to approve taxes to support internal improvements and common schools, statewide liquor prohibition, the post–Civil War revival of local option, or the explosion of initiative, referendum, and recall during the Progressive Era, dissenters argued for limits to majority rule and popular political empowerment, the protection of minority rights, and representative as opposed to direct democracy. At times these arguments proved persuasive to legislators, state constitution

makers, and jurists who decided against direct democracy. As evidenced
by the growth of direct democracy in the late nineteenth and early twentieth centuries and its ongoing use, however, this position was just as often
relegated to minority reports and dissenting opinions.[53]

Nonetheless, much like the Sabbath politics surrounding Sunday
laws, the liquor politics surrounding local option sparked debates that
critically energized and reshaped vital components of the American
countermajoritarian tradition, lending legitimacy to a vision of democracy that was not strictly majoritarian and included minority rights.
While local option seemed to mesh with the democratic faith in majority
rule and popular political empowerment, the challenge of liquor dealers
and their allies pushed many to reassess that faith. Especially for workingmen, immigrants, and partisan Democrats, who might otherwise
have been strong proponents of majoritarian democracy's egalitarian
promise, local option brought them face to face with the democratic
credo falling into the wrong hands and being used to justify excessive
state power and limitations on popular freedom. Those who questioned
local option turned to the thinking of James Madison, John Calhoun,
Edmund Burke, and other conservatives with reservations about
unbridled majority rule. Elites harboring their own reservations about
democracy like James Bayard were likely happy to advance conservative
arguments traditionally used to oppose democratization and to protect
the rights of elites and slaveholders as they rebuffed local option. But
other professed democrats no doubt winced as they employed the positions of renowned antidemocrats to lead their struggle against moral
majoritarianism. Contemporaries noted these "peculiar" connections.
"The old, high toned Federal party," observed the *Pittsburgh Gazette*,
"hardly assumed higher ground in removing active, responsible, delegated power, from the people." Many who opposed local option in the
late 1840s and continued to object to ballot-box legislation with pleas for
representative institutions and minority rights, however, did not seek to
oppose democracy or return to the elitist Federalist-style deferential politics. Instead, they saw a debate over different types of popular self-rule
in which they favored its representative over its direct form. To them, it
better ensured freedom within governments of popular sovereignty by
helping avert "the tyranny of the changeable majority."[54]

4

Mixed Marriages, Motley Schools, and the Struggle for Racial Equality

IN 1840, SEVENTEEN-YEAR-OLD Eunice Ross became another pioneer in the antebellum struggle for minority rights. Ross sparked one of the nation's first conflicts over racially segregated public schools by applying for admission to Nantucket, Massachusetts's all-white high school. Though the local school committee found Ross "amply qualified for admission," the majority of local voters assembled at a town meeting instructed the committee to deny her admission. Ross could attend the "African School" that educated black children separately, but only white children, the voters declared, should attend the high school. Seeing segregation as a badge of black inferiority and an affront to racial equality, local black residents and supportive white abolitionists would join Ross and mount a prolonged fight for the right of all black children to attend any of the island town's schools alongside white children regardless of the wishes of the local majority.[1]

While Sabbath and temperance reformers turned to majority rule to advance their causes in the 1840s, radical abolitionists found that democracy's great postulate posed a formidable obstacle. In their national campaign against slavery they certainly hoped to transform public opinion so an antislavery majority might one day stamp out the South's peculiar institution. But while fighting for the equal rights of black northerners— another crucial arm of their crusade—abolitionists found themselves both in the decided minority and confronted with majoritarian rationales for policies that to them exhibited the same racial prejudice that undergirded slavery. Their opponents argued that policies separating blacks and whites in marriage and in the schools properly reflected the moral sensibilities of an overwhelming majority of Americans who loathed interracial contact. To them, legalized segregation was at once moral—it prevented licentiousness (sex across the color line) and implemented God's demand that the races be kept apart—and democratic—it was sanctioned by majorities. Implicitly breaking with Sabbath and temperance reformers and implicitly joining opponents of Sunday and local option laws as fellow moral minorities, abolitionists rejected such majoritarian omnipotence and advocated for the rights of minorities. In this case, abolitionists challenged the ability of majorities to strike at the social equality of a racial minority—black men, women, and children—in law.

The abolitionists' challenges in Massachusetts to the legal ban on interracial marriage and to racially segregated schools were fundamental. Not only was the Bay State at the vanguard of radical abolitionism and therefore in the national spotlight of antislavery politics, but unlike most other northern states that legally restricted black settlement and withheld voting rights from black men, Massachusetts allowed blacks to settle and authorized the men among them to vote. Yet they and their white abolitionist allies found that basic political inclusion did not equate to democracy and freedom. Like those who opposed Sunday laws and local option in the 1840s, black and white abolitionists found that possessing the vote in a two-party political system afforded few guarantees for the rights of minorities. As the other moral minorities of the age had done, these activists advocated for minority rights in the court of public opinion and before several seats of government. More than just early and precedent-setting battles in the long struggle for civil rights, conflicts over legalized segregation in Massachusetts brought abolitionists and their allies to confront the ascendant fusion of majoritarian democracy and racial prejudice. Moreover, these issues of race emerged in the 1840s alongside conflicts over temperance and Sabbath-keeping as critical sites where some Americans would question the dominant faith in majority rule and begin to implement grass-roots tactics to defend the rights of minorities within American democracy. As the other moral minorities of the era discovered, the road to rights protection would prove long and arduous.[2]

THE ABOLITIONISTS' STRUGGLE for minority rights served the essential second objective of their reform enterprise: the eradication of racial prejudice. In the 1830s, as white radicals boldly broadcast their call for the immediate, uncompensated emancipation of all slaves, they joined black activists in rejecting the colonization schemes that had been the hallmark of early white antislavery. Positing that white prejudice against blacks was ineffaceable, colonizationists had insisted that emancipated blacks be removed from American soil. White radicals and most black northerners, however, found expatriation abhorrent and offered a vision of postemancipation America that was composed of both whites and blacks and free of racism. The trouble was that the United States in the 1830s brimmed with prejudice, and the northern "free" states were no exception. In fact, to such observers as Alexis de Tocqueville, racial prejudice seemed "stronger in those states that have abolished slavery than in those where it still exists." For abolitionists, the fulfillment of their reform agenda required, as the Massachusetts *Abolitionist* announced in 1839, a "war" against "the peculiar American *colorphobic* prejudice" that was "to the death."[3]

This war was fought on multiple fronts. Believing that defeating prejudice was tied to the elevation of the free black community, black and white abolitionists had at first advocated socioeconomic and moral uplift. Early on black activists used churches and local associations to promote communal and self-help strategies, and leaders bolstered these efforts at the black conventions that met intermittently during the antebellum period. By the 1830s, white abolitionists would join them and promote the same values of moral respectability among black northerners—hard work, virtue, thrift, temperance, and education—that sustained white reform crusades and united the burgeoning white middle class.[4] In the meantime, abolitionists sought to cure white America's "colorphobia" by demanding that white Christians judge others not by "their complexion" but by their "moral and intellectual character." This had particular implications for black socioeconomic advancement. "Paths of honest and honorable industry" formerly closed to blacks should be opened. White mechanics and farmers, abolitionists instructed, should "receive colored journeymen and colored apprentices...on the same terms as if they were white." White women had a role to play as well. As the 1839 Anti-Slavery Convention of American Women advised, black women should be invited to participate in "every social advantage, moral, literary, and religious" with white women. Such fellowship, they hoped, would "roll back this tide of cruel prejudice."[5]

Abolitionists realized that defeating prejudice was also a problem of law. As part of its grass-roots petition campaign of the 1830s that called on Congress to outlaw slavery and the slave trade in Washington, DC, the American Anti-Slavery Society targeted northern state policies that inscribed prejudice into law by placing disabilities on black men and

women. In many states, they echoed black conventions in demanding voting rights for black males and the abolition of "black laws" that restricted
black settlement. They also sought the right of blacks to testify against
whites in court as well as for black men to serve on juries. These legal
limitations, abolitionists argued, kept free black northerners in the lim-
inal space between freedom and slavery. They excluded blacks from the
democratic polity, codified black inferiority, and legitimated white racism.
For the United States to be a truly free democracy, such measures needed
to be eradicated.[6]

Black Bay Staters had most of the legal and political rights denied to
their brethren elsewhere, so when abolitionists there delivered petitions to
the state legislature calling for the repeal of all state laws making "any distinction among its inhabitants, on account of COLOR," only one common
measure glaringly applied to Massachusetts as well: the prohibition against
interracial marriage. The initial law, part of an early eighteenth-century
slave code, intended to order the developing system of racial slavery that
interracial marriage, sex, and especially the production of mixed-race children would threaten. Though slavery died in Massachusetts during the
Revolution, the legislature retooled the law in 1786, barring the marriage
of "any white person" with "any Negro, Indian or Mulatto" and mandating a hefty $50 fine for any official or clergymen who solemnized these
unions.[7] Such leading radicals as David Walker, William Lloyd Garrison,
and Lydia Maria Child had earlier objected to such "tyrannical" measures,
and from 1838 until 1843, abolitionists made repeal of the Massachusetts
law a pillar of their larger governmental reform agenda.[8] As reformers had
in other arenas, abolitionists accused the law of sanctioning immorality: it
codified the "unmanly and unchristian" prejudice that infected the North
and that provided the "foundation" for slavery in the South. Horrifically,
the most immoral of Americans—slaveholders—could "point to" the
Massachusetts statute book to justify slavery. Abolitionists implemented
a policy-focused political style, using petitions, the press, and public
meetings to condemn the law and urge the legislature to repeal it. Only
then might the Commonwealth redeem its stained "moral and religious
character."[9]

Repeal did not come easy. Interracial marriage, long a taboo in early
American culture, had become one of the age's most widely discussed
immoralities courtesy of antiabolitionists. Bursting on to the scene in the
1830s, antiabolitionists warned that abolitionists countenanced "amalgamation," what pundit J. K. Paulding defined as "indiscriminate marriages,

between the whites and blacks, accompanied of course by a communion of social and civil rights" (fig. 4.1). For the bulk of white northerners who detested blacks and believed that God abhorred racial mixture, little could be worse. And antiabolitionist spokesmen like Paulding knew it. They advanced the bugaboo of "amalgamation," along with its companion question—"Would you have your daughter marry a nigger?"—to undermine abolitionists' reform agenda, to incite antiabolitionist mobs, and to validate everyday hostilities toward black northerners and white abolitionists. Their efforts helped ensure that antiamalgamation remained a pillar of white moral respectability. Any whites willing to marry across the color line, Paulding raved, were "traitors to the whiteskin, influenced by madbrained fanaticism, or the victims of licentious and ungovernable passions."[10]

While the antiamalgamation maxim reflected real fears held by white northerners, its moralistic appeal and sexual overtones helped obscure the power structure behind antiabolitionism. At the top, politicians, editors,

FIGURE 4.1 *An Amalgamation Waltz* (1839). Courtesy of the American Antiquarian Society. Antiabolitionists insisted that radical abolitionists' push to end slavery and promote racial equality would embolden black men to seek out white women as sexual and marital partners. Such immorality, they protested, would threaten the purity of the white race and the survival of American democracy.

businessmen, and clergymen deployed it to scapegoat blacks and white abolitionists, all the while hoping to enhance their careers and to protect their professional interests from a disruptive reform. As with Sunday laws and liquor bans, Christian morals often hid dubious motives with frightening implications, in this case of wider controls over black and white. The popular appeal of the amalgamation bugbear was, however, formidable because it suggested that abolitionists threatened white superiority. Blacks comprised only a tiny fraction of the northern population, but their presence elevated even the poorest whites, including the rising number of European immigrants, from the bottom rung of the social ladder, freeing many of job and marital competition with blacks. Open marriage would threaten that protective barrier. By demonizing abolitionists as amalgamators and blacks as innately immoral, antiabolitionists urged white males to protect the "purity" of their households, particularly their "young females," from black men who emboldened by abolitionism were eager to copulate with white women. The antiamalgamationist maxim, then, afforded white men an opportunity to assert masculinity in defense of their families and their race and gave white women space to affirm feminine virtue.[11]

In demanding repeal of the ban on interracial marriage, abolitionists entered extremely hostile territory and produced an almost inevitable "excitement" that reverberated beyond Massachusetts. What they faced was not just another moral majority of the day. Indeed, most abolitionists were part of other reform efforts—temperance, in particular—that aimed to instill particular moral behavior in the masses. What they faced was a moralized racial majority of nearly all white men and women, even in Massachusetts, who viewed black men and women as innately immoral and unfit for association with whites. As a result, nearly all abolitionists, for all their radicalism, failed to advocate interracial marriage. A few, William Lloyd Garrison most notably, proclaimed that there was "nothing unnatural in the amalgamation of our species," but most hoped to avoid the abuse that Garrison's candor invited. In one familiar chide, the *Boston Olive Branch* blustered that "Garrison's taste is *very* singular; he likes the peculiar *odor* of the negro, and advocates sexual amalgamation with the black daughters of Ham." When mobs dragged Garrison through the streets, abolitionists fearing for their lives steadfastly denied any wish to promote interracial marriage. To French visitor Gustave de Beaumont, it was, in fact, the unwillingness of abolitionists to repudiate what he saw as the foolish and oppressive taboo against interracial marriage that most explicitly illustrated the tyranny of the majority in American democracy. Indeed, instead of tackling the antiamalgamation maxim head on, abolitionists deflected criticism by arguing that slavery, not abolition, bred amalgamation. "The whole South is a much heap of amalgamation," Garrison's *Liberator* declared, because "unprincipled masters" and their sons ravished "female slaves" giving rise to mixed-race children—"the uncomely, illegitimate, bastard hue of the 'peculiar institution.'" Only ending slavery would end amalgamation.[12]

Sidestepping the issue of amalgamation was far more difficult when calling for the repeal of the ban on interracial marriage since antiabolitionists eagerly took the opportunity to ridicule the abolitionist petitioners as hypersexual amalgamators (fig. 4.2). This was most blatant in 1839 when both Whig and Democratic politicos put the white women abolitionists who spearheaded the petition drive in their crosshairs. These

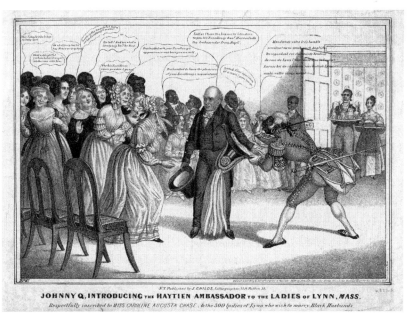

JOHNNY Q, INTRODUCING the HAYTIEN AMBASSADOR to the LADIES of LYNN, *MASS.*
Respectfully inscribed to MISS CAROLINE AUGUSTA CHASE, & the 500 ladies of Lynn who wish to marry Black Husbands

FIGURE 4.2 *Johnny Q, Introducing the Haytien Ambassador to the Ladies of Lynn* (1839). Courtesy of The Library Company of Philadelphia. Antiabolitionists lampooned the white female abolitionists who directed the early petition drive for the repeal of the Massachusetts law banning interracial marriage. Here the abolitionist women of Lynn are eager to make the acquaintance of the Haitian ambassador, whom former US president and antislavery sympathizer John Quincy Adams is introducing. American black men, the artist suggested, hoped to receive the same sexual attention from white women.

"politicians in petticoats," they charged, had left "their appropriate sphere" by transgressing the gender divide in presuming to have something to say about public policy. They had also crossed racial and sexual barriers. To the *Boston Morning Post*, Caroline Augusta Chase and the over seven hundred other petitioners from the Lynn Women's Anti-Slavery Society clearly had had no luck with white men and were now "willing to try *de colored race.*" Legislators similarly questioned the female petitioners' virtue and invited them to withdraw their names from petitions "lest future historians should form an erroneous estimate of the manners and morals of the age."[13] Those legislators who advocated repeal also risked vilification. George Bradburn, a Nantucket Whig who deemed the intermarriage law an affront to "freedom and equality" and championed repeal, was one such victim. Noting that Bradburn was a widower, the *Boston Phoenix* suggested that perhaps the legislature should pass a "special act" to allow him to marry "any *fair* daughter of Ethiopia for whom he feels a tender passion."[14] No such law was passed.

Abolitionists and their legislative allies persisted in the face of such criticism, maintaining that it was equality they were after, not amalgamation. The problem with the ban on interracial marriage was not that it prevented interracial marriage. Law or no law, such unions, most abolitionists in fact argued, were unlikely to occur because of the strength of public opinion against them. The chief problem was that the law distinguished between "citizens on account of complexion" and, in doing so, created a racial hierarchy at war with "humanity," "justice," and the broad egalitarian values of Christianity and republicanism. "Neither the colored people nor the white petitioners," the *National Anti-Slavery Standard* carefully explained from New York City, "have wished for the repeal of this law because they think 'amalgamation' desirable...the principal reason...is, that the *statute was a record of contempt for the colored race.*" This was, abolitionist John A. Collins declared, a question "of HUMAN RIGHTS, not of matrimony."[15]

Defenders of the ban vehemently disagreed. Ignoring the law's roots in slavery, they argued that there was no inequality at work in the provision, only the promotion of good Christian morals. The law, one legislative committee maintained, acted alike on both black and white citizens "without discrimination," making not "the slightest superiority in one race or inferiority in another." It applied "to all colors, to all races, spreading its protection for morality and purity over every member of the community." Others, like the *Hampshire Republican*, returned to the standard antiabolitionist contention that it was not in "the design of the Creator" for marriages to "take place between Negroes and whites." The legislature rightfully implemented God's law "to preserve the purity and morality of the people" by restraining the "depraved appetites" of those who would cross the color line. Representative George Lunt was even more forceful. To him, interracial marriage was akin to "incest and marriages within prohibited degrees." If the legislature repealed one ban, what would keep it from repealing other restraints on licentiousness? Beyond moral purity, also at stake to antirepealers was the purity and superiority of the white race. "The mixed blood is depraved, the intellect is inferior," one Boston legislator thundered. "We pass laws for the preservation of the heath hen and of certain fisheries…[and] to improve…the breed of cattle or sheep, or pigs." Why would we not "preserve our own race from the certain deterioration"? The intermarriage law was simply good race management. For antirepealers it almost went without saying that these ends were well supported in public opinion. "The common feeling of men," observed Nathan Hale, the Whig editor of the *Boston Weekly Messenger* and loudest opponent of repeal, "revolts at the idea" of blacks and whites intermarrying. If law in a democratic polity properly reflected public opinion, why should this one not stand?[16]

Abolitionists' arguments, however, presupposed limits on legislative power, and that the legislature, in making distinctions between citizens on grounds of color—even those supported in public opinion—had exceeded the scope of its authority and violated the state constitution. As abolitionists eagerly pointed out, the Massachusetts Constitution, unlike the US Constitution, made no compromises with slavery and explicitly incorporated the promises of the Declaration of Independence. The first provision of its Declaration of Rights proclaimed that "all men are born free and equal, and have certain natural, essential and unalienable rights; among which may be reckoning the right of enjoying and defending their lives and liberties; that of acquiring, possessing and protecting property; in fine, that of seeking and obtaining their safety and happiness." Referring to the famed Quok Walker cases of the 1780s, abolitionists emphasized how this provision had "abolished slavery at a blow" in Massachusetts. It should now, they insisted, abolish the state's intermarriage ban.[17]

Abolitionists and their supporters parsed the constitutional provision. Some contended that the law, by interfering with marital choice, interfered with the right to pursue happiness. Others maintained that the law violated property rights, especially when the "innocent" offspring produced by the few interracial unions were legally branded as "illegitimate" and denied inheritances. Most, however, focused on the "all men are born free and equal" provision, which the prohibition on interracial marriage, they claimed, violated by enshrining white superiority and black inferiority in law.[18] Countering antirepealers who insisted that the ban applied equally to all races, a prorepeal legislative committee explained, "The law must necessarily bear hardest upon the race which is lowest in social position, which is least numerous, least cultivated, least wealthy, and which has most to gain by forming ties that may connect its individuals with the intelligence, the cultivation, and the power of the stronger race." As another commentator explained, the law was "a standing insult to the people of color, just as a law would be which should forbid intermarriages between the professional and mechanical classes, a law which every body would feel to be an intentional insult to the latter." When considering the history of black degradation and present social standing of most blacks, the racial distinction signaled hierarchy. Hierarchy constituted constitutional violation.[19]

As they advanced equality as a moral and constitutional value that should invalidate the intermarriage ban and even as they steadfastly denied any interest in promoting amalgamation, abolitionists insisted that marital choice was not an issue of morals but one of "taste." While a true moral standard—like racial equality or antislavery—might properly be the subject of law, a standard of taste was not. Capturing this sentiment, the *Northampton Courier* maintained that "the choice between the white and the colored is a matter of *taste*. Other matters may be questions of religion, morality, education, . . . and the like, but color is entirely a matter of taste, or perhaps more properly of *fancy*." As the law allowed all sorts of questionable marriages—"the most refined and virtuous lady" may "marry an ignorant, vulgar, unprincipled white *fellow*" or "a drunken white debauchee"—why prevent whites from marrying blacks? To Lydia Maria Child, free marital choice was much like the freedom to choose a religion. The state, she affirmed, should not "be invested with the power to control the affections, any more than the consciences of citizens. A man has at least as good a right to choose his wife, as he has to choose his religion. His taste may not suit his neighbors; but so long as his deportment is correct, they have no right to interfere with his concerns." For nonabolitionists, especially Democrats who would come to support repeal, many with little interest in racial equality, this argument proved especially attractive. Reminiscent of how many Democrats rejected Sunday and local option measures, some thought it better if state governments just stayed out of this regulatory arena. "Private *taste*, and a common respect for the opinions of mankind," the *Brooklyn Eagle* sardonically opined, "are sufficient 'regulators' in this matter; and if the former incline a romantic youth to take to his bosom an Ethiopian damsel, do let him enjoy the luxury undisturbed." There was no need for government to interfere in this ultimately private choice.[20]

If some Democrats offered some measure of consistency across the varied debates over moral regulations in the 1840s, abolitionists were somewhat less consistent. Certainly, a small contingent opposed Sunday legislation on the grounds of religious freedom, but in shifting the discussion of interracial marriage away from a moral standard to one of taste, most abolitionists kept the door open for certain morals to be enshrined in public policy. Clearly, they wanted their radical moral standard of racial equality cemented into government practice, and many, no doubt, looked forward to a day when the abolition of slavery was a moral pillar embedded in national law. Most abolitionists also supported the local option legislation of the 1840s and the prohibition measures of the 1850s—efforts that attempted to enshrine the moral norm of teetotalism, purportedly the will of the majority, in policy.

In the context of the marriage law, however, abolitionists maintained that a standard of taste was not a proper basis of law, even if countenanced by majorities. On this they joined the growing chorus of opponents of uninhibited majority rule. In 1840, a legislative committee supporting the abolitionist petitioners and advocating repeal crystallized this position in a report submitted by state legislator George T. Davis and rumored to have been ghostwritten by George Bradburn of Nantucket. Though "well aware of the strength of the social prejudice in which this law took its origin, and still finds its support," the legislature should not, the report declared, "sanction the principle that the tastes of the majority shall be the measure of the rights of the minority." Majorities were not clothed with absolute power, and especially when mere matters of "taste" were at issue, they could not impair minority rights. Ironically, this position to some extent echoed the stance taken by opponents of restrictive liquor legislation who declared that it was not for majorities to tell other citizens what to eat or drink.

Abolitionists, however, took a somewhat distinctive step because their repudiation of majority rule ultimately involved two different minorities. First, their efforts to some extent protected anyone (regardless of racial identity) willing to cross the color line in marriage or to support those who did. Majorities could not inhibit their "taste" in marriage partners. Second and, to them, far more important, they sought to protect black northerners, an unequivocal numerical minority—a racial minority—whom they argued were rendered unequal by the marriage law's differentiation between black and white citizens. For abolitionists and their supporters, majorities could not establish social hierarchies. "According to the theory of our government and the letter of our constitution, the races whose intermixture is prohibited" by the marriage law "are entitled to stand as citizens upon a footing of entire civil equality." The "spirit of caste" could not be clothed with "the authority of law" even if sanctioned by the majority of the people. In this case, morality had a religious and constitutional basis—equality—that necessarily came before the majority.[21]

These arguments reflected abolitionists' broader concerns about the linkage between majoritarian democracy and racial prejudice, which abolitionists understood as the white majority's oppression of the black minority. In 1837, for example, abolitionist Elizur Wright Jr. praised Gustave de Beaumont's novel *Marie, or Slavery in the United States* for its shrewd assessment of public opinion's power to legitimate racial prejudice and degrade black men and women. Inspired by Beaumont, Wright protested, "Let it be understood, that, in the model republic of the world, there is a minority…which has nothing to expect but to be trampled upon without mercy." This majoritarian oppression of black men and women, he declared, was "a reproach to republicanism" that held up "the tottering thrones of all Europe." Abolitionists adapted these general assessments to prejudice in the law, which they attributed to the corrupt and immoral sentiments of the white majority. As Lydia Maria Child explained, "Where the laws are made by the people, a majority of course approve them; else they would soon by changed. It must therefore in candor be admitted, that the *laws* of a State speak the prevailing *sentiments* of the inhabitants." For them, doing away with laws imbued with prejudice demanded either that the sentiments of majorities be changed or that majorities be prevented from enacting policies steeped in prejudice. In their struggle to repeal the marriage law, abolitionists at once sought to change public opinion about the law while simultaneously advancing a political and constitutional rationale for limiting the power of majorities to protect the rights of the black minority.[22]

The abolitionist camps taking form by the early 1840s—Garrisonian and political abolitionists—added different perspectives on the problem of unrestrained majority rule. On the one hand, Garrison insisted that democracy needed to be more than majority rule. To him, genuine popular sovereignty could only be achieved through adherence to true Christian values, including racial equality. In reviewing an election sermon that praised the "sovereignty of the whole people," he protested that "in this country, it is not 'the people,' but the majority...that rule, 'for better, for worse,'—and the minority agree to succumb." By contrast, Garrison insisted, "Christianity has no minority. Its exactors are peace, its officers righteousness, its walls salvation, and its gates praise. Its laws admit of no modification, and its regulations are of the most perfect character." Garrison's perfectionist vision of the Christian government of God would fuel his broader tactics of nonresistance, particularly his advocacy of disunion with the slaveholding South. His concern with the rights of minorities, however, proved critical as Garrisonians—despite their often anti-institutional stance—remained concerned about public policy and fought to repeal the intermarriage ban and other forms of legalized prejudice. As Garrison later announced, "They who are for trampling on the rights of the minority, in order to benefit the majority, are to be registered as the monsters of their race. Might is never right, excepting when it sees in every human being, 'a man and a brother,' and protects him with a divine fidelity." Majorities could only legitimately advance equality, never inequality.[23]

On the other hand, the political abolitionists who broke with the Garrisonians to form the Liberty Party struggled to forge a minority-based political movement—a new third party in a two-party political culture that demanded majoritarian success. For the Massachusetts Abolition Society, the idea that abolitionists as well as black men and women were a "minority" was self-evident. "WE ARE A MINORITY!" the *Massachusetts Abolitionist* declared. "Our whole struggle has been for the rights of minorities," and this scenario necessitated their foray into electoral politics. "The only security, in a popular government, against that most odious of all despotism—the despotism of a majority—is in the fearless action of the minority." Taking "abolitionism to the polls," no matter "how few we are," would eventually prove the "omnipotent" power of "a 'Right minded minority'" and ensure the security of "minorities in their rights." Protecting the rights of the minority, political abolitionists argued, was the "one grand end of civil government" and the highest democratic enterprise.[24]

Though black abolitionists remained comparatively quiet in the public debate over the intermarriage law, they too had developed an assessment

of majoritarian democracy by the early 1840s. The most powerful exposition came from James McCune Smith, a doctor, intellectual, and leading
activist who Frederick Douglass would later say understood "the whole
struggle between freedom and slavery" better than any person in America.
In 1841, Smith's lecture *The Destiny of the People of Color* provided a foundational statement of black Americans' standing as "a minority...dis-
tinguished by a difference of complexion" in a democracy governed by
majority rule. Whether in slavery in the South or in "half bondage" in
the North, black men and women were "an oppressed minority" excluded
from "the common equality of the human family" and held in "servitude
by a majority who pretend to be Republican in their form of Government."
To Smith, the "irresponsible rule of the multitude"—the "most awful of
tyrannies"—needed to be resisted. The doctrine that "might makes right"
needed to be replaced with the doctrine "right makes right." Looking to
census data showing that the black population was not keeping up with
the growing "white population," Smith had no expectation that black
Americans, even with "their political rights...restored," would gain "paramount political influence...at the ballot box." To obtain equal rights,
black men and women needed to battle in the realm of public opinion—to
"reason down the prejudices which bar us from rights." Only through
righteous ideas and untiring activism would the black minority succeed
in their "struggle for liberty" against the white majority. Success, Smith
insisted, would purify the American republic and "save the [republican]
form of government."[25]

As all camps of abolitionists moved against the intermarriage law in
Massachusetts, they asked the state legislature, an elective body theo-
retically accountable to public opinion and majorities, to act in defense
of minority rights. After several years of near repeals and much debate,
legislators in 1843 finally repealed the law. The high-profile attempted
retrieval of the fugitive slave George Latimer in Massachusetts and the
controversial jailing of northern black seamen in southern ports spurred a
rise in antislavery sentiment on which abolitionists' capitalized. So too did
Garrisonian lobbyists who not only persisted in their yearly petition campaigns but also made repeal "the test question" that they put before candidates for state legislature. Some legislators, no doubt, were eager to end
this annual onslaught that supplied, as one critic protested, yet another
"topic for turbulent and inflammatory discussion" that cost "the commonwealth thousands of dollars." Persistence could pay off. Additionally, the
inroads in electoral politics made by political abolitionists of the Liberty

Party proved crucial. The three-party election of 1843 resulted in no clear legislative majority, and as part of the haggling over legislative control Liberty Partyites supported Democratic control in exchange for the repeal of the intermarriage law. A minority third party holding the balance of power in the legislature had helped push through what they saw as an advance for the rights of the black minority.[26]

Detractors, of course, saw no such advance and took the opportunity to ridicule abolitionists and the Massachusetts legislature for encouraging amalgamation. Wisconsin's *Racine Advocate* derided the Massachusetts legislature for passing "an amalgamation law," while one watchful white Virginian mocked that "the milk and molasses color will hereafter be fashionable in the Bay State."[27] Nathan Hale of the *Boston Messenger* warned that Massachusetts would soon "be thought the paradise of colored people" and bring a mass migration of black men who would put white women at risk. Other politicos took the opportunity to exploit racial fears and chastise their partisan opponents. James Watson Webb's conservative Whig *New York Courier and Enquirer*, for example, excoriated Massachusetts Democrats for affording white women "the legal luxury of being married to…an Ethiopian as black as burnt cork!" The end of the intermarriage prohibition, declared the *Cattaraugus Republican*, "will bring about amalgamation as soon as the fiercest abolitionist can desire."[28]

In the meantime, abolitionists of all stripes celebrated. At the Essex County Anti-Slavery Meeting, William Lloyd Garrison, Frederick Douglass, and other Garrisonians applauded their own resolve, while political abolitionists as far off as Ann Arbor, Michigan, credited the "influence" of the Liberty Party. More broadly, abolitionists united in praising the victory over prejudice. It signaled, according to the *National Anti-Slavery Standard*, that the American republic would "inevitably outgrow [its] irrational and unjust prejudice." Indeed, at the second World Anti-Slavery Convention meeting in London, Hiram H. Kellogg of the Illinois State Anti-Slavery Society gladly spread the news about "the progress of legislation favourable to liberty" in Massachusetts. Notably it was a liberty that was to be protected by democratic government even if counter to the wishes of popular majorities. As a correspondent to Cincinnati's *Philanthropist* proclaimed, "however strong may still be the prejudices of the whites against the blacks," the Massachusetts legislature has ensured that "the colored man may here feel that he is civilly, if not socially a freeman, an equal with his fairer-faced neighbor." Popular prejudices could not legitimate the denial of equal legal rights to the small minority of black men and women. This was a "signal victory."[29]

IN THE MEANTIME, Massachusetts' black citizens took matters into their own hands in a wave of local opposition to the state's segregated public schools. The movement to create free public (or common) schools had flourished in New England and especially in Massachusetts in the 1830s and 1840s, where attendance rose sharply. Yet if black children gained access to the fruits of public education it was often in segregated settings. Black activists saw education as the key to black socioeconomic advancement, respectability, and the most essential path to combating racism, and some, in fact, had preached the virtues of separate schools in the early nineteenth century. By the 1830s, however, abolitionists—black and white—began to look upon segregated schools as another badge of servitude and source of oppression. Beginning in three of Massachusetts' largest communities—Nantucket, Salem, and Boston—abolitionists challenged segregation and contributed to the era's emergent popular minority-rights activism. In these local theaters yet simultaneously, rights-activists practiced an extrapartisan mode of democratic engagement in which they petitioned local school boards, organized boycotts, held public meetings, and published protests to change policy. Their controversial crusade recruited ever more abolitionists and rose into the state legislature and the courts, becoming a spectacle beyond the state. As Garrison's *Liberator* opined, the school question raised "issues" that "will have an influence upon the destinies of many more than our own colored fellow-citizens." Essential "issues" were, again, the power of majorities and the rights of minorities.[30]

When in 1840 seventeen-year-old Eunice Ross demanded admission to Nantucket's all-white high school and William Lloyd Garrison, Wendell Phillips, and William Cooper Nell petitioned the city of Boston "to grant equal school rights" to black children, they knew they were entering dangerous territory. The schoolhouse had already proven an extremely contentious venue in the era's divisive racial climate (fig. 4.3). When white abolitionist Simeon Jocelyn, for example, proposed to open a manual labor college for black men in 1831, appalled local whites in New Haven, Connecticut, including students and faculty at Yale, made sure the project never got off the ground. In Canaan, New Hampshire, local oxen helped irate whites yank the schoolhouse of Noyes Academy off its foundation because black and white pupils were educated there together. Most infamously, Quaker schoolteacher Prudence Crandall caused a maelstrom

FIGURE 4.3 *Colored Schools Broken Up* from the *Anti-Slavery Almanac* (1839). Courtesy of The Library Company of Philadelphia. The mixture of black and white children in schools sparked outrage and violence from local white citizens in several communities during the 1830s.

in Canterbury, Connecticut, when she admitted black girls to her female academy. Angry white parents withdrew their daughters, but local outrage continued as Crandall, with the support of William Lloyd Garrison, enticed young black women from afar to attend her now all-black school. Locals dumped animal feces in her well, pelted her house with eggs, and lobbied the state legislature for assistance. To them, Crandall's "nigger school" would ruin their property values and "break down the barriers which God has placed between blacks and whites." When the legislature responded with a law prohibiting the operation of "a school for out-of-state blacks without permission of the local community," Crandall was quickly prosecuted and convicted. Her conviction was overturned and the Black Law was soon repealed, but she never dared to reopen her school. As Massachusetts abolitionists moved against segregation in the 1840s, they too sparked an uproar.[31]

Black and white abolitionists again put their moral commitments to promoting racial equality and to defeating prejudice at the forefront of the crusade. As they sought to change public opinion and public policy with public meetings, petitions, and editorials, they insisted that the "blasting disease" of prejudice that sustained slavery was also behind school segregation. Separate schools degraded black children by branding them with "inferiority and unfitness to associate with the mass," and they also injured white children by teaching them prejudice. Segregation, the minority of the Boston Primary School Committee announced, fostered "feelings of repugnance and contempt for the colored race as degraded inferiors, whom they may, or must, treat as such." Absent segregation, abolitionists and their supporters argued, white children would be less likely to develop prejudice and instead would learn to judge their fellow citizens by their "character" alone. Integration, then, would cleanse "the springs of instruction," improve the standing of black Americans, and help rid future generations of white Americans of their diabolical prejudice.[32]

Defenders of segregation appeared at public meetings and wrote editorials (often anonymously) of their own. They too disseminated moral concerns to convince the public and policymakers that segregation was imperative. Amalgamation once again proved the moral raison d'être. Integrated schools would be a steppingstone to intermarriage and consequently, racial and social disorder. Responding to grass-roots desegregation crusades, the *Boston Olive Branch*, for example, called upon "good men and heaven [to] defend us from such a social intercourse of the two races, as might destroy the usefulness of our excellent schools, or lead to the abomination of the unnatural amalgamation of two races, *whom God intended should ever be distinct.*" Extending the olive branch even further, the author announced, "There is as much propriety in Negroes marrying with the ourang outang, as there is of the matrimonial amalgamation of the Saxon and the negro races; and motley schools are the forerunners and producers of such amalgamation." Not only would "motley schools" cause racial decline, but it would upset the entire American social order. As the *Olive Branch* concluded, "Give the negro his liberty, but KEEP HIM IN HIS PLACE."[33]

Debates over the intermarriage law had centered on the regulatory power of the legislature, but school segregation focused on the power of local school committees, to which local activists turned their attention. With the school law, the state legislature had empowered local school committees to regulate school systems, and even for segregationists, this power could not prevent black children from receiving an education. The question was whether school committees could separate black and white children. Segregationists thought so. To an unnamed speaker at a Nantucket town meeting in 1843, the committee's ability to separate black and white children was not unlike its ability to ban "children having disease and infection." This analogy, pregnant with allusions to the degraded black body and the threat it posed to pure white children, was far from uncommon. Another Nantucketer writing under the pseudonym "Fair Play" declared, "We say that the presence of coloured children is as obnoxious to us, and even more so to some of us, than the presence of contagious disease. Some dislike canker-rash, measles, whopping cough, and other contagious diseases more than they do colored children, others dislike the colored children the most." Whether separating the diseased from the healthy or the degraded from the superior, school boards properly protected the health, morals, and welfare of the community.[34]

The bitter opposition of school boards showed how deeply entrenched prejudice was in northern communities, and it also exposed how majoritarian democracy and racial prejudice could be mutually reinforcing. Segregationists insisted that school boards needed to implement the will of the "vast majority of our citizens" who found blacks "very obnoxious." "Most of the white people" and "the majority of the colored," Boston's Primary School Committee claimed, supported segregation. "Every body," an anonymous Nantucketer declared, "feels that separation is the mandate of God." Beyond the rhetoric, Nantucket's segregationists used town meetings to instruct their school committee to uphold segregation. Reminiscent of temperance reformers' claims during the contemporary debates over local option, Nantucket segregationists saw no leeway for elected officials, in this case the school committeemen, to exercise their own judgment. They were beholden to the majority will explicitly expressed at the town meeting. If the committee did not continue separate schools, one editorialist held, "The peculiar opinions of a minority are gratified, the sovereign is defeated, and that fundamental principle of democracy, 'the greatest good of the greatest number,' is overborne by the few." Indeed, in defending their "obedience to the manifest will of the town," the members of Nantucket's school committee explained that they "had no right to gratify the wish of a small portion of the citizens for a social amalgamation offensive to all the rest." Segregation was within their legal power; it was perfectly democratic because the majority demanded it.[35]

For local integrationists and their abolitionist allies, this was another area where majorities should not rule. The Massachusetts Constitution and broad Christian and republican values, they repeatedly argued, all mandated equality and prohibited school committees—even if supported by majorities—from treating the black children as anything less than equals. At one of the many public meetings called to combat segregation, abolitionists and their supporters in Nantucket declared segregation an unconstitutional and illegal "exercise of power by the majority." In a public protest read aloud by George Bradburn, the former state legislator who had battled the intermarriage law, local activists explained that the state constitution "neither makes nor tolerates any distinction among its citizens, on account of differences of race, of color, or of outward condition." Before the constitution, "as before the omnipotent God, the black man and his children stand as the equals of the white man and his children." No school committee or popular majority could violate "this noble instrument" or "our boasted doctrine of democratic equality." The minority of the Boston Primary School Committee agreed and emphasized that America's republican political order was predicated on the absence of social divisions in law and the existence of equal "legal rights." "It is the peculiar advantage of our republican system," they argued, "that it confers civil equality...and creates no difference, between rich and poor, learned and ignorant, white and black." While never denying that distinctions might actually exist in society along racial and class lines, integrationists insisted, as James B. Congdon of New Bedford did, that everyone deserved "equality before the law."[36]

Beyond the state constitution, the most important law at issue was the school law, which abolitionists maintained also outlawed social hierarchy and, thus, segregation. The "equality of privileges," a meeting of black Bostonians resolved, is "the vital principle of the school system of Massachusetts." It was "the object of our school law," another integrationist argued, "that our system of free schools is to be one of *absolute* equality. The right to attend any town school can only be limited by the qualifications of the scholar. Any other rule, would tend, sooner or later, to an unequal and partial dispensation of the benefits of the school system." In an advisory opinion on segregation solicited by the Salem School Committee, prominent white lawyer Richard Fletcher echoed these themes. A chief virtue of the free school system was that "all classes of the community mingle together. The rich and the poor meet upon terms of equality, and are prepared to discharge the duties of life by the same instructions.... It is the principle of equality, cherished in the free schools, on which our free government and free institutions rest." If equality were destroyed in the schools by the infiltration of aristocracy, free society would be threatened. "The rich alone would obtain knowledge and power, and the poor would be ignorant and degraded. The rich would oppress the poor, and the poor would war against the rich, and our free institutions would inevitably be destroyed in the conflict." According to Fletcher, racial hierarchy too threatened the destruction of the school system and republican society.[37]

Local integrationists also drew inspiration from judicial precedent, and most critically *Commonwealth v. Dedham*. This 1819 decision by the Massachusetts Supreme Judicial Court had nothing to do with racial segregation. At issue was whether a town with multiple school districts could offer the benefit of grammar school education to children in one geographic area without offering it to children living in other sections of the town. The Court found that state law demanded that residents deserved equal school privileges, which meant that all should have the ability to attend every gradation of schooling. The details of the case mattered in the 1840s, especially as the gradation of schools was at issue in the local contests over racial segregation. Perhaps even more important were the words Justice Wilde used to justify his decision. "The schools," he wrote, "required by the statute, are to be maintained for the benefit of the whole town: as it is the wise policy of the law to give *all* the inhabitants *equal* privileges, for the education of their children in the public schools. Nor is it in the power of the *majority*, to deprive the *minority* of this privilege."[38] First appearing in the pages of the *Nantucket Inquirer* in 1843 as an anonymous editorialist demanded school integration, Wilde's words proved inspirational for abolitionists more than two decades after they were written. They provided an explicit statement about the inability of majorities to strike at the equality of the minority. When Richard Fletcher advised the Salem School Committee in 1844 that the law mandated desegregation, he turned to *Commonwealth v. Dedham* and made its protections for minorities apply explicitly to the black minority. Others would follow his lead.[39]

Integrationists hoped to shift public opinion on the question of black rights, but they especially targeted school committee members and offered a perspective on the relationship of school committees and public opinion at odds with segregationists' vision. Reminiscent of the arguments that surfaced during local option debates about the importance of independent elected officials, black Nantucketers meeting in 1842 argued that school committees needed to stand above majorities if their wishes conflicted with the state constitution and the school law. The school committee had a "duty which necessarily devolves upon them, by virtue of their being a School Committee—the agents of the whole community—to attend to the department of what is called 'Common School Education,' and to see that the law in reference to their charge is carried out." The editor of Nantucket's Democratic organ, *The Islander*, agreed. "The School

Committee," he maintained, "are in some respects state officers, and are not called upon to obey the will of those who elect them only. They are responsible to the state as well as to the town; to the state, because they are bound to see that its laws with regard to education are enforced; and to the town, that they be governed by the dictates of a wise economy in enforcing those laws." School committees, apart from voters, town meetings, and majorities, rightly protected minorities by upholding the law and the constitution.[40]

In Salem this approach seemed to work. Spurred by a black boycott of the town's black school and armed with Fletcher's advisory opinion, the school committee integrated the public schools there in 1844.[41] Activists were not as successful in Nantucket and Boston. Despite a brief victory in 1844 when the school committee desegregated Nantucket schools, integrationists there continued to meet resistance. Local residents responded by turning the integrationist committee out of office and returning a segregationist committee at the next election. For Nantucket integrationists, representative democracy in the form of the school committee had failed to protect black rights, as had the direct democracy of the town meeting system of government, which continued to instruct the school committee to maintain separate schools. After segregation was reinstated in 1845, Nantucket residents petitioned the state legislature for help in defending the right of black children "to equal instruction with other children" in the common schools.

Aware that the legislature recently had repealed the intermarriage law, Nantucket abolitionists hoped the legislature would continue its defense of black rights. Led by prominent black abolitionist Edward J. Pompey and black businessman and former ship captain Absalom Boston (fig. 4.4), Nantucket's 104 black petitioners protested, "They can have no instruction from the town, unless they submit to insults and outrages upon their rights...and for no other reason but color." Having been informed by "some of the first lawyers in the Commonwealth...that they can get no redress through the law as it is," they asked the legislature for "some enactment, which will protect all children in their equal right to the schools." These black petitioners were very specific about from whom they needed protection: "the majorities of School Committees, or of those who assemble in town meetings." Implicit in their plea to the legislature was not only that something was wrong with the current school law, but also that something was wrong with democracy if popular and representative "majorities" could control their rights, particularly without redress in court.[42]

FIGURE 4.4   Absalom Boston. Courtesy of the Nantucket Historical Association Research Library. Successful businessman and former sea captain Absalom Boston was a pivotal leader in the struggle against school segregation in Nantucket.

The legislature responded with a law that authorized parents to bring suits for damages if their child was unlawfully excluded from a public school. If local school boards and local majorities refused to respect the equal rights of the minority, the court system would come to their aid. The New York–based *National Anti-Slavery Standard* continued to make the struggle national news and credited the labor of prominent abolitionists William Lloyd Garrison, Wendell Phillips, and Ellis Gray Loring, as well as white Nantucketers John T. Shaw and George Gardner, local abolitionist leaders who had supported black activists' integrationist crusade. According to the *Standard*, these abolitionists had "frequent and repeated interviews with the Committees both of the Senate and House." In the Massachusetts Senate, abolitionists found an ally in Henry Wilson, a Liberty Partyite and later a US senator and the vice president of the United States. Wilson echoed the arguments distilled in the local school debates in Nantucket, Salem, and Boston, which included citing the Court's pronouncement in *Commonwealth v. Dedham* that "the majority could not deprive the minority" of equal educational privileges. "The [school] law gives all equal rights," he argued, "but these rights are invaded, and there is no mode of redress." The legislature must, he announced, watch over "the rights of the poorest and the humblest" and protect black children "from the tyranny of prejudice and false taste." The state legislature rightly protected minorities from local majorities.[43]

The final text of the new law proved important. It read: "Any child, unlawfully excluded from public school instruction in this commonwealth, shall recover damages therefore against the city or town by which such public instruction is supported." As the *National Anti-Slavery Standard* noted, "The law was originally worded, 'any child unlawfully excluded from *any public school*,' but the word 'instruction' was added, in reality to defeat the purpose of the bill, and still confine the colored children to separate schools." Many lawyers, they continued, still felt the law was good enough to achieve its objective. "It remains to be seen," the *Standard* concluded, "whether the courts will carry out the system of free school instruction in the spirit in which it was originally instituted, or bow to the petty and vulgar prejudices of the day, to suit the aristocratic tastes of two or three large towns." The *Liberator* also echoed concern that the new law might be useless. "Abolitionists," they observed, "forced on a reluctant Legislature a law, giving to all color equal rights in the public schools; so worded, however, by its enemies, that it...leaves it somewhat questionable whether it can be enforced."[44] They would soon have their answer.

Two groups used the new law to challenge segregation with mixed results. First in Nantucket, Absalom Boston quickly initiated a test suit against the town on behalf of his daughter, Phebe Ann Boston, who was excluded from an all-white school. Taking an active interest in the case, the *Liberator* wrote, "As questions of a similar character have caused some discussion in other places, the progress and results of this suit will be watched with no little interest." The Baltimore-based *Niles' National Register* agreed. The ultimate decision in the case "will be an important one, as a precedent." There would be no decision. The threat of Boston's suit in conjunction with continued local agitation and a breakdown in party allegiances spurred a reversal in policy—what the *Nantucket Inquirer* termed a "Moral Revolution." The hotly contested and widely reported elections for school board in 1846 centered on the question of segregation. "Whig and Democratic lines," the *Inquirer* explained, "were not at all attended to. On both sides, members of the two political parties were earnestly laboring together." When the smoke cleared, a majority of Nantucket voters had cast ballots for the slate of integrationist candidates. The new board speedily admitted black children to previously all-white schools. Nantucket schools would remain integrated. Six years of grass-roots activism had brought the local majority to sanction the protection of the rights of the black minority.[45]

The victory in Nantucket did little to help the black children who remained barred from Boston's white schools. Since the early 1840s, black and white abolitionists had lobbied the city's school committee for "equal school rights" and urged local blacks to boycott the Smith School, where the city's black children were educated separately. Armed with the school law of 1845, a black printer and activist named Benjamin Roberts took action. On four previous occasions Roberts had unsuccessfully sought the admission of his daughter Sarah to the white primary school closest to their home. He was ready for a fifth round. Assisted by black abolitionist and lawyer Robert Morris as well as white lawyer and future US senator Charles Sumner (fig. 4.5), Roberts first sought damages in the Common Pleas Court. Losing there, he then appealed to the Massachusetts Supreme Judicial Court to test the constitutionality of school segregation.

FIGURE 4.5   Charles Sumner. Courtesy of the Library of Congress.

Before the Court, Charles Sumner made a wide-reaching argument against segregation that synthesized, crystallized, and elaborated on the range of arguments made by black and white abolitionists and other integrationists since at least the early 1840s. Looking to the promises of "equality before the law" enshrined in the Declaration of Independence, the natural rights provisions of the Massachusetts Constitution, and the egalitarian premises of the school law, Sumner passionately maintained that school committees could not create the racial caste distinctions that accompanied the separation of black and white children. A central implication of Sumner's argument was his elevation of "equality" as the fundamental aspect of American democracy, one more fundamental than majority rule. Indeed, Sumner demanded that the Court adhere to its own precedent—the *Commonwealth v. Dedham* decision—by recognizing it was not "in the power of the majority to deprive the minority" of equal school rights. Benjamin Roberts printed Sumner's argument in pamphlet form, and both the abolitionist and mainstream press broadcast his plea for equality and minority rights widely. Segregation, the *Liberator* wrote, "will be long matter of debate in this and other States, and the comprehensive view of Mr. Sumner will long be a treasure-house for other laborers to draw from."[46]

In *Roberts v. City of Boston* the Massachusetts Supreme Judicial Court, however, had little to say about the rights of minorities, and notoriously, the prominent chief justice, Lemuel Shaw, upheld segregation. Shaw conceded that "colored persons...are entitled by law, in this commonwealth, to equal rights, constitutional and political, civil and social." "The question" for Shaw was "whether the regulation in question, which provides separate schools for colored children, is a violation of any of these rights." Shaw thought not. Echoing segregationists in Salem, Nantucket, and Boston, Shaw gave wide latitude to local school committees to "make all the reasonable rules, for organizing such schools and regulating and conducting them." Shaw gave birth to the infamous doctrine—"separate but equal"—that would be adopted by the US Supreme Court in *Plessy v. Ferguson* (1896) and obstruct civil-rights activists for the next century. In his opinion, however, Shaw suggested that if the legislature crafted "a somewhat more specific rule," the practice of racial segregation could be restricted. Shaw alluded to the wording of the 1845 school law, which had been altered by segregationists to limit the effectiveness of suits for damages. In the absence of a more specific rule, one explicitly outlawing race-based segregation, Shaw found that the school law "has vested the power in the committee to regulate the system of distribution and classification." Again deferring to school committees, Shaw wrote, "The committee, apparently upon great deliberation, have come to the conclusion, that the good of both classes of schools will be best promoted, by maintaining the separate primary schools for colored and for white children, and we can perceive no ground to doubt, that this is the honest result of their experience and judgment." If the school committee deemed it appropriate, segregation could continue.[47]

Abolitionists had found no protection for the black minority from the state's highest court, but this hardly ended their crusade. As Frederick Douglass would later remember, the *Roberts* decision "did not place a quietus upon the anti-exclusive movement. It only animated its ardent friends to redoubled diligence, and a renewed determination to conquer."[48] Indeed, while the *Roberts* case was before the courts, black abolitionists had begun to formalize their movement. William Cooper Nell (fig. 4.6), William Wells Brown, William J. Watkins, Benjamin Roberts,

FIGURE 4.6   William Cooper Nell. Courtesy of the Massachusetts Historical Society. Abolitionist William Cooper Nell formed the pioneering Equal School Rights Committee to end the segregation of public schools in Boston.

John T. Hilton, and others organized a special association—the Equal School Rights Committee—to spearhead the effort. The group established a leadership structure and held repeated mass meetings to grow support, especially within the local black community. They published their views in newspapers and sent special delegations to antislavery conventions. In the aftermath of *Roberts*, the association also initiated a massive petition campaign directed at the state legislature and sent Benjamin Roberts throughout the state gathering signatures. All of this heightened activity cost money, and the association established an "Equal School Rights fund" and solicited pledges from "friends" of the cause. They also held fundraisers, some of which featured black children (fig. 4.7). In supporting one of these events, Garrison's *Liberator* explained that "funds are much needed at the present time, and every one can cast in his mite, and at the same time be more than compensated by a rich mental and musical feast." When the association publicly thanked the "donors for their generous aid," the list of names included elite white abolitionists and ordinary black

EQUAL SCHOOL RIGHTS.

An Elocutionary and Musical Entertainment in aid of the above glorious struggle will be given at Washingtonian Hall, Bromfield Street, on TUESDAY EVENING, Nov. 27th, *commencing at 7 1-2 o'clock.*

The exercises to consist of declamations, original and selected, and favorite colloquies, by volunteers from the Young Men's Literary Society, blended with a choice selection of Vocal and Instrumental Music, by Mrs. A. M. Nahar, Miss C. L. Howard, Mr. Wm G Alled, and others, who have generously tendered their valuable services. The whole, it is hoped, offering a sufficient inducement to secure a large audience of the friends of impartial freedom.

Tickets 12 1-2 cts. each, to be obtained at 21 Cornhill, of the Committee, and at the door.

ISAAC H. SNOWDON, ⎫
WM. C. NELL,   ⎬ *Com.*
WM. T. RAYMOND,   ⎭
Boston, Nov. 23, 1849.

FIGURE 4.7 *Equal School Rights* from *The Liberator*, November 23, 1849. Courtesy of The Library Company of Philadelphia. The Equal School Rights Committee publicized its activities, including its fundraising events, in William Lloyd Garrison's *Liberator*.

citizens. The work of this pioneering minority-rights association, though led by leading black abolitionists, had a popular base and remained to some extent interracial and class-diverse.[49]

The Equal School Rights Committee persevered in the face of obstacles and defeats. Its petition campaign in the early 1850s fell on deaf ears before the legislature, and opposition to their crusade from within the black community distracted the movement. Perhaps even more damaging, the Fugitive Slave Law of 1850 unleashed a reign of terror on the local black community, threatening to return many to slavery, including some active in the movement for equal school rights. Nonetheless, by 1853 the movement re-emerged when Boston school officials dismissed a mixed-race student named Edward H. Pindall from an all-white school where he had "passed" as white for "a day or two" before his black ancestry was discovered. Represented by black attorney Robert Morris, Pindall's father bought suit. Though no damages were awarded in court, Boston's Committee on Public Instruction issued a report that suggested that segregation was illegal. William Cooper Nell again sprang to action, calling on black parents to petition that their children be admitted to local schools regardless of race and to seek legal redress against school committeemen if they were denied. In the meantime, Nell set out for what would be one final petition campaign to the state legislature for "equal school rights."[50]

Victory finally came on April 28, 1855, when the Massachusetts legislature passed a law explicitly prohibiting school authorities from making distinctions between students "on account of race, color, or religious opinions." The law was a product of grass-roots minority-rights politics capitalizing on a favorable partisan political climate. With Nell at the helm, the Equal School Rights Committee saw that "some dozen petitions or more" were sent to the State House demanding that the legislature mandate desegregation in the public schools. They came from around the state and bore the names of more than fifteen hundred men and women, black and white, all of whom had by signing their name become meaningful participants in the growing crusade for minority rights. Just as important for the success of their efforts, the petitions arrived at a state legislature newly dominated by the Know-Nothing Party, which in Massachusetts was filled with antislavery sympathizers. The Know-Nothing's inherent anti-Catholic, anti-immigrant, and temperance sentiments had combined with rising antislavery sentiment brought by the rendition of fugitive slave Anthony Burns in Boston and the Kansas-Nebraska Act of 1854 to sweep their party into the legislature. Such political abolitionists as Henry Wilson, a former member of the Free Soil Party, found a temporary home with the Know-Nothings. Led by Charles W. Slack, antislavery Know-Nothings pushed through the desegregation law with surprisingly little opposition. When the public schools opened their doors in the fall of 1855, they would do so irrespective of race.[51]

These events brought the usual pattern of abolitionist celebrations and antiabolitionist ridicule. To the *New York Herald*, the Massachusetts legislature had put the "children of the African race on a footing of equality with the descendants of the original Puritans."

> Now the blood of the Winthrops, the Otisses, the Lymans, the Endicotts and the Eliots is in a fair way to be amalgamated with the Sambos, the Catos and the Pompeys…. The wooliest head and the thickest lips had an equal chance for education to this time with the whitest skin and the strongest Saxon peculiarities; but now the niggers are really just as good as white folks. The North is to be Africanized. Amalgamation has commenced. New England heads the column. God save the Commonwealth of Massachusetts.

By contrast, black New Yorkers hailed the bright star of Massachusetts and looked "forward to the day when the State of New York will follow her example." Abolitionists in Ohio made similar pronouncements and applauded "the persistent and faithful labors of the colored people themselves and a few of their especial friends."[52]

The efforts of the Equal School Rights Committee in Massachusetts inspired others to organize and take action against segregation. In Rhode Island, abolitionists led by businessman George T. Downing began a decade-long campaign to defeat segregated schools. Unsurprisingly, these activists encountered majoritarian rationales for maintaining segregation. In 1859, the *Providence Journal* declared that "the fact that so great a majority…are in favor of the schools as they now exist, outweighs, in our judgment, all the equal rights and all the finely turned periods about the claims of humanity." Drawing inspiration from Providence's Francis Wayland and his *Elements of Moral Philosophy*, local abolitionists emphasized that "the majority" had no "right to do anything which violates the principle of the entire social equality" of any members of society. Indeed, minorities—in this case, the black minority—had rights of which "majorities" could "not dispose." This vision of freedom, equality, and democracy would continue to undergird their ongoing crusade against school segregation.[53]

As one anonymous black activist suggested in the midst of the school fight in Nantucket, the struggle to protect the equal rights of the black minority was also about legitimating and affirming the potential of democratic government worldwide. "We are" duty-bound, he argued, "to maintain public liberty, and by the example of our own systems to convince the *world* that order, law, religion and morality, the right of conscience, the right of person and the right of property, may all be preserved and be cared for in the most perfect manner, by a government purely elective." Should there be any "errors" within American democracy—errors like the oppression of racial minorities—"we are *bound* to correct them, and if any practices exist contrary to the principles of justice and humanity within the reach of our laws, or our influence, we are inexcusable if we do not exert ourselves to restrain and abolish them." To survive and flourish in a world of doubters, democracy required untrammeled vigilance, continuous reform, and protections for minorities. The struggles over the ban on interracial marriage and segregated schools in Massachusetts provided abolitionists with foundations upon which to build elsewhere. They would also stand beside the popular battles of other moral minorities during the antebellum period that joined in challenging majoritarian omnipotence and attempting to secure a place for minority rights within American democracy.[54]

5

"Jim Crow Conveyances" and the Politics of Integrating the Public

WHEN WILLIAM WELLS BROWN set foot on British soil in 1849, the prejudice he had so long endured in his native land seemed to vanish. In the American South he had been "bought and sold as a slave," and in the "so-called Free States," he was treated as "one born to occupy an inferior position." But after nine days aboard an Atlantic steamer, he was, by his own account, "recognized as a man, and an equal." In Britain, he declared, "the very dogs in the streets appeared conscious of my manhood." Five years later, however, Brown's manhood was again in question when he returned to the United States. After landing in Philadelphia he hailed an omnibus to take him to another part of the city. The conductor admitted his two white companions who had traveled with him from Europe but told Brown, "We don't allow niggers to ride in here." Though Brown and his comrades had taken "the same car . . . from London to Liverpool . . . and had crossed the Atlantic in the same steamer," in America they could not ride together. How was it, Brown wondered, that he enjoyed equal rights in "monarchical Europe" yet in his native democracy was treated worse than foreigners? The answer was clear: slavery and "Negrophobia" had rendered American democracy "hypocritical." Brown might have returned to Europe, but he instead remained to rejoin abolitionists in their crusade to purify American democracy.[1]

An essential part of that crusade entailed fighting for the equal rights of America's black minority in the North. In addition to taking aim at bans on interracial marriage and segregated schools, black and white activists challenged the practice of racial discrimination in public transportation. Like the conductor who refused to admit Brown to the omnibus, owners and operators of steamboats, railroads, streetcars, and other conveyances throughout the North regularly excluded black passengers or consigned them to second-rate accommodations. To abolitionists, these practices reflected the same prejudice that permitted southern slavery to exist. They also stymied black northerners' travel, hampering their freedom of movement and obstructing the creation of an interracial, egalitarian, and to them, truly democratic public. Most white northerners were little alarmed by these practices. They insisted that black men and women, if allowed to travel at all, should be kept apart from white passengers. At stake for them was not only the threat of amalgamation but also a vision of America's increasingly mobile society that had little place for the presence of black men and women on equal terms.

Like segregated schools and bans on interracial marriage, public transportation emerged as a key issue that sparked debates over the rights of black northerners and the power of majorities to create racial hierarchies. Where these other issues had forced participants to wrestle with the power of such explicitly governmental institutions as state legislatures, school boards, and town meetings, public transit raised questions about the power of businesses that served the public. Were steamboat companies and railroad corporations fundamentally private entities that could exclude or segregate black riders if their owners saw fit? Or, did these businesses have special responsibilities to the traveling public? And what "public"? Here the common law had something to say about this, but so too did public opinion and above all majority rule. Should majorities govern the social environment of public travel as they governed electoral politics and policymaking? In this case, should transportation companies bow to the assumed moral proclivities of the white traveling majority by excluding or segregating black travelers? Alternatively, should all persons travel together on equal terms, thereby rendering the majority's preferences irrelevant? As supporters and opponents of "Jim Crow conveyances" gave conflicting answers to these pressing questions, they extended America's ongoing battles over majority rule and minority rights to public travel.[2]

Amid this quest for integration, abolitionists in Massachusetts, New York, Michigan, and elsewhere expanded the range of tactics of minority-rights advocacy. Campaigns for public opinion and petition drives aiming at converting the political powers were still vital tools, but visible scenes of resistance in the spaces of travel became critical, as did civil litigation against transportation companies. Though black activists and their white allies sometimes raised constitutional objections when taking segregation to court, they and their attorneys brandished a different legal weapon—the common law of common carriers—to demand that judges and juries find against segregation. While implementing these methods, black leaders also contributed to the maturation of rights politics in the 1850s by founding institutions explicitly dedicated to local rights advocacy. The most important of these—New York City's Legal Rights Association—built upon the example of William Cooper Nell's Equal School Rights Committee. In many ways, it also reflected the associations formed by opponents of liquor prohibition and Sunday legislation during the same decade. Collectively, these varied groups would bestow this essential institution of modern democratic politics—the rights association—to subsequent groups seeking to defend their rights and interests. Part of this institution's origins lay in the earliest fights against racially segregated public transit.

THE GREAT TRANSPORTATION revolution of the early nineteenth century was from its beginning racially structured. Technological developments and the rage for internal improvements proliferated roads, turnpikes, steamboats, canals, railroads, and streetcars that brought the American nation closer together. As increasing numbers of Americans, especially members of the burgeoning white middle class, took part in public travel in all its forms, they increasingly associated mobility with freedom. Americans' victory over the tyranny of distance, however, brought demands for boundaries. New modes of transit created such intimate public spaces as steamboat cabins and railroad cars in which the rising tide of travelers encountered one another, conversed, consumed meals, slept, and otherwise passed the time on journeys long and short. The new spaces produced anxieties, particularly as travelers were brought face to face with strangers. To accommodate their patrons, companies instituted several forms of segregation that reinforced dominant cultural conventions. Embracing the rise of "separate spheres," for example, they provided separate cabins and "ladies" cars for unaccompanied women and women traveling with male companions. To some extent, companies also embraced class barriers by offering differently priced tickets for varying levels of accommodation. They also segregated by race.[3]

Like Protestant churches that relegated blacks to the notorious "negro pew" and schools that separated black and white children, public transit followed a pattern of racial exclusion and segregation that reflected a culture teeming with prejudice and moral fears of racial mixture. Aboard the stagecoaches that traversed rutty roads and muddy highways, drivers either rejected black riders or required them to sit "on the outside," often with luggage. On oceangoing ships, canal packets, and steamboats, captains and ticket agents either refused black travelers or excluded them from enclosed cabins. Unless sympathetic black crewmembers offered them shelter, blacks typically remained on ship decks exposed to rain, wind, extreme temperatures, and rough seas. At mealtime, they found themselves barred from the communal tables inside and told to procure meals directly from the "cook in the kitchen" and only after white passengers had eaten.[4]

Railroads with tiered accommodations routinely prohibited black riders from occupying the first-class or ladies' cars, even if they paid the fare that gave white passengers access. Conductors relegated blacks to cramped and unclean second-class cars known variously as the "dirt," "dog," or "Jim Crow" cars after the minstrel show's popular caricature of black Americans. A white traveler describing one of these "rough, close, dismal dirty car[s]" thought it resembled "more a cage for wild beasts, than any thing else." The car "had never been painted or cleaned," and the ceiling was "so low that no person of ordinary height could stand erect." Many of these compartments were windowless, making summer travel often unbearable; others were so porous that they became virtual "cold prison[s]" in winter months. At least that was how W. P. Johnson described the "worn out and open" car that he and two female companions rode in from Camden to Trenton, New Jersey, in 1841. They paid "the highest price charged," but the conductor barred them from the "tight and heated car" reserved only for whites.[5]

The horse-drawn omnibuses and streetcars that came to crisscross northern cities also made life difficult for blacks. If carried at all, blacks regularly stood on outside platforms or boarded only cars bearing signs that read "Colored People Allowed in This Car," which ran far less frequently than whites-only cars. As a result, the omnibuses that helped facilitate the geographical expansion of cities often restricted black residents' ability to take advantage of the same housing and employment opportunities opened for whites. A black resident of Brooklyn who made a living "scrubbing stores and houses" for wealthy white Manhattanites, for example, "dared not [ride in the cars], as the white folks made such a fuss about colored folks riding in them." She chose to make the long, often painful walk instead. Some white urbanites, many of whom probably rode in their own coaches and not aboard the public cars, lamented these circumstances. Denying blacks "the right of cheap transit," noted one employer, prevented whites from sending their black domestics "to a distance on any business," thereby limiting their "usefulness" and perhaps hampering their employability.[6]

Black northerners did not encounter a uniform system of discrimination. Practices changed over time and varied by region, state, and city, particular companies, the season, and likely even the moods of conductors, captains, and ticket agents. In one instance in 1838, abolitionist Charles B. Ray celebrated his seventeen-hour journey from New York to Boston because neither the steamer he took to Providence nor the train he rode to Boston denied him any of the rights afforded white travelers. Yet three months later abolitionist David Ruggles met entirely different circumstances on his way to Boston. Though taking the same steamer as Ray, he was confined to the deck. When boarding a rail car in Stonington, Connecticut, to complete the journey, a conductor, who accused him of being "a d—d abolitionist," forced him into the "jim crow car." Having paid "full fare" and been guaranteed equal privileges, Ruggles protested this "Highway Robbery" and cautioned abolitionists against taking "the Stonington Rail Road."[7]

While modern travel in its early days remained unpredictable for most travelers, white riders, to a greater extent, knew what to expect and could plan accordingly. The omnipresent threat of discrimination denied black travelers that simple luxury. It also kept many from straying too far from home. In newspapers and by word of mouth, black travelers exposed the varied conditions of travel and recommended friendly and unfriendly lines, but these efforts only brought some certainty. On an outward journey blacks might travel without incident; on their return they might be denied passage or forced to endure unpleasant conditions. At still other moments, they might seat themselves in a first-class car only to be told that "no nigger should be in the car" and instructed to leave before a company employee dragged them out (fig. 5.1). Irregularities and the possibility of violence only added to everyday expressions of hostility from whites who passed "sneers and jests" or exhibited "a preference not to sit on the same seat" as a black rider. Overall, if blacks wished to partake in the transportation revolution's fruits, they either had to endure inconsistencies and insults or seek out alternative, often slower and more costly modes of transit.[8]

The spaces of travel provided glaring everyday places where categories of racial identity and hierarchy were visible. As white men, women, and

NEGRO EXPULSION FROM RAILWAY CAR, PHILADELPHIA.

FIGURE 5.1 *Negro Expulsion from Railway Car.* Courtesy of the Library of Congress. Black men and women were routinely subjected to harassment and discrimination aboard northern public conveyances. Immigrant and working-class white employees of the rail car and streetcar companies enforced segregation.

children of various class and ethnic backgrounds stepped into cars reserved only for whites or witnessed the removal of black travelers, they learned and affirmed the privileges of their own superior racial status. Meanwhile, excluded blacks or those forced into second-class accommodations discovered their own humiliating, subordinate status; others with lighter skin found a place where they might pass for white. Gendered identities were also in play. When denying black women access to ladies' cars, for example, conductors questioned their status as respectable females. They challenged black men's "manhood," not only when barring them from cars and cabins, but also by preventing them as husbands and fathers from protecting their wives and children from company agents' verbal and physical abuse. Conversely, resisting discrimination, as black women and men would increasingly come to do, could affirm their respectable femininity, manhood, and commitments to racial equality.[9]

Behind this inchoate system was not only a broader culture seemingly obsessed with racial identity, but also the power of transportation companies and their "mercenary captains and petty officers" to determine race and to control the social environment of modern travel. Especially for company employees, who were mostly white men and, especially in eastern cities, often of immigrant background, enforcing segregation allowed these masters of small worlds to assert both masculine and white identities. As one opponent of Jim Crow cars protested, these businesses and their henchmen prevented passengers from determining their own racial identity. "If every man does not judge of his own color... to suit them," the company intervenes "by sorting them out, seizing all whose complexions are not of the right shade and dragging them forth by main strength, and thrusting them like goats into their appropriate pens." What right, some critics asked, did these businesses have to assess and categorize travelers by skin color?[10]

To segregation's many defenders, the companies had not just the right but an actual obligation. Racial exclusion, separation, and categorization meshed well with dominant visions of progress and freedom that presupposed white supremacy. Would not any other arrangement be a "step toward practical amalgamation"? Segregationists' moral and sexualized fears of racial mixture were set off by the crowded conditions of travel that might leave, as one columnist shockingly observed, "a negro wench tightly sandwiched between two ladies." Respectable white passengers, especially the "ladies," often claimed to find close contact with biologically and morally degraded black passengers repulsive. As the Philadelphia *Pennsylvanian* observed:

> To sleep, to eat and to ride in public conveyances with negroes are three things not very pleasant to do, nor would any decent person willingly be placed in such intimate association with them. The first two, fortunately for our comfort, may be easily avoided, but the last is sometimes forced upon us by conductors on the city railway cars.

In these situations, white travelers protested the great "insult," cried "AMALGAMATION," and claimed that black bodies contaminated cars and cabins with the "disagreeable smell" that came from "nigger blood." The sooner transport companies respected the preference of "the white public" for separation, the *New York Globe* noted, the better it would be for their profits.[11]

Black and white abolitionists, however, responded by asserting their own preference for equality in transportation as early as the late 1820s. Discrimination in travel was yet another "anti-republican and anti-Christian" practice that exposed American democracy's hypocrisy and undercut the nation's identity as a land "where all men are free and equal." As they had in debates over the Massachusetts ban on interracial marriage and segregated schools, such leading abolitionists as Maria Weston Chapman maintained that the bigoted operation of public conveyances jeopardized northern states' identities as "free states." Some slaves escaping to the North echoed these indictments. As Harriet Jacobs remembered, exclusion from a first-class rail car provided "the first chill to [her] enthusiasm about the Free States." Restrictions on black mobility in the North seemed like a return to slaveowners' control of slaves' locomotion that left them confined to particular locales and required to carry a pass, which any white person could demand to see, when traveling. The ability to travel aboard public conveyances unencumbered by prejudice became something of the antithesis of slavery and a symbol of freedom and progress (fig. 5.2). As Frederick Douglass affirmed, "the lash of proscription" in public travel "has a sting for the soul hardly less severe than that which bites the flesh and draws the blood from the back of the plantation slave." True freedom required equal access to the world of movement.[12]

Abolitionists also dismissed segregationists' fears of amalgamation and their olfactory sensitivities, insisting that their real problem was encountering blacks as equals. Slaveholders, George Bradburn noted, had traveled with their slaves in New England without objection. "But when a free citizen of Massachusetts, having a colored skin, dares to step into one of these vehicles...why, our nobility turn up their noses, and talk of odor!" It was not that black men and women were innately immoral or offensive to whites; rather, without slavery, white northerners needed Jim Crow accommodations to mark their superior status. If they genuinely worried about the presence of unsavory passengers, integrationists protested, white riders would not regularly sit near unclean whites, those in "a state of beastly intoxication," or "German or Irish women, with a quarter of mutton or a load of codfish."[13]

Amid these indictments, integrationists repeatedly revealed their frustration that blacks' performance of middle-class respectability and their status as native-born citizens did not gain them access to the spaces that

FIGURE 5.2 *Get Off the Tracks* (1844). Courtesy of the Library of Congress. Radical abolitionists linked their fights against slavery and prejudice with the progressive spirit of the age that rail travel symbolized. To them, racial discrimination in travel countered the progress promised by modern travel.

nearly all whites, including immigrants, drunks, and the poor, could enter. As Henry Scott, a successful black businessman, complained:

> Here you advertise your public coaches, your railroads and cars. I will take my trunk and go to the depot, well dressed as I always am. I shall undertake to go in your cars...and although my pockets are well lined with money, and my person civil, you will say, "you cannot go in our cars with others who pay the same price." The car master will then say, "we will show you where you can ride—come ride here." I answer, I do not as a gentleman wish to ride in a *dirt car*. I wish to use my privileges as other men do. I wish to ride with decent and respectable gentlemen. "Ah!" says he, "you are a colored man."

To Scott, his racial identity wrongly negated the "privileges" that should accompany his gentlemanly status. As he and other critics saw it, education, industry, "refinement," and wealth should afford any traveler "the courtesies and facilities of other persons." Class should trump race aboard the conveyances and throughout American society.[14]

By the early 1840s, black activists and their many white abolitionist collaborators had had enough. Prominent abolitionist David Ruggles was among the first to spearhead an integrationist crusade. The movement began in Massachusetts as Ruggles and others took aim at the state's three segregated rail lines. In July 1841, Ruggles paid for the best accommodations aboard the New Bedford and Taunton Branch railroad, only to be ordered out of the first-class car. He refused, proclaimed his right to ride, and soon found himself surrounded by railroad employees who dragged him out. Similar encounters followed, several involving such leading black abolitionists as Frederick Douglass, William Cooper Nell, and Mary Newhall Green, the secretary of the Lynn Anti-Slavery Society. Still other incidents involved white abolitionists who questioned segregation or attempted to join their black friends in Jim Crow cars. These often calculated acts of disobedience brought violent reprisals from railroad employees, bodily injuries for abolitionists, and property damage for the railroads. "In dragging me out," Frederick Douglass proudly remembered, "it must have cost the company twenty-five or thirty dollars, for I tore up seats and all."[15]

Forging tactics as they went along, these integrationists printed resistance narratives, published letters to the railroads' stockholders and directors, held meetings, organized boycotts, and petitioned the state legislature, asking that it intervene to integrate travel. They used the existing abolitionist infrastructure—local associations and the abolitionist press, especially William Lloyd Garrison's *Liberator*—to mobilize the growing coalition and to attract national attention. Indeed, active engagement in the public sphere, as with the era's other movements for minority rights, was a component of their political engagement and vision of democracy. So too was court action driven by test cases. David Ruggles and Daniel Mann, a white dentist who was "violently dragged" from the Eastern Railroad after protesting the removal of a black man, initiated the two most important early suits. With the help of white attorneys, they put segregation on trial by suing the employees who had ejected them for assault and battery, seeking damages. More importantly, they wanted railroads "to explain, under oath, the object of their" policy separating black and white passengers and wanted local justices to rule on its legitimacy. Though judges in both cases discharged the employees, the suits successfully ferreted out railroads' rationale for segregation while starting a public conversation about the companies' legal duties and power.[16]

Railroads and other modes of public transportation had a special common-law status as "common carriers." Racial egalitarians would turn to this status time and time again as they struggled against segregation during the nineteenth century. Along with other businesses providing public accommodations, such as hotels, restaurants, and theaters, common carriers were required to accept most all passengers, permitted to make regulations governing the conditions of travel and the conduct of travelers, and authorized to eject any passengers who violated these regulations. Among other requirements, regulations had to be "reasonable" and made public. For railroads and their employees, the posted regulation empowering conductors to seat passengers where they saw fit allowed them to segregate passengers by race. For abolitionists, this use of a vague regulation was not only unreasonable but despotic, arbitrary, and even unconstitutional.[17]

In courtrooms and the public debates that ensued from these high-profile ejections, defenders offered two additional rationales for segregation's reasonableness. First, they maintained that railroads were "private" and could enact whatever regulations they deemed necessary for their business interests. In Ruggles's case, Judge Henry Crapo of the New Bedford Police Court argued that rail cars were "private property" and that companies could establish regulations that were "not repugnant to any existing law of the Commonwealth." Second, segregationists turned to custom, public opinion, and majority rule. In Mann's case, the Eastern Railroad's attorney maintained that corporations could make regulations that "their own interests and the public good" required. "The established usage and the public sentiment of the community" authorized segregation. Persuaded, Judge Simmons of the Boston Police Court released the conductor "on the ground that public opinion required the separate negro car." Outside the courtroom, white residents of Salem who organized to defend segregation agreed. Mixing black and white passengers would diminish "the comfort and convenience of a very large majority of passengers." The minority of blacks who sought first-class accommodations and the minority of whites who were comfortable riding with blacks should bow to the majority's preferences. Majority rule should govern the nation's most intimate public spaces just as it governed its political institutions.[18]

Integrationists offered their own rationales that would exert influence long after struggles over Jim Crow moved beyond Massachusetts. First, they argued that railroad corporations were public entities with "no right to make arbitrary distinctions between individuals" or to deny equal rights to anyone. Their public nature made corporations accountable to the state constitutional provision declaring "every citizen (black or white)...free and equal." Since the Massachusetts Constitution "recognize[d] no distinction among its citizens on account of color," neither could the state's railroad corporations. Reaching even wider, abolitionists insisted that the removal of black and especially white passengers revealed the "TYRANNY OF CORPORATIONS" and their ability to plunder "the sacred rights of the people." Echoing recent Democratic assaults on the Second Bank of the United States, abolitionists called upon the people to subdue these "overbearing and unprincipled monopol[ies] of wealth and power and wrong." Unless railroads respected travelers' equal rights, abolitionists insisted, they would add to those seeking to "destroy all corporate rights" by making "their charters worthless."[19]

Second, abolitionists built upon the position they advanced in debates over the ban on interracial marriage and segregated schools: the rule of majorities should not be absolute and the rights of minorities should not be "graduated by the state of public opinion." To the Massachusetts Anti-Slavery Society, deference to "popular caprice" overlooked "the great object of government, which is to protect the weak against the strong, and to shield the rights of the minority from the encroachments of the majority." This same spirit, John Collins protested, had "banished" the Puritans "to the American Wilderness," justified the Puritan abuse of the Quakers, and undergirded "every murderous act of the Spanish Inquisition." Whether openly perpetrating religious or racial tyrannies or acting behind a screen of state law, the schoolhouse, or the rail car, public opinion's oppression of unpopular minorities needed to end.[20]

Abolitionist leaders Wendell Phillips, Charles Lenox Remond, and Ellis Gray Loring put the problem of minority rights on prominent display in 1842 when a special state legislative committee, formed in response to integrationists' petitions, held public hearings and invited their testimony. Before a "large audience" of legislators "and ladies and gentlemen generally," Phillips urged legislative intervention, while Remond insisted that neither "complexion" nor the whims of majorities should be "made the criterion of rights." It was Loring, however, who provided the capstone statement of abolitionists' quarrel with majority rule. A prominent attorney and a committed Garrisonian abolitionist, Loring urged the legislature to determine whether railroad corporations' race regulations were "consistent with the public good." At present, various justices of the peace answered this question by turning to the democratic dictum that "the majority ought to rule." These justices, Loring reported, had found "riding with colored men disagreeable to the majority" and promptly concluded that the public good required segregation. To Loring, however, the public good and the will of the majority were not synonymous, especially when the equal rights of minorities were at stake. "Are all our rights," he pointedly asked, "at the mercy of a majority?" "Our Constitution and our laws," he declared, "are framed mainly to protect the rights of the *minority*, and to say to the majority, 'Thus far shalt thou go, and no farther.'" As he and other integrationists saw it, the legislature had to intervene to ensure that the corporations it chartered acted in accordance not with the wishes of the majority but with the state constitution that rightfully protected the rights of minorities.[21]

To drive the point home, Loring, like other moral minorities of the age, tied abolitionists' struggle against majority rule to the traditional fear that democracies would threaten property rights. "You allow," he reminded his audience, "no uncertainty to overhang questions relating to your property. You would not allow your property to be confiscated, because it was the taste of the majority to take it from you; if not, why are your other rights to be left at the mercy of every man's taste? Surely there are rights as valuable as money!" Loring's strategic argument aimed both at political conservatives continuing to harbor reservations about democratic empowerment and at the rising white middle class who cherished propertied independence in an age of increasing economic uncertainty. The same spirit that would authorize majorities to govern the spaces of travel with absolute impunity, he implied, could empower indebted and propertyless majorities to strike at the rights of the propertied classes. As with contemporaries making this point on behalf of moral minorities, Loring's reference to "confiscated" property likely conjured fears of the violent rumblings of Rhode Island's Dorrites and New York's Anti-Renters and perhaps also the controversial federal bankruptcy legislation recently enacted by Congress. Anyone who believed in the sanctity of property rights and had any concerns about these developments, Loring suggested, should also believe in the right of black men and women to travel aboard public conveyances without interference from popular majorities, whether real or imagined. Once again, conservative arguments about property rights could aid ante-bellum America's moral minorities.[22]

In suggesting that there were "rights as valuable as money," Loring also contributed to a transformation in the cultural conceptions of tyranni-cal majorities and vulnerable minorities as well as the broadening signifi-cance of minority rights. Loring and some integrationists might have held actual concerns about poor majorities redistributing wealth. But their real issue was the power of the white segregationist majority to create racial hierarchies. Such action, activists protested, publicly demeaned black men and women, striking at their respectability and self-worth by impairing their equal rights to travel. Despite Loring's attempt to downplay their monetary value, these rights, as integrationists well knew, carried signifi-cant socioeconomic value. In the age of market capitalism, restrictions on black movement were particularly problematic because travel had become an essential attribute of business, work, religion, reform, and politi-cal life. Black preachers needed to minister to geographically dispersed congregants; newspaper editors needed to discern and spread the news; businessmen needed to engage in the often distant world of commerce; workers needed to travel from their homes to increasingly distant places of employment. Restricting the actual mobility of black men and women could impair their social standing, hamper their economic survival, and curtail their social mobility, especially their coveted rise into the ranks of the middle class.

For blacks participating in abolitionism, a movement dependent upon people and information moving across space, outright exclusion from public travel obstructed their participation and so too did segre-gation. Reformers regularly traveled in groups and filled their journeys with camaraderie and strategizing. Forced racial separation when travel-ing could hinder the development of interracial alliances. Realizing this, Gerrit Smith, a leading white political abolitionist committed to cultivat-ing friendships across the color line, avoided public conveyances when-ever possible. This was the only way, he explained to Frederick Douglass, to live the theory of "racial equality." Not all abolitionists, however, had Smith's means to access alternate routes of travel. With local courts enlist-ing majority rule to reject integration, their hope was that the legislature would protect the rights of the black minority.[23]

Many state legislators heeded abolitionists' pleas for intervention. A committee headed by Libertyite Seth Sprague Jr. crafted a law barring

railroad corporations from making "any distinction" or giving "a preference in accommodation to any one or more persons over others, on account
of descent, sect, or color." The law mandated the fine and imprisonment
for employees who assaulted any person "for the purpose of depriving
him of his right or privilege, in any car or other rail-road accommodation," and made such employees liable for civil damages. The committee
asserted that railroads had violated the state constitution and travelers'
rights, and it justified intervention because of corporations' distinctly public nature. They were "established by State authority, supported in some
cases by State loans, protected always and specially by legislation." The
committee did this for the "very purpose of protecting minorities from
the tastes of the majorities." While abolitionists applauded, their opponents, including some white southerners, balked. The proposed measure,
Macon, Georgia's *Weekly Telegraph* maintained, would promote an "amalgamation" that would "mingle the two bloods and restore the original cop-
per color of this continent." Next the legislature would compel "tavern
keepers to put the two races in the same bed." The death of America's
white republic would follow.[24]

The law nearly passed in the 1842 and 1843 legislative sessions, but a
last-minute amendment introduced in 1843, which would have applied
the law to all corporations, killed the measure. Abolitionists called upon
voters to teach those who sank the bill "that there is too much of the
spirit of liberty in the popular heart" by removing them from office. In
the meantime, Charles Francis Adams and other state legislators with
antislavery leanings threatened railroads that they must abandon Jim
Crow cars lest "their charters" be stripped. These threats, instigated by
the minority-rights politics that abolitionists began in rail cars and took
to the public, the courts, and the legislature, eradicated rail car segregation in Massachusetts.[25]

THE SAME YEAR that David Ruggles resisted segregation in Massachusetts,
Thomas Downing did the same in New York City. A black abolitionist and
"celebrated oyster vender," Downing scarcely had taken a seat aboard the
Harlem Railroad when an agent told him to leave. Downing refused, and
"the agent and driver immediately seized hold of him, dragged him out,
and assisted by two other men, gave him a severe beating, and inflicted
a wound in his neck."[26] Downing sued the agent and driver for assault
and battery. When the all-white jury ruled against him, Charles B. Ray's
Colored American observed, "There appears to us to be...but little hope

in the case of our people, in the courts of justice in this city…in any case which comes in contact with a corrupt public sentiment." "We advise our people," Ray concluded, "to keep out of legal trials."[27]

Thirteen years later, two women on their way to church would spark a chain of events that would bring leading black New Yorkers to reject that advice and to organize a movement to desegregate public transit in America's largest city. It began on a Sunday in July 1854, when schoolteacher Elizabeth Jennings and her friend Sarah E. Adams boarded the Third Avenue horse-drawn trolley car on their way to the First Colored Congregational Church. Upon entering the car, the Irish-born conductor ordered them out, telling them to wait for the next car that had "[their] people in it." Already late, Jennings and Adams refused to alight. As Jennings and the conductor argued, the driver grew impatient, leading the conductor to allow the two women aboard. He warned them, however, that he would remove them if any passengers objected. Refusing to bow to his insults, Jennings announced that she was, unlike him, "a respectable person, born and raised in New York" who never before had been treated so crudely. The enraged conductor grabbed both women and pulled them out of the car. Jennings fearlessly climbed back aboard. Unable to keep the car segregated himself, the conductor ordered the driver to enlist the aid of the state. A police officer entered the car and pushed Jennings out, taunting her "to get redress" if she could.[28]

Beyond her brazen act of resistance, Jennings was no ordinary New Yorker. She hailed from a middle-class black family with strong abolitionist commitments and a history of combating racial prejudice. Her father, Thomas Jennings, was a successful businessman, a longtime abolitionist, and a leader in the early black convention movement. Her brother, a Boston dentist named Thomas Jennings Jr., was among the many passengers forcibly removed from segregated rail cars in Massachusetts the previous decade.[29] Seeing another of his children victimized by prejudice, Jennings determined to strike back. He joined local blacks who met to condemn the "intolerant" streetcar company and to explore the possibility of bringing "the whole affair before the legal authorities." Seeking public support, they published their proceedings and Elizabeth's resistance narrative in the *New York Tribune* as well as *Frederick Douglass' Paper*. The local *National Anti-Slavery Standard* applauded the efforts, as did distant black Californians who declared that they too would "resist" such outrages "until we secure our rights."[30] With an eye on bringing suit against the streetcar company, Thomas Jennings crafted an appeal to black New Yorkers, asking them for pecuniary aid. More than the injuries Elizabeth sustained, at stake in this lawsuit would be "the rights of our people."[31]

Though the burgeoning New York movement involved far fewer white abolitionists than the earlier Massachusetts effort, black New Yorkers still depended on the help of white attorneys willing to represent them in court. Jennings sought out one-time Whig congressman and aboli- tionist attorney Erastus Culver, who passed the case to his young asso- ciate Chester A. Arthur, the future Republican president of the United States. In February 1855, before the Brooklyn Circuit of the New York State Supreme Court, Arthur sought $500 in damages and pointed Judge William Rockwell to the common law of common carriers. Taking the bait, Rockwell instructed the jury that the Third Avenue Company was "liable for the acts of their agents" and bound as common carriers "to carry all respectable persons." "Colored persons," he announced, "had the same rights as others" and "could neither be excluded by any rules of the Company, nor by force or violence." The jury ruled in Jennings's favor and awarded her $225. To many black New Yorkers and their supporters, especially Horace Greeley's *New York Tribune*, this "Wholesome Verdict" was a major triumph. Milwaukee's *Weekly Wisconsin* agreed. It was time "the absurd and foolish prejudice against colored persons was rebuked, and their rights defended." This "proper decision" was an excellent start.[32]

This victory provided the basis for further grass-roots mobilization and institution-building in New York. The verdict did not mean every carrier would voluntarily invite black passengers to travel on the same terms as whites, nor did it mean that state or local officials would ensure integra- tion. Ejections continued. In response, Thomas Jennings, joined by two other black leaders, James W. C. Pennington and James McCune Smith (fig. 5.3), announced "the formation of a 'Legal Rights League'" to ensure the integration of local public transit. Frederick Douglass spurred them on from Rochester, and McCune Smith informed his influential friend Gerrit Smith. "We colored men are organizing a society," he wrote, "to raise a fund to test our legal rights in traveling &c. &c. in the Courts of Law. Oh that I could infuse an '*Esprit de Corps*' in my black brethren!"[33]

McCune Smith's parting lament spoke to his long-standing desire for a wider group of black northerners to join the cause of their own advance- ment, and it also underscores the importance he and others saw in their new association—the Legal Rights Association (LRA). In 1841 Smith himself had articulated the difficulties blacks were destined to face as a racial minority in a political system governed by majority rule, but he had

FIGURE 5.3   James McCune Smith. Courtesy of The Library Company of Philadelphia. Longtime abolitionist champion Dr. James McCune Smith provided much of the intellectual backing for black New Yorkers' pioneering Legal Rights Association.

then left merely implicit the need for black northerners to unite if their "struggle for liberty" was to succeed.[34] More than a decade later and just months before Elizabeth Jennings's incident, Smith suddenly became more explicit. "The great hindrance to the advancement of the free colored people," he announced in *Frederick Douglass' Paper*, "is the want of unity in action." Black northerners needed either to treat a "wrong to one" as a "wrong to all" or to find "some general form of oppression continuous in character" that they could all "combine and continuously struggle until we are free and equal." To Smith, the latter was clearly the "PUBLIC OPIN-ION" that treated black men and women as lesser human beings. A student of American democracy, he recognized that "public opinion is the King of today and rules our land." With "combined *will*" blacks needed to "attack public opinion in detail; and each specific victory will strengthen our hands and perfect our organization for the next." A year later, Smith had found in streetcar segregation a form of oppression that blacks could unite against and found in the *Jennings* decision a victory upon which they could build. The moment was ripe to improve their "organization," and the LRA was his answer. It would bind black New Yorkers to defeat streetcar segregation and constitute an important front in the larger battle of the black minority to secure freedom and equal standing in the court of public opinion.[35]

Smith had experienced discrimination while traveling, as had James W. C. Pennington, the other cofounder of the LRA (fig. 5.4). Born a slave in Maryland, Pennington by the mid-1850s was a recognized black leader. After escaping slavery, he relocated to New York and soon joined Thomas Jennings at the black conventions of the early 1830s. He became a minister and ascended the abolitionist ranks, twice traveling to Europe to represent American abolitionists. On his second journey, Pennington published his own slave narrative and received an honorary doctorate of divinity from the University of Heidelberg. Like other black Americans

FIGURE 5.4   James W. C. Pennington. Courtesy of The Library Company of Philadelphia. Abolitionist leader Rev. James W. C. Pennington orchestrated the Legal Rights Association's early campaign against streetcar segregation in New York City.

who traveled abroad, he too had a declining tolerance for discrimination upon his return from a culture seemingly devoid of racism. Throughout the early 1850s he protested segregation aboard ferries and streetcars and scoffed at the continuing rationale for excluding blacks—that "the majority of the public would object to" their presence. By 1855, he was ready to defeat this tyrannical majority.[36]

The creation of the LRA was a pivotal event in the burgeoning minority-rights politics of the mid-nineteenth century, which built on abolitionists' efforts to uplift free blacks, shelter fugitive slaves, and combat interracial marriage bans, black laws, and suffrage restrictions. No doubt the Equal School Rights Committee formed by William Cooper Nell to defeat segregated schools in Boston provided a model. Their choice of title—"rights association"—may also have been influenced by the contemporary proliferation of southern rights associations, liquor dealer associations, and women's rights associations.[37] But the LRA had more direct roots in the work of Hezekiah Grice, a black Baltimorean who had originated the idea for the black convention movement. In 1831, he spurred other black leaders to form a "Legal Rights Association," which solicited written opinions on the "rights and citizenship of the free black" from prominent white statesmen and attorneys William Wirt, John Sargent, and Horace Binney. All three men declined to weigh in on such a controversial topic, but Grice's efforts influenced Jennings, Smith, and Pennington. At least according to the *Anglo-African*, Grice deserved credit for inaugurating "two of the leading ideas on which our people have since acted"—the convention movement and "the struggle for legal rights." By 1855, the LRA had taken up the latter cause, implementing a new strategy of rights advocacy that differed from the black convention movement's focus on annual meetings and petitioning. The LRA's reliance upon local mobilization, organized civil disobedience, and strategic legal challenges would serve as a vital model for future efforts to secure minority rights.[38]

The LRA's leaders sought to persuade local officials that the *Jennings* decision bound all the city's public carriers and to convince their black brethren to assert their right to ride. Through petitions and public letters, Pennington urged New York's mayor, Fernando Wood, to "restrain" streetcar companies from removing black passengers and to instruct the police not to aid conductors in removing blacks. Pennington used the abolitionist press and his pulpit to rally local blacks to the cause, urging them to "show a bold front in this and other kindred matters of equal importance." The LRA's leaders also initiated a disobedience campaign. They encouraged black men and women to enter the cars, resist ejection, and seek legal redress, and they sought to jump-start this effort by capitalizing on the "Anniversary Week" in May 1855 that made New York City the epicenter of the broad struggle against slavery. Between the numerous meetings, abolitionist visitors would ride the streetcars, and the LRA's leaders determined to put their local battle on a national stage. To structure the effort, Pennington published instructions in *Frederick Douglass' Paper* for black men and women to board New York's ferries and streetcars with confidence. "If any driver or conductor molests you," Pennington explained, "have him arrested, or call upon Dr. Smith, 55 West Broadway, Mr. T. L. Jenning[s], 167 Church-st., or myself, 29 Sixth-av., and we will enter your complaint at the Mayor's office." The LRA's leaders were ready for battle.[39]

One of the first encounters involved Sidney McFarlan, who boarded the Sixth Avenue Railroad's "white persons" train, as he put it, to "test the question whether persons of his shade could ride on the white folks' car, or not." After being ejected, McFarlan had the conductor and driver arrested. In front of a full courtroom, a police court judge dismissed his case and repudiated the LRA's tactics, claiming that McFarland improperly had "provoked the assault." Nonetheless, "a number of others" continued to enter the cars, and on May 24, 1855, Pennington himself joined the fray. After he refused to leave a Sixth Avenue whites-only car, a "ferocious" driver "forcibly laid hold of him and ejected him." After finding no relief in police court, Pennington announced his intent, as newspapers as far away as Indiana reported, "to test the validity of this exclusion" before the Superior Court of New York. His case, which took over eighteen months to come to trial, became the LRA's most widely discussed legal challenge.[40]

Pennington's ordeal brought some to examine even more fundamental questions of democracy, namely the power of majorities. Segregationists continued to proclaim that transit companies should follow the majority's wishes and that the black minority should not force themselves "in where a large majority do not wish." This gave Frederick Douglass pause. Pennington's incident prompted him to muse publicly about French visitor Gustave de Beaumont's observations about racism and democracy. To Douglass, "the spirit which dragged Dr. Pennington from the *public* car" was analogous to that which drove "the colored man from the lower floor of [America's] Christian (?)...churches." It was Beaumont, Douglass informed his readers, who along with his travel companion, Alexis de Tocqueville, had tied the power of democratic majorities to America's degradation of blacks. "In a congregation of fashionable people," Beaumont wrote in his antislavery novel *Marie*, "the majority will necessarily have a mind to shut the door against the people of color: the majority willing so, nothing can hinder it." For Douglass and perhaps many of his readers, Pennington's case proved Beaumont correct by again exposing the majoritarian underpinnings of black inequality. To them, the LRA's battle was not only against streetcar companies and racism. It was for the rights of the black minority and against the absolute rule of majorities that was corrupting "*democracy*" itself.[41]

In the months following Pennington's altercation, LRA leaders continued to develop the tactics essential to their rights campaign. In August 1855, "the most intelligent colored citizens in our vicinity," according to the *Tribune*, assembled in Brooklyn, selected Thomas Jennings as president, and signed a constitution. From that point, expanding the membership became their priority. Success would rest on the group's ability to reshape white opinion on the question of black rights *and* to obtain a following of black men and women who were committed mind, body, and purse to the cause. At weekly meetings participants gave and heard speeches, discussed the changing conditions of transit, debated resolutions, and crafted petitions urging the state legislature to intervene on behalf of black riders.[42]

Disobedience and civil litigation, however, remained the centerpieces of the LRA's rights politics. LRA members agreed to take seats aboard streetcars and if "hindered, molested, questioned, or in any way treated different from other citizens" to seek legal redress. Though the LRA left no official records, making the full extent of this campaign difficult to assess, newspaper evidence reveals that members regularly confronted discrimination and initiated lawsuits through the early 1860s. The LRA, of course, hoped this approach would yield favorable rulings, and it took advantage of New York City's expansive system of lower courts by initiating suits that tested the positions of varied juries and judges. Beyond seeking victories in the courts, the LRA's litigious ways pestered the companies that refused to integrate (as well as their agents who ejected black riders), testing their resolve in the process. These courtroom dramas also provided continued spectacles that ensured segregation would remain before the public.[43]

A key obstacle to this court-centered crusade was cost. From the outset, the LRA established a legal defense fund that members could access should they challenge segregation in court. Members paid an "initiation fee of 25 cents and five cents monthly dues" and dropped spare change in a contribution box that circulated at meetings. Black women, who participated in meetings, fought Jim Crow conveyances in the streets, and served as litigants in several lawsuits, also played a vital fundraising role. Building on the efforts of Nell's Equal School Rights Committee, the LRA's "Female Branch" held annual galas commemorating "the decision by Judge Rockwell" in the *Jennings* case. Ticket sales helped grow the LRA's coffers, but equally important, the gathering allowed politics and pleasure to mix. The three hundred attendees in 1856, for example, supported the cause while socializing, consuming an "excellent" meal, and engaging in "promenading and vocal music." These all-night festivals, the *Tribune* observed in 1858, were essential "to keep alive the interest in the Society."[44]

Despite their best efforts, the LRA did not convince most black New Yorkers to join the association. Of the more than 12,000 local blacks, the association only ever brought a few hundred participants to any one of its functions, and its expenses, wealthy oysterman Thomas Downing grumbled, "had to be borne by a few only." The LRA also had to weather public criticisms, including those of unconverted local blacks. Most notably, Joseph R. Rolin, a black man reared in an elite white family, repudiated the LRA's efforts in print and even attempted to derail an LRA meeting in person. To Rolin, the association's so-called leaders were self-aggrandizing tools of white abolitionists. The approach of "forcing ourselves" into cars and resorting to courts of law was unmanly and made "us, the minority, the enemy of the white majority." "I am a man of peace," Rolin declared, "and seek no rights that are not given to me by public consent, and do not believe in those acquired by force of law." Real men would adopt a strategy of self-help and education so that the next generation could be "useful and respectable members of society." Only through patience, uplift, and avoiding "angry strife with the majority" would the black minority defeat prejudice and secure their rights.[45]

Rolin was not alone. At the peak of the LRA's action in 1855, a commentator in the *New York Times* declared the LRA's approach "the least judicious of several possible ones." It unrealistically hoped for a "sudden revolution" and foolishly proposed "to carry the most elevated positions in society by storm; to contest the ascent to positive equality, by one petty skirmish after another, reckoning on a final victory over that last enemy which is to be overcome, the prejudice of color, by some final and forcible *coup de main*." According to this author, prejudices were unconquerable, and the LRA's "litigious and vexatious plans" would only strengthen them. Black New Yorkers would be better off concentrating on "self-elevation, by moral and educational means." Alluding to colonization schemes, the author suggested that blacks should remember that they had chosen "to remain among the whites." If unwilling to leave the United States, blacks instead might follow the Mormons and use "portions of our own vast territory" to found their own community. In other words, a better way for minorities to establish their rights was to flee hostile environments and to form separate communities. Barring such geographic "segregation," if "the negro…chooses to remain," he should "accept the terms of his choice with all possible patience." Only "time" would mitigate "the popular aversion against color."[46]

These critics no doubt represented many Americans, black and white, who rejected the LRA's aggressive style of rights advocacy. Many probably agreed that it was better for black northerners to avoid conflict, accept the status quo, work hard, and hope that equality would come in due time. Alternatively, the reference to the Mormons' exodus to Utah signaled that for some northerners, emigration was a legitimate tactic that oppressed minorities should consider. Even among some black activists, emigrationism—a position scorned by earlier black leaders—had gained adherents as life for black northerners seemed to worsen in the 1850s, not least because of the terrors of the Fugitive Slave Law of 1850. For Martin Delany, the foremost emigrationist of the era, the key reason blacks should consider leaving the United States was because of their "political position"—they likely would always be a minority. It was their "numerical feebleness" that made "equality of rights" seem an impossibility. Better to go "where the black and colored man comprise, by population, and constitute by necessity of members, the *ruling element* of the body politic." To Delany and his followers, it was not the American West where black majorities would rule but rather in the Caribbean and Central and South America. As conditions for black northerners continued to worsen in the late 1850s, the LRA would come to count emigrationists in its leadership corps, including militant abolitionist Henry Highland Garnet. Nonetheless, its mode of minority-rights advocacy, which was predicated on gaining equal access to a racially integrated American public, contrasted with the exit strategies that the Mormons initiated and those that Delany and others sought to implement. When the abolition of slavery brought far greater numbers of black Americans to advocate for rights as minorities, the LRA's strategies to shape law and public opinion would provide a useful guide.[47]

IN DECEMBER 1856, James Pennington stood before the "ladies and gentlemen" of the LRA and announced that "the time had come" to "present themselves in solid phalanx to demand" their equal right to the cars. The Sixth Avenue Railroad Company had "staved off the testing of this question" for some time, but his long-awaited case was scheduled to be tried in Superior Court. At the outset of the three-day trial, the LRA's lead attorney, Frederick A. Tallmadge, a former Whig congressman turned Republican partisan, narrowed the issue. The LRA's members saw their effort as a part of the larger national struggle against slavery and prejudice, but Tallmadge assured the jury that they would hear no "abolition harangue" nor any discussion of "Sharp's rifles" and the violent civil war raging in Kansas. The case was meant "to test" the "simple question" of black citizens' right to ride in the public conveyances on equal terms with whites. Black New Yorkers, he assured the amalgamation-sensitive, did "not expect to be invited to sit at their tables or share their beds." The only "equality" claimed was in "the right of passage." Waldo Hutchins, the streetcar company's attorney, would later dangle the threat of amalgamation before the jury, but his opening statement concerned the LRA's novel tactics. To him, the case was misnamed. Instead of being called *James W. C. Pennington v. The Sixth Avenue Railroad*, it should be called "The Colored People of the City of New York vs. The Sixth Avenue Railroad." It was, Hutchins explained, the "Legal Rights Association who bring this suit." They paid the costs, "raised by contributions, and Mr. Pennington is merely the instrument," chosen because he is "one of the most respectable colored men in this City." Would the jury, he implicitly asked, sanction the LRA's calculating, meddlesome ways?[48]

With the facts of Pennington's ejection agreed upon, the case quickly centered on the common law's demands and the reasonableness of the company's regulation excluding blacks from whites-only cars. The LRA's attorneys argued that it was unreasonable because common carriers were bound to carry all travelers equally. The Sixth Avenue Company's attorneys countered that it was entirely reasonable to separate and categorize passengers, provided that all riders were amply accommodated. Blacks could ride "on the front platform" of all cars and inside the cars allowing blacks that passed "every half-hour." The company's policy merely accommodated the "great prejudice" of many whites and was little different from railroads' common, uncontested practice of refusing to admit "gentlemen unaccompanied by ladies" to ladies' cars.[49]

Once again the judge's charge to the jury made all the difference, and Judge John Slosson, a jurist of Whig-Republican leanings, all but sealed the LRA's fate. As Chester Arthur had in the *Jennings* case, the LRA's second attorney, Edward John Phelps, urged Slosson to declare that "as a matter of law the company [had] no right to exclude one class of persons as a class from their cars." Taking comfort in the likely possibility that "a higher tribunal" would soon decide the question, Slosson declared, "The right of citizens to be carried is not absolute." The jury would decide whether Pennington had the "right to sit...promiscuously with the whites" or whether the company had reasonably excluded "the colored people." The jury also needed to consider "the probable effect upon the [company's] capital, business and interests, of admitting blacks" on terms of "equality" with whites. After deliberating for several hours, the jury decided in favor of the company. Rumor had it that the jury felt "the admission of colored persons would tend to diminish the profits of the Company."[50]

Reactions varied. To James Gordon Bennett's *New York Herald*, a southern sympathizer and champion of minority rights when it came to liquor dealers and opponents of Sunday legislation, the verdict perfectly and "unquestionably harmonize[d] with the law of public opinion in these latitudes." Any higher court would have to sustain the decision and protect whites from having to ride "on a footing of equality with 'niggers.'" Meanwhile, Pittsburgh's *Presbyterian Banner and Advocate*, supporters of liquor prohibition and Sabbath legislation, insisted that "well-dressed and well-behaved" blacks should be allowed to ride on equal terms. When added to the numerous disabilities blacks encountered, this insult helped explain why blacks "do not, as a people, rise to a superior social position." For the *Cincinnati Daily Enquirer*, the decision illustrated "one of the evils of the anti-slavery agitation"—namely that it pushed northerners to treat "free colored people" worse than southerners treated slaves. Because abolitionists gallingly questioned the natural superiority of the white race, white northerners were induced to "regard the negro with hostility, jealousy and prejudice." Only the end of the abolitionist movement (and the cessation of the LRA's agitation), the author implied, would improve the condition of northern blacks.[51]

Commentator after commentator expected an appeal, but it never materialized, owing in part to the LRA's trouble amassing funds. On the eve of his own case, Pennington, perhaps sensing defeat, wrote to wealthy political abolitionist Gerrit Smith. Lamenting that the LRA lacked "the pecuniary means" to combat the "powerful corporations" that controlled the conveyances, he asked Smith to serve as their attorney should an appeal be made. This may have been an indirect way of asking Smith for money, or perhaps Pennington genuinely hoped Smith would take on the LRA's case, presumably pro bono. How Smith responded is unknown, but it seems unlikely that he offered his support, as the LRA never took any of its cases to the New York Court of Appeals. Nevertheless, its members would continue to combat segregation locally. If Pleasant Smith's remarks are any indication, these efforts took on even greater urgency as the decade continued. When asked in his own lawsuit in 1858 if he belonged "to the Legal Rights Association," he proclaimed, "I belong to an association that can't be defeated."[52]

GERRIT SMITH WAS not being insensitive. Just as his associate Edward C. Delavan had underwritten many of the temperance movement's costs, Smith had used his fortune to underwrite many costs of the era's reform crusades, especially abolition. In late 1856, his reluctance to aid the LRA might have been linked to the fact that he had already received a similar request. Earlier that year, William Howard Day had asked Smith to subsidize his challenge to discriminatory public transit in the Midwest (fig. 5.5). Whether Smith helped Day is also uncertain, but if Smith had, he might have wanted to await the outcome of Day's litigation before supporting the

FIGURE 5.5   William Howard Day, *Documenting the American South*. University of North Carolina at Chapel Hill Library. With the support of the Detroit black community, abolitionist activist William Howard Day challenged segregated travel before the Michigan Supreme Court.

LRA's appeal.[53] Day's battle began in September 1855 when he and his wife sought passage aboard the steamboat *Arrow* for their journey from Detroit to Toledo. Told that they would be forbidden from entering the ship's cabin, the pair refused to countenance prejudice. They traveled instead by land and brought suit against John Owen, the steamboat's owner. Like Elizabeth Jennings, Day was no ordinary black northerner. Born free, he graduated from Oberlin College, became a prominent fixture in the abolitionist movement in the 1850s, and regularly associated with other leaders in the struggle for black rights, including James McCune Smith and James Pennington. Like them, Day initiated his battle against discrimination "for the colored people generally" and found support in Detroit's black community. The LRA's class-action approach had migrated west.[54]

After losing in the Wayne County Circuit Court, Day appealed to the Michigan Supreme Court, which in 1858 was a four-judge elected court comprised completely of Republicans. This composition may have given the Days some cause for optimism, as black activists were more likely to find support among antislavery Republicans. Yet it was no guarantee for success, as Republican hostility to slavery's expansion brought no necessary commitment to racial equality. Segregationist steamboat owner John Owen, in fact, was a Republican.[55] In court, Day's attorneys, themselves Republicans, predictably argued that denying him access to the cabin violated the common law of common carriers. Owen's attorney, Samuel T. Douglass, a Democrat who recently had vacated his seat on the Michigan Supreme Court, countered that the common law only required Owen to carry Day, not to provide him "with accommodation on any particular part of the boat." Not only, he explained, was the exclusion of "colored persons" from cabins a "custom of navigation" on the Detroit River and Lake Erie, it was "the custom of the country." Allowing such intercourse "would have been offensive to the other cabin passengers," and it was Owen's duty "to make all reasonable regulations" for "the safety, convenience, comfort, or interests, either of the passengers or carriers." Preventing Day from entering the cabin was reasonable; the common law did not demand otherwise.

Ruling against Day, the Michigan Supreme Court upheld the power of common carriers to exclude blacks from steamboat cabins. Speaking for the unanimous bench, Justice Randolph Manning explained that there was a difference between the "right to be carried" and "the privileges of a passenger on board of the boat." Had Owen "refused to carry [Day] generally, he would be liable" for damages; merely excluding Day from the cabin was entirely reasonable. In judging reasonability, Manning returned to a standard that was all too familiar to abolitionists: what was best for the "large majority of passengers." According to the Court, the "reasonableness of the rule" depends "on the effect the carrying of such persons in the cabin would have...on the accommodation of the mass of" travelers. The good of the community was what mattered, not a few "particular individuals" who might "incommode the community at large." Once again, the majority ruled.[56]

Reported throughout the country, the *Day* decision was another blow in abolitionists' fight for equal rights. For some elated antiabolitionists the decision showed that abolitionists' court-centered, minority-rights politics had backfired. As one Detroit segregationist opined:

> When it is remembered that this case was started by the abolitionists for the purpose of placing upon record the decision of the Supreme Court of the right of the negro to equal privileges with whites on public conveyances in Michigan—that they have borne the expenses of the suit—the extent of their mortification and anger at what they call the absurd decision...can better be imagined than described.[57]

Much like Lemuel Shaw's decision in *Roberts v. City of Boston, Day v. Owen* became a damning precedent that future members of the bench and bar would cite to legitimate racial discrimination, including the southern legal regime of Jim Crow that emerged in the late nineteenth century. More immediately, the precedent likely made some activists think twice before appealing other cases to high courts. To undo the damage, activists would need civil rights legislation, constitutional change, or a court willing to overturn precedent. In the explosive sectional environment of the late 1850s, all seemed highly unlikely.[58]

Day v. Owen also showed how minority-rights politics could become fodder for partisan controversy, which at the time was shaped by another divisive court opinion triggered by a black litigant—the US Supreme Court's *Dred Scott v. Sandford*. A Missouri slave, Scott sued for his freedom based on the fact that his owner voluntarily took him to free territory. Seeing an opportunity, the Court attempted to settle vexing questions of black citizenship and the status of slavery in the territories. Chief Justice Roger Taney limited Congress's ability to restrict slavery's expansion and also declared that blacks living in the United States were not citizens and had no right to sue in federal court. Not only did Scott lose his appeal before the nation's highest judicial authority, but his effort to free himself through court action unwittingly jeopardized the rights of all black Americans, slave or free. As Taney infamously announced, blacks "had no rights which the white man was bound to respect."[59]

Dred Scott unleashed a frenzy of commentary and became the centerpiece of partisan conflict in the late 1850s. Republicans, whose free soil platform opposed slavery's western expansion, condemned the decision, while most Democrats demanded obedience. Some supporters insisted that any debates about the rights of free blacks, including aboard public transit, should be closed. At least one local northern judge agreed. In another challenge to segregation in New York, a black hairdresser named Maria Jenkins sued a conductor who had ejected her from a Sixth Avenue car. In his charge to the jury, Judge Albert A. Thompson, a Democrat, proclaimed that "the Dred Scott decision" was "sound law" and that blacks did "not possess the same rights and privileges as white men." Jenkins had "no right to a seat," and the conductor was right "to expel her."[60]

While in William Howard Day's case neither the attorneys nor the jurists had mentioned *Dred Scott*, that decision loomed large in the aftermath. The *Detroit Free Press*, the state's leading Democratic daily, used *Day v. Owen* to play the race card and to deride the Republican Party. The *Free Press* spun the decision this way: in *Day*, a Republican-controlled state high court, more than any other court in the country, had "fully and entirely sustained the Dred Scott decision." Actually, they claimed, the Michigan Supreme Court had "gone beyond" it. Setting the tone for much of the nation, the *Free Press* painted the decision as evidence of Democratic vindication and Republican hypocrisy. The editorialists chided Republicans for trying to explain away the decision by resorting to "various technical points." To them, the ruling was actually quite simple. It sustained Owen in refusing to carry Day in the cabin because, first, "Day *was a negro,*—not that he was a filthy negro, or an ill-dressed negro, or offensive because of insobriety or disease,—*but that he was a negro*"; and second, Day's presence in the cabin would have been disagreeable to whites. There was no other conclusion to draw than that "negroes [were] an inferior and degraded race." In *Dred Scott*, the US Supreme Court had ruled that blacks were politically unequal with whites, but Michigan's court had found "the negro" to be socially and "morally" inferior. This decision, the *Free Press* glowed, was "eminently right," and the newspaper would "sustain it" as it had sustained *Dred Scott*. But what would Republicans do? They adamantly had rejected *Dred Scott*, but now their own court had ruled "in accordance with the principles of the democratic party and the Dred Scott decision itself." How could Republicans assail *Dred Scott* any longer without assailing their own court? Simply put, black persons had no rights, minority or otherwise.[61]

Even though Republicans charged Democrats with misleading the public, the *Free Press*'s spin proved widely influential. As the *Cleveland Plain Dealer* blustered, "Black Republican courts [in Michigan] have made a decision far more degrading to the black man than the Dred Scott decision." White southerners joined in as well, again showing how abolitionists' minority-rights politics easily played into the sectional divide. To Galveston, Texas's *Civilian and Gazette Weekly, Day v. Owen* proved that "negroes" were "not citizens of the United States, either at the North or the South." To Macon, Georgia's *Weekly Telegraph*, the decision showed that the "free soil uproar" had infected the North with a hypocritical abolitionism. Overstating the extent of white northerners' interest in racial equality, the *Telegraph* chastised northerners for preaching "negro equality" in one moment and then forcing "some poor free negro out of his seat in a car, steamboat or omnibus" in the next. If further evidence of northern humbuggery was needed, white southerners needed only look to "the streets of New York," where white northerners would "stand a law suit rather than 'ride with a nigger.'" Should Republicans succeed in carrying out their abolitionist designs, "The negro would have neither place to sit or stand—nor air to breathe—nor food to eat—nor shelter nor clothes to cover him." All of these necessities, the author's proslavery critique implied, were more readily available to slaves in the South.[62]

In the face of hostile verdicts and the tendency of their failures to be pulled into the heated partisan and sectional rhetoric of the age, black men and women persisted in their fight. Court action remained an essential tool, albeit with continued mixed results. In 1859, a black man threatened to sue New Jersey's Morris and Essex Railroad following his "unwarranted" ejection. In Ohio, two black ministers did the same after being removed from the sleeping car on the Little Miami Railroad. A "mulatto" woman ejected from a Cincinnati streetcar received a favorable decision from the Hamilton Common Pleas Court. Amid the secession crisis in early 1861, black Philadelphians were not as fortunate. Judge John I. Hare of the District Court of Philadelphia denied George W. Goines's claim against the streetcar conductor who had expelled him, finding the company's rule banning black riders to be "a wise one." When establishing rules for the "association of men in public," it was right, Hare explained, to consult public opinion. In this case, forcing the "two races"—one vastly "superior" and the other only "emerging from the shades of barbarism"—to associate would only exacerbate the existing "repulsion and antipathy" between them. Better for society, and especially for the "weaker" black population, that whites rode and blacks did not.[63]

As with other disappointing decisions, abolitionists responded with outrage. Writing to the *Christian Recorder*, Philadelphia black leader William Still described the ruling as "a second edition of the Dred Scott decision." A "pro-slavery" judge had taken "especial delight in showing that colored people have no rights that white men are bound to respect." But Still's analysis went further. More than the shadow of *Dred Scott* and the judge's cruelty, much of the blame for the odious decision rested with George W. Goines. A "great mistake," Still explained, had been made "in urging this suit...before proper preliminary steps were resorted to; such as the aid of the press, the co-operation of influential persons, the use of petitions, the securing of the very ablest counsels, &c." All of these tools of the era's burgeoning minority-rights politics were available to Goines, and in fact, some Philadelphians already had made progress on these fronts. Rushing to court, however, had "wofully damaged" the cause. "Railroads and public places will feel now," Still explained, "that they can reject us by law, whereas before, they had nothing more than a corrupt public sentiment to stand upon." Still wanted to be clear. He did not oppose "contending for our rights in the courts." But when a case affected "the entire colored community," it was necessary "to bring to bear all the influence imaginable, to win the day." Too much was at stake not to employ "wise management and earnest effort."[64]

Dred Scott, Day v. Owen, and *Goines v. M'Candless* made William Still and other activists painfully aware that there was more to securing minority rights than "entering a suit." As the secession crisis gave way to Civil War, black men and women in Philadelphia, San Francisco, and Washington, DC, continued to battle to integrate the spaces of public travel, and most would adopt the broader range of techniques that activists in Massachusetts and New York had pioneered. In Philadelphia, for example, Still and other black leaders founded the Social, Civil, and Statistical Association of the Colored People of Philadelphia, complete with a "car committee" that targeted segregation.[65] Black leaders began to call for these tactics to be extended to causes other than travel. Amid black Californians' struggle for the right to testify in courts, for example, Philip A. Bell, a transplanted New Yorker and associate of LRA cofounder

James McCune Smith, urged his brethren to move beyond the costly and "cumbersome" method of using conventions to lobby for rights. Instead, blacks should form "Legal Rights Associations" in each county, complete with "Female Branches," and all coordinated by a central association and executive board lodged in San Francisco. Rights associations would bring black Californians to do what they most needed to do to achieve equal rights: "Above all, *organize!* organize!! ORGANIZE!!!"[66]

SINCE 1855, THE Legal Rights Association had organized to integrate New York's public conveyances and to guard any victories they achieved. And victories there were. In 1856, Sarah Williams won a verdict in the local Supreme Court after her expulsion from the Empire Stage Line. When John W. Hunter's skirmish with a Sixth Avenue conductor went to fisticuffs a year and a half later, a judge of the Court of Special Sessions dismissed assault charges against Hunter because blacks, he maintained, could not be banned from the cars. Peter S. Porter's success came some- what differently. While serving as the LRA's treasurer in late 1856, he and five black women were violently removed from an Eighth Avenue car, and when Porter threatened a lawsuit, the company ended its discriminatory ways rather than go to court.[67]

The LRA's efforts did not, however, yield a neat, progressive increase in rights. The Sixth Avenue Company, which withstood Pennington's famous challenge, continuously ran whites-only cars and expelled black riders. Other lines backtracked. In 1858, the formerly integrated Fourth Avenue Company banned black riders after one black youth "was taken sick," likely from overindulgence, aboard their streetcar on New Year's Day. The Eighth Avenue Railroad Company also reversed its course. Peter S. Porter had spurred this line's integration, but in the summer of 1863 the mobs of New York City's draft riots changed the situation. Rioters victimized black New Yorkers and also targeted the city's infra- structure, tearing down telegraph lines and ripping up the streetcar tracks. Ostensibly to keep future mobs from spewing their racist venom toward the company, the Eighth Avenue line moved to prohibit black riders.[68]

If the turbulence of wartime had endangered black New Yorkers and threatened their rights in public, it also opened opportunities. By the time of the draft riots, the war to preserve the Union had already transformed into a war of emancipation. Tied to Lincoln's Emancipation Proclamation was the provision to bring black men into the Union army, and as black men began to join and fight, some inevitably returned to northern cities. Would they be allowed to ride the conveyances on equal terms? In the winter of 1864, when a conductor on the Fourth Avenue Railroad ousted a black soldier who had lost his leg in combat, the outraged *Tribune* called upon the public and the legislature "to reflect upon" the absurdity of a nation that asked black men to risk their lives in battle while ejecting them from the cars. When the Fourth Avenue Company rescinded its prohibition on black riders a few weeks later, papers as far as Madison, Wisconsin, took note. Only two discriminatory lines remained.[69]

A new opportunity arose when Ellen Anderson was dragged from an Eighth Avenue car in June 1864. Black women had been valued litigants in the LRA's crusade, but Anderson was especially treasured. A close friend of LRA leader Peter S. Porter, Anderson was the widow of a black soldier who had died in Beaufort, South Carolina, while serving the Union cause. In something of a twist on the LRA's tactics, Anderson's attorney, Charles C. Whitehead, brought suit not against the conductor or the company but instead against the policeman who had aided in Anderson's ejection. Before the Board of Police Commissioners, Whitehead clarified the goal of the case: to "test" whether policemen could "eject a person from the cars on account of color." More than representing Ellen Anderson, Whitehead appeared in court for all those "whose feelings had often been much shocked by these *fracas* in the street cars, sometimes at the very moment the colored regiments were marching down the streets on their way to the war." Anderson herself helped drive the point home by dressing in black mourning attire for her appearance before the police commissioners. Would the commissioners trample on the grave of a valiant soldier—and every other black man currently donning the Union blues— by authorizing government officers to eject black men and women from public streetcars?[70]

Led by Republican Thomas C. Acton, the Board of Police Commissioners reprimanded the officer and effectively ended police support of Jim Crow conveyances. As Acton explained, "no law" prevented black men and women from "riding in the cars," and there was no "order requiring policemen to do the dirty work of these conductors." Officers existed "to preserve the peace," and in this case, the officer should "have arrested the conductor [rather] than the woman." In the face of bad publicity and the end of state support for segregation, the Eighth Avenue Company announced that blacks thereafter would be allowed in all of its cars. Scarcely more than a week later—nearly ten years to the day after Elizabeth Jennings's ejection began the LRA's struggle—the Sixth Avenue Railroad Company followed suit and abolished "the distinction of color in their cars." The LRA had finally won its war.[71]

Just as they had with many of the LRA's battles, newspapers nationwide took an active interest in these developments, perhaps none more so than Philadelphia's *Christian Recorder*, which hoped the news would inspire readers to persevere in their own struggle to integrate Philadelphia's streetcars. The Democratic *Brooklyn Eagle*, by contrast, chastised the *Tribune* and the other "champions of unlimited license for the negro" for having another "negro spasm" over the Anderson case. It was doubtful, the *Eagle* insisted, that Anderson was really "the wife of a brave colored soldier." This claim was made only "to create sympathy" for an innocent woman harmed who, in reality, had sparked the incident by defying "the conductor to put her out" and "acting like a virago." Furthermore, it was not surprising that the Republican police commissioners bought the act. No doubt speaking for many Americans who remained unconvinced by the ideas of racial equality that had ascended during the war, the *Eagle* concluded that "so long as any prejudice does exist against the company of negroes, it is folly to attempt to remove it by forcing the negro into the presence of those who object to it." The police commissioners and the abolitionists would only make matters worse.[72]

To other pundits, the tactics behind Anderson's case were genius. As one correspondent to Garrison's *Liberator* proudly announced, the "disappearance of the last vestige of caste in our street conveyances...was due, in a large degree, to the public indignation excited by the forcible expulsion of a colored soldier's widow." Certainly, the wartime climate and Ellen Anderson's status as a soldier's widow facilitated the final defeat of segregation. Yet as much credit goes to the decade-long struggle of the LRA—perhaps black activists' most important contribution to the maturing popular minority-rights politics of the 1850s. Along with such supportive organs as the *Tribune*, the LRA mobilized a critical portion of the black community, kept the issue before the public, and provided a powerful example for those fighting for rights elsewhere.[73]

6

America's First Wet Crusade and the Sunday Question Redux

AS THE SUMMER sun set on June 27, 1855, fireworks exploded over Chicago. Thousands of residents had spent the day celebrating the defeat of a proposed state law banning the sale of alcohol. After the morning rains subsided, they came from all corners to join an "immense procession." Michael Diversey, the successful German-born owner of the Chicago Brewery, led the crowd down Michigan Street to West Division and then on to South Randolph and Clark Street. Men and boys hoisted banners with slogans written in both English and German. Triumphant music from local bands set the pace, and along the way "thousands of...wives and daughters" joined in. When the march reached Dearborn Park, the great "Anti-Prohibition Demonstration" that followed came to constitute, at that point, the largest gathering ever held there. One hundred guns were fired, and organizers called the crowd to order. Prominent figures gave speeches and read resolutions condemning prohibition as fanatical legislation hostile to the "well established principles of personal freedom and equal rights." That the hastily constructed platform from which the day's orators spoke collapsed in the middle of the proceedings did little to crush the crowd's resolve. They would hold themselves "in readiness to meet the same issues" should they emerge again, and they urged others to do the same. "The friends of constitutional liberty everywhere," they proclaimed, needed to muster "renewed energy and vigilance in the cause of freedom" to ensure the survival of "free government."[1]

While abolitionists were forging a minority-rights politics to battle for racial equality, others were deploying similar tactics to combat temperance and Sabbath reformers' renewed crusades in the 1850s. From Maine to California, diverse opponents of liquor prohibition and of renewed Sunday surveillance joined in initiating a massive defense of rights that built upon the foundational struggles over local option and Sunday laws in the 1840s. Realizing that well-organized moralists and overbearing state and local governments might long threaten their interests, foes of restrictive liquor and Sunday regulations began to move beyond ad hoc responses. They mobilized larger segments of society to repel hostile legislation while regularizing tactics to press their cases before the public, elected officials, and the courts. A "large class" of citizens, a freethinker observed in 1855, "are getting restless under the religious, political, and social despotisms which are imposed upon them by majorities." Like advocates of racial equality in the 1850s, they created formal and sometimes lasting grass-roots, nonpartisan political associations. Representing liquor dealers and self-described religious liberals and hoisting (sometimes literally) the banner of minority rights, these associations signaled the historic emergence of these groups as organized forces in American political life. In the process, mid-nineteenth-century Americans increasingly came to counter the theory of democracy authorizing the uninhibited rule of the majority—the theory they saw legitimating punitive liquor and Sabbath regulations—with constitutional defenses of minority rights. As the antiprohibitionist *New Yorker Staats Zeitung* editorialized, the time had come to dispense with the "theory of the absolute, uncontrolled will of the majority." Along with racial egalitarians, these other moral minorities would make grass-roots, minority-rights politics a major and well-publicized part of democratic engagement.[2]

IT STARTED IN Maine. When New York held its first local referenda on liquor licenses in 1846, the Maine legislature took a different path, prohibiting the manufacture and sale of alcohol statewide. Lacking teeth, the law went largely unenforced, driving temperance champions to demand a more stringent measure. Taking the lead was Neal Dow, a man whom one historian describes as "almost a caricature of the fanatical Yankee reformer: small in stature, vain, thrifty, even though his tannery, banks, and real estate holdings made him wealthy, and utterly self-righteous." In 1850, Dow became president of the Maine Temperance Society, and a year later, voters broke party lines to elect him as the antiliquor mayor of Portland. Dow had been working on a new prohibitory bill, and in 1851, he shopped his handiwork to the state legislature. Solid support came from the small contingent of antislavery Free Soilers, and foreshadowing later temperance tactics, Dow exploited divisions within the Whig and Democratic parties to forge a prohibitionist majority in both houses of the legislature. With his pending re-election in mind, Democratic governor John Hubbard signed prohibition into law even though he was known to hit the bottle from time to time. Dow—the "Napoleon of Temperance"— got to work seeing the so-called Maine Law enforced and bragged about its successes to all who would listen.[3]

Glowing reports about the Maine Law miracle traveled throughout the United States as well as to Canada and Great Britain, and temperance reformers inundated the public with this propaganda. In the Maine Law a proper device had at last been devised to end the hated license system, to put "the *rum power*" out of business, to help control unruly urban, immigrant, and working-class populations, and to dry up all the evils—crime, vice, poverty, the abuse of wives and children, high taxes—that flowed from drink and continued to threaten the republic.[4] To the New Haven–based *New Englander*, the long struggle against demon rum had proven that "moral suasion alone" could not bring temperance's complete victory. Maine's approach rightly employed "the strong arm of the law" by proscribing both the manufacture and sale of alcohol and by empowering ordinary citizens along with the usual authorities to enforce it. Armed with an easily obtained search warrant, prohibitionists could enter a business or dwelling suspected of housing illegal liquor and dump any contraband they discovered "into the gutter" (fig. 6.1). Presbyterian pastor Samuel H. Hall boasted to a receptive Michigan audience that the Maine Law was unlike "all previous legislation upon the subject of intemperance." It closed legal loopholes, ensured violators received quick trials that favored prosecutors, and meted out stiff fines and prison sentences to guilty parties. "The people," the law's supporters affirmed, "have determined to carry it through." Legal power combined with popular support would defeat the monster alcohol.[5]

Across the North and parts of the upper South, elite and middle-class temperance men and women intensified their single-issue, grass-roots pressure politics to make America dry. They were abuzz with mass meetings, speaking tours, propaganda campaigns, and new associations like Salem, Iowa's Ladies Maine Law Society. Influential newspapers like Horace Greeley's *New York Tribune* lent support. A torrent of petitions signed by men, women, and children flooded state legislatures, and elections returned growing phalanxes of Maine Law supporters into state offices. Reformers organized independent slates of prohibitionists

FIGURE 6.1 *Three Cheers for Maine!* (1852). Courtesy of the Library Company of Philadelphia. America's first experiment with alcohol prohibition occurred in the 1850s when thirteen state legislatures passed so-called Maine Laws. Temperance reformers cheered the powerful laws that authorized the destruction of illegal alcohol.

in some areas, but they more often continued to work with candidates from existing parties. After seeking pledges from candidates to back prohibition, reformers implored voters to support only *"true* Temperance men"—committed prohibitionists—regardless of party affiliation. As the Pennsylvania State Temperance Convention explained, "If of two candidates, the Democrat is in favor of Prohibition, and the Whig is opposed, *vote for the Democrat.* If the Whig is in favor, and the Democrat is opposed, *vote for the Whig!*" Ideally, this approach, which privileged public policy over party, would make the Maine Law "the *main issue*" in state elections and allow voters to return "a large majority" of prohibitionists to state assemblies. "If united and resolute," the *New York Evangelist* opined in 1852, prohibitionists could "hold the balance of power in every election" and force every northern legislature to pass a Maine Law.[6]

The *Evangelist* was prescient. By 1855 twelve additional northern states and territories from New Hampshire to Iowa (and including Delaware) had enacted prohibition. Several others had come extremely close. "In almost every State in the Union," the *Boston Traveller* announced, the

Maine Law "has become a political question, controlling to a greater or less extent, all party movements and elections." This course of events wreaked havoc on the party system that had structured much of American electoral politics since the 1830s and which was already threatened by sectional issues. Recognizing the divisive nature of prohibition, most Whig and Democratic leaders had hoped to steer clear of the issue, but prohibition-ists forced the issue, breaking traditional party lines as members of both parties supported the Maine Law. These developments sped the demise of the northern Whig Party, which was already weakened by the national party's sectional divisions over slavery. It also helped fuel the rise of the Know-Nothing Party, which organized anti-Catholic and nativist senti-ment and used prohibition and the persistent linkage between alcohol and immigrants to bolster its brief but meaningful success in the mid-1850s. Eventually, a new political party—the Republican Party—would emerge from the ashes of the Second Party System, a system finally destroyed by prohibition politics. Party dissolution, however, was only one important political consequence of the Maine Law.[7]

Though partisan instability and reformers' electoral machinations powered the passage of prohibition, advocates insisted that Maine Laws were the "public, emphatic and deliberate expression of the views of the majority upon a great moral question." In fact, prohibitionists lauded their ability to circumvent the obstructive party system and reveal the majority's true policy proclivities. This was how democracy was supposed to work. After Indiana went dry in 1855, for example, the state's Central Temperance Committee advised local leaders,

> Let it be known in your speeches that the unanimity with which the law was passed, receiving the votes of both parties, in the last Legislature proves conclusively that it is demanded by a large majority of the people in this State—rises above all party consider-ations—and refutes the oft repeated declaration of its enemies, that the enactment of such a law would be in defiance of the wishes of a large majority of the people.

As they had done during the local option episode, reformers insisted that the wet minority should gladly yield to the Maine Law because, as one prohibition rally proclaimed, "in a republic, where the majorities govern, there is no excuse for rebellious opposition to the laws." To make sure of it, temperance forces organized special associations to see prohibition enforced. The most prominent of these, the Carson League, pooled funds not only to offset the costs of litigation generated by prohibition but also to compensate clandestine informers who provided evidence of illegal sales of alcohol. Prohibitionists would stop at nothing to see that the majority's measure succeeded and to prove that democracy could defeat drink.[8]

Yet unsurprisingly, the enactment of a new law, despite its heralded power and widespread support, failed to bring universal obedience. Thousands of Americans in "dry" states continued to make, sell, possess, and consume alcohol, and many defended their right to do so. As in the local option episode but far surpassing it, antiprohibitionists practiced both secret and public evasion, and the more creative episodes garnered national media attention. Patrick Donohoe, a resident of North Adams, Massachusetts, for example, made the papers after several gallons of liquor were found concealed inside his hollowed-out "cellar wall." A Maine man's unsuccessful attempt to smuggle liquor to Portland in a coffin brought repeated reports of an onlooker quipping that "the coffin in this case contained not the *body*, but the *spirit*." Enterprising businessmen supplemented these "ingenious tactics" by setting up shop on the wet side of a dry state's border. Indiana dealers sold liquor on the Ohio River aboard boats tied to the wet Kentucky shore. When Connecticut went dry, residents of Norwich considered purchasing an island in New York waters but "within a stone's throw of the Connecticut shore." With "no law against the rum traffic in New York" at that time, the *Norwich Courier* predicted a "firey inundation" would "roll in upon us from the fountain to be opened on this neighboring island."[9]

Circumvention was only the beginning. Angry Bostonians hung Neal Dow and their Democratic and prohibitionist governor, George S. Boutwell, in effigy, while Germans in DuBois County, Indiana, burned effigies of their governor and state senator. Others vandalized the property of prohibitionists. In Binghamton, New York, the homes of Maine Law men were "disfigured with tar and filth, their fruit trees quilled, and their fences injured." Those who enforced prohibition also risked retaliation, including the two Rhode Island magistrates who found their barns in flames. In Chester, Massachusetts antiprohibitionists formed "what they called a Tiger League," blew up a Methodist church, burned a gristmill, and "disfigured the horses" of members of the Carson League. Attempts at enforcement turned violent as prohibitionists, sometimes wielding "hatchets and pick axes," barged into homes and businesses suspected of harboring liquor aiming to destroy what they found, only to meet resistance.

Added to these altercations were well-publicized riots, including one in Portland, Maine, in 1855. When a largely Irish-born crowd demanded access to alcohol rumored to be held in City Hall and refused to disperse, Neal Dow ordered the militia to fire. One man was killed; several others were injured. Some saw the deadly melee as proof of immigrants' inability to hold their liquor and of the righteousness of prohibition, yet others fretted that the Maine Law had ushered in a prohibitionist "reign of terror."[10]

Less lethally, antiprohibitionists organized grass-roots movements across the northern states to repel Maine Laws and to protect their right to drink and sell alcohol. Their efforts comprised America's first true wet crusade as well as a turning point in the expansion of the minority-rights politics of the mid-nineteenth century. As in the previous decade's local option battle, the most consequential actors were liquor dealers, brewers, hotelkeepers, and others whose livelihoods depended on the sale of alcoholic beverages. Though plenty of native-born Americans worked in the alcohol industry, by the early 1850s it was dominated by Irish and German immigrants, who had flocked to the United States because of famine and Europe's failed democratic revolutions of 1848. A range of other influential men joined the leadership corps, but newspaper editors and local politicos, who were often but not always of Democratic partisan leanings, were the most common. In Kalamazoo, Michigan, for example, antiprohibitionists were directed by Irish-born hotelier Phelix Duffie, a Democratic newspaper editor named Samuel N. Gantt, and Salmon C. Hall, a surveyor and former state legislator. In Chicago, prominent German brewer Michael Diversey was aided, among others, by Alfred Dutch, a Whig newspaper editor, and Francis A. Hoffman, a Prussian-born Lutheran clergyman who would later help organize Illinois's Republican Party. Looking northward to Milwaukee, the mostly German antiprohibitionists there were led by Moritz Schoeffler, a Democratic newspaper editor and the son-in-law of Jacob Best, a brewer whose business would eventually be renamed the Pabst Brewing Company. In New York City, the veritable capital of antiprohibition, hotel-owner Richard French, who had led liquor dealers' earlier opposition to local option, re-emerged alongside wine merchant Phillip W. Engs. Both were wealthy and native born.[11]

The backbone of their rights crusade was popular mobilization that prominently exposed how antebellum moral minorities relied upon a democratic public sphere that tolerated dissent. The highly participatory side of opposition to Maine Laws quickly dwarfed the scale and scope of the organized resistance that had helped rebuff local option laws. It emerged most conspicuously at the meetings and rallies that sprung up in Boston; Brooklyn; Lancaster, Pennsylvania; Dubuque, Iowa; Marion County, Indiana; and countless places in between. Organizers typically invited all interested participants "without distinction of party" and generally regardless of religion and national origin, though Germans sometimes held their own meetings in addition to attending mixed gatherings. An often motley crew responded. Immigrant and homegrown men (and to a much lesser extent, women); Catholics and Protestants; freethinkers and self-described liberals; business owners and wage workers—all filled halls, parks, and other public spaces to defend their cultural traditions, their habits and addictions, their financial interests, their manhood, and their vision of free democracy. By the time prohibition was in retreat in 1856, these gatherings had pulled thousands upon thousands of Americans into public life, many of whom might not have taken such public stands on issues of policy. The threat of prohibition proved a powerful force for recruitment, as did the spectacle of an antiprohibitionism that often appropriated the pageantry of party rallies and included bands, banners, and specially written songs; the firing of guns and cannon; parades and torchlight processions; fireworks and bonfires (fig. 6.2).[12]

Beyond the ballyhoo, antiprohibitionist kingpins adopted an approach designed to illustrate the strength of their cause, bolster its respectability, and influence public opinion and policymakers. They eagerly differentiated their assemblies from riotous and violent resistance to prohibition by styling their proceedings formally and by involving elite men whose names appeared on public lists of officers. Depending on the location and the composition of the crowd, proceedings were conducted in English, both English and German, or sometimes only in German. Once called to order, participants selected officers, created special committees, heard speeches, approved resolutions, and signed their names to petitions calling for legislators and "all political parties to denounce" the Maine Laws. Despite antiprohibitionists' best efforts to be respectable, temperance advocates ridiculed their gatherings as the work of unmanly drunkards and murderous rum-sellers (fig. 6.3). Although antiprohibitionist crowds typically contained a wide range of dissenters, to critics, opposition to Maine Laws was the product of "the hordes of European and degraded immigration," especially the infidels, the Catholics, "the low Irish," and the "beer-guzzling" Germans. Real men and true Americans would never dare show their faces at these "Bacchanalian orgies."[13]

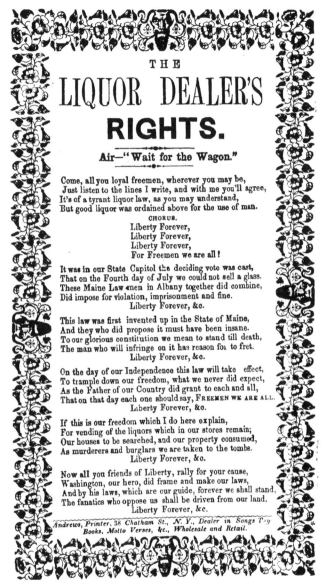

FIGURE 6.2 *Liquor Dealer's Rights* (1855). Courtesy of the Library of Congress. Those attending the anti-Maine Law rallies of the 1850s sang songs that protested prohibition, ridiculed fanatical temperance reformers, and called for Americans to defend popular liberty and constitutional rights.

The Opposer of Temperance.
You uphold the rum-traders madly,
While you cannot *hold up* yourself;
You swallow their poison, and gladly
You aid them in robbing your pelf.

FIGURE 6.3 *The Opposer of the Maine Law* (1855). Courtesy of The Library Company of Philadelphia. Prohibitionists lambasted opponents of Maine Laws as unmanly and subhuman drunkards. To them, popular resistance to prohibition only benefited the liquor dealers who placed personal financial gain above the public good.

Where temperance reformers had long used centralized institutions and propaganda machines to lobby legislatures and coordinate their efforts across space, antiprohibitionists worked at a disadvantage. As an antireform movement fought to preserve the status quo—to keep alcohol legal—its initial efforts proved reactionary and fairly decentralized. But their unity and effectiveness grew steadily. Media coverage of local events (even when scornful) made opposition to Maine Laws national news and helped unite far-flung dissenters. So too did the handful of short-lived specialized newspapers, including Illinois's *Anti-Prohibitionist* and Columbus, Ohio's *Common Sense Against the Maine Law*.[14] Pundits such as G. J. Beebe also helped promote unity across state lines. An outspoken antireformer, a staunch advocate of the separation of church and state, and, as one admirer described, a "champion of human rights," he edited the widely distributed *Banner of Liberty* in Middletown, New York. In its pages Beebe protested nativism, the Sabbath reform, and abolitionism. He skewered the "pretendedly pious and benevolent moral reformers" and condemned Bible reading in schools, the employment of legislative chaplains, demands for racial equality, and most prominently, liquor prohibition. So committed was Beebe to defeating Maine Laws that he took his act on the road, traveling throughout the Mid-Atlantic and Midwest and stump-speaking at anti-Maine Law gatherings. He also challenged temperance leaders to public debates, and for a time, teetotalers accepted. These showdowns climaxed in 1853 when Beebe faced off against temperance stalwart Charles Jewett in several Ohio communities in front of thousands of men and women. Before touring Indiana the following year, Beebe suggested a similar course of debates, only to be turned down by the state temperance society. He would preach the antiprohibitionist gospel unopposed.[15]

Ideas also connected antiprohibitionists. In debates, pamphlets, editorials, speeches, resolutions, petitions, and banners, they and their allies disseminated a multipronged critique of Maine Laws and their advocates. They complained about the inevitable economic disaster that would ensue if the multi-million-dollar alcohol industry was outlawed. Tavern owners and saloon keepers would be thrown out of work. Liquor-pedaling grocers would be forced to close shop, as would the many hotels whose "most substantial source of revenue" came from the bar. Add to that the thousands of men employed in distilling and brewing as well as the farmers who supplied them grain. Livelihoods would be destroyed, homes broken up, and families ruined. Economic misery would accompany the Maine Law but so would the misery of abstinence that would fall disproportionately on "the poor." Opponents cried class warfare in other ways, especially when pointing to the loophole in prohibitory laws, inserted to avoid federal constitutional questions, that allowed the purchase of imported alcohol. To Phelim Lynch of the *Irish-American* and others, the effect was to authorize the "rich man" to buy expensive foreign wines and spirits while arresting "the poor laborer" for seeking cheap beer and liquor in the form he could afford it, by the glass.[16]

Antiprohibitionists insisted that reformers had again taken a wrong turn in seeking to eradicate intemperance by law. Though many claimed to support the general goals of the temperance movement, they insisted that moral suasion was the only feasible way to get Americans to drink less. Legal coercion, they said, would only result in increased consumption. Humans' craving for "stimulants," some argued, was so strong that prohibition would cause "riot and bloodshed." If prohibition somehow proved enforceable, any positive effects would be negated when drinkers inevitably turned to other stimulants: strong tea and coffee, "more tobacco chewing and smoking," and, some suggested, even "the frightful relief of opium." What was so bad about alcohol anyway? Moderate consumption, antiprohibitionists emphasized, not only had a long-standing, legitimate, and legal place in American history but also was ordained by God. Look to your Bibles, one Ohioan demanded, referencing a litany of biblical passages. Was it not "anti-Christian" to take away "the moral privileges" of drinking wine that Christ himself had sanctioned? Antiprohibitionists conceded that the few habitual drunkards should be dealt with by law, but they insisted that the many moderate drinkers should be at liberty to chart their own path. "Morals and morality," German Protestant theologian Edward Graf concluded, would "only thrive in the soil of moral freedom." Prohibition would poison that soil.[17]

Indeed, a centerpiece of the antiprohibitionist position was that fanatical reformers and overbearing state legislatures were improperly expanding their power and violating the personal liberty of all Americans—and especially American men—"to judge what is best for them to drink." The state's Maine Law, angry Michiganders explained, "proceeds upon the principle that the people of this State are not capable of controlling or regulating their own appetite" and that the government should do it for them. Antiprohibitionists regularly compared prohibition to the long-repudiated sumptuary laws of the early modern period, which regulated fashion and consumer choices, often according to social class. "The same authority that attempts to dictate what a man shall drink," one critic warned, "will soon prescribe what he shall eat and what he shall wear—it will fix the model of his house and the style of his hat, the cut of his coat and the length of his shoes." Hammering on this threat of the slippery slope, Icahabod Lindsay threatened that reformers would next take "our tobacco," and then, referencing the contemporary penchant for dietary reform, "restrict our diet to brown bread!" If the Maine Law was not resisted now, nothing would prevent future prohibitions and reform-conjured commandments until "finally the legislature in its motherly care of the people" would compel all citizens "to attend one particular church." All of these decisions rightfully belonged to individuals not the state.[18]

Even more broadly, antiprohibitionists argued that something was wrong with America's political system if state legislatures could eradicate a legal species of property (alcohol), turn once law-abiding businessmen into criminals, authorize government officers and fanatical reformers to invade "the sanctity of the home" looking for booze, and hamper "the right of trial by Jury." These "anti-republican" features of Maine Laws violated "the constitutional and legal rights of all" and subverted "the free institutions of our country." To a German Catholic priest in Cincinnati and other immigrants, prohibition exemplified the "fanaticism, intolerance, and ultra-views on politics and religion" that flourished in the world's lone democracy. Edward Graf similarly worried that the damage done to America's reputation as a "land of civil and political liberty" would facilitate "the triumph of the friends of absolutism in the old world." They would see "nothing less than the abolition of personal liberty! of the freedom of trade and traffic! of the freedom of property!" and scoff at America's unfree democracy.[19]

Antiprohibitionists also united in dubbing prohibition the work of tyrannical majorities and in viewing themselves as an oppressed minority. This had occurred in the earlier local option episode and given rise to arguments about the delegation of legislative power and the ability of representative democracy to protect minority rights. In states like Pennsylvania, Michigan, and Illinois where state legislatures presented voters with referenda on prohibition, these arguments reappeared. Elsewhere, however, antiprohibitionists continued to emphasize the duty of elected officials to act with the welfare of the whole and the rights of the minorities in mind. An anonymous pamphleteer in Boston maintained:

> Our Legislature is not invested with the law-making prerogative merely to consult the will of the *majority*; they have higher purposes to subserve, in attaining the ends of justice and equal rights, in protecting the interests of the weak as well as of the strong, and in guarding the rights of the *minority* from popular innovation. The minority, however meager, have rights which may not be wrested from them; the majority are neither absolute in power, nor infallible in judgment.

When state legislatures bowed to "popular innovation" and ignored minority rights by passing prohibitory statutes, antiprohibitionists lambasted them and shifted their rhetoric to warn about the dangers of omnipotent legislatures. When more than ten thousand New Yorkers assembled to protest prohibition on the eve of its implementation, it was no accident that the banner adorning the stage announced Thomas Jefferson's admonition: "I DO NOT FEAR EXECUTIVE ENCROACHMENT, BUT THE TYRANNY OF LEGISLATIVE MAJORITIES." Prohibition showed that American government's most majoritarian branch could be its most dangerous, especially if legislators shirked their responsibility to protect minorities.[20]

But in the era of the Maine Law, the discussion of majority rule and minority rights became more open-ended as a much larger group regularly turned to the rhetoric of majority tyranny and minority rights to crucify prohibition. As the moral minorities combating Sunday laws and race regulations had done, antiprohibitionists questioned whether popular majorities actually supported prohibition, and they routinely claimed that the public was in no way ready for such a draconian measure. Nevertheless, they unabashedly tackled the repeated claims that prohibition was legitimate because it embodied the moral sense of the majority. To them, American democracy had to be more than majority rule. It had to guard against what prohibition so obviously was: the paradigmatic display of the "Tyranny of the Majority." As antiprohibitionists broadcast their arguments, they contributed mightily to making the dangers of majority rule a widespread and popular concern among ordinary Americans. As one incensed resident of Portland, Maine, put it, "The paradox, that Democracy is the straightest road to destruction, and that no tyranny is so terrible as that of a majority of a free people, never received a better illustration than it has here." Indeed, alcohol and the question of its prohibition, perhaps more than any other policy issue before the Civil War, brought home the perilous place of minority rights within America's burgeoning democracy.[21]

Notably, antiprohibitionist concerns about majority tyranny came from across the antiprohibitionist spectrum, knew no geographic boundaries, and had varied focuses. Opponents, for example, insisted that there were certain rights that democratic majorities could not touch. Alcohol consumption, Virginia's *Danville Register* argued, was one of those touchy moral questions "in which the minority have rights as well as the majority, and rights which a majority" could not be "trample upon." A correspondent to the *Detroit Free Press* agreed. Prohibition was clearly "subversive of equality of rights, and is as much a tyranny as though instituted by an individual, instead of a majority; for rights exist, irrespective of... majorities." Antiprohibitionists also suggested that the fate of America's democratic experiment was at stake. Illinois's *Anti-Prohibitionist* compared Maine-Lawism to ancient history and reminded readers that the leading causes of "the downfall of ancient Republics" was "a capricious and violent majority" violating "the rights of the minority." More than just defending their prized ability to drink beer, such German revolutionaries as Wilhelm Weitling condemned America's majorities for being more tyrannical than the worst despots of the Old World. Having just fled the extensive tyrannies of princes and monarchies in Europe, they keenly understood that even a majority tyranny, once begun, would be hard to stop. "Majorities," traveling antiprohibitionist G. J. Beebe warned, "may be as tyrannical as monarchs or oligarchies." Or they could be worse.[22]

Worse for Beebe was the redistribution of wealth. Like others defending the rights of moral minorities in the mid-nineteenth century, Beebe turned to this long-standing conservative bugaboo as he repudiated prohibitionist's strict majoritarianism. "Suppose a majority," he posited, "should vote in favor of an equal division of property, would it therefore be right and republican, to take the property earned by one man or his ancestors and give it to his indolent and profligate neighbors?" Certainly not, Beebe declared. And in no way should Americans, especially the many who cared about the sanctity of their present or future property rights, allow prohibitionist majorities to take away liquor dealers' hard-earned property. The precedent of majorities taking one form of property, Beebe insinuated, could authorize another, potentially greater taking and lead to social instability and democracy's destruction. Once again, the classic arguments against majority rule could be strategically deployed to aid moral minorities, and once again, moral minorities could transform the older arguments by making them applicable to new people and new situations. Nonetheless, arguments such as Beebe's, though in service of the antiprohibitionist cause, also bolstered the older position. Whether Beebe had any larger motives is unclear, but in strategically suggesting that no one in their right mind could countenance "an equal division of property," he, like others, helped normalize that position while limiting what some would see as democracy's capacity to promote economic justice. For antiprohibitionists, however, the economic justice that interested them was not a redistribution of wealth. It was their ability to operate their businesses and to purchase and consume alcohol unencumbered by a democratic state beholden to moral reformers and popular majorities.[23]

As with local option, many Democrats voted for and supported prohibition. Nonetheless, many others opposed it and again played a prominent role in criticizing absolute majority rule. Still the mouthpiece of the party, the *Democratic Review* again found reason to defend minorities, arguing that the Maine Law exposed how mere "principles" of liberty and "unprescriptible rights" were "a miserably insufficient shield against the strong arm of a rampant majority." Some Democrats, however, had problems with this line of argument. P. T. Barnum, the great American showman and longtime follower of Andrew Jackson, was among them. When the Democratic *Hartford Times* dubbed the Maine Law "a law which NO MAJORITY has any RIGHT to pass," Barnum took issue. "Does not democracy," he asked in a public appeal, "declare that the majority shall govern, and that the minority shall peaceably abide by the laws enacted by a majority?" This was, after all, not only the regular refrain of prohibitionists but also the creed Andrew Jackson had announced at the birth of the Democratic Party. "Does any democrat suppose," Barnum asked, "that the good old democratic *Hartford Times*, as it was conducted twenty-five years ago, would have put forth such principles as those above quoted, and de-clared [sic] them to be the principles of '*democracy?*'" So miffed was Barnum that he abandoned the Democratic Party and eventually joined the Republicans. To other Democrats, however, Barnum and the prohibitionists missed the important caveats in the democratic creed. "We agree," the *Democratic Review* explained, that American democracy "must be found in the voice of the majority." It needed to be "controlled and checked, however, by certain fixed forms and limitations—otherwise individuals would have no freedom, and minorities would enjoy no rights." Whether Democrats or not, antiprohibitionists, like other antebellum moral minorities, would look to state constitutions to provide those limitations and to protect their freedom.[24]

In this climactic moment in the grand struggle with the new moral majority, some antiprohibitionists drawn to think about the nature of American democracy in the Maine Law era probed even deeper and condemned the power of the temperance crusade in political life. Early on in the fight, businessmen in New York produced an important pamphlet that ridiculed the Maine Law as a clear "despotism of the popular majority" and urged all Americans to consider whether "the power of the majority over the minority, in this country, [was] unlimited?" They also, however, reminded their countrymen of the engine behind prohibition—the rise of reform associations and their influential tactics. Though not constituting "a controlling majority in our popular elections," the *Appeal* argued, reformers were able to "create one, by adding their votes in concert, in behalf of any public candidate whom they may deign to favor." This "balance of power" approach to lobbying, in their view, had corrupted normal democratic processes and facilitated democratic despotism. The "rapid growth and political perversion" of reform societies, they concluded, was "the most alarming and ominous development that has yet appeared in our grand experiment in self-government." The resultant prohibitory laws proved Alexis de Tocqueville's admonition in *Democracy in America* that "*the unlimited authority of the majority*" might destroy "*the free institutions of America.*"[25]

Curiously enough, Tocqueville had lauded associational life and American's "freedom of association" as "a necessary guarantee against the tyranny of the majority." Several decades later, however, antiprohibitionists were revising Tocqueville as they theorized about American democracy while experiencing its workings on the ground. Associations, they protested, had facilitated majority tyranny. Notably, they did not call for such associational life to be outlawed or for democracy to be abandoned. Tocqueville might have missed the potential of association-driven despotism, but he had correctly sensed the power of associations to protect minority rights. Indeed, in conjunction with the popular antiprohibitionism and finally antimajoritarianism that they had helped to spur, alcohol-peddling entrepreneurs embraced the "freedom of association" to wage an industry-wide defense. Just as black activists were elaborating a specific organizational form—the rights association—to defeat segregation, liquor dealers turned to specialized associations to defend their rights as a distinct minority. It was a pivotal moment not only for the political organization of the alcohol industry but also for the broader maturation of minority-rights politics that was occurring in the 1850s.[26]

Liquor dealers' organizational efforts, of course, built upon the work of those who opposed local option in the 1840s. The rise of absolute prohibition, however, convinced dealers both that such ad hoc responses would not suffice and that the party system, especially the Democratic Party, could not adequately protect their interests. Formal and "permanent" institutions "without regard to party, creed, or sect" were needed to pressure partisan politicians and to guard against hostile legislation and relentless

reformers. Their associations went by many names. In California, industry leaders formed the Anti Maine Liquor Law Club, while Pennsylvanians
joined "Liquor Leagues." Cincinnati's brewers, winemakers, and liquor
dealers mixed in a Free Traders Association. Delawareans created a Liquor
Dealer's Association and invited "all persons opposed to sumptuary laws,
and all persons possessing a property interest in the sale of liquors, to concert together and mutually agree upon the measures to be taken hereafter,
more effectually to protect our property and preserve our civil liberties
from the destructive consequences of the misrule of a Maine Law despotism." By 1855, the proliferation of these institutions could not be missed.
From the other side of the Atlantic, the London *Patriot* reported that "the
Liquor Excitement was increasingly rapidly throughout the United States,
and in all the cities and large towns the liquor dealers were organizing
associations."[27]

These associations brought together a cross section of the alcohol
industry: large dealers and small dealers; native-born owners of high-end
hotels and immigrant operators of breweries and corner grog shops; real
estate moguls who rented space to liquor-based establishments and their
tenants who ran groceries and beer gardens. Or as the *Boston Times* put
it, they included "the millionaire importer down to the three-cent dealer."
Their joint interest in squashing prohibition united business competi-
tors, cut across ethnic and religious identities, and blurred lines of party
affiliation, though wet Democrats again remained prominent. Their mode
of organization followed a general trend. The brewers and dealers who
formed the Wisconsin Free Trade Society in 1853, for example, crafted a
constitution that outlined the association's goals, the structure of their
organization, and the responsibilities of officers and members. Members
paid an initiation fee and agreed to pay weekly dues. Prohibitionists ridiculed such associations as akin to "organizations among thieves, gamblers
and counterfeiters" but nonetheless recognized, as the *Chicago Tribune*
did, that they were "a mighty power to contend against." That was their
purpose. To the liquor interest and the larger antiprohibitionist minority
they represented, these associations seemed a reasonable way to protect
their personal and collective freedom.[28]

Once organized, these "avowedly political association[s]" employed a
single-issue, pressure politics of their own. In the several states where
prohibition was to be decided by referendums, liquor forces actively cam-
paigned to keep their states wet, but more generally, they entered the
fragmented partisan arena to lobby for their cause. Mimicking the style

of their temperance adversaries, they demanded that sitting legislators oppose prohibition and questioned candidates of all parties about their prohibitionist proclivities. They would, the dealers of Albany, New York, resolved, "support no man, by our votes or influence…who will lend himself to such absurd and unconstitutional enactments." In some areas, dealers assembled their own tickets composed of candidates "of whatever party" and urged members to toe the anti-Maine Law party line. Their efforts forced politicians and party organizations to take antiprohibitionist sentiment seriously and, when successful, typically garnered the most consistent support from wet Democrats eager to repudiate prohibition and to earn the immigrant vote. Their pressure, however, would also make many Republicans weary of prohibition.[29]

The industry's preemptive efforts did not always succeed in staving off prohibition. As state after state followed Maine's example, dealers' activities intensified and their associations, if they had been created earlier, became instantly popular as a once-imagined threat became imminent. The thrust of their political engagement also noticeably shifted away from lobbying and elections and toward questioning the constitutionality of Maine Laws in formal courts and in the court of public opinion. Since the birth of the Maine Law, antiprohibitionists had raised constitutional objections and gone to court, but the fullest and most broadly publicized effort developed throughout the state of New York in 1855. There liquor dealers had organized during the local option episode, and they reenergized in 1851 at the dawn of the Maine Law era. But in the months between prohibition's enactment in April 1855 and its implementation on the Fourth of July, interest in the associations exploded. Cities and small towns throughout the state sported their own societies, and in New York City, dealers organized by ward and held nightly meetings. Members poured in at such a high rate, the supportive *New York Herald* reported, that it was "impossible to transact any other business." The associations, however, quickly managed to do what antisegregationists often had difficulty doing in their crusades for minority rights—raise immense sums of money to establish a legal defense fund. And the nation was watching. As the *Atlanta Daily Intelligencer* reported in April 1855, New York was "the battle ground where the hottest contest" over prohibition "will be waged." The future of Maine Laws hung in the balance.[30]

Dealers could not challenge New York's Maine Law in court until someone was actually arrested, so in the months before implementation, they raised constitutional objections in the court of public opinion. Making use of their extensive funds, they solicited opinions at the rumored price tag of $1,000 from prominent lawyers and jurists who condemned Maine Laws as unconstitutional and predicted that high courts would inevitably declare them void. Dealers published these opinions in newspapers, including German-language papers, and the Albany-based Metropolitan Society for the Protection of Private and Constitutional Rights assembled over thirteen opinions in a lengthy pamphlet and distributed it widely. These efforts saturated public discourse with constitutional arguments about search and seizure, property rights, the due process of law, and the meaning of various state constitutional provisions and their relationship to New York's Maine Law. As the Irish-American *Citizen* reported, "The constitutionality of the Prohibitory Liquor Law continues to be the all absorbing subject of discussion and conjecture in this State." Prohibitionists sneered that "hawk-eyed lawyers" would write just about anything for the right fee, but nonetheless, by the time prohibition went into effect, dealers had made its constitutionality an open question. As one Boston paper described, "The opinions of lawyers...adverse to the constitutionality of the law, have operated to embarrass proceedings, and will prevent the full execution of the [Maine Law] until a final decision is obtained from the duly constituted judicial authorities."[31]

The other essential use of liquor dealers' joint funds was to obtain decisions against prohibition in the courts. Part of their strategy was to "clog" the court system with "liquor cases" to prevent "all other business," but they chiefly sought to "test the constitutionality" of the state's Maine Law. As in the age's other minority-rights crusades, test cases required planning and agreement on tactics. Dealers got to work "skillfully perfecting their organizations" and committed themselves to civil disobedience—to selling in the face of the law. To educate their various members, the Law Committee of the New York General Liquor Dealers' Association "issued a circular of instructions to the various liquor dealers of the City" detailing the actions to be taken if an enforcement attempt was made against them. The instructions were designed to ensure that causes for legal action would exist after an arrest was made and also that public officers were treated "with respect" and without violence. "Such conduct," the committee wrote, was "reprehensible and impolitic." If members stopped selling liquor once prohibition took effect or violently resisted enforcement, they did so "under pain of being expelled."[32]

The threat of expulsion exposed the internally coercive aspects of dealers' minority-rights politics and the marked lack of individualism inherent in their collective crusade. Expulsion meant a loss of one's investment in the association and also the inability to access the associations' legal defense fund. Liquor associations used their financial resources to hire "eminent counsel" and to pay bail and other court costs. In this way, all members had an interest in the arrest, fine, and imprisonment of any members. All members obviously had an interest in the outcome of litigation, especially as cases were appealed to the state high courts. All of these activities were not done in secret but rather were national news. When the dealers in Buffalo, for example, agreed to continue selling alcohol "and if prosecuted to carry the matter to the Courts," papers as far off as Georgia reported it.[33]

Throughout the Maine Law era, businessmen went to court to challenge prohibitory laws with mixed success, but by 1855, they had turned it into a highly organized affair. In New York, the two most important cases appealed to the Court of Appeals were born of liquor dealers' grass-roots minority-rights politics. *People v. Toynbee* featured Thomas Toynbee, the owner of Toynbee's Hotel in Brooklyn and the president of the Kings County Liquor Dealers' Association. *Wynehamer v. The People* might have begun simply with the sale of a glass of brandy at James G. Wynehamer's bar. More plausibly, it originated with the association of German and American liquor dealers, distillers, grocers, and brewers who combined in Buffalo to challenge prohibition. Both Toynbee and Wynehamer did as liquor dealers' associations directed: they sold alcohol in the face of the prohibitory law, accepted arrest without hostility, and set the wheels of the legal defense fund in motion.[34]

After obtaining contradictory rulings in the lower courts, the New York Court of Appeals heard both cases on appeal and ultimately declared the prohibitory law unconstitutional. Elected as part of the anti-immigrant and prohibitionist Know-Nothing Party, Judge George F. Comstock might have been expected to uphold the law, but instead he authored the lead opinion voiding it. Joined by the Court's Democrats, Comstock announced in his *Wynehamer* opinion that alcohol was a species of property "as much entitled to the protection of the constitution as lands, houses or chattels of any description." Turning to the state constitutional provision stipulating that "no persons shall be deprived of life, liberty or property without due process of law," Comstock ruled that the state legislature had overstepped the "constitutional limits of the legislative power." It had denied due process by annihilating "the value of property"—property in liquor—that was previously legal. The constitution, Comstock reasoned, was "intended

188MORAL MINORITIES

expressly to shield private rights from the exercise of arbitrary power." The Court must protect "the essential right of the citizen to his property"—liquor dealers as well as land moguls—by exercising judicial review.[35]

It was a great victory for the liquor dealers and a major blow for temperance activists. New York's first experiment with prohibition officially ended and most other Maine Law states followed down the path of repeal. The decision implicitly validated dealers' mode of minority-rights advocacy and explicitly endorsed their overall democratic ideology that emphasized constitutional limits to majority rule. Comstock said as much in his opinion in *Wynehamer*. The state constitution, he wrote, protected

> the sanctity of private property, as against theories of public good, eminently applicable to our own condition and times. In a government like ours, theories of public good or public necessity may be so plausible, or even so truthful, as to command popular majorities. But whether truthful or plausible merely, and by whatever numbers they are assented to, there are some absolute private rights beyond their reach, and among these the constitution places the right of property.

Comstock conceded that liquor was dangerous and that prohibitionists had laudable intentions. Nonetheless, he saw greater dangers in a democratic government that gave unlimited power to the sentiments of "popular majorities." The position that antiprohibitionists had advanced since the dawn of the Maine Law era—that certain rights existed regardless of the whims of majorities—now had the assent of one of the nation's most influential high courts.[36]

Support came in Indiana as well. There associated dealers scored the era's other major judicial victory against prohibition. In *Beebe v. State*, Samuel E. Perkins, a Democrat, declared that constitutional restrictions on legislatures existed "to protect the minority from the oppression of the majority." Perhaps even more than Comstock, Perkins suggested that Indiana's Maine Law exposed new concerns with majority tyranny, even though the protection of property—the classic concern with tyrannical majorities—was still at the heart of the constitutionalism that protected minorities. "It is easy to see," he wrote, "that when the people are smarting under losses from depreciated bank paper, a feeling might be aroused, that would...return a majority to the legislature which would declare all banks a nuisance, confiscate their paper and the buildings from which it issued."

Such a direct assault of the needy majority on the wealthy minority, he implied, would obviously be unconstitutional. Perkins declared, however, that "the same constitution...protects the dealer in beer." In other words, there were different species of property worthy of constitutional protection, and there were different types of majorities that could threaten property rights. If moral majorities endangered the property of moral minorities, the courts rightly interfered to uphold constitutional protections.[37]

Comstock, Perkins, and other jurists likely had more than beer in mind. As they were crafting their decisions, the contentious issue of slavery was upending national politics, had sparked a bloody civil war in Kansas, and had given rise to a new sectional, antislavery party, the Republican Party. Popular antislavery majorities preaching free soil and threatening slaveholders' peculiar property rights, they no doubt believed, could threaten the survival of Union and thus, of American democracy itself. The extent to which the politics of slavery explicitly shaped their opinions in *Wynehamer* and *Beebe* is unclear. There is no doubt, however, that prohibition raised issues also fundamental to the slavery controversy—not least, majoritarian democracy's potential to destroy property rights. Again, the links are murky, but it was no accident that Chief Justice Roger Taney used the logic of substantive due process, which Comstock had used in *Wynehamer* to protect liquor dealers' rights, to protect slaveholders' rights in his *Dred Scott* decision the following year. Not surprisingly, the Democrats who applauded the end of prohibition were the loudest in preaching respect for the Supreme Court's *Dred Scott* decision.[38]

For the liquor dealers who had waged a defensive war against prohibition, their goal was not to produce a legal precedent that would help protect slaveholders' rights. Jurists might have taken that opportunity as a result of their resistance. But the proalcohol minority applauded Comstock's explicit limitation of "popular majorities" first and foremost because they had experienced the rapacious power of majoritarian democracy in the form of liquor prohibition. To them, America's constitutional democracy functioned properly when courts protected minorities. As one supporter explained, a "chance majority" had enacted New York's Maine Law "to oppress and severely injure a minority of the people of this State—namely, the liquor dealers." The dealers appealed to the Court of Appeals, whose members thankfully found prohibition "to be one of the cases where the rights of a minority were intended to be shielded by the constitution." That no subsequent legislature was "willing to pass another prohibitory law" proved the "wisdom" of the Court's decision. In New York, Indiana, and elsewhere, prohibitionists vehemently disagreed and again lobbied for legislatures to enshrine the supposed "will of the majority"—prohibitionism—in law. Theirs would be an uphill battle.[39]

In the meantime, organized liquor dealers showed few signs of disbanding, even as legislators—both Democrats and Republicans—proved unwilling to reenact prohibition in the late antebellum period. For all the temperance talk about the reprehensible existence of a Rum Power in public life, if such a force existed prior to the Maine Law era, it initially proved underequipped to handle the powerful prohibitionists. Yet Maine Laws, if they failed to eradicate alcohol consumption, ironically succeeded in forcing proalcohol interests to unite in new, powerful ways—ways that gave the constitutional rights of minorities a prominent place in public discussion. In the aftermath of prohibition, these businessmen would remain organized and continue to advocate for their rights as a vulnerable minority. And prohibition was not the only threat. When the New York legislature passed a restrictive license law in 1857, the dealers knew exactly what to do. They met, raised money, voiced opposition, employed counsel to challenge "the constitutionality of the law," determined to sell in violation of the law, and agreed that members who were arrested would be defended by the association. Believing that their "interests" were "of more importance than the mere gratification of party pride and party success," they looked past party allegiances to lobby for a just license law. Liquor dealer associations and their tactics proliferated through the remainder of the nineteenth century. They continued to figure prominently in continuing the tradition of popular minority-rights politics and making it a core component of American democracy.[40]

TWO YEARS AFTER New York's Court of Appeals declared prohibition unconstitutional, the California Supreme Court decided the fate of its state's Sunday law. For some time Protestant moralists had demanded that the Christian Sabbath be guarded from the bustle of the Gold Rush, and in 1858 the legislature responded by banning a range of business activity on Sundays. Among the first to be arrested for violating the new law was M. Newman, a Jewish clothier in Sacramento. Newman appealed his conviction to California's highest court, arguing that the Sunday law violated the state constitution's protections of religious liberty and property rights. Two of three judges agreed. Responding to claims that the law for "the better observance of the Sabbath" merely established a secular day of rest, they held that the legislature, by forcing citizens to stop working

Sundays, had infringed upon their "right to acquire property." Believing, however, that the law fundamentally established "a compulsory religious observance," the Court also declared that the legislature had violated "as much the religious freedom of the Christian as of the Jew." "If there be a single individual in the State who professes a particular faith," Justice Burnett proclaimed, "he is as much within the sacred protection of the Constitution as if he agreed with the great majority of his fellow-citizens."[41]

Newman was able to do what those who had battled Sunday laws the previous decade had been unable to do: convince a state high court to protect the rights of religious and moral minorities by declaring Sunday legislation unconstitutional. It was an important moment, and veterans of the earlier fight were elated. The freethinking *Boston Investigator* was glad to see its view of Sunday laws finally endorsed by a state high court. The editors of the Seventh Day Baptist *Sabbath Recorder* enthusiastically covered the victory, as did Jewish leader Isaac Leeser. By 1858, this old guard was joined by a growing chorus of increasingly vociferous opponents of Sunday laws. Germans in Utica, New York, for example, praised the California court for offering "other States a worthy example." In Cincinnati, Isaac Mayer Wise, German immigrant and rising leader of American Reformed Judaism, proudly broadcast the decision in his newspaper, the *Israelite*. In Brooklyn, an anti-Sunday law activist named J. L. Hatch invited the "friends of Civil and Religious Liberty" to attend his discourse commemorating the decision.[42]

The expansion of dissent was also evident on the streets of Sacramento where saloon-keepers, shopkeepers, cigar dealers, and barbers eagerly joined a procession to celebrate the Court's ruling, for Newman's fight had been theirs. Members of these trades had followed the trend popularized by liquor dealers during the Maine Law era and formed special associations, raised money, and hired attorneys. Newman, in fact, had "thrown himself into the breach to test" the constitutionality of the Sunday law not merely for other Jews but "on behalf of the traders in his line."[43] Liquor dealers were especially involved. The American association and the German association in San Francisco combined into "a permanent society" and agreed to use joint funds to defend themselves from prosecution. It probably came as no surprise that attorney Solomon Heydenfeldt argued Newman's case. Not only was he Jewish and a former member of the California Supreme Court, but he had previously agreed to represent the liquor dealers when they tested the Sunday law. As it turned out, Newman's suit rendered their effort unnecessary.[44]

Driving all of this action was yet another era of contested Sunday sur-veillance that had emerged not just in California but throughout the nation. Since the late 1840s, Sunday enforcers had initiated bouts of enforcement, including several that occurred amid the Know-Nothing ascendancy of the mid-1850s. But the real action occurred later in the decade as the demise of both Know-Nothingism and prohibition sent nativists, temper-ance reformers, evangelical clergymen, and other elite and middle-class Protestants looking for other ways to institute moral order. Catalyzed by the economic panic of 1857, a burst of religious revivalism, and various local contexts, these citizens reorganized the Sabbath reform and lobbied authorities to enforce Sunday laws. As in California, their efforts sparked resistance from a diverse group who preferred that they be left free to spend Sundays as they pleased. The ensuing conflict gave rise to what contemporaries regularly called "The Sunday Question." As a correspon-dent to the *New York Times* wrote in 1859, "In New-York, Philadelphia, Baltimore, Chicago, St. Louis and elsewhere, the inevitable Slavery ques-tion yields place to Sunday matters."[45]

As they had for decades, Sabbath reformers looked to the protection of the Christian Sabbath as the key to ensuring the popular religiosity and morality essential for the survival of their "free, Christian, and Protestant nation." And in the late 1850s, it seemed that the Sabbath was again under assault. Much on their long list of concerns was familiar, but it reflected the continued urbanization, cultural diversification, and economic mod-ernization of American society. Instead of a day of worship, rest, and quiet contemplation, reformers protested, Sunday was becoming a day of rau-cous amusement, gratuitous commerce and travel, and general debauch-ery lubricated by alcohol. Shouting news-venders hawked Sunday papers often a stone's throw from churches. Manufacturing and printing establish-ments continued to operate. Young men raced horses through the streets and noisily paraded fire engines. Steamboats, railroads, and streetcars enticed "city rowdies and pleasure-seekers" to crisscross cities and to dis-turb the peace of "suburban villages." Businesses remained open, includ-ing the groceries, taverns, and grog shops frequented by immigrants and workers. The German fondness for beer, music, and heterosocial Sunday leisure was conspicuously displayed at the theaters and gardens that pro-liferated during the 1850s (fig. 6.4). To make matters worse, their owners scandalously employed "pretty waiter girls" and flaunted their "attrac-tions" in sensational advertisements. A steppingstone to more shocking vices, Sabbath-breaking would spell national Armageddon if not quelled.[46]

A GERMAN BEER GARDEN IN NEW YORK CITY ON SUNDAY EVENING.

FIGURE 6.4 *A German Beer Garden in New York City on Sunday Evening* from *Harper's Weekly*, October 15, 1859. Courtesy of The Library Company of Philadelphia. To Sabbath reformers and their allies, German beer gardens were spaces of immorality, especially when men, women, children, and alcohol mixed in them on Sundays. To German immigrants, beer gardens were essential leisure spaces and a key part of the cultural heritage that they brought to America.

Following the usual pattern, reformers organized associations, initiated public-opinion campaigns, urged good Protestants to vote only for "Sabbath-honoring legislators," and petitioned city officials and state legislatures to protect the Sabbath.[47] As they unabashedly pushed authorities to enforce Sunday bans on recreation, drink, travel, and business, they again turned to arguments about the Christian nation and majority rule. Elected officials often mimicked their rhetoric. As one Pennsylvania legislative committee declared, "We are a Christian people, and not a Mohammedan, a Pagan, or an atheistic people." The Christian majority had the privilege of legal protection "in the exercise of their religious rights." Indeed, Sunday laws were especially proper in a government that "recognizes the will of the majority as its fundamental law." Minorities, once again, needed to obey.[48]

Especially as officials heeded the calls of reformers, foes of the Sabbath reform sprang to action, holding protest meetings, raising objections in

print, and petitioning officials to repeal the Sunday laws. As with popular antiprohibitionism, this grass-roots movement mobilized a substantial and socially varied lot and revealed the rising popularization and
diversification of minority-rights politics that was occurring in the 1850s.
At a meeting called in Philadelphia, for example, some 15,000 persons
attended "without distinction of party" and cheered as "The Quaker, the
German, the Jew and the professional man all stood upon the platform
and severally denounced the present Sunday enactments." The diversity of opposition exposed one of the leading arguments against Sunday
laws: mandating strict Sabbath-keeping was antiquated in an increasingly
pluralistic society. The *Revue de l'Ouest*, a French-language newspaper, for
example, argued that St. Louis had "a cosmopolitan character, a little more
German than Yankee, a little more European than American, a little more
skeptic than Presbyterian, a little more given to laughter than bigoted and
fanatic." Sunday laws were especially inappropriate in such environments
and clearly would never work.[49]

Opponents also protested inconsistent enforcement and Protestant
hypocrisy. How was it, the *Baltimore Sun* asked, that "negroes and boys"
were arrested "for pitching cents and playing cards on Sundays" while "the
systematic operations of the professional gambler" were permitted seven
days a week? Where, in other words, were the priorities of reformers and
municipal governments? Others protested that Sunday laws specifically
targeted the working classes. In Cincinnati, where reformers sought to
halt omnibuses on Sundays, opponents protested that such a move "would
put the poor to a disadvantage as compared with the rich." Unless Sunday
laws were equally "enforced against the coachman who drives the rich
man's carriage, the cook who roasts his Sunday turkey, and the housemaid
who makes the beds on that day," they should not be enforced against the
working classes. Radical abolitionists, who had their hands full in the late
1850s, remained fairly quiet during this round of the Sunday question.
Some nonetheless lambasted "the great evangelical fraternity" for again
concerning themselves with Sabbath-keeping while remaining relatively
indifferent to the truly great moral question of the day—slavery.[50]

Once again, opponents protested that Sunday laws were an affront to
civil liberties, religious freedom, the separation of church and state, and
constitutional protections of equal religious rights. Sunday laws, as one
Chicagoean put it, were "a remnant of Theocratical Government," constituted "a State Religion in the United States, notwithstanding the Bill of
Rights and the Declaration of Independence," and violated the "Liberty of

conscience, of Personal Liberty and Happiness, of Freedom of Trade, and of the Right of Every Man to his Labor." German residents of Lafayette, Indiana, similarly resolved that this "meddling of the State with church matters" contradicted "the Constitution of this country" and "the interests of a Republican form of Government."[51]

As Jews and Seventh Day Baptists had the previous decade, the widening opposition also mounted an explicit constitutional defense of their rights as minorities and again asked the public to consider the proper limits to majority rule. Germans in Davenport, Iowa, for example, took issue with the "friends of the Sunday law" for insisting "that the majority must rule." Far from absolute, majority rule, they held, needed to harmonize with the Iowa Constitution's command that prohibited the state legislature from making laws "respecting an establishment of religion, or prohibiting free exercise thereof." Invoking Thomas Jefferson, they argued that this provision "intended an entire *separation of the church and the State*" and banned the state from interfering "*with religious duties*" that were properly left "to the *consciences* of the citizens." As other moral minorities had done, these Iowans offered hypotheticals "if the rule of the majority were unrestrained and unlimited": a Catholic majority might mandate "kneeling, or prohibiting the use of meat on Friday"; a Jewish majority might command the observance of their Saturday Sabbath, require "circumcision," or prohibit "the eating of bacon." Fortunately, however, the state constitution protected religious freedom and thus kept Iowans' Saturdays free, their diets flexible, and their penises intact. The same constitution should guarantee free Sundays, even if the majority supported restrictions.[52]

Anti-Sunday law activism and linked debates over majority rule emerged throughout the North and parts of the urban South, but New York City became a national focal point. There the nationally influential and well-financed New York Sabbath Committee (NYSC) initiated the action. This group counted prominent members of the "bench, bar and pulpit, and the commercial...classes" among its members. President Norman White, for example, was a New England–born Presbyterian who had prospered in paper manufacturing among other business enterprises. A former Whig state senator and self-appointed steward of the city, Recording Secretary James W. Beekman had gained his substantial real estate fortune the old-fashioned way: he inherited it. No doubt these elites saw in the Sabbath crusade not only a way to honor their maker but also a way to protect the value of their fortunes from the threat of urban disorder. With municipal government dominated by Democrats and generally beholden to unruly

immigrant voters, the NYSC took advantage of a controversial development in the city's policing. In 1857, the upstate Republican-controlled
state legislature passed the Metropolitan Police Act, which created a police
force for New York administered by state appointees. Locals protested
this invasion on home rule, and after Mayor Fernando Wood mustered a
municipally controlled police force, a "municipal civil war" erupted. The
unrest helped legitimate the NYSC's demands, but more importantly,
reformers lobbied the Metropolitan Police to do what they were charged to
do: enforce the Sunday laws.[53]

The NYSC elicited the ire of many New Yorkers but perhaps no one
more than J. L. Hatch. A Congregationalist clergyman, Hatch had fallen
out of favor with more than one congregation for preaching the desirabil-
ity of "Christians engaging in dancing and other amusements," suggesting that the Sabbath was "intended as a day of recreation," and opposing
Sunday laws. With views too liberal for most Congregationalists, Hatch
was disciplined for "errors in doctrinal belief" and eventually expelled from
the pastorate.[54] In the meantime he found a new calling as New York's
(and perhaps the nation's) leading challenger of Sunday laws. In 1858,
he founded a landmark rights organization—the American Society for
Promoting Civil and Religious Liberty (ASPCRL)—which was nonde-
nominational and nonpartisan in orientation. The society was necessary,
Hatch explained, because "civil and religious liberty" were consistently
endangered by so-called reformers who sought "to secure the adoption
and enforcement by government of their peculiar views respecting Sunday
observance, temperance and other vexed questions of religion and morality, upon which the community is divided." Like the era's other emergent
minority-rights associations, the ASPCRL aimed to grow its membership
and to influence public opinion and policymakers. Hatch organized meetings and lectures, published letters in newspapers, and circulated a free
pamphlet that argued that the Sabbath was "a festival appointed for recreation and enjoyment" (fig. 6.5). He also challenged reformers to debate
the issue of Sunday laws (they declined) and lobbied the commissioners of
Central Park to schedule musical performances on Sundays.[55]

In just over a year, Hatch amassed over one thousand followers and
had gained the backing of the *New York Herald*, which had supported
antiprohibitionists and not coincidentally published a controversial
Sunday edition. In 1859, the ASPCRL countered the NYSC's petitions to
the Metropolitan Police with a lengthy remonstrance of their own that
cited the California Supreme Court's decision in *Ex Parte Newman* and

FIGURE 6.5 J. L. Hatch, *Sunday Laws* (New York, 1859). Courtesy of the Library of Congress. Those attending anti-Sunday law meetings sang J. L. Hatch's songs that mocked Sunday laws as archaic and unfit for a modern, pluralistic America.

urged authorities not to enforce the "unconstitutional" Sunday laws. The document was signed by 750 Germans and Jews and 550 native-born Americans, including such cultural leaders as Charles Shaum, a German Lutheran minister; prominent Seventh Day Baptists William B. Maxson (fig. 6.6.) and George B. Utter; and Wilhelm Kopp, the editor of the *New-Yorker Demokrat.*[56] The polyglot ASPCRL was soon joined by a second grass-roots association—the German Association for Resisting All Arbitrary Sunday and Prohibitory Laws (GARASPL)—directed by Andreas Willmann, a future leader of New York's German Republicans, and attorney John J. Freedman, and composed "mostly of proprietors of lager bier saloons." This association's emergence reflected the fact that Germans had become a chief target of Sabbath enforcers and highlighted the essential role the growing German community—Protestants, Jews, Catholics, and freethinkers; Democrats and Republicans—played in the anti-Sunday law movement in New York and elsewhere.[57]

The GARASPL also reflected rising divisions among alcohol-purveying entrepreneurs in New York that were exacerbated by Sunday laws. The liquor dealer associations that repelled the Maine Law had included Germans and non-Germans, and in other locales (as, for example, in California) these interethnic groups battled Sunday laws. After 1857, however, the New York associations were beset with infighting and had their hands full combating the draconian license law and the continued threat of prohibition. Members had no love for Sunday laws and had little intention of adhering to their strictures, but with a more dangerous threat of prohibition still looming, they proved at first unwilling to risk damaging the antiprohibitionist cause by publicly challenging the Sunday laws. German lager-beer purveyors, who were especially sensitive to Sunday interference, moved into the vacuum, mobilized New York's substantial German community, and sought to contest the Sunday laws "by every legal means" possible.[58]

The ASPCRL's and GARASPL's joint campaign began with a well-publicized mass meeting in September 1859 that invited citizens opposed to Sunday laws—men and women, regardless of "sect or party"—to Volks Garden in the Bowery. German men dominated the crowd, but Jews and Seventh Day Baptists as well as members of the French and Italian communities also made a showing. Combining "pleasure with business," attendees heard music, drank beer, and smoked meerschaums and cigars. They also chose officers and listened to speeches (in both English and German) that condemned Sabbath

FIGURE 6.6   William B. Maxson. From the archives of the Seventh Day Baptist Historical Society, Janesville, WI. Prominent minister William B. Maxson represented the Seventh Day Baptists in New York's anti-Sunday law crusade during the late 1850s.

reformers and Sunday laws, defended religious freedom, and called for limits to majority rule. The crowd approved a lengthy set of resolutions that demanded the repeal of the Sunday laws and applauded the decision of the California Supreme Court. Notably, the group also adopted the Seventh Day Baptist's *Appeal to the Friends of Equal Rights and Religious Freedom*, first published in 1846 during the earlier contestation over Sunday legislation, as the sentiment of the meeting. Attendees committed themselves to continued activism and legal resistance, and future public meetings would help sustain the popular wing of the movement. Meanwhile, a special committee would spearhead the group's lobbying effort.[59]

A new legal development in the spring of 1860 changed the landscape of the anti-Sunday law crusade. At the behest of reformers, the Republican-dominated state legislature passed a new law banning theatrical performances on Sundays. Sabbath reformers had long tar-geted Sunday performances as a particularly bothersome vice, and they fumed that theater owners skirted the Sunday laws by billing their events as "sacred concerts." The new measure meant to close the loophole and stipulated a substantial $500 fine.[60] It spawned new associational activity among German theatrical managers, heightened critical commentary in the German-language press, spurred new attempts to evade the law, and brought a spate of arrests that led to several highly publicized legal cases in New York and Brooklyn.[61]

At the center of the controversy was Gustav Lindenmuller, a former German revolutionary, an outspoken opponent of the Maine Law, an avid Republican, and the owner of the Odeon Theater in the Bowery. In the aftermath of the new law, Lindenmuller not only led fellow the-ater managers in planning resistance, which included taxing the sale of beer to form a legal defense fund. He also instituted a new tactic at the Odeon. He hung a sign near the entrance that identified his theater as the meeting house for the "German Shaker Association," whose mem-bers worshipped with dramatic performances and beer. The *Tribune* described their rituals:

> The worshippers, both male and female, instead of sitting uprightly and reverently in conventional church-ships, were sitting face to face around altars, very similar in structure and usage to the wooden tables usually found in lager beer saloons, partaking of an amber-colored fluid from broad-bottomed goblets, listening to music discoursed by a brass band in the chancel, and only shaking with hearty Scandinavian laughter.

To Lindenmuller and his congregants, this was not that unlike the Catholics who legally worshipped "with organ, incense, full bands of music, and every ceremony of pomp and splendor which mortal imagination can con-ceive." Why couldn't the German Shakers form their own religion just as "the Seventh Day Baptists, the Jews, and the Shakers" had? Despite the self-proclaimed religious nature of his theater, Lindenmuller was arrested and served with an injunction to cease all Sunday performances. His "test case" would be the New York anti-Sunday law movement's most impor-tant. Newspapers across America followed these battles closely, and, as before, minority rights became the theater of American democracy.[62]

Lindenmuller appealed his conviction to the Supreme Court of New York and challenged the constitutionality of the Sunday Theater Law. His prominent attorney, James T. Brady, cited *Ex Parte Newman* and maintained that the law violated the New York state constitution's guarantees of "the free exercise and enjoyment of religious profession and worship." Pointing to *Wynehamer v. The People*, Brady also argued that the law violated Lindenmuller's property rights because it impeded his ability to earn money on the most profitable day of the week. The Court disagreed. The judges dismissed the suggestion that Lindenmuller's German Shaker Association was a legitimate religion, and they generally ignored arguments about property rights. Echoing the long-standing defense of Sunday laws, the Court found that because the law mandated no compulsory "religious observance," it did not infringe upon Lindenmuller's religious freedom. The legislature had properly "restrained the people from secular pursuits and from practices...deemed hurtful to the morals and good order of society." It was similar, Justice Allen maintained, to laws banning gambling, lotteries, profanity, and polygamy, which rightly limited citizens' "natural rights" for society's benefit. The construction of religious freedom Lindenmuller proposed, he feared, would authorize a man to "go naked through the streets, establish houses of prostitution *ad libitum* and keep a faro-bank on every corner." Protecting Sunday laws from the anti-Sunday law crusade (and its brand of minority-rights activism) would keep Americans clothed and prevent American society from becoming a licentious den of sin.[63]

New York's opponents of Sunday laws might have appealed to the Court of Appeals, but the demands of the Civil War, which called militiaman Lindenmuller to service, interfered. To the glory of Sabbath reformers, *Lindenmuller v. The People* would remain the leading statement of the constitutionality of New York's Sunday laws. As the *Daily National Intelligencer* announced, this decision should be "highly satisfactory to all Christians and all right-minded citizens." The German theater opened "for German Jews and infidels" was rightly closed on Sundays.[64]

WITH THE CIVIL WAR raging in 1861, it seemed to the Seventh Day Baptists that the "Sunday Question" might subside. "Sunday," the editors of the *Sabbath Recorder* reported, "does not appear to receive much attention from 'the powers that be' in these times. Troops are shipped, barracks are built, and warlike operations generally are carried forward with as much vigor on Sunday as on any other day of the week." The demands of wartime would transform the American Sunday by accelerating the rise of industrial capitalism, but the battle over Sunday laws would nevertheless continue, even in rough-and-tumble California, where the state supreme court had declared the Sunday law unconstitutional. There, resolute reformers convinced the state legislature in 1861 to enact a new Sunday law. Liquor dealers promptly tested the new measure, and counter to its earlier decision, the Supreme Court ruled that the Act for the Observance of the Sabbath neither infringed upon the rights of religion or property as guaranteed by the state constitution. The San Francisco Sabbath Committee lauded the law—"enacted in obedience to the wishes of a large majority of our citizens, and confirmed by the highest judicial authority as constitutionally binding upon all the people"—as "an auspicious step in the Sabbath cause." War and reform now went hand in hand.[65]

Plenty of other Californians were outraged, including a Jewish lawyer named Joseph R. Brandon. Writing to the *Daily Alta California*, Brandon protested that the Sunday law was discriminatory, a violation of the "free exercise of religion," and an embarrassment to American boastings of "freedom and equality." Brandon could have left it at that, but instead he did what other moral minorities in the mid-nineteenth century had so often done: he made a more expansive argument that struck at the supposed ideological core of American democracy's golden age. Sunday laws represented not a free self-governing society but rather epitomized what was unfree about American democracy: "the power of majorities to oppress the minority." To bolster his indictment, Brandon might have chosen the words of James Madison or Alexis de Tocqueville. He might even have summoned British political theorist John Stuart Mill, who published *On Liberty* in 1859, which explored the problem of the "tyranny of the majority" within modern democracies. Showing the transatlantic impact of moral minorities' activism, Mill notably pointed to Maine Law prohibition and Sabbath legislation as two quintessential examples of majority tyranny.

Brandon, however, quoted from John Calhoun's posthumously published *Disquisition on Government*, which sought to remedy the problem of majority tyranny that was especially plaguing southern slaveholders and threatening the Union. This, of course, was not the first time that conservative, proslavery political thought had been mustered by antebellum opponents of moral regulations. Indeed, with Calhoun in his arsenal, Brandon fired back that whether actually supported by majorities or not, Sunday laws violated several state constitutional provisions that existed to protect the rights of "the *minority.*" In this case, the California Supreme Court had failed to interpret the state constitution to achieve that noble purpose. This unfortunate course of events, Brandon concluded, had proven John Calhoun correct: mere constitutional provisions would never sufficiently "prevent the major and dominant party in a State from abusing its powers." The Sunday law ordeal had made Brandon painfully aware of what *"feeble a shelter"* constitutional barriers provided *"the right of the minority"* from *"the shafts of fanaticism and bigotry."*[66]

By 1861, Calhoun's theories had shaped many white southerners' decision to secede from the Union in the aftermath of Lincoln's election. Calhoun and other white southerners had long feared for their peculiar property rights—their rights to own slaves—in the face of a growing national majority dedicated to free labor and hostile to slavery's expansion. With the White House to be inhabited by a northern Republican with known antislavery convictions, it would not be long, they surmised, before the federal government interfered with slavery. To slaveholders, secession and the formation of a new nation unequivocally committed to slavery seemed the best way to protect their rights as a minority. Their decision, of course, would do exactly the opposite, as Lincoln's war to preserve the Union transformed into a war of emancipation. The Thirteenth Amendment to the US Constitution would constitutionalize perhaps the largest single moment of property redistribution in the history of American democracy: taking slave property from white slave-owners and transferring it to freedmen and women as self-owning individuals. With the aid of secession and war, the classical danger of democracy—that a propertyless (in this case slave-less) majority would take and redistribute the property of the propertied minority—had finally come to significant fruition in the United States.

When turning to Calhoun in California, however, Brandon not only expressed little concern for slaveholders' rights but was also not advocating secession for Jews and the other minorities harmed by Sunday legislation. Indeed, rather than leaving democracy or hoping for its downfall, Brandon counseled vigilant minority-rights activism. He channeled the wisdom of other mid-nineteenth-century moral minorities, including Rabbi Isaac Mayer Wise, who had declared during debates over Sunday legislation that "liberty must be guarded by vigilance, and injustice must be repulsed by sound argument." As Brandon himself recognized, there was a "higher tribunal" than the California Supreme Court and to it Brandon appealed on behalf of "a large minority of citizens." He explained: "This tribunal is the sense of justice and right which subsists in the educated, intelligent and unprincipled mind, which often moulds public opinion; and where justice last lingers when it has been smothered or silenced in its public seats." Winning or losing in court was not the end of the battle for minority rights within American democracy. The question of minority rights was ultimately a fight for public opinion that required powerful ideas, activism, and vigilance directed at both the institutions of government as well as the people themselves. The battle for the rights of minorities was an eminently democratic battle. In the minds of moral minorities like Brandon, it was also a battle for democracy itself.[67]

By publishing his essay in a major newspaper—an essay reprinted in San Francisco's Jewish newspaper and Isaac Leeser's Philadelphia-based *Occident*—Brandon had joined this crusade for a democracy that respected minority rights. Others in California and beyond, even those who may have eschewed his provocative use of Calhoun, were nonetheless with Brandon. The San Francisco Association of Retail Liquor Dealers continued to agitate against Sunday laws, as did local cigar dealers and liquor dealers in Stockton and Sacramento. On the other side of the aisle of moral politics, the Sabbath reformers preaching majority rule pressed the state legislature to improve California's existing Sunday law. In the meantime, the New York Sabbath Committee organized a National Sabbath Convention in 1863 and called reformers from throughout the nation to devise means for promoting national Sabbath observance. The Sabbath Question was far from resolved, as was the battle between majority rule and minority rights.[68]

THE GRASS-ROOTS MINORITY-RIGHTS politics that had come of age before the Civil War established popular conflict between majority rule and minority rights as a defining attribute of American democracy. Struggles over Sunday laws, restrictive liquor regulations, and racial segregation— struggles born of the explosion of moral reform in the early nineteenth century—brought thousands of Americans into the public sphere to debate divisive policy questions, to consider limits to majority rule, and to join popular crusades for their rights. Liquor dealers and drinkers, racial egalitarians, Jews and Seventh Day Baptists, and the era's other everyday moral minorities played the most fundamental roles in these developments. By boldly resisting laws and practices they deemed oppressive and willfully defying the religious, temperate, and racist majorities of the day, they transformed minority rights from the comparatively narrow concern of propertied aristocrats, slaveholders, and intellectuals into the rallying cry of growing groups of socioeconomically diverse Americans. Indeed, by the onset of the Civil War, moral minorities had democratized America's countermajoritarian tradition. In the process, they developed political practices for defending the rights of minorities within democracy. Moral minorities used forceful rhetoric on behalf of legal and constitutional rights to shape public opinion and to influence policymakers and jurists. They created a new institutional form—the rights association—that worked outside of political parties and helped organize an array of grass-roots, rights-oriented political tactics. And, in key instances, their efforts had led to statutes and court rulings upon which later minority-rights activists would draw inspiration and build. These were major contributions to political practice in the "golden age" of American democracy. There would be no going back.

Epilogue

MAKING DEMOCRACY SAFE FOR MINORITIES

IN THE SUMMER of 2013, the US Supreme Court shot off its usual end-of-the-term fireworks. Among the controversial decisions that year were two dealing with same-sex marriage, an issue that had become one of the most hotly debated moral questions of the early twenty-first century. In *United States v. Windsor,* the Court invalidated the section of the federal Defense of Marriage Act (DOMA) that defined "marriage" as a "legal union between one man and one woman." A Republican-led Congress had passed the measure in 1996 to protect "traditional" marriage from the threat that some states might authorize same-sex marriage. President Bill Clinton, a Democrat, signed it into law. Seventeen years later, the US Supreme Court declared the law unconstitutional. Speaking for the Court's majority, Justice Anthony Kennedy declared that because the "purpose and effect" of DOMA was "to disparage and to injure" same-sex couples, it denied them "the equal protection of the laws" guaranteed by the liberty provision of the US Constitution's Fifth Amendment. The second case, *Hollingsworth v. Perry,* was decided on technical grounds. Citing issues of standing, the Court refused to rule on the constitutionality of Proposition 8, a California ballot initiative passed by voters in 2008 that prevented official use of the term "marriage" for same-sex unions. In effect, the Court's decision left in place the trial court's ruling that allowed two same-sex couples to marry.[1]

As news of the decisions quickly spread, the media and activists began making sense of the historic day within the recent battles over same-sex marriage as well as the longer history of the gay-rights movement. Cameras panned to the victorious litigants in the cases, their attorneys, and the activists who had assembled outside of the Supreme Court's chambers in Washington, DC. They also showed the reactions of patrons of New York's Stonewall Inn, the gay bar that in 1969 was the site of a public demonstration often credited with sparking the modern gay liberation movement. Meanwhile, celebrations erupted across the country and especially in historically gay neighborhoods, including Miami's South Beach, Chicago's Boystown, and San Francisco's Castro District, the neighborhood that had given rise to Harvey Milk, the nation's first openly gay politician. In a *New York Times* op-ed, activist historian George Chauncey reminded Americans that the decisions were the product of a long struggle for gay rights and also that marriage was neither the first nor the last issue that had and would continue to animate the movement.[2]

This response was correct, of course, but it was only the most immediate and narrow context with which to understand the rulings. The Court's decisions and the battle for gay rights were only some of the latest events in a much longer and broader history of popular minority-rights politics that had been a fixture of the American political tradition since the mid-nineteenth century. That history began when reformers injected divisive moral questions of right and wrong into American public life. Those questions prompted dissent and generated conflicts that exposed contrasting visions of the proper social and cultural contours of American society and of the role of the state in securing those visions. Indeed, the gay-rights activists of the twenty-first century had much in common not only with the mid-nineteenth-century racial egalitarians who fought pioneering battles against bans on interracial marriage, but also the minorities who challenged restrictive liquor and Sabbath regulations. Though the particular issues had changed, the grass-roots struggles over freedom and equality that stirred nineteenth-century democracy and those trying to live within it continued to operate in similar ways in the early twenty-first century.

Had the varied moral minorities of the mid-nineteenth century somehow been transported to the late twentieth and early twenty-first centuries, they would have been surprised by the issues of gay rights and same-sex marriage but otherwise would have found much that was familiar. Most obviously, they would have seen the same democratic tension between majority rule and minority rights—a tension again fueled by unmistakably moral issues—that was at the core of their struggles 150 years earlier.

The congressmen who backed DOMA in 1996, for example, justified their rejection of same-sex marriage in majoritarian terms:

> Civil laws that permit only heterosexual marriage reflect and honor a collective moral judgment about human sexuality. This judgment entails both moral disapproval of homosexuality, and a moral conviction that heterosexuality better comports with traditional (especially Judeo-Christian) morality.

Similarly, following the passage of California's Proposition 8 in 2008, Maggie Gallagher of the National Organization for Marriage drew majoritarian conclusions. "The majority of people," she insisted, "recognize that same-sex marriage is not a civil right." Therefore, banning it was entirely justified.[3]

Meanwhile, defenders of gay rights insisted that the moral sensibilities of majorities could not be enshrined in law if they hampered minority rights. In the landmark 2003 case, *Lawrence v. Texas*, for example, the US Supreme Court observed that while state antisodomy laws might reflect dominant "moral principles," "the majority" could not "use the power of the State to enforce these views on the whole society." Likewise, gay-rights activists opposing the penchant to decide same-sex marriage by initiative and referendum maintained, as one activist in New Jersey did, that "it should never be up to the majority to vote on the rights of the minority." An editorialist in the *Philadelphia Inquirer* agreed. If racial segregation had been decided by referendum, the writer contended, "black folks in the South would likely still be drinking from 'colored' water fountains." Whether pertaining to racial minorities, sexual minorities, or others, direct democracy was an inappropriate approach to resolving questions involving fundamental issues of freedom and equal rights. "American democracy," the author concluded, "doesn't mean the majority always rules; The rights of the minority must be protected." And to this author, legislators often needed to stand apart from the wishes of majorities and play that protective role. The liquor dealers and their allies who had first opposed direct democracy in the 1840s could not have said it any better.[4]

Beyond the ideas embedded within these twenty-first century debates, the mid-nineteenth-century opponents of liquor, Sabbath, and race regulations would also have recognized the modes of political engagement employed on both sides of the issue. And they likely would have been impressed if not amazed by the scale at which grass-roots rights activism came to operate. Religiously grounded groups such as the National Organization for Marriage, the Family Research Council, and the American Family Association emerged to oppose gay-rights efforts, to trumpet morals, and to protect opposite-sex marriage. Meanwhile, gay-rights activists employed an organized, popular minority-rights politics in the style pioneered more than 150 years earlier. In California, for example, the American Foundation for Equal Rights (AFER) formed for the specific purpose of challenging Proposition 8. It did what the moral minorities of the mid-nineteenth century had done; it initiated test cases with specially chosen litigants and assembled high-powered legal teams. Like many antebellum moral minorities, the AFER conspicuously presented itself in nonpartisan style. It employed two lead attorneys, one with Republican credentials and the other with Democratic, and proudly announced that these lawyers had faced off thirteen years earlier in *Bush v. Gore*, in which partisan opponents George W. Bush and Al Gore had battled for the presidency.

As in the mid-nineteenth century, rights advocacy in the courtroom was only one major part of the overall crusade. Gay-rights activists, like so many minority-rights crusaders before them, knew that theirs was ultimately a democratic battle for public opinion. They aimed to convince the majority that the rights of the gay minority deserved recognition and equal protection. Activists went to the ever-expanding playbook, holding rallies and celebrations, crafting editorials for newspapers and magazines, appearing on television and radio, and offering commentary on websites and social-media sites. Interweaved was the critical aspect of fundraising—something else of which nineteenth-century rights activists knew the value. The AFER, for example, gained the support of those with deep pockets, solicited other donations of all sizes, organized an art auction, and secured the services of rock legend Elton John, who held a private concert to benefit the cause. Such major efforts were bolstered by a range of smaller ones, including those of California winemakers who created a special wine—Same Sex Meritage (figs. E.1 and E.2)—and donated a portion of the proceeds to Freedom to Marry, another emergent rights organization. In 2013, it seemed that the public-opinion campaigns were paying dividends. Polls showed that a majority of Americans favored same-sex marriage, up from only 37 percent four years earlier. As Richard Kim of *The Nation* put it, "Gay marriage isn't winning the day because of some singularly persuasive legal argument; it's winning because the battleground has shifted from the court of law to the court of public opinion."

FIGURE E.I Same Sex Meritage (front label).

The founder of Freedom to Marry, Evan Wolfson, wasn't shy about this strategy. "Building a critical mass of states and a critical mass of public support—that's how social movements succeed." The battle for rights very much remained a battle to have those rights recognized in public opinion.[5]

Same Sex Meritage
2010 California Red Table Wine

United States citizens should have two irrevocable freedoms--to marry the person they love and to purchase an awesome wine at a reasonable price. With every bottle of Same Sex Meritage you purchase and enjoy, you support those who are currently forbidden from marrying the people they love and want to spend their lives with. This prohibition is unquestionably a violation of civil rights, and we will dispute it until all loving and committed couples enjoy the freedom to marry in the USA. Same Sex Meritage supports the progressive movement on this issue by pledging a portion of revenue to Freedom To Marry, the campaign to win marriage nationwide: working to win more states, growing the majority for marriage, and overturning federal marriage discrimination.

This California Meritage rivals its Old World inspirations by staying stylistically true to the philosophy that blended wines bring out the best from the grape better than the components alone. Drink Same Sex Meritage because, in doing so, you are supporting the fight for increased civil rights by toasting to brighter futures for us all. Go to freedomtomarry.org and samesexmeritage.com to find out about how you can become more involved with this key campaign. Thank you for your support!

Matt Gold & Josh Stein
Co-Founders, Same Sex Meritage

Love Is For Everyone
Eat, drink and be married!

Vinted and Bottled by
Stein Family Wines ° Napa, CA

GOVERNMENT WARNING:
(1) ACCORDING TO THE SURGEON GENERAL, WOMEN SHOULD NOT DRINK ALCOHOLIC BEVERAGES DURING PREGNANCY BECAUSE OF THE RISK OF BIRTH DEFECTS.
(2) CONSUMPTION OF ALCOHOLIC BEVERAGES IMPAIRS YOUR ABILITY TO DRIVE A CAR OR OPERATE MACHINERY, AND MAY CAUSE HEALTH PROBLEMS.
CONTAINS SULFITES

SameSexMeritage.com

Alc. 13.5% By Vol.

FIGURE E.2 Same Sex Meritage (back label). Courtesy of Matt Gold and Josh Stein, cofounders, Same Sex Meritage. In explaining their "cause wine" benefiting Freedom to Marry, winemakers Matt Gold and Josh Stein maintained that Americans should have the freedom both to marry and to buy great wine. The moral minorities of the mid-nineteenth century fought groundbreaking battles to ensure both of these freedoms.

THE HISTORICAL TRAJECTORY of minority-rights politics from the mid-nineteenth century to the gay-rights struggles of the twenty-first century was neither straight nor simple. The intervening history was highly complex and, like the minority-rights politics of the pre–Civil War period, shaped by diverse historical actors and vital historical contexts. Yet the two eras—the distant past and the recent past—are connected by the long history of popular, minority-rights activism, a history that had its most substantial foundations in antebellum America, when a range of minorities refused to bow to the supposed moral proclivities of majorities.

Without detailing the subsequent history of minority rights, it is important to recognize that the struggles of the mid-nineteenth century were not random or passing phenomenon only to be built upon by the black freedom struggle of the 1950s and 1960s or gay-rights activism more recently. The pre–Civil War tradition of popular minority-rights activism never subsided. Perhaps not surprisingly, racial egalitarians, religious minorities, drinkers, and alcohol-peddling entrepreneurs again played essential roles, in large part because the moralized issues of race, religion, and alcohol continued to divide the American public into majorities and minorities. These issues, and no doubt others, ensured that majority tyranny and minority rights remained persistent concerns for a diverse lot of Americans. They guaranteed that moral politics, and the popular minority-rights politics they continued to spawn, endured as significant and highly participatory parts of democratic political life into the twentieth century.

After emancipation, not all black Americans were content to let their political and civil rights be determined by the white majority or the whims of party politics, and black-rights groups, beginning with the National Equal Rights League (NERL), emerged to do battle. That black men and women were a minority within the nation (and most of the states) remained a self-evident political problem that justified their organization outside of political parties. Leading activist William D. Forten made this case at the NERL's first annual meeting in 1865. "The necessity for us," he argued, "who are a minority... to form combinations to resist the overriding tyranny of a united, powerful, and unprincipled majority" was so obvious that any "further lingering" on the topic was a waste of time. With the Republican Party instructing blacks to "wait" because any attempt to do them "justice" would jeopardize "the interests" of the party, Forten counseled his brethren to support the NERL with their "money," "labor," and "influence."[6]

The NERL built upon the grass-roots rights activism initiated by abolitionists before the Civil War. The idea for this organization, in fact, probably came from Henry Highland Garnett, a leader in the New York Legal Rights Association's crusade against segregation in the late 1850s. The NERL nationalized such foundational efforts. In Washington, DC, veterans of earlier struggles, including William Howard Day and George T. Downing, lobbied for black voting rights and called upon old allies, especially Senator Charles Sumner, to protect black civil rights with national legislation. The NERL also spurred the creation of state and local leagues modeled on the early rights organizations. Whether in New Orleans, New Brunswick, New Jersey, or San Joaquin, California, these groups ensured that grass-roots involvement remained vital to the continuing struggle for "civil and political equality." Members brandished the usual weapons— "the newspaper, the lecture, the petition"—to reshape "public opinion" and to lobby public officials. Critically, these groups hired attorneys, practiced civil disobedience, and initiated test cases to challenge discrimination in schools, transportation, and public places. Their efforts met with mixed success. But by the end of Reconstruction, ERLs helped nationalize the practice of turning to courts (local, state, and federal) and of arguing for equal rights with a growing range of legal tools, including the newly minted Fourteenth Amendment.[7]

A range of other national and local rights organizations followed the NERL. At times, black activists called upon the tactics and memory of antebellum struggles to motivate the black community. T. Thomas Fortune, for example, sued a New York hotel in 1890 for refusing him service to boost his Afro-American League. Elizabeth Jennings offered her support. Writing to the *New York Age*, she reminded readers of her legal victory against streetcar segregation in 1855, which had seeded the New York Legal Rights Association (NYLRA). Only through this type of "public spirit," she agreed, would black Americans defeat "discrimination." In the twentieth century, the National Association for the Advancement of Colored People (NAACP) carried the torch of minority-rights activism lit by Jennings and others. Like its forbearers, the NAACP recognized the struggle as one for the purification of democracy through the protection of minority rights. "The Negro," the NAACP reported in 1927, "represents the 'shock troops' in behalf of all the minority groups in America, which test the reality of American democracy." As the civil rights movement blossomed and then fractured in the 1950s and 1960s, the pre–Civil War experience could again prove instructive. In 1968, the NAACP's *Crisis* reprinted a

New York Tribune article from 1858 that described the NYLRA. It documents, *The Crisis* noted, "an early, effective and little known effort on the part of New York Negroes to secure their rights more than a century ago. Then, as now, the city's black population organized to strike down racial barriers." That tradition must continue.[8]

The crusade for black civil rights, as before, was only one engine behind the expansion of minority-rights politics. Major conflicts over religion also played that role. Local battles over Sunday laws persisted as reinvigorated moral reformers pressed for stricter Sunday-closing legislation, especially in the nation's immigrant-laden cities. That America was a "Christian nation" and that such measures were supported by "the majority" continued to justify Sunday surveillance. As one Milwaukeean announced in 1889, "The majority of the people of this country [are] in favor of a Sunday law and the state [has] an indisputable right to enforce such a law at the command of the majority." Whether in Milwaukee, St. Louis, Indianapolis, New York, or elsewhere, familiar groups resisted: alcohol-purveying businessmen, drinkers, Catholics, Jews, Seventh Day Baptists (and now Seventh-day Adventists), and a range of immigrants, especially the swelling population of Germans. Collectively, these groups employed the usual tactics as they battled for the "rights of the minority."[9]

New groups joined the fight, and none was more important than the National Liberal League (NLL) and its host of local auxiliaries. Formed in the 1870s to counter Protestant moralists' attempt to amend the national Constitution and establish the United States as a Christian nation, the NLL soon challenged an array of perceived church-state infractions, including Sunday laws and religion in public schools. Veterans of earlier struggles joined the leadership corps. They included Jewish leader Isaac M. Wise and J. L. Hatch, founder of the American Society for Promoting Civil and Religious Liberty that had crusaded against New York's Sunday laws in the 1850s. As before, their battle was for minority rights. "Equal religious rights and liberties," the NLL's founding platform announced, "do not depend in the slightest degree upon conformity to the opinions of the majority." Carrie Burnham Kilgore, a NLL activist who later became Pennsylvania's first female attorney, cemented this position in an address titled "Democracy" given at the NLL's organizing convention. No hackneyed salute to American institutions, Kilgore found "the American Republic...in imminent peril" because of the "despotism of the majority." The "founders of the Republic," she reminded her audience, had warned of it; Tocqueville predicted it could bring about America's downfall. To Kilgore, the problem remained in 1876. Her chief examples, not coincidentally, were Sunday laws and the Sunday closing of Philadelphia's Centennial Exposition. Sanctioned by the Christian majority, these practices illustrated "the barbaric motto, 'might makes right'; as is every application of the majority rule which ignores the rights of the minority." The NLL needed to safeguard minorities' "fundamental rights" by fully separating church and state.[10]

Conflict over alcohol followed the general trend. Temperance reformers regrouped after the Civil War, forming new organizations including the National Prohibition Party and the Woman's Christian Temperance Union. As they convinced lawmakers to restrict booze, proalcohol forces mobilized. The liquor dealer associations that had proven so critical in the battle against the Maine Laws returned and increasingly operated on the state and eventually national level. German brewers got an earlier start, forming the United States Brewers' Association (USBA) in response to federal alcohol taxes during the Civil War. The USBA united the industry, countered prohibitionists' propaganda campaigns, aided local struggles against temperance, and initiated test cases to challenge prohibitory laws. Beginning in the 1870s, Germans and their allies formed "Personal Liberty Leagues" in cities to bolster the popular appeal of antiprohibitionism and to preserve the "rights of the minority." Temperance sympathizers objected. Any "combination to resist the enactment of laws expressing a majority wish," the *Philadelphia North American* declared in 1882, was immoral and antidemocratic. "As well may the Mormon claim indulgence in his polygamist practices, on the ground that such social conditions suit him, as the new Leaguers may claim privilege to disregard Sabbath observances and override liquor regulations." By the mid-1880s, the proliferation of alcohol-rights organizations was in full evidence. "Under the names of associations, leagues, unions, and the like," the Connecticut Temperance Union lamented, "they are to be found everywhere, and wherever found they are active and aggressive." It was time, temperance men and women argued, for "the American people" to destroy "this impudent minority."[11]

With the passage of the Eighteenth Amendment and the implementation of national prohibition, temperance crusaders thought they had succeeded in doing just that. But even a national constitutional amendment couldn't stop drink, nor could it quiet arguments about majority rule and minority rights. In a telling moment in 1927, prominent attorney Clarence Darrow debated Wayne B. Wheeler, the chief counsel of the Anti-Saloon League, before a crowd of twenty-five hundred at New York's Carnegie Hall. The question of the day: should Prohibition continue? Yet again, issues of majority rule and minority rights took center stage. For Wheeler, the Prohibition amendment embodied democracy because it was the "will of the majority." As the "majority of the people" still believed in it, Prohibition should stand. Darrow, however, complained that a cadre of temperance activists had pushed through the Prohibition amendment and robbed the Constitution of its most fundamental purpose: "to give some sort of protection...against the caprice and the bigotry of a given majority." Only by repealing Prohibition would the Constitution be restored. As Darrow made his case, he notably referenced two other violations of constitutionally pro-tected minority rights: first, the denial of black Americans' rights, north and south; and second, Sunday laws. The three issues that had most given rise to popular minority-rights activism in the mid-nineteenth century remained, to him, troublingly unresolved in the late 1920s. Fortunately, from his perspective, the tradition of activism remained to purge majoritarian oppression from American democracy.[12]

With the passage of the Twenty-First Amendment and the decline of the prohibition movement, the vital contributions of antitemper-ance forces to the making of American democracy's tradition of popular minority-rights activism have faded from popular memory. By contrast, the continuing struggles for black civil rights and religious freedom in the twentieth century remain well known. They played pivotal roles in shaping the trend to see "minorities" as fixed social groups with histo-ries of oppression, particularly racial and religious prejudice. Since the US Supreme Court famously referred to "discrete and insular minorities" in a footnote in 1938, the list of American "minorities" has expanded to include other nonwhite racial groups, women, indigenous peoples, gays and lesbians, the disabled, and others. These groups transformed and expanded America's minority-rights tradition and played essential roles in keeping the tension between majority rule and minority rights at the heart of American democracy.[13]

These widely recognized minorities were not the only ones in the twentieth century to embrace the modes of political action pioneered by the mid-nineteenth-century opponents of Sabbath, liquor, and race regula-tions. Rights associations and legal defense funds represent the interests of wide-ranging parts of the political and cultural spectrum. In fundamen-tal ways, the National Organization for Women, Americans United for the Separation of Church and State, and Lambda Legal practice a mode of politics strikingly similar to the National Rifle Association and the Home School Legal Defense Association, just to name a few. All work beyond party and use now-basic tools of democratic rights-advocacy—grass-roots mobilization, public-opinion campaigns, legislative lobbying, and court action. Antebellum moral minorities' most important tactics are a mainstream part of modern democracy.

These tactics extend beyond the United States. Of late, the rising democratic polities throughout the world have struggled with the tension between majority rule and minority rights, especially while dealing with problems of social diversity, cultural pluralism, and religious and moral conflict. Battles over gay rights, for example, are an increasingly global phenomenon spawning heated debate and popular rights-activism. In 2009, an international gay rights organization called upon the Indian High Court to overturn a long-standing antisodomy law. The Court agreed, using striking language that antebellum moral minorities would have appreciated. "Moral indignation, howsoever strong, is not a valid basis for overriding individuals' fundamental rights of dignity and privacy. In our scheme of things Constitutional morality must outweigh the argument of public morality, even if it be the majoritarian view." By contrast, Lech Walesa, the historical champion of Polish democracy and winner of the Nobel Peace Prize, sparked controversy in 2013 by suggesting that Poland's gay community should take a backseat in political life. As he put it, "A minority should not impose itself on the majority." Sexuality is only one of many issues. In the emerging democracies of the Middle East, recurring battles between Muslim majorities and Christian minorities threatened political stability and the return of autocracy in the aftermath of the Arab Spring of 2011. As was the case in nineteenth-century America, many learned that there is more to democracy than voting, elections, and majority rule. Without guarantees for "individual and minority rights," one pundit observed, the emergence of "illiberal democracy and the tyranny of the majority" was a likely possibility. The solution, according to another commentator, was for Middle Easterners to "commit themselves to equal rights for religious minorities."[14]

If the formative era of popular minority-rights politics is any guide, constitutional guarantees and loose commitments to minority rights only go so far. Those interested in promoting sustainable democracies and protecting the rights of minorities—present and future, moral and otherwise—might consider the approach of the mid-nineteenth-century moral minorities: vigilant activism and persistent organization coupled with compelling arguments about the moral sanctity of human equality and constitutional freedom. Underlying their approach was a steadfast commitment to democracy, even in the face of persistent democratic oppression. Building on their example might help the rights of varied minorities, and democracy itself, stand a chance of remaining legitimate in a world in which many believe that the only true rights are those of real or imagined majorities.

Notes

INTRODUCTION

1. "The Anti-Sabbatarian Movement," *New York Herald*, Sep. 14, 1859; "Anti-Sabbatarian Meeting," *New York Times*, Sep. 14, 1859; "Anti-Sabbath Agitation," *New York Tribune*, Sep. 14, 1859.

2. George T. Downing et al., *To the Friends of Equal Rights in Rhode Island* (Providence, 1859), 1, 5, 7–8.

3. Alexander Hamilton, James Madison, and John Jay, *The Federalist* [1787–1788], ed. J. R. Pole (Indianapolis, IN, 2005), 49–50. On these themes, see especially Jennifer Nedelsky, *Private Property and the Limits of American Constitutionalism: The Madisonian Framework and Its Legacy* (Chicago, 1990); Jack Rakove, *Original Meanings: Politics and Ideas in the Making of the Constitution* (New York, 1996); Alexander Keyssar, *The Right to Vote: The Contested History of Democracy in the United States* (New York, 2000); Robin Einhorn, *American Taxation, American Slavery* (Chicago, 2006); James H. Read, *Majority Rule versus Consensus: The Political Thought of John C. Calhoun* (Lawrence, KS, 2009).

4. Long before Edmund Morgan's influential explication of "popular sovereignty" as a "fiction" helping those in power legitimate their influence in democracy, historian Charles Beard suggested that "majority rule" similarly functioned as a "fiction." As this history shows, defenders of Sabbath, liquor, and race regulations in the mid-nineteenth century strategically used "majority rule" to legitimate their pet measures. Antebellum moral minorities did explore the fiction of "majority rule," especially as they lamented the difficulty of determining what "the majority" truly wanted and the disproportionate power of the opinion-makers within the burgeoning democratic political culture. Nonetheless, they also took "majority rule" at face value, combating it head on with the language of majority tyranny and minority rights. See Charles A. Beard, "The Fiction of Majority Rule," *Atlantic Monthly* 140 (Dec. 1927), 831–836; Edmund S. Morgan, *Inventing the People: The Rise of Popular Sovereignty in England and America* (New York, 1988).

5. Alexis de Tocqueville, *Democracy in America* [1835], ed. J. P. Mayer, George Lawrence, translation (New York, 1966), 254–256; Gustave de Beaumont, *Marie or, Slavery in the United States* [1835], Barbara Chapman, translation (Baltimore, 1999), 251.

6. Morton Keller, *America's Three Regimes: A New Political History* (New York, 2007), 88. Sean Wilentz's prize-winning synthesis, *The Rise of American Democracy*, exemplifies the scholarly trend of viewing the ascension of majority rule to the ideological core of American political life as the defining political development of the age. Wilentz, *The Rise of American Democracy: Jefferson to Lincoln* (New York, 2005). For scholars highlighting concerns about minority rights from opponents of democratization and slaveholders, see Arthur Schlesinger Jr., *The Age of Jackson* (Boston, 1945), 401–421; Daniel T. Rodgers, *Contested Truths: Keywords in American Politics since Independence* (Cambridge, MA, 1987), 80–111; Richard E. Ellis, *The Union at Risk: Jacksonian Democracy, States' Rights and the Nullification Crisis* (New York, 1987); Lacy K. Ford Jr., "Inventing the Concurrent Majority: Madison, Calhoun, and the Problem of Majoritarianism in American Political Thought," *Journal of Southern History* 60 (1994), 19–58; Manisha Sinha, *The Counterrevolution of Slavery: Politics and Ideology in Antebellum South Carolina* (Chapel Hill, 2000); Keyssar, *Right to Vote*; Wilentz, *Rise of American Democracy*; Einhorn, *American Taxation, American Slavery*. A recent exception to this trend is W. Caleb McDaniel, *The Problem of Democracy in the Age of Slavery: Garrisonian Abolitionists and Transatlantic Reform* (Baton Rouge, LA, 2013).

7. Scholars have long highlighted the impact of evangelical reform on the partisan political environment. More recently they have noted the essential role played by reform movements in democratizing nineteenth-century public life. This book builds on their efforts while highlighting the importance of antireformers and the problems of minority rights raised by reform enterprises. On reform and party politics, see especially Daniel Walker Howe, "The Evangelical Movement and Political Culture in the North during the Second Party System," *Journal of American History* 77 (1991), 1216–1239; Richard Carwardine, *Evangelicals and Politics in Antebellum America* (New Haven, CT, 1993). Important recent appraisals of the political nature of reform include Richard S. Newman, *The Transformation of American Abolitionism: Fighting Slavery in the Early Republic* (Chapel Hill, 2002); Johann Neem, *Creating a Nation of Joiners: Democracy and Civil Society in Early National Massachusetts* (Cambridge, MA, 2008); McDaniel, *Problem of Democracy*. More generally, this book joins other scholars expanding the boundaries of political history, particularly beyond voting and political parties. For recent examples, see Mary P. Ryan, *Civic Wars: Democracy and Public Life in the American City during the Nineteenth Century* (Berkeley, CA, 1997); Kimberly K. Smith, *The Dominion of Voice: Riot, Reason, and Romance in Antebellum Politics* (Lawrence, KS, 1999); Sinha, *Counterrevolution of*

Slavery; Reeve Huston, *Land and Freedom: Rural Society, Popular Protest, and Party Politics in Antebellum New York* (New York, 2000); Mark Voss-Hubbard, *Beyond Party: Cultures of Antipartisanship in Northern Politics before the Civil War* (Baltimore, 2002); Ronald P. Formisano, *For the People: American Populist Movements from the Revolution to the 1850s* (Chapel Hill, 2008); Reeve Huston, "What We Talk about When We Talk about Democracy: Reengaging the American Democratic Tradition," *Commonplace* 9 (Oct. 2008); Christian G. Fritz, *American Sovereigns: The People and America's Constitutional Tradition before the Civil War* (New York, 2008); Jason Frank, *Constituent Moments: Enacting the People in Postrevolutionary America* (Durham, NC, 2010). For more traditional appraisals of nineteenth-century political life, see Joel Silbey, *The American Political Nation, 1838–1893* (Stanford, CA, 1991); Michael E. McGerr, *The Decline of Popular Politics: The American North, 1865–1928* (New York, 1986), 3–41. For a critique of the party period paradigm, see Glenn C. Altschuler and Stuart M. Blumin, *Rude Republic: Americans and Their Politics in the Nineteenth Century* (Princeton, NJ, 2000).

8. In this way, this history textures recent scholarship describing a historical tradition of "popular constitutionalism" in which "the people themselves" exercised constitutional authority alongside courts. It shows how "the people" and "the courts" were not necessarily antithetical institutions in antebellum America. Rather, it shows competing interest groups—some claiming majority status and others minority status—advancing their agenda in courts as well as in the wider public sphere. See especially Larry D. Kramer, *The People Themselves: Popular Constitutionalism and Judicial Review* (New York, 2004).

9. Historian Daniel T. Rodgers, for example, suggests that the most consequential rights claims of the era were those for "the social rights of workers, women, and slaves." Rodgers, "Rights Consciousness in American History," in *The Bill of Rights in Modern America*, ed. David J. Bodenhamer and James W. Ely Jr. (Indianapolis, 2008), 9. For examples of this vast and important scholarly literature, see Edmund S. Morgan, *American Slavery, American Freedom: The Ordeal of Colonial Virginia* (New York, 1975); Hendrik Hartog, "The Constitution of Aspiration and 'The Rights That Belong to Us All,'" *Journal of American History* 74 (Dec. 1987), 1013–1034; Thomas Bender, ed., *The Antislavery Debate: Capitalism and Abolitionism as a Problem in Historical Interpretation* (Berkeley, CA, 1992); Eric Foner, "The Meaning of Freedom in the Age of Emancipation," *Journal of American History* 81 (Sep. 1994), 435–460; Foner, *The Story of American Freedom* (New York, 1998); Elizabeth B. Clark, "'The Sacred Rights of the Weak': Pain, Sympathy, and the Culture of Individual Rights in Antebellum America," *Journal of American History* 82 (Sep. 1995), 463–493; Amy Dru Stanley, *From Bondage to Contract: Wage Labor, Marriage, and the Market in the Age of Slave Emancipation* (New York, 1998); Seth Rockman, *Scraping By: Wage Labor, Slavery, and Survival in Early Baltimore* (Baltimore, 2008); Kate Masur, *An Example for*

All the Land: Emancipation and the Struggle over Equality in Washington, D.C. (Chapel Hill, 2010); Susan J. Pearson, *The Rights of the Defenseless: Protecting Animals and Children in Gilded Age America* (Chicago, 2011); Stacey Smith, *Freedom's Frontier: California and the Struggle over Unfree Labor, Emancipation, and Reconstruction* (Chapel Hill, 2013). On voting rights, see variously Phyllis F. Field, *The Politics of Race in New York: The Struggle for Black Suffrage in the Civil War Era* (Ithaca, NY, 1982); Keyssar, *The Right to Vote*; Ellen Carol DuBois, *Feminism and Suffrage: The Emergence of an Independent Women's Movement in America, 1848–1869* (Ithaca, NY, 1978).

10. In focusing on issues that contemporaries regarded as "moral issues," I join with other scholars emphasizing the importance of such issues in American public life. For examples, see James Morone, *Hellfire Nation: The Politics of Sin in American History* (New Haven, 2003); Sarah Gordon, *The Mormon Question: Polygamy and Constitutional Conflict in Nineteenth Century America* (Chapel Hill, 2002); Donna Dennis, *Licentious Gotham: Erotic Publishing and its Prosecution in Nineteenth-Century New York* (Cambridge, MA, 2009).

11. In this way, I join legal historians in exploring how law shaped the "conditions of freedom" in nineteenth-century America. I differently highlight how resistance to regulation released popular political energies and shaped both the conditions and conceptions of freedom. See especially J. Willard Hurst, *Law and the Conditions of Freedom in the Nineteenth-Century United States* (Madison, WI, 1956); William J. Novak, *The People's Welfare: Law and Regulation in Nineteenth-Century America* (Chapel Hill, 1996).

12. For scholarship on these twentieth-century developments, see Robert M. Cover, "The Origins of Judicial Activism in the Protection of Minorities," *Yale Law Journal* 91 (Jun. 1982), 1287–1316; Michael J. Klarman, "Rethinking the Civil Rights and Civil Liberties Revolutions," *Virginia Law Review* 82 (Feb. 1996), 1–67; Akhil Reed Amar, *The Bill of Rights: Creation and Reconstruction* (New Haven, CT, 1998); Mary Ann Glendon, *Rights Talk: The Impoverishment of Political Discourse* (New York, 1991); James T. Patterson, "The Rise of Rights and Rights Consciousness in American Politics, 1930s–1970s," in *Contesting Democracy: Substance and Structure in American Political History, 1775–2000*, ed. Byron E. Shafer and Anthony J. Badger (Lawrence, KS, 2001), 201–223; Mark Tushnet, "The Rights Revolution in the Twentieth Century," in *The Cambridge History of Law in America*, vol. 3, ed. Michael Grossberg and Christopher Tomlins (New York, 2008), 377–402; John D. Skrentny, *The Minority Rights Revolution* (Cambridge, MA, 2002); Rodgers, "Rights Consciousness," 19–22. Some scholars of twentieth-century civil liberties and civil rights have begun to push this traditional story backwards. See especially David Rabban, *Free Speech in its Forgotten Years, 1870–1920* (New York, 1997); Jacquelyn Dowd Hall, "The Long Civil Rights Movement and the Political Uses of the Past," *Journal of American History* 91 (Mar. 2005), 1233–1263; Michael Willrich, "'The Least Vaccinated of

Any Civilized Country': Personal Liberty and Public Health in the Progressive Era," *Journal of Policy History* 20 (2008), 76–93.

13. Notably, this study does not tackle every "rights movement" in the mid-nineteenth century, including battles for voting rights, all aspects of the battle for black rights, women's rights, worker's rights, and the rights of indigenous peoples. Rather I focus on only those struggles in which I discovered that the ideas of majority tyranny and minority rights played an explicit and significant role. For examples of scholarship exploring these other important movements, see DuBois, *Feminism and Suffrage*; Nancy Isenberg, *Sex and Citizenship in Antebellum America* (Chapel Hill, 1998); Patrick Rael, *Black Identity and Black Protest in the Antebellum North* (Chapel Hill, 2002); Dana Weiner, *Race and Rights: Fighting Slavery and Prejudice in the Old Northwest, 1830–1870* (DeKalb, IL, 2013); William G. McLoughlin, *Cherokee Renascence in the New Republic* (Princeton, NJ, 1986); Donald M. Nielsen, "The Mashpee Indian Revolt of 1833," *New England Quarterly* 58 (Sep. 1985), 400–420; Mary Hershberger, "Mobilizing Women, Anticipating Abolition: The Struggle against Indian Removal in the 1830s," *Journal of American History* 86 (Jun. 1999), 15–40; Sean Wilentz, *Chants Democratic: New York City and the Rise of the American Working Class, 1788–1850* (New York, 1984); David Montgomery, *Citizen Worker: The Experience of Workers in the United States with Democracy and the Free Market during the Nineteenth Century* (Cambridge, 1995).

14. This study urges other scholars to explore alternate venues in the nineteenth century where challenges to majority rule were explicitly made and to search consciously for self-understood minority groups in history. For scholars conceptualizing "minority history" as histories of those groups deemed "minorities" in the late-twentieth century, see Patricia Nelson Limerick, "Has 'Minority' History Transformed the Historical Discourse?" *AHA Perspectives* (Nov. 1997); Dipesh Chakrabarty, "Minority Histories, Subaltern Pasts," *AHA Perspectives* (Nov. 1997).

CHAPTER 1

1. Lyman Beecher, *The Memory of Our Fathers: A Sermon Delivered at Plymouth, on the Twenty-Second of December, 1827* (Boston, 1828), 38, 6, 22, 32, 26–28, 16, 39.

2. Beecher, *Memory of Our Fathers*, 19, 30–32; "Review of Reports on Sunday Mails," *Christian Spectator*, Mar. 1, 1829 (emphasis in original); J. M. Peck, *The Principles and Tendencies of Democracy: An Address, Made in Belleville, St. Clair County, Illinois* (Belleville, IL, 1839), 10; Thomas H. Skinner, *Religion and Liberty: A Discourse* (New York, 1841), iii. For overviews of early nineteenth-century reform, see Ronald G. Walters, *American Reformers, 1815–1860* (New York, 1978); Robert H. Abzug, *Cosmos Crumbling: American Reform and the Religious Imagination* (New York, 1994); Steven Mintz, *Moralists and Modernizers: America's Pre–Civil*

War Reformers (Baltimore, 1995); Michael P. Young, *Bearing Witness against Sin: The Evangelical Birth of the American Social Movement* (Chicago, 2006).

3. This chapter's emphasis on the political underpinnings and nature of antebellum reform builds on several recent appraisals. See especially Richard S. Newman, *The Transformation of American Abolitionism: Fighting Slavery in the Early Republic* (Chapel Hill, 2002); Johann Neem, *Creating a Nation of Joiners: Democracy and Civil Society in Early National Massachusetts* (Cambridge, MA, 2008), 81–113; John L. Brooke, "Cultures of Nationalism, Movements of Reform, and the Composite-Federal Polity from Revolutionary Settlement to Antebellum Crisis," *Journal of the Early Republic* 29 (Spr. 2009), 1–33.

4. Francis Wayland, *The Duties of An American Citizen* (Boston, 1825), 27–28; George W. Bethune, *Our Liberties: Their Danger, and the Means of Preserving Them* (Philadelphia, 1835), 6.

5. Bethune, *Our Liberties*, 6; Mintz, *Moralists and Modernizers*, 3; Walters, *American Reformers*, 3–6; Paul Boyer, *Urban Masses and Moral Order in America, 1820–1920* (Cambridge, MA, 1978), 3–21; Eric R. Schlereth, "Fits of Political Religion: Stalking Infidelity and the Politics of Moral Reform in Antebellum America," *Early American Studies* 5 (Fall 2007), 288–323. For recent synthetic treatments of the vast transformations of the early nineteenth century, see especially Daniel Walker Howe, *What Hath God Wrought: The Transformation of America, 1815–1848* (New York, 2007); Christopher Clark, *Social Change in America: From the Revolution to the Civil War* (Chicago, 2007).

6. Howe, *What Hath God Wrought*, 166–167; W. J. Rorabaugh, *The Alcoholic Republic: An American Tradition* (New York, 1979), 21; J. W. Barber, *The Drunkard's Progress* (New Haven, CT, 1826); Thomas R. Pegram, *Battling Demon Rum: The Struggle for a Dry America, 1800–1933* (Chicago, 1998), 20.

7. Job R. Tyson, *A Brief Survey of the Great Extent and Evil Tendencies of the Lottery System, as Existing in the United States* (Philadelphia, 1833), 33; John Samuel, *Fortune's Merry Wheel: The Lottery in America* (Cambridge, MA, 1960).

8. Bethune, *Our Liberties*, 17; John M. Krebs, *Righteousness the Foundation of National Prosperity: A Sermon* (New York, 1835), 20–21; Joseph R. Underwood, *An Address Delivered to the Colonization Society of Kentucky, at Frankfort, Jan. 15, 1835* (Frankfort, KY, 1835), 8; Theodore Frelinghuysen, *An Oration: Delivered at Princeton, New Jersey, Nov. 16, 1824, before the New-Jersey Colonization Society* (Princeton, NJ, 1824), 6, 14; James Brewer Stewart, *Holy Warriors: The Abolitionists and American Slavery*, rev. ed. (New York, 1996), 30–50.

9. "Review of Reports on Sunday Mails," *Quarterly Christian Spectator*, Mar. 1, 1829 (emphasis in original); William James, *The Moral Responsibility of the American Nation: A Discourse, Delivered in Rochester, July 4, 1828* (Rochester, NY, 1828), 10–13; Perry Miller, *The Life of the Mind in America from the Revolution to the Civil War* (New York, 1965), 67–72; John G. West, *The Politics of Revelation and Reason: Religion and Civic Life in the New Nation* (Lawrence, KS, 1996), 117–119.

"Change in the nature of politics," notes historian Ronald Walters, "had almost
as much significance for antebellum reform as did the economic transformation of the United States." Walters, *American Reformers*, 6.

10. Donald M. Scott, *From Office to Profession: The New England Ministry, 1750–1850*
(Philadelphia, 1978), 24–35; Jon Butler, *Awash in a Sea of Faith: Christianizing
the American People* (Cambridge, MA, 1990), 267–268; Clifford Griffin,
Their Brothers' Keepers: Moral Stewardship in the United States, 1800–1865
(New Brunswick, NJ, 1960), 3–22; Marshall Foletta, *Coming to Terms with
Democracy: Federalist Intellectuals and the Shaping of an American Culture*
(Charlottesville, VA, 2001), 135–142; Abzug, *Cosmos Crumbling*, 135–145; Paul
Goodman, *Of One Blood: Abolitionism and the Origins of Racial Equality* (Berkeley,
CA, 1998), 36–44; W. Caleb McDaniel, *The Problem of Democracy in the Age of
Slavery: Garrisonian Abolitionists and Transatlantic Reform* (Baton Rouge, LA,
2013), 21–44.

11. Daniel T. Rodgers, *Contested Truths: Keywords in American Politics since
Independence* (Cambridge, MA, 1987), 80–111; Harry L. Watson, *Liberty and
Power: The Politics of Jacksonian America* (New York, 1990), 49–51; Alexander
Keyssar, *The Right to Vote: The Contested History of Democracy in the United States*
(New York, 2000); Sean Wilentz, *The Rise of American Democracy: Jefferson to
Lincoln* (New York, 2005).

12. Watson, *Liberty and Power*, 97–98, 80–84; Wilentz, *Rise of American Democracy*;
Robert V. Remini, *Andrew Jackson: The Course of American Democracy, 1833–1845*,
vol. 3 (Baltimore, MD, 1984), 317; Remini, *The Legacy of Andrew Jackson: Essays
on Democracy, Indian Removal, and Slavery* (Baton Rouge, 1988), 7–44; Lynn
Hudson Parsons, *The Birth of Modern Politics: Andrew Jackson, John Quincy
Adams, and the Election of 1828* (New York, 2009).

13. See especially Michael Wallace, "Changing Concepts of Party in the United
States: New York, 1815–1828," *American Historical Review* 74 (1968), 453–491;
William E. Gienapp, "'Politics Seem to Enter into Everything': Political Culture
in the North, 1840–1860," in *Essays in Antebellum Politics, 1840–1860*, ed.
Stephen E. Maizlish and John J. Kushma (College Station, TX, 1982); Ronald
P. Formisano, *The Transformation of Political Culture: Massachusetts Parties,
1790s–1840s* (New York, 1983); Joel Silbey, *The American Political Nation, 1838–
1893* (Stanford, CA, 1991).

14. Horace Bushnell, "American Politics," *American National Preacher* 14 (Dec.
1840), 204; Horace Bushnell, *Politics under the Law of God: A Discourse delivered in the North Congregational Church, Hartford, on the Annual Fast of 1844*
(Hartford, 1844), 23; Nathaniel Gage, *Sins and Dangers of the Times: A Sermon,
Delivered in Haverhill, Mass.* (Haverhill, MA, 1838), 25.

15. John H. Harvey, *Party Spirit: An Address before the Society of Alumni of Hanover
College at their Second Anniversary, Sept. 27, 1837* (South Hanover, IN, 1837), 9,
6; "Public Sentiment," *Christian Advocate and Journal*, Mar. 13, 1835; Samuel

T. Spear, *The Politico-Social Foundations of Our Republic: A Sermon* (New York, 1845), 12; Bushnell, "American Politics," 199; Bushnell, *Politics under the Law of God*, 23; Richard Carwardine, *Evangelicals and Politics in Antebellum America* (New Haven, CT, 1993), 1–49. On women and party politics, see especially Mary Ryan, *Women in Public: Between Banners and Ballots, 1825–1880* (Baltimore, 1990); Elizabeth Varon, *We Mean to Be Counted: White Women and Politics in Antebellum Virginia* (Chapel Hill, 1998), 71–102.

16. "Review of Reports on Sunday Mails," *Christian Spectator*, Mar. 1, 1829; "Infidelity in the United States," *Free Enquirer*, Feb. 2, 1834; Lyman Beecher, *A Plea for the West* (Cincinnati, 1835), 48; Mark Tucker, *A Discourse Preached on Thanksgiving Day, in the Beneficent Congregational Meeting-House, Providence, July 21, 1842* (Providence, 1842), 7; Heman Humphrey, *Parallel Between Intemperance and the Slave-Trade* (New York, 1828), 13–14; Griffin, *Their Brothers' Keepers*, 60; Walters, *American Reformers*, 8; Daniel Walker Howe, "The Evangelical Movement and Political Culture in the North during the Second Party System," *Journal of American History* 77 (1991), 1216–1239.

17. Wayland, *Duties of An American Citizen*, 36–37.

18. *The Politics of Aristotle* (Chapel Hill, 1997), 89–91, 94; J. G. A. Pocock, *The Machiavellian Moment: Florentine Political Thought and the Atlantic Republican Tradition* (Princeton, NJ, 1975).

19. Elisha P. Douglass, *Rebels and Democrats: The Struggle for Equal Political Rights and Majority Rule during the American Revolution* (Chapel Hill, 1955), 13–16; Gordon Wood, *Creation of the American Republic, 1776–1787* (Chapel Hill, 1969), 223–224, 239–240; Eric Foner, *Tom Paine and Revolutionary America* (New York, 1976), ch. 2; Wilentz, *Rise of American Democracy*, 15–31.

20. Foner, *Tom Paine*, 122; Marc W. Kruman, *Between Authority and Liberty: State Constitution Making in Revolutionary America* (Chapel Hill, 1997), 144–148.

21. John Adams, *A Defence of the Constitutions of the United States of America* [1787–1788] (New York, 1971), I, 3, III, 353, 291, 216–217, 225–226. On the political thought of John Adams, see Wood, *Creation of the American Republic*, 567–592; C. Bradley Thompson, *John Adams and the Spirit of Liberty* (Lawrence, KS, 1998).

22. James Madison, "Vices of the Political System of the United States," in *The Writings of James Madison*, vol. 2 [1783–1787] (New York, 1901), 366–367; Wood, *Creation of the American Republic*; Jack N. Rakove, *Original Meanings: Politics and Ideas in the Making of the Constitution* (New York, 1996), 35–56; Woody Holton, *Unruly Americans and the Origins of the Constitution* (New York, 2007).

23. Madison, "Vices of the Political System," 368–369; Alexander Hamilton, James Madison, and John Jay, *The Federalist* [1787–1788], ed. J. R. Pole (Indianapolis, 2005), 48–51.

24. *Reports of the Proceedings and Debates of the Convention of 1821, Assembled for the Purpose of Amending the Constitution of the State of New-York* (Albany, 1821), 221; *Journal of Debates and Proceedings In the Convention of Delegates, Chosen*

to Revise the Constitution of Massachusetts [1820–1821] (Boston, 1853), 276–279; Merrill D. Peterson, ed., *Democracy, Liberty, and Property: The State Constitutional Conventions of the 1820s* (New York, 1966); Keyssar, *The Right to Vote*; Wilentz, *Rise of American Democracy*. On populist uprisings of the period, see especially Ronald P. Formisano, *For the People: American Populist Movements from the Revolution to the 1850s* (Chapel Hill, 2008).

25. Lyman Beecher, *Six Sermons on the Nature, Occasions, Signs, Evils, and Remedy of Intemperance* (Boston, 1829), 57–58; Merle Curti, *The Social Ideas of American Educators* (Paterson, NJ, 1959), 135; Michael Schudson, *The Good Citizen: A History of American Civic Life* (New York, 1998), 92; Horace Mann, "The Necessity of Education in a Republican Government," in *Lectures on Education* (Boston, 1845), 142–143; Bethune, *Our Liberties*, 14–15.

26. *Journal of Debates and Proceedings . . . of Massachusetts*, 307, 314, 317, 309–310, 312; Merrill D. Peterson, *The Great Triumvirate: Webster, Clay, and Calhoun* (New York, 1987), 104–106. Webster was tapping into the Revolutionary-era republican rationale to support changes in inheritance law, particularly the abolition of primogeniture and entail. See Stanley N. Katz, "Republicanism and the Law of Inheritance in the American Revolutionary Era," *Michigan Law Review* 76 (1977–1978), 15; Holly Brewer, "Entailing Aristocracy in Colonial Virginia: 'Ancient Feudal Restraints' and Revolutionary Reform," *William and Mary Quarterly* 54 (Apr. 1997), 307–346.

27. Wilentz, *Rise of American Democracy*, 188; Alexis de Tocqueville, *Democracy in America* [1835], ed. J. P. Mayer, George Lawrence, translation (New York, 1966), 9, 248, 210–211; Morton J. Horwitz, "Tocqueville and the Tyranny of the Majority," *Review of Politics* 28 (1966), 293–307.

28. Beecher, *Memory of Our Fathers*, 8–9; Albert Barnes, *The Connexion of Temperance with Republican Freedom: An Oration* (Philadelphia, 1835), 9–10.

29. *Lotteries Exposed. Or An Inquiry into the Consequences Attending Them in a General and Individual Point of View* (Philadelphia, 1827), 5–6; *The Proceedings and Constitution of the Pennsylvania Branch of the General Union for Promoting the Observance of the Christian Sabbath* (Philadelphia, 1828), 15.

30. Albert Barnes, "The Supremacy of the Laws," *American National Preacher* 12 (1838), 128; Harvey, *Party Spirit*, 6.

31. Francis Wayland, *The Elements of Political Economy* (Boston, 1840), 119.

32. "Public Sentiment," *Christian Advocate and Journal*, Mar. 13, 1835; Beecher, *Memory of Our Fathers*, 17.

33. On the Second Great Awakening, see especially Donald G. Mathews, "The Second Great Awakening as an Organizing Process, 1780–1830," *American Quarterly* 21 (Spr. 1969), 23–43; Nathan O. Hatch, *The Democratization of American Christianity* (New Haven, CT, 1989); Butler, *Awash in a Sea of Faith*, 257–288.

34. Beecher, *Memory of Our Fathers*, 30–32; Boyer, *Urban Masses and Moral Order*, 13; Mintz, *Moralists and Modernizers*, 50–78; Pegram, *Battling Demon Rum*, 19;

Walters, *American Reformers*, 81. For a thorough treatment of reform in the South and Midwest, see John W. Quist, *Restless Visionaries: The Social Roots of Antebellum Reform in Alabama and Michigan* (Baton Rouge, 1998).

35. Charles G. Finney, *Lectures on Revivals of Religion* (New York, 1835), 167; Neem, *Creating a Nation of Joiners*, 81–113; Brooke, "Cultures of Nationalism," 1–33. On reformers' middle-class orientation, see Paul E. Johnson, *A Shopkeeper's Millennium: Society and Revivals in Rochester, New York, 1815–1837* (New York, 1978); Boyer, *Urban Masses and Moral Order*; Mary P. Ryan, *Cradle of the Middle Class: The Family in Oneida County, New York, 1790–1865* (New York, 1981); John S. Gilkeson, *Middle-Class Providence, 1820–1940* (Princeton, NJ, 1986); Christine Stansell, *City of Women: Sex and Class in New York, 1789–1860* (Chicago, 1987); Randolph A. Roth, *The Democratic Dilemma: Religion, Reform, and the Social Order in the Connecticut River Valley of Vermont, 1791–1850* (New York, 1987); Stuart M. Blumin, *The Emergence of the Middle Class: Social Experience in the American City, 1760–1900* (New York, 1989).

36. John R. Bodo, *The Protestant Clergy and Public Issues, 1812–1848* (Princeton, NJ, 1954), 53; William W. Brown, *A Lecture Delivered Before the Female Anti-Slavery Society of Salem* (Boston, 1847) reprinted in *The Narrative of William W. Brown—a Fugitive Slave* [1848] (Mineola, NY, 2003), 90; Spear, *Politico-Social Foundations*, 11–12; Carwardine, *Evangelicals and Politics*, 22–26. Even Garrison expected "to see abolition at the ballot-box" after the "moral vision of the people" was reformed such that it became "the duty of every voter to be an abolitionist." See "Reply to James G. Birney," *Liberator*, Jun. 28, 1839. For a recent appraisal of Garrisonian political thought and behavior, see McDaniel, *Problem of Slavery*.

37. Beecher, *Memory of Our Fathers*, 37; Ezra Stiles Ely, *The Duty of Christian Freemen to Elect Christian Magistrates* (Philadelphia, 1828); Bodo, *Protestant Clergy*, 46–47; Mintz, *Moralists and Modernizers*, 50; West, *Politics of Revelation and Reason*, 128–133.

38. Carwardine, *Evangelicals and Politics*, 126–127; West, *Politics of Revelation and Reason*, 134–135; "Fourth of July," *The Correspondent*, Jul. 7, 1827; Schlereth, "Fits of Political Religion," 288–323; William Ellery Channing, "Remarks on Associations," in *The Works of William E. Channing*, vol. 1 (Boston, 1846), 305–308; Neem, *Creating a Nation of Joiners*, 114–115.

39. [Theodore Frelinghuysen], *An Inquiry Into the Moral and Religious Character of the American Government* (New York, 1838), 208; Lyman Beecher, "Pre-Eminent Importance of the Christian Sabbath," *National Preacher* 3 (1829), 156; Heman Humphrey, *Essays upon the Origin, Perpetuity, Change, and Proper Observance of the Sabbath* (New York, 1829), 96–97; Eviatar Zerubavel, *The Seven Day Circle: The History and Meaning of the Week* (Chicago, 1985), 28–35. On the Sunday mails controversy, see especially Bertram Wyatt-Brown, "Prelude to Abolitionism: Sabbatarian Politics and the Rise of the Second Party System," *Journal of American History* 58 (1971), 316–341; Richard R. John, "Taking Sabbatarianism Seriously: The Postal System, the Sabbath, and the

Transformation of American Political Culture," *Journal of the Early Republic* 10 (1990), 517–567; West, *Politics of Revelation and Reason*, 137–170.

40. *Proceedings and Constitution of the Pennsylvania Branch*, 11; West, *Politics of Revelation and Reason*, 148–159; "Review of Reports on Sunday Mails," *Quarterly Christian Spectator*, Mar. 1, 1829, 157.

41. On early petition efforts, see especially Newman, *Transformation of American Abolitionism*, 39–59. On the later petition campaign, see especially Russel B. Nye, *Fettered Freedom: Civil Liberties and the Slavery Controversy, 1830–1860* (Chicago, 1963), 41–67; Stewart, *Holy Warriors*, 81–85; Don E. Fehrenbacher, *The Slaveholding Republic: An Account of the United States Government's Relations to Slavery* (New York, 2001), 49–88; Susan Zaeske, *Signatures of Citizenship: Petitioning, Antislavery, and Women's Political Identity* (Chapel Hill, 2003).

42. Abzug, *Cosmos Crumbling*, 14; "Slavery in the District of Columbia," *The Abolitionist* (Sep. 1833), 139–140; "Slavery and the Slave Trade in the District of Columbia," *The Abolitionist* (Oct. 1833), 154; William Jay, *A View of the Action of the Federal Government, in Behalf of Slavery* [1839], in *Miscellaneous Writings on Slavery* (Boston, 1853), 216.

43. Nye, *Fettered Freedom*, 44–45; Daniel Wirls, " 'The Only Mode of Avoiding Everlasting Debate': The Overlooked Senate Gag Rule for Antislavery Petitions," *Journal of the Early Republic* 27 (Spring 2007), 115–138; Stewart, *Holy Warriors*, 82–84; William Lee Miller, *Arguing about Slavery: The Great Battle in the United States Congress* (New York, 1996).

44. Walters, *American Reformers*, 136–137; Mark A. Vargas, "The Progressive Agent of Mischief: The Whiskey Ration and Temperance in the United States Army," *Historian* 67 (2005), 199–216.

45. American Temperance Society, *On the Immorality of the Traffic in Ardent Spirit* [appendix to *Fifth Report*] (New York, 1832), 198–220; "The Traffic in Ardent Spirit, to be Used as a Drink, is a Violation of the Law of God, and is an Immorality," *Seventh Annual Report of the American Temperance Society—1834*, contained within *Permanent Temperance Documents*, vol. 1, 57; *Sixth Annual Report of the American Temperance Society*, 44–46. On early license laws, see Sharon Salinger, *Taverns and Drinking in Early America* (Baltimore, 2002); William J. Novak, *The People's Welfare: Law and Regulation in Nineteenth-Century America* (Chapel Hill, 1996).

46. Ian Tyrrell, *Sobering Up: From Temperance to Prohibition in Antebellum America, 1800–1860* (Westport, CT, 1979), 227–232, 243; *Seventh Annual Report of the American Temperance Society*, 6; "License, License," *Journal of the American Temperance Union* 5 (Jun. 1841), 90; John A. Krout, *The Origins of Prohibition* (New York, 1925), 273–274.

47. *Report of the Executive Committee of the American Temperance Union, 1840* (New York, 1840), 11; Tyrrell, *Sobering Up*, 237–239; Robert L. Hampel, *Temperance and Prohibition in Massachusetts, 1813–1852* (Ann Arbor, MI, 1982), 79–94.

48. "Mr. Adams and the Massachusetts License Law," *Niles' National Register*, Aug. 31, 1839; Formisano, *Transformation of Political Culture*, 298–299; "The License Law-Extract from Governor Morton's Message," *Liberator*, Feb. 14, 1840; *Report of the Executive Committee of the American Temperance Union, 1841* (New York, 1841), 20; "The License Law-Political Action," *Liberator*, Feb. 21, 1840.

CHAPTER 2

1. "The Sunday Laws," *Workingman's Advocate* (New York), Jun. 29, 1844; "Ejecting an Alderman," *New York Herald*, Jun. 25, 1844; "Sunday Keeping in New York," *Sabbath Recorder* (New York) (hereafter *SR*), Jul. 4, 1844.

2. On the Sabbath in colonial America, see Winton U. Solberg, *Redeem the Time: The Puritan Sabbath in Early America* (Cambridge, MA, 1977). For a broad investigation of Sunday laws, see Andrew J. King, "Sunday Law in the Nineteenth Century," *Albany Law Review* 64 (2000), 675–772.

3. Sunday laws were not the only area of public policy that generated questions about the religious character of the American nation and its government in the nineteenth century, though they were particularly important in giving rise to debates about majority rule and to minority-rights activism. For examples of scholarship investigating other arenas of conflict, see Mark De Wolfe Howe, *The Garden and the Wilderness: Religion and Government in American Constitutional History* (Chicago, 1965); Morton Borden, *Jews, Turks, and Infidels* (Chapel Hill, 1984); Sarah B. Gordon, "Blasphemy and the Law of Religious Liberty in Nineteenth-Century America," *American Quarterly* 52 (2000), 682–719; Philip Hamburger, *Separation of Church and State* (Cambridge, MA, 2002); Ronald P. Formisano and Stephen Pickering, "The Christian Nation Debate and Witness Competency," *Journal of the Early Republic* 29 (Summer 2009), 219–248; Steven K. Green, *The Second Disestablishment: Church and State in Nineteenth-Century America* (New York, 2010).

4. *Abstract of the Proceedings of the National Lord's Day Convention, held in the City of Baltimore, on the 27th and 28th November, 1844* (Baltimore, 1845), 4–5; "National Lord's Day Convention," *New York Evangelist*, Dec. 5, 1844.

5. "Observance of the Sabbath," *Pittsburgh Gazette*, Oct. 27, 1846; "Sabbath Convention," *Pittsburgh Gazette*, Oct. 29, 1844; "Sabbath Convention," *Pittsburgh Gazette*, Sep. 20, 1845; Willard Hall, *A Plea for the Sabbath; addressed to the Legal Profession in the United States, by Judge Hall, of Delaware* (Baltimore, 1845); Frederick L. Bronner, "The Observance of the Sabbath in the United States, 1800–1865" (PhD diss., Harvard University, 1937); Roy Z. Chamlee Jr., "The Sabbath Crusade: 1810–1920" (PhD diss., George Washington University, 1968), 122–135; J. Thomas Jable, "Aspects of Moral Reform in Early Nineteenth-Century Pennsylvania," *Pennsylvania Magazine of History and Biography* 102 (1978), 344–363; John Gilkeson, *Middle-Class Providence, 1820–1940* (Princeton, NJ,

1986), 68–69; John Paul Rossing, "A Cultural History of Nineteenth Century American Sabbath Reform Movements" (PhD diss., Emory University, 1994), 117–159; Richard Olin Johnson, "Free from the Rigor of the Law: Challenges to the Anglo-American Sabbath in Nineteenth-Century America" (PhD diss., Graduate Theological Union, 2001), 53–55; Alexis McCrossen, *Holy Day, Holiday: The American Sunday* (Ithaca, NY, 2002), 26–27. Rossing observes that the Sabbath reform was "a male movement. At a time when women were active in the temperance movement, the abolition movement, and the peace movement, the leaders of the Sabbath reform were all men." Rossing, "Nineteenth Century American Sabbath," 146.

6. "Sabbath Violations in New-York," *New York Evangelist*, Jul. 28, 1842; "Critical Notices," *American Biblical Repository* 5 (Jan. 1841), 236–237; *Proceedings of the New York State Sabbath Convention, held at Saratoga Springs* (Albany, NY, 1844), 27; Chamlee, "The Sabbath Crusade," 83–98.

7. "Sabbath Association," *Pittsburgh Gazette*, Nov. 23, 1844; *Proceedings of the Sabbath Convention held at the City of Rochester*, (Rochester, NY, 1842), 43. *Proceedings of the State Sabbath Convention; held at Harrisburg* (Philadelphia, 1844), 35; *Proceedings of the Lord's Day Convention Assembled in the City of Washington, on the 24th and 25th of February, 1846* (Washington, DC, 1846), 6–7; "Regard for the Sabbath," *Pittsburgh Gazette*, Dec. 1, 1845; *Proceedings of the New York State Sabbath Convention, held at Saratoga Springs*, 6; "For the Pittsburgh Gazette," *Pittsburgh Gazette*, Dec. 27, 1845; Rossing, "Nineteenth Century American Sabbath," 143–145.

8. "Observance of the Sabbath," *Pittsburgh Gazette*, Oct. 27, 1846; Stanley Nadel, *Little Germany: Ethnicity, Religion, and Class in New York City, 1845–80* (Chicago, 1990), 104–116, 132–133; McCrossen, *Holy Day, Holiday*, 41–46.

9. "Sabbath Violations in New-York," *New York Evangelist*, Jul. 28, 1842; "Licensed to Ruin Souls," *New York Evangelist*, Jun. 26, 1845; Kingsbury, *The Sabbath*, 363; Johnson, "Free from the Rigor," 61; "Sunday in France," *American Protestant Vindicator*, Jan. 15, 1845; Johnson, "Free from the Rigor," 58–61.

10. *Proceedings of the New York State Sabbath Convention, held at Saratoga Springs*, 14; "For the Pittsburgh Gazette," *Pittsburgh Gazette*, Dec. 27, 1845; Philip S. Foner, *History of the Labor Movement in the United States*, vol. 1, *From Colonial Times to the Founding of the American Federation of Labor* (New York, 1947), 211.

11. *Proceedings of the Sabbath Convention held at the City of Rochester*, 16; *Second Annual Report of the Philadelphia Sabbath Association* (Philadelphia, 1843), 11; Mark Hopkins, *The Sabbath and Free Institutions: A Paper Read before the National Sabbath Convention, Saratoga, Aug. 13, 1863* (New York, 1863), 26–27.

12. *Abstract of the Proceedings of the State Sabbath Convention of Alabama* (Mobile, AL, 1846), 8, 17, 19; Richard C. Wade, *Slavery in the Cities: The South 1820–1860* (New York, 1964), 145–160; Ellen Eslinger, "Antebellum Liquor Reform in Lexington, Virginia: The Story of a Small Southern Town," *Virginia Magazine*

of *History and Biography* 99 (Apr. 1991), 163–186; Thomas D. Morris, *Southern Slavery and the Law, 1619–1860* (Chapel Hill, 1996), 338. On Sundays in slavery, see Kenneth M. Stampp, *The Peculiar Institution: Slavery in the Ante-Bellum South* (New York, 1956), 79, 166–172, 218; Peter Kolchin, *American Slavery, 1619–1877* (New York, 2003), 107, 130.

13. *Proceedings of the Sabbath Convention held at the City of Rochester,* 43–44; "Sabbath Convention," *Brooklyn Eagle,* Jul. 25, 1842; *Proceedings of the Sabbath Convention held at the City of Rochester,* 68; *Christian Observer* (Louisville, KY), Jun. 14, 1844; "Address," *Weekly Messenger* (Chambersburg, PA), Jul. 10, 1844; *Proceedings of the State Sabbath Convention; held at Harrisburg,* 36; "Legislation for the Sabbath," *Christian Observer,* Dec. 19, 1845.

14. *Proceedings of the National Lord's Day Convention,* 63–64; "Sabbath Convention," *New England Puritan,* Aug. 26, 1841; "Protection of the Sabbath," *New York Evangelist,* Feb. 2, 1843.

15. "The 'Sabbath' Question," *United States Catholic Magazine and Monthly Review* 4 (Apr. 1845), 224–225; "Lady Critics," *Catholic Magazine and Monthly Review* 4 (Oct. 1845), 675.

16. "The Mayor's Speech," *Workingman's Advocate* (New York), May 18, 1844; Edward K. Spann, *The New Metropolis: New York City, 1840–1857* (New York, 1981), 36–40; Sean Wilentz, *Chants Democratic: New York City and the Rise of the American Working Class, 1788–1850* (New York, 1984), 322; Richard J. Carwardine, *Evangelicals and Politics in Antebellum America* (New Haven, CT, 1993), 84–85. For the broader context, see Billington, *Protestant Crusade,* 193–219; Vincent P. Lannie, *Public School Money and Parochial Education: Bishop Hughes, Governor Seward, and the New York School Controversy* (Cleveland, 1968); Hamburger, *Separation of Church and State,* 229; Green, *The Second Disestablishment,* 251–271.

17. "Sunday Laws," *Workingman's Advocate* (New York), Jun. 1, 1844; "City Reform," *Workingman's Advocate,* Jun. 8, 1844; Teresa Anne Murphy, *Ten Hours' Labor: Religion, Reform, and Gender in Early New England* (Ithaca, NY, 1992); 164–176; Jama Lazerow, *Religion and the Working Class in Antebellum America* (Washington, DC, 1995), 49–51.

18. "Thoughts on Religious Liberty," *The Knickerbocker* 26 (Sep. 1845), 230–231 (emphasis in original).

19. "Spartan Doctrines," *Workingman's Advocate,* Oct. 5, 1844; "Thoughts on Religious Liberty," *The Knickerbocker* 26 (Sep. 1845), 229; "The Sunday Law—Stopping Omnibuses," *Boston Investigator,* Aug. 4, 1841.

20. "Thoughts on Religious Liberty," *The Knickerbocker* 26 (Sep. 1845), 229–230.

21. "Lady Critics," *Catholic Magazine and Monthly Review* 4 (Oct. 1845), 675. During the earlier conflict over the Sunday mails, Richard Johnson's report similarly pointed to these groups to expose the absurdity of any notion of American religious conformity. Now, instead of being used to justify the federal policy of distributing the mail on Sundays, Jews and Seventh Day Baptists were used

to delegitimate state and local Sunday laws. See *Report of the Committee on Post-Offices and Post-roads of the United States Senate* (1829) as found in *Social Theories of Jacksonian Democracy*, ed. J. S. Blau (Indianapolis, 2003), 276.

22. "The Christian Sabbath," *SR*, Jul. 31, 1845; *Proceedings of the Sabbath Convention at Hollidaysburg, September 23, 1846* (Philadelphia, 1846), 4–5.

23. [Theodore Frelinghuysen], *An Inquiry into the Moral and Religious Character of the American Government* (New York, 1838), 191–193; "Mr. Editor," *Cincinnati Daily Times*, Sep. 30, 1845; "The Christian Sabbath," *SR*, Jul. 31, 1845.

24. "Central Seventh-day Baptist Association," *SR*, Jul. 4, 1844 (emphasis in original).

25. "The Festival of Sunday a Human Ordinance," *SR*, Jun. 5, 1845; "The Sabbatarians or Seventh-day Baptists," *SR*, May 13, 1847; "The Lord's Day Not the Sabbath," *SR*, Jul. 4, 1844; "Observations of a Tourist—No. 3," *SR*, Dec. 19, 1844; "Legislation in Favor of Sabbath-keepers," *SR*, Jul. 10, 1845; "Reasons for Opposing Sunday Legislation—No. 12," *SR*, Apr. 23, 1846.

26. "The Israelites of South Carolina," *Occident and American Jewish Advocate* (hereafter *OAJA*) 2 (Jan. 1845), 496–510; "The Israelites and the Governor of S.C.," *SR*, Jan. 9, 1845; "The Israelites of Charleston," *Episcopal Recorder*, Dec. 21, 1844; Naomi Cohen, *Jews in Christian America: The Pursuit of Religious Equality* (New York, 1992), 49–50; Drew Gilpin Faust, *James Henry Hammond and the Old South: A Design for Mastery* (Baton Rouge, 1982), 249.

27. *Constitution and Proceedings of the Charleston Society for the Due Observance of the Lord's Day* (Charleston, 1843), 7–8, 14–15; "Richmond, Virginia," *OAJA* 3 (Nov. 1845); "Sunday Legislation," *OAJA* 3 (Feb. 1846), 561–567; "Sunday Legislation," *OAJA* 4 (Sep. 1846), 297–302; Myron Berman, *Richmond's Jewry* (Charlottesville, VA, 1979), 49–53; Cohen, *Encounter with Emancipation*, 80–81; "Observance of the Sabbath," *Western Washingtonian and Sons of Temperance Record* (Cincinnati), Aug. 23, 1845; "The City Council," *Western Washingtonian and Sons of Temperance Record*, Sep. 6, 1845; "Several Jews," *Cincinnati Daily Times*, Aug. 27, 1845; "Thirteen Israelites," *Western Washingtonian*, Sep. 20, 1845; "Violation of Sunday," *SR*, Sep. 4, 1845; "Sunday-Keeping in Cincinnati," *SR*, Sep. 11, 1845; "Police Reports," *Cincinnati Daily Times*, Sep. 6, 1845; "Sunday," *Fort Wayne* (IN) *Times and Peoples Press*, Oct. 18, 1845; "The Sunday Ordinance," *Cincinnati Daily Enquirer*, Aug. 14, 1845.

28. "The German Seventh-day Baptists," *SR*, Jun. 17, 1847; *SR*, Jun. 24, 1847; *SR*, Jul. 1, 1847; *SR*, Jul. 8, 1847; Charles Treher, *Snow Hill Cloister* (Allentown, PA, 1968); Corliss Fitz Randolph, "The German Seventh Day Baptists," in *Seventh Day Baptists in Europe and America* [1910] (New York, 1980); E. G. Alderfer, *The Ephrata Commune: An Early American Counterculture* (Pittsburgh, 1985), 173–183.

29. "Persecution in Pennsylvania," *SR*, Sep. 18, 1845; "A Plain Statement," *SR*, Apr. 2, 1846; "Served them Right," *Adams Sentinel and General Advertiser* (Gettysburg,

PA), Aug. 25, 1845; Davis, *General History of the Sabbatarian Churches*, 254–255; Randolph, "German Seventh Day Baptists," 1222–1223.

30. "How It Works," *SR*, Jan. 29, 1846; "Persecution in Pennsylvania," *SR*, Sep. 18, 1845.

31. "Sunday Legislation," *OAJA* 3 (Feb. 1846), 561.

32. Lance J. Sussman, *Isaac Leeser and the Making of American Judaism* (Detroit, 1995); Jonathan D. Sarna, *American Judaism: A History* (New Haven, CT, 2004), 76–82; Hasia R. Diner, *The Jews of the United States, 1654 to 2000* (Berkeley, CA, 2004), 118–122.

33. Isaac Leeser, *The Claims of the Jews to an Equality of Rights* (Philadelphia, 1840), 51, 91, 17; Cohen, *Jews in Christian America*, 44–45; "Sunday Legislation," *OAJA* 3 (Feb. 1846), 561.

34. "The Dangers of Our Position," *OAJA* 2 (Jan. 1845).

35. "Sunday Laws," *Sunday Times and Noah's Weekly Messenger* (New York), Feb. 13, 1848; Jonathan Sarna, *Jacksonian Jew: The Two Worlds of Mordecai Noah* (New York, 1981), 134–135.

36. *Minutes of the Seventh-Day Baptist General Conference held at Shiloh, New Jersey* (New York, 1846), 7–9; "The German Seventh-Day Baptists," *SR*, Jun. 17, 1847; "Equal Religious Privileges," *SR*, Jan. 21, 1847; *Religious Liberty Endangered by Legislative Enactments: An Appeal to the Friends of Equal Rights and Religious Freedom, in the United States, From the Seventh-Day Baptist General Conference* (New York, 1846).

37. For examples, see "Sunday Laws," *Boston Investigator*, Jun. 2, 1847; "State Laws in Reference to the Sabbath," Dec. 29, 1847; "Anti-Sabbath Convention," Feb. 2, 1848.

38. Garrison likely was influenced by the Motts, whose Quakerism brought them to believe that strict Sabbath observance was a Jewish institution of the Old Testament revoked in the New Testament by the "purely spiritual reign of Christ." Garrison's controversial stance also exacerbated the pending split in the abolitionist movement as more traditional evangelical abolitionists like Lewis and Arthur Tappan could not countenance his position on the Sabbath. "Lyman Beecher," *Liberator*, Jul. 23, 1836; Wendell Phillips Garrison and Francis Jackson Garrison, *William Lloyd Garrison, 1805–1879: The Story of His Life Told by His Children*, vol. 2, *1835–1840* (New York, 1885), 106–113; Walter M. Merrill, *Against Wind and Tide: A Biography of Wm. Lloyd Garrison* (Cambridge, MA, 1963), 131–132; Chamlee, "The Sabbath Crusade," 188–210; William L. Van Deburg, "William Lloyd Garrison and the 'Pro-Slavery Priesthood': The Changing Beliefs of an Evangelical Reformer, 1830–1840," *Journal of the American Academy of Religion* 43 (Jun. 1975), 233–234; Robert H. Abzug, *Cosmos Crumbling: American Reform and the Religious Imagination* (New York, 1994), 180; Rossing, "Nineteenth Century American Sabbath," 150–155; McCrossen, *Holy Day, Holiday*, 28–29; Johnson, "Free from the Rigor," 96–117. On women active in the Garrisonian resistance to Sabbath reformers and the relationship to women's rights, see

Nancy Isenberg, *Sex and Citizenship in Antebellum America* (Chapel Hill, 1998), 75–101.

39. Rossing, "Nineteenth Century American Sabbath," 153; McCrossen, *Holy Day, Holiday*, 30–32; Henry Parkhurst, *Proceedings of the Anti-Sabbath Convention, Held in the Melodeon, March 23d and 24th* [1848] (Port Washington, NY, 1971); "C.C. Burleigh in Prison," *SR*, Mar. 23, 1847; "C.C. Burleigh in Prison," *New York Tribune*, Mar. 20, 1847.

40. "Religious Equality," *OAJA* 5 (Jan. 1848), 500; "The United States Not A Christian State," *OAJA* 7 (Feb. 1850), 563–564; "Sunday Legislation," *OAJA* 3 (Feb. 1846), 561; W. L. Fisher, *History of the Institution of the Sabbath Day* (Philadelphia, 1845), 43–51; Burleigh, *Sabbath Question*, 7.

41. "Equality of Religious Rights," *SR*, Dec. 24, 1846; "Sunday Legislation," *OAJA* 3 (Feb. 1846), 561–562; "Sunday Legislation Anti-Republican—No.5," *SR*, Feb. 5, 1846; "Richmond, Virginia," *OAJA* 3 (Nov. 1845); "Religious Equality," *OAJA* 5 (Jan. 1848), 500; "Johnson's Sunday-Mail Report," *SR*, Feb. 4, 1847; "The General Conference," *SR*, Sep. 17, 1846; "Sunday Legislation," *OAJA* 3 (Feb. 1846), 566.

42. "Petitions for Equal Religious Privileges," *SR*, Jan. 14, 1847; "Pennsylvania Sunday Laws," *SR*, May 27, 1847; "Liberty of Conscience," *SR*, Jan. 27, 1848; "Religious Equality," *OAJA* 5 (Jan. 1848), 499–500; Fisher, *Institution of the Sabbath Day*, 43–51; "Sunday Legislation," *OAJA* 3 (Feb. 1846), 565.

43. "Enforcing Sabbaths By Civil Penalties," *SR*, Sep. 11, 1845; "Tax Upon Conscience," *SR*, Feb 17, 1848; "Triumph of Constitutional Rights," *SR*, Feb. 4, 1847; "The General Conference," *SR*, Sep. 17, 1846 (emphasis in originals).

44. "Legislation in Favor of Sunday," *SR*, Mar. 27, 1845; *Religious Liberty Endangered by Legislative Enactments*, 16; "Sunday Legislation Anti-Republican—No. 5," *SR*, Feb. 5, 1846.

45. "The Right of Legislatures to Enforce Sabbaths," *SR*, Jul. 20, 1846; *Proceedings of the Anti-Sabbath Convention*, 8.

46. "Ultraism," *Boston Quarterly Review* 1 (Jul. 1838), 377–384; "Religion and Politics," *Boston Quarterly Review* 1 (Jul. 1838), 326, 321–322; Arthur M. Schelesinger Jr., *Orestes A. Brownson: A Pilgrim's Progress* (Boston, 1939), 112–123; Schelesinger Jr., *The Age of Jackson* (New York, 1945), 401–406; Patrick W. Carey, *Orestes A. Brownson: American Religious Weathervane* (Grand Rapids, MI, 2004), 81–83.

47. *Religious Liberty Endangered by Legislative Enactments*, 14; "Church and State," *SR*, Mar. 5, 1846.

48. James Madison, *Memorial and Remonstrance Against Religious Assessments* in *The Mind of the Founder: Sources of the Political Thought of James Madison*, ed. Marvin Meyers (Hanover, NH, 1981), 7; John G. West Jr., *The Politics of Revelation and Reason: Religion and Civic Life in the New Nation* (Lawrence, KS, 1996), 67–73.

49. "A Plea for Sunday Freedom," *Liberator*, Jan. 24, 1845; "Church and State," *SR*, Mar. 5, 1846; "Sunday Legislation," *OAJA* 3 (Feb. 1846), 562–563; "The Right of Legislatures to Enforce Sabbaths," *SR*, Jul. 20, 1846.

50. "Violation of Sunday Laws at Charleston," *OAJA* 4 (Mar. 1847); *City Council of Charleston v. S.A. Benjamin*, 2 Strob. 508 (1848).

51. *Cincinnati v. Rice*, 15 Ohio 225 (1846); "Triumph of Constitutional Rights," *SR*, Feb. 4, 1847.

52. Hans L. Trefousse, *Thaddeus Stevens: Nineteenth-Century Egalitarian* (Chapel Hill, 1997).

53. *The Argument of Thaddeus Stevens, Esq. Before the Supreme Court of PA., at Harrisburg, in the case of Jacob Specht vs. The Commonwealth* (Lancaster, PA, 1848), 4–9; *Specht v. Commonwealth*, 8 Barr. 312 (1848), 314–316.

54. *Argument of Thaddeus Stevens*, 12–14.

55. 8 Barr 312, 320–321.

56. 8 Barr 312, 322–323.

57. 8 Barr 312, 322, 324–326.

58. "The Courts," *Niles' National Register*, Jul. 19, 1848.

59. "Religious Rights Repudiated," *SR*, Jul. 13, 1848; "Political Inequality," *OAJA* 6 (Aug. 1848), 217.

60. "Pennsylvania Sunday Law—Inconsistencies," *SR*, Mar. 22, 1849. For general notice of the decision, see "Constitutionality of the Pennsylvania Sabbath Law," *Baltimore Sun*, Jul. 10, 1848; "Pennsylvania Sabbath Law," *Alexandria* (VA) *Gazette*, Jul. 11, 1848; "Constitutionality of the Sabbath Law," *New Bedford* (MA) *Mercury*, Jul. 14, 1848; "Constitutionality of the Sabbath Law," *Nantucket* (MA) *Inquirer*, Jul. 18, 1848; "Constitutionality of the Pennsylvania Sabbath Law," *New London* (CT) *Daily Chronicle*, Jul. 18, 1848; "Constitutionality of the Sabbath Law," *Farmer's Cabinet* (Amherst, NH), Jul. 20, 1848; "Christian Sabbath," *Charleston Gospel Messenger and Protestant Episcopal Register* 25 (Feb. 1849), 338.

61. "Opinions in the Press," *SR*, Aug. 17, 1848; "Political Inequality," *OAJA* 6 (Sep. 1848), 274; "Sunday Laws—Protection," *SR*, Nov. 9, 1848.

62. "Sabbath Laws in Pennsylvania," *Democratic Review* 23 (Nov. 1848), 433, 443, 438.

63. "The Lord's Day, The Christian Sabbath," *Methodist Quarterly Review* 1 (Jan. 1849), 40.

64. "Doings in Pennsylvania," *SR*, Oct. 12, 1848; "Progress of Persecution in Pennsylvania," *SR*, Oct. 26, 1848; "The Christian Sabbath, As Sanctioned by the Supreme Court of Pennsylvania," *OAJA* 6 (Nov. 1848), 413; "Petition of German Seventh Day Baptists," *Liberator*, Apr. 27, 1849.

65. *Report Relative to the Observance of the Sabbath, Made to the House of Representatives* (Harrisburg, 1850), 3–4.

66. "The German Sabbath-Keepers," *SR*, Dec. 13, 1849.

CHAPTER 3

1. "Judge Lynch in Ann Arbor," *Signal of Liberty* (Ann Arbor, MI), Aug. 11, 1845; "Eleventh Anniversary of the American Temperance Union," *Journal of the American Temperance Union* (hereafter *JATU*) 11 (Jun. 1847), 81–82; John A. Krout, *The Origins of Prohibition* (New York, 1925), 276–278.

2. "The New License Law," *New York Tribune*, Mar. 17, 1845; "To the Friends of Temperance in the State of New York," *Albany Patriot*, May 7, 1845; "The License System," *North American* (Philadelphia), Jan. 30, 1847; Maryland General Assembly, "Report of the Select Committee on the License Law, February 13th, 1847" (Annapolis, 1847), 12.

3. On early uses of direct democracy, see Frederick A. Cleveland, *The Growth of Democracy in the United States* (Chicago, 1898), 181–229; Charles Sumner Lobingier, *The People's Law or Popular Participation in Law-Making* (New York, 1909), 349–357; Ellis Paxson Oberholtzer, *The Referendum in America* (New York, 1911); John J. Dinan, *The American State Constitutional Tradition* (Lawrence, KS, 2006), 29–84. For temperance scholarship discussing local option, see Ian Tyrrell, *Sobering Up: From Temperance to Prohibition in Antebellum America, 1800–1860* (Westport, CT, 1979), 243; W. J. Rorabaugh, "Prohibition as Progress: New York State's License Elections, 1846," *Journal of Social History* 14 (1981), 425–443; Jed Dannenbaum, *Drink and Disorder: Temperance Reform in Cincinnati from the Washingtonian Revival to the WCTU* (Chicago, 1984), 85–105; John W. Quist, *Restless Visionaries: The Social Roots of Antebellum Reform in Alabama and Michigan* (Baton Rouge, 1998), 202–209, 252–260; Thomas R. Pegram, *Battling Demon Rum: The Struggle for a Dry America, 1800–1933* (Chicago, 1998), 35–38.

4. "Pennsylvania," *JATU* 11 (Jul. 1847), 108; "The German Rumsellers," *JATU* 8 (Apr. 1844), 58; "Foreign Population," *JATU* 9 (Mar. 1845), 33; Robert Ernst, *Immigrant Life in New York City, 1825–1863* (New York, 1949), 90–91; Stanley Baron, *Brewed in America: A History of Beer and Ale in the United States* (Boston, 1962), 175–183.

5. "Oneida County," *JATU* 10 (Feb. 1846), 30; Krout, *The Origins of Prohibition*, 278–282; "A Voice from the Ladies of Buffalo," *JATU* 10 (Jun. 1846), 91; Tyrrell, *Sobering Up*, 88–89; Jack S. Blocker, *American Temperance Movements: Cycles of Reform* (Boston, 1989), 13–14.

6. *The Balance, or "License," or "No License," Examiner* (Albany, 1846); *Appeal to the Voters of the State of New York, Together with Extracts of the Proceedings of the Conventions held at Albany and Rochester, Relative to the License Question* (Albany, 1845). On Delavan, see W. J. Rorabaugh, "Delavan, Edward Cornelius," http://www.anb.org/articles/15/15-00171.html, *American National Biography Online*, Feb. 2000; Tyrrell, *Sobering Up*, 88–89; Blocker, *American Temperance Movements*, 13–14.

7. "The License Question," *JATU* 8 (Nov. 1844), 170; Tyrrell, *Sobering Up*, 91–92, 225–243; Paul E. Johnson, *A Shopkeeper's Millennium: Society and Revivals in Rochester, New York, 1815–1837* (New York, 1978), 129–133.

8. "The License Law," *Albany Evening Journal*, Mar. 15, 1845; "The License Question," *North American* (Philadelphia), Jun. 8, 1846; "The License Law," *Albany Argus*, Apr. 26, 1845; "Law-Moral Suasion," *JATU* 7 (Sep. 1843), 134; "The License System," *North American* (Philadelphia), Jan. 30, 1847; "Governor Slade on the License Question," *JATU* 9 (Feb. 1845), 28. On the Washingtonian temperance movement, see Krout, *The Origins of Prohibition*, 182–222; Tyrrell, *Sobering Up*, 159–190; Dannenbaum, *Drink and Disorder*, 32–68; Sean Wilentz, *Chants Democratic: New York City and the Rise of the American Working Class, 1788–1850* (New York, 1984), 306–314; Teresa Anne Murphy, *Ten Hours' Labor: Religion, Reform, and Gender in Early New England* (Ithaca, NY, 1992), 101–130; Pegram, *Battling Demon Rum*, 26–32.

9. Morris County Temperance Society, *License! Or No License! Addressed to the Citizens of New Jersey in View of the Election on the 1st Tuesday in Dec. 1847* (New York, 1847), 6 (emphasis in original); "State Temperance Convention," *New York Tribune*, Jan. 22, 1848; Henry Harbaugh, *A Word In Season, or a Plea for Legislative Aid, in Putting Down the Evils of Intemperance* (Chambersburg, PA, 1846), 16–17; Pennsylvania State Temperance Society, *Address to the People of the Commonwealth of Pennsylvania, Relative to the License Question* (Philadelphia, 1846), 7; "The Temperance Cause," *Pittsburgh Gazette*, Nov. 5, 1845; "Temperance Meeting at the Tabernacle, Last Evening," *New York Herald*, Mar. 28, 1845; "Liberty! Liberty!!," *Ohio Washingtonian Organ & Sons of Temperance Record*, Aug. 9, 1846, 413.

10. "The License Law," *Geneva* (NY) *Courier*, Apr. 29, 1845. On immigrants, nativism, and temperance, see Ray Allen Billington, *The Protestant Crusade, 1800–1860: A Study in the Origins of American Nativism* (New York, 1938), 193–219; Kathleen Neils Conzen, *Immigrant Milwaukee, 1836–1860: Accommodation & Community in a Frontier City* (Cambridge, MA, 1976); Dannenbaum, *Drink and Disorder*; David Gerber, *The Making of An American Pluralism: Buffalo, New York, 1825–1860* (Chicago, 1989). On temperance as an ethno-cultural issue in the Second Party System, see Lee Benson, *The Concept of Jacksonian Democracy: New York as a Test Case* (Princeton, NJ, 1961); Ronald P. Formisano, *The Birth of Mass Political Parties: Michigan, 1827–1861* (Princeton, NJ, 1971); Herbert Ershkowitz and William G. Shade, "Consensus or Conflict? Political Behavior in the State Legislatures during the Jacksonian Era," *Journal of American History*, 58 (1971), 591–622; Daniel Walker Howe, "The Evangelical Movement and Political Culture in the North during the Second Party System," *Journal of American History* 77 (1991), 1216–1239.

11. "The License Law," *Albany Evening Journal*, Mar. 15, 1845; *Report of the Select Committee on a Petition to Amend the Excise Laws, No. 40* (Albany, 1837), 2; L. Ray

Gunn, *The Decline of Authority: Public Economic Policy and Political Development in New York State, 1800–1860* (Ithaca, NY, 1988), 144–169; Dinan, *American State Constitutional Tradition,* 68–76.

12. "Law—Moral Suasion," *JATU* 7 (Sep. 1843), 134; "Doctrine of Instruction," *New Englander & Yale Review* 1 (Apr. 1843), 193; Edward Skeen, "Vox Populi, Vox Dei: The Compensation Act of 1816 and the Rise of Popular Politics," *Journal of the Early Republic* 6 (Fall 1986), 253–274; Skeen, "An Uncertain 'Right': State Legislatures and the Doctrine of Instruction," *Mid-America* 73 (Jan. 1991), 29–47. For earlier background of these debates, see J. R. Pole, *Political Representation in England and the Origins of the American Republic* (Berkeley, CA, 1966); Gordon Wood, *Creation of the American Republic, 1776–1787* (Chapel Hill, 1969); Edmund S. Morgan, *Inventing the People: The Rise of Popular Sovereignty in England and America* (New York, 1988); John Phillip Reid, *The Concept of Representation in the Age of the American Revolution* (Chicago, 1989).

13. "Albany County," *JATU* 10 (Apr. 1846), 54; "Law-Moral Suasion," *JATU* 7 (Sep. 1843), 134; "Maryland State Temperance Society," *JATU* 10 (Mar. 1846), 46.

14. "Pennsylvania Responding," *JATU* 10 (Aug. 1846), 125; Lyman Beecher, *Six Sermons on the Nature, Occasions, Signs, Evils, and Remedy of Intemperance* (Boston, 1826); Joseph Gusfield, *Symbolic Crusade: Status Politics and the American Temperance Movement* (Chicago, 1963), 39–44; "The License Law," *Albany Argus,* Apr. 10, 1845; "Temperance Meeting at the Tabernacle Last Evening—Triumph of the Excise Law," *New York Tribune,* Mar. 25, 1847; "License by the Towns," *JATU* 8 (May 1844), 73; "We notice…," *Signal of Liberty* (Ann Arbor, MI), Mar. 24, 1845.

15. "Proceedings of the Ladies' Temperance Convention," *Delaware Gazette,* Mar. 23 1847; "Female Influence," *JATU* 11 (May 1847), 74; "A Glorious Victory! The Teetotalers Triumphant!!," *The Pearl* (New York), Jun. 6, 1846; "Something more about the Rights of Woman," *The Pearl,* Aug. 1, 1846. On women and temperance, see Barbara Leslie Epstein, *The Politics of Domesticity: Women, Evangelicalism, and Temperance in Nineteenth-Century America* (Middletown, CT, 1981); Ian R. Tyrrell, "Women and Temperance in Antebellum America, 1830–1860," *Civil War History* 28 (1982), 128–152; Nancy A. Hewitt, *Women's Activism and Social Change: Rochester, New York, 1822–1872* (Ithaca, NY, 1984); Lori Ginzberg, *Women and the Work of Benevolence: Morality, Politics, and Class in Nineteenth-Century America* (New Haven, CT, 1990); Nancy Isenberg, *Sex and Citizenship in Antebellum America* (Chapel Hill, 1998). On woman's suffrage and the New York Constitutional Convention of 1846, see Lori D. Ginzberg, *Untidy Origins: A Story of Woman's Rights in Antebellum New York* (Chapel Hill, 2005).

16. "Oneida County," *JATU* 10 (Feb. 1846), 30; "The License Question," *New York Tribune,* Apr. 17, 1845; "Report of the Select Committee, Relative to Granting License to Sell Liquor," *Reports Made to the Senate & House of Representatives of*

the State of Illinois (Springfield, 1847), 186; Maryland General Assembly, "Report of the Select Committee," 12.

17. "Mass Meeting at Poughkeepsie," *JATU* 9 (Nov. 1845), 163; "A Green Field," *Milwaukee Sentinel & Gazette*, Apr. 19, 1847; Frederick Grimke, *The Nature and Tendency of Free Institutions* [1848], ed. John William Ward (Cambridge, MA, 1968), 321; *Report of the Secretary of State in answer to a resolution of the Assembly relative to the elections on the subject of licensing the sale of intoxicating drinks* (Albany, 1847); Rorabaugh, "Prohibition as Progress." The states asking voters to decide the license question at the ballot box were New York, Vermont, Rhode Island, Connecticut, New Jersey, Pennsylvania, Delaware, Indiana, Michigan, Iowa, Wisconsin, and Ohio. For an overview of the election results throughout the United States, see "Eleventh Anniversary of the American Temperance Union," *JATU* 11 (Jun. 1847), 81–82.

18. J. L. O'Sullivan, *Report of the Minority of the Select Committee on the Bill entitled "An act relating to licensing retailers of intoxicating liquors,"* No. 294 (Albany, 1841), 6.

19. "Introduction," *United States Magazine & Democratic Review* 1 (Oct. 1837), 9, 3; O'Sullivan, "Report," *New York Morning News*, Mar. 29, 1845; "Intemperate Temperance," *New York Morning News*, Mar. 28, 1845. On O'Sullivan, see Arthur M. Schlesinger Jr., *The Age of Jackson* (Boston, 1945), 371–373; Edward L. Widmer, *Young America: The Flowering of Democracy in New York City* (New York, 1999); Robert D. Sampson, *John L. O'Sullivan & His Times* (Kent, OH, 2003).

20. "The Ultraism of the Age," *New York Herald*, Apr. 15, 1845; "Mr. Editor," *Pittsburgh Daily Morning Post*, Jan. 1, 1847; "The Power of the State," *Albany Atlas*, Apr. 4, 1845; "Legislating over Morals," *Albany Atlas*, Mar. 25, 1845; Gunn, *Decline of Authority*, 155; "The Excise Bill," *Brooklyn Eagle*, Apr. 12, 1845. The composition of the 1845 New York General Assembly that voted for local option with little opposition, for example, contained sixty-seven Democrats, forty-six Whigs, and fifteen "Native American." "The Legislature," *Daily Plebian* (New York), Jan. 6, 1845.

21. A. B. Grosh, "To A.S., Norwich, N.Y.," *Evangelical Magazine and Gospel Advocate*, Apr. 3, 1846, 111; "'Save Me from My Friends,'" *Young America* (New York), Mar. 7, 1846; "Temperance Efforts," *Young America*, May 24, 1845; "Squirming of the Rumsellers," *New York Evangelist*, Jun. 18, 1846; "Novel Discussion," *Brooklyn Eagle*, Dec. 17, 1845; "New York," *Niles National Register* (Baltimore), May 3, 1845; "Demonstration at the Tabernacle," *New York Organ*, Jan. 30, 1847; "Excise Law—New York Legislature," *JATU* 10 (Nov. 1846), 168; "Temperance and Politics," *New York Tribune*, May 25, 1847; "Indiana," *JATU* 12 (Apr. 1848), 62.

22. "Rumsellers' Petition," *JATU* 11 (Feb. 1847), 25; "Meeting of Rumsellers," *New York Tribune*, Feb. 4, 1846; "The License Bill," *JATU* 9 (Apr. 1845), 58; "Organized Opposition," *JATU* 10 (Mar. 1846), 41; "The New Legislature," *JATU* 10 (Oct. 1846), 152; "Shall Liquor Dealers Rule the State?," *JATU* 10 (Dec. 1846),

188; "Address of the Tradesmen's Mutual Benefit Society," *New York Herald*, Nov. 2, 1846.

23. "The Striped Pig Outdone," *Dwights American Magazine*, Jul. 25, 1846; "One of the Results of the New Excise Law," *Brooklyn Eagle*, Feb. 2, 1847; "Constitutional Question," *JATU* 10 (Jul. 1846), 105. For examples of legal cases and arguments, see "Grog-Shop Indictments in Brooklyn," *JATU* 10 (Oct. 1846), 149; *People v. Townsey*, 5 Denio 70 (1847); *Hodgman v. The People*, 4 Denio 235 (1847); "Important Decision in Relation to the Excise Law," *JATU* 11 (Feb. 1847), 20; *People v. Safford*, 5 Denio 112 (1847); *Nevin v. Ladue*, 3 Denio 43 (1846); *Nevin v. Ladue*, 3 Denio 437 (1846); "License Law, Beer, &c.," *JATU* 10 (Jul. 1846), 99; "Important Decision Under the License Law," *JATU* 10 (Dec. 1846), 183.

24. *License Cases*, 46 U.S. 504 (1847); Harold M. Hyman and William M. Wiecek, *Equal Justice under Law: Constitutional Development, 1835–1875* (New York, 1982), 24, 80–82; William J. Novak, *The People's Welfare: Law and Regulation in Nineteenth-Century America* (Chapel Hill, 1996), 176–177, 324–325.

25. "The Great Decision," *JATU* 11 (Apr. 1847), 56; "Decision of the Supreme Court," *JATU* 11 (May 1847), 67; "Circular," *JATU* 11 (Apr. 1847), 56; *An Appeal to the Citizens of the State of Ohio*, 14; "The Great Decision," *JATU* 11 (Apr. 1847), 56; "The Excise Laws Sustained," *New York Tribune*, Mar. 13, 1847; "Important Decision," *Brooklyn Eagle*, Mar. 9, 1847; "License Laws," *Pittsburgh Daily Morning Post*, Apr. 23, 1847.

26. "An Act," *Blue Hen's Chicken & Delaware Democratic Whig* (Wilmington), Mar. 5, 1847; "No Title," *Delaware Gazette* (Wilmington), Mar. 16, 1847; "To the Public," *Blue Hen's Chicken & Delaware Democratic Whig*, Mar. 5, 1847; "To the Citizens of New Castle County and the State of Delaware," *Delaware Gazette*, Mar. 26, 1847; "Republicanism and Equal Rights v. Tyranny and Oppression, No. 2," *Delaware Gazette*, Apr. 2, 1847. For temperance in Delaware, see Charles H. Bohner, "Rum and Reform: Temperance in Delaware Politics," *Delaware History* 5 (1953), 237–269.

27. "Death of Amos H. Wickersham," *Local Intelligencer* (Wilmington), Oct. 17, 1854; "New Castle County Temperance Convention," *Delaware State Journal* (Wilmington), Jul. 3, 1846; "New Castle County Temperance Convention," Mar. 24, 1846; "To the People of New Castle County," *Delaware Gazette*, Oct. 23, 1846; "To the citizens of New Castle County," *Delaware State Journal*, Nov. 3, 1846; "To the citizens of New Castle County," *Delaware Gazette*, Nov. 6, 1846; Amos H. Wickersham, "To the People of New Castle County," *Delaware Gazette*, Oct. 23, 1846 (emphasis in original).

28. "Doctrine of Instruction," *New Englander*, 193; Skeen, "Vox Populi, Vox Dei," 270–271.

29. "Messrs. Editors," *Delaware Gazette*, Nov. 6, 1846.

30. Bayard would later become a stalwart in the conservative wing of the Democratic Party and a three-term US senator during the turbulent 1850s

and Civil War era. On the Bayards and Delaware's patrician politics, see "The Bayards of Delaware," *New York Evangelist*, Jun. 24, 1880; Roy Franklin Nichols, *The Disruption of American Democracy* (New York, 1948), 19–20; Jean H. Baker, *Affairs of Party: The Political Culture of Northern Democrats in the Mid-Nineteenth Century* [1983] (New York, 1998), 196–211; Joanna Dunlap Cowden, *"Heaven Will Frown on Such a Cause Like This": Six Democrats Who Opposed Lincoln's War* (Lanham, MD, 2001).

31. *Steward v. Jefferson*, 3 Del. 335 (1841); John Locke, *Second Treatise on Government* [1690], ed. C. B. Macpherson (Indianapolis, 1980), 74–75.

32. "No Title," *Delaware Gazette*, Mar. 16, 1847; "Messrs. Editors," *Delaware Gazette*, Mar. 19, 1847; "Republicanism and Equal Rights vs. Tyranny and Oppression, No.1," *Delaware Gazette*, Mar. 19, 1847; "Republicanism and Equal Rights vs. Tyranny and Oppression, No.2," *Delaware Gazette*, Apr. 2, 1847 (emphasis in originals).

33. J. R. Pole, ed., *The Federalist* [1787–1788] (Indianapolis, 2005), 51–52; George Sidney Camp, *Democracy* (New York, 1841), 185–186, 194–195.

34. "Temperance Convention," *Delaware Gazette*, Mar. 23, 1847; "License and Its Advocates," *Delaware Gazette*, Mar. 20, 1847; "Proceedings of the Ladies' Temperance Convention," *Delaware Gazette*, Mar. 23 1847. On the results of the Delaware license election, see "The License Election," *Delaware Gazette*, Apr. 9, 1847; "Delaware.—Victory!," *JATU* 11 (May 1847), 73.

35. "The License Question," *Delaware Gazette*, May 7, 1847; "Legislature of the State of New York," *JATU* 11 (Jun. 1847), 92.

36. *Report of the Majority of the Committee on the Internal Affairs of Towns and Counties, on the petitions and papers relative to the repeal of the Excise Law of 1845,* (Albany, NY, 1847), 2–4, 11–16.

37. "Messrs. Editors," *Delaware Gazette*, Jul. 30, 1847; *Rice v. Foster*, 4 Del. 479 (1847). On the relationship of Bayard and Clayton, see Joseph P. Comegys, *Memoir of John M. Clayton* (Wilmington, 1882), 33–34. On Clayton, see Richard Arden Wire, "John M. Clayton and the Search for Order: A Study in Whig Politics and Diplomacy" (PhD diss., University of Maryland, 1971); John A. Munroe, *History of Delaware* (Newark, DE, 1979), 115–117; Michael Holt, *The Rise and Fall of the American Whig Party: Jacksonian Politics and the Onset of the Civil War* (New York, 1999), 565–566.

38. "Speech of Mr. Clayton," *Delaware Gazette*, Jun. 18, 1847; 4 Del. 479.

39. "Speech of Mr. Clayton," *Delaware Gazette*, Jun. 18, 1847.

40. "Speech of Mr. Clayton," *Delaware Gazette*, Jun. 18, 1847. On debates over capital punishment in the 1840s, see David Brion Davis, "The Movement to Abolish Capital Punishment in America, 1787–1861," *American Historical Review* 63 (1957), 23–46; Louis P. Masur, *Rites of Execution: Capital Punishment and the Transformation of American Culture, 1776–1865* (New York, 1989). On the Anti-Rent Wars and land reform politics in the 1840s, see Reeve Huston, *Land*

and Freedom: Rural Society, Popular Protest, and Party Politics in Antebellum New York (New York, 2002); Charles W. McCurdy, *The Anti-Rent Era in New York Law and Politics, 1839–1865* (Chapel Hill, 2001); Mark A. Lause, *Young America: Land, Labor, and the Republican Community* (Urbana, IL, 2005).

41. "Speech of Mr. Clayton," *Delaware Gazette*, Jun. 18, 1847. On slavery in Delaware and the 1847 gradual abolition bill, see Munroe, *History of Delaware*, 120; John A. Munroe, "The Negro in Delaware," *South Atlantic Quarterly* 56 (1957), 428–444; Patience Essah, *A House Divided: Slavery and Emancipation in Delaware, 1638–1865* (Charlottesville, VA, 1996), 158–161; William H. Williams, *Slavery and Freedom in Delaware, 1639–1865* (Wilmington, DE, 1996), 172–173. On the problem of slaves and interstate travel, see Paul Finkelman, *An Imperfect Union: Slavery, Federalism, and Comity* (Chapel Hill, 1981).

42. "Speech of Mr. Clayton," *Delaware Gazette*, Jun. 18, 1847; Willard Carl Klunder, "Lewis Cass & Slavery Expansion: 'The Father of Popular Sovereignty' & Ideological Infanticide," *Civil War History* 32 (Dec. 1986), 296; Essah, *A House Divided*, 161.

43. "Popular Government," *Delaware Gazette*, May 28, 1847.

44. 4 Del. 479, 499, 488; William M. Wiecek, *The Guarantee Clause of the U.S. Constitution* (Ithaca, NY, 1972), 252–253, 261–262.

45. 4 Del. 479, 488–489, 498–499 (emphasis in original).

46. 4 Del. 479, 485–489.

47. Pole, *The Federalist*, 49–50. See especially Wood, *Creation of the American Republic*; Jennifer Nedelsky, *Private Property and the Limits of American Constitutionalism: The Madisonian Framework and Its Legacy* (Chicago, 1990); Jack Rakove, *Original Meanings: Politics and Ideas in the Making of the Constitution* (New York, 1996); Woody Holton, *Unruly Americans and the Origins of the Constitution* (New York, 2007).

48. "Messrs. Editors," *Delaware Gazette*, Jul. 30, 1847; "Delaware License Law," *JATU* 11 (Jul. 1847), 109; "The Vote of the People," *JATU* 11 (Aug. 1847), 120.

49. "Temperance and Elective Legislation," *North American* (Philadelphia), Jun.18, 1847; "Mr. Clayton's speech on the New License Law," *North American*, Jun. 17, 1847; "The License Law Pronounced Unconstitutional," *Democratic Union* (Harrisburg), Jun. 20, 1847.

50. "The License Law Pronounced Unconstitutional," *Adams Sentinel* (Gettysburg, PA), Jun. 28, 1847; *Parker v. Commonwealth*, 6 Pa. 507 (1847); "The License Question," *Pittsburgh Gazette*, Nov. 10, 1847; "Unconstitutionality of License Law," *Daily National Intelligencer* (Washington, DC), Nov. 15, 1847; "The License Question in New Jersey," *Geneva* (NY) *Gazette*, Dec. 18, 1847; *Report of the Majority of the Committee of Assembly, to which were referred the Petitions for the Repeal of the License Law of the Last Legislature* (Trenton, NJ, 1848), 10; "Temperance in Bermuda," *JATU* 12 (Jun. 1848), 92. For other antebellum local option cases where the arguments legitimated in *Rice v. Foster* and *Parker v. Commonwealth*

were employed (with mixed results), see *Garner v. State*, 8 Blackf. 568 (1848); "Indiana," *JATU* 12 (Apr. 1848), 62; *Maize v. State*, 4 Ind. 342 (1853); "Illinois," *JATU* 14 (Mar. 1850), 46; *Geebrick v. State*, 5 Iowa 491 (1857); "The Constitutional Question," *JATU* 12 (Oct. 1848), 154; *State v. Copeland*, 3 R.I. 33 (1854); *State v. Swisher*, 17 Tex. 441 (1856); *Bancroft v. Dumas*, 21 Vt. 456 (1849).

51. "State Temperance Convention," *Northern Christian Advocate* (Auburn, NY), Jan. 26, 1848; "Recent Developments," *JATU* 12 (Apr. 1848), 56; "Twelfth Anniversary," *JATU* 12 (Jun. 1848), 83. See chapter 6, below.

52. On popular sovereignty and Bleeding Kansas, see David M. Potter, *The Impending Crisis, 1848–1861* (New York, 1976); Michael A. Morrison, *Slavery and the American West: The Eclipse of Manifest Destiny and the Coming of the Civil War* (Chapel Hill, 1997); Nicole Etcheson, *Bleeding Kansas: Contested Liberty in the Civil War Era* (Lawrence, KS, 2004); Elizabeth R. Varon, *Disunion! The Coming of the American Civil War, 1789–1859* (Chapel Hill, 2008).

53. For examples of the mixed success of antebellum legal challenges to ballot-box legislation, see *Commonwealth v. Judges of Quarter Sessions*, 8 Pa. 391 (1848); *Commonwealth v. Painter*, 10 Pa. 214 (1849); *Caldwell v. Reynolds*, 10 Ill. 1 (1848); *Johnson v. Rich*, 9 Barb. 680 (1851); *Thorne v. Cramer*, 15 Barb. 112 (1851); *Railroad Co. v. Commissioners of Clinton County*, 1 Ohio St. 77 (1852); *State v. Scott*, 17 Mo. 521 (1853); *State v. Field*, 17 Mo. 529 (1853); *Sharpless v. Mayor of Philadelphia*, 21 Pa. 147 (1853); *Moers v. City of Reading*, 21 Pa. 1853 (1853); *Bradley v. Baxter*, 15 Barb. 122 (1853); *Barto v. Himrod*, 8 NY 483 (1853); Thomas Cooley, *A Treatise on Constitutional Limitations Which Rest Upon the Legislative Power of the States of the American Union*, 5th ed. (Boston, 1883), 139–148.

54. "The License Question," *Pittsburgh Gazette*, Nov. 10, 1847; *Ex Parte Wall*, 48 Cal. 279, 314, 316 (1874).

CHAPTER 4

1. Petition of Eunice F. Ross in aid of E. J. Pompey presented Feb. 26, 1845, Massachusetts State Archives.

2. This chapter builds on the important work of such scholars as Paul Finkelman and J. Morgan Kousser. See especially Finkelman, "Prelude to the Fourteenth Amendment: Black Legal Rights in the Antebellum North," *Rutgers Law Journal* 17 (1985–1986), 415–482; Kousser, "'The Supremacy of Equal Rights': The Struggle against Racial Discrimination in Antebellum Massachusetts and the Foundations of the Fourteenth Amendment," *Northwestern University Law Review* 82 (1987–1988), 941–1010.

3. Alexis de Tocqueville, *Democracy in America* [1835], ed. J. P. Mayer, George Lawrence, translation (New York, 1969), 343; "Prejudice," *Massachusetts Abolitionist*, Jun. 13, 1839. On black northerners, see especially Leon Litwack, *North of Slavery: The Negro in the Free States, 1790–1860* (Chicago, 1961); James Oliver Horton and Lois E. Horton, *In Hope of Liberty: Culture, Community, and*

Protest among Northern Free Blacks, 1700–1860 (New York, 1997); Patrick Rael, *Black Identity and Black Protest in the Antebellum North* (Chapel Hill, 2002), 12–27.

4. George Fredrickson, *The Black Image in the White Mind: The Debate on Afro-American Character and Destiny, 1817–1914* (Middletown, CT, 1971), 36–42; Jane H. Pease and William H. Pease, *They Who Would Be Free: Blacks' Search for Freedom, 1830–1861* (New York, 1974); Horton and Horton, *In Hope of Liberty*, 220–224; Rael, *Black Identity and Black Protest*, 118–208.

5. "Help for the Colored Man! Who Will Take Hold?," *Massachusetts Abolitionist*, Oct. 10, 1839; "Colorphobia," *Massachusetts Abolitionist*, Jun. 27, 1839; *Proceedings of the Third Anti-Slavery Convention of American Women, held in Philadelphia, May 1st, 2d and 3d, 1839* (Philadelphia, 1839), 8, 23–24; Paul Goodman, *Of One Blood: Abolitionism and the Origins of Racial Equality* (Berkeley, CA, 1998).

6. See Litwack, *North of Slavery*, 64–97; Eugene H. Berwanger, *The Frontier against Slavery: Western Anti-Negro Prejudice and the Slavery Extension Controversy* (Urbana, IL, 1967); Pease and Pease, *They Who Would Be Free*; Phyllis F. Field, *The Politics of Race in New York: The Struggle for Black Suffrage in the Civil War Era* (Ithaca, NY, 1982); Paul Finkelman, ed., *Slavery in the Courtroom: An Annotated Bibliography of American Cases* (Washington, DC, 1985); Finkelman, "Prelude to the Fourteenth Amendment," 415–482; Stephen Middleton, *The Black Laws of the Old Northwest: A Documentary History* (Westport, CT, 1992); David N. Gellman and David Quigley, eds., *Jim Crow New York: A Documentary History of Race and Citizenship, 1777–1877* (New York, 2003); Stephen Middleton, *The Black Laws: Race and the Legal Process in Early Ohio* (Athens, GA, 2005); Dana Weiner, *Race and Rights: Fighting Slavery and Prejudice in the Old Northwest, 1830–1870* (DeKalb, IL, 2013).

7. *Acts and Resolves of the Massachusetts Bay, 1692–1704*, vol. 1 (Boston, 1869), 578; *Massachusetts Statutes, 1786*, Ch. 3, Sec. 7; David H. Fowler, *Northern Attitudes towards Interracial Marriage: Legislation and Public Opinion in the Middle Atlantic and the States of the Old Northwest, 1780–1930* (New York, 1987), 47–52; Joanne Pope Melish, *Disowning Slavery: Gradual Emancipation and "Race" in New England, 1780–1860* (Ithaca, NY, 1998), 122–125; Andrew Kull, *The Color-Blind Constitution* (Cambridge, MA, 1992), 24–25.

8. "Legislative," *Liberator*, Jan. 8, 1831; "Look At This!!!," *Liberator*, Feb. 5, 1831; David Walker, *Appeal to the Coloured Citizens of the World, but in particular, and very expressly, to those of the United States of America* [1829] (New York, 1965), 9; Lydia Maria Child, *An Appeal in Favor of that Class of Americans Called Africans* (Boston, 1833), 209–210. For useful overviews of this battle, see Louis Ruchames, "Race, Marriage, and Abolition in Massachusetts," *Journal of Negro History* 40 (1955), 250–273; George A. Levesque, *Black Boston: African American Life and Culture in Urban America, 1750–1860* (New York, 1994), 137–148.

9. "The Marriage Bill," *Liberator*, Jun. 11, 1831; "The Marriage Law," *Liberator*, Jan. 29, 1841; "The Petitions," *Liberator*, Dec. 23, 1842; "Equal Laws—The Lynn

Petition," *Liberator*, Feb. 22, 1839; "The Marriage Law," *Liberator*, Jan. 28, 1832; "Bradford A.S. Society," *Liberator*, Apr. 12, 1839.

10. J. K. Paulding, *Slavery in the United States* (New York, 1836), 61–62; "Colorphobia," *Massachusetts Abolitionist*, Jun. 27, 1839; Winthrop D. Jordan, *White over Black: American Attitudes toward the Negro, 1550-1812*, 2nd ed. (Chapel Hill, 2012), 542–569; Linda K. Kerber, "Abolitionists and Amalgamators: The New York City Race Riots of 1834," *New York History* 48 (1967), 28–39; Lorman Ratner, *Powder Keg: Northern Opposition to the Antislavery Movement, 1831–1840* (New York, 1968); Leonard L. Richards, *"Gentlemen of Property and Standing": Anti-abolition Mobs in Jacksonian America* (New York, 1970); Leslie M. Harris, "From Abolitionist Amalgamators to 'Rulers of the Five Points': The Discourse of Interracial Sex and Reform in Antebellum New York City," in *Sex, Love, Race: Crossing Boundaries in North American History*, ed. Martha Hodes (New York, 1999), 191–212.

11. "Anti-Amalgamation Law," *Liberator*, Feb. 20, 1836; Kerber, "Abolitionists and Amalgamators"; Paul Gilje, *The Road to Mobocracy: Popular Disorder in New York City, 1763–1834* (Chapel Hill, 1987), 162–170; Rael, *Black Identity and Black Protest*, 169–173.

12. "The Marriage Law," *Liberator*, May 7, 1831; "Garrison's Taste," *Liberator*, Sep. 12, 1845; Gustave de Beaumont, *Marie or, Slavery in the United States* [1835], Barbara Chapman, translation (Baltimore, 1999), 251; "'Amalgamation!'" *Liberator*, May 10, 1839; "The Marriage Law," *Liberator*, May 21, 1831; Ronald G. Walters, "The Erotic South: Civilization and Sexuality in American Abolitionism," *American Quarterly* 25 (May 1973), 177–210.

13. "Unequal Laws—The Lynn Petition," *Pennsylvania Freeman*, Feb. 28, 1839; "The Marriage Law," *Liberator*, Feb. 15, 1839; "Massachusetts Legislature," *The Emancipator* (New York), Feb. 28, 1839; *Massachusetts Legislature. House Reports, 1839. No. 28*, 16; Ruchames, "Race, Marriage, and Abolition," 257; George A. Levesque, "'Politicians in Petticoats': Interracial Sex and Legislative Politics in Antebellum Massachusetts," *New England Journal of Black Studies* 1 (1983), 40–59; Kull, *Color-Blind Constitution*, 22–23.

14. George Bradburn, "The Anti-Marriage Law in Massachusetts," in *The Legion of Liberty! And the Force of Truth* (New York, 1857), 109; "Amalgamation," *Liberator*, Feb. 7, 1840; "Mr. Bradburn," *Liberator*, Mar. 6, 1841.

15. "Petitions," *Massachusetts Abolitionist*, Sep. 26, 1839; "Worcester County, South Division," *Massachusetts Abolitionist*, Apr. 4, 1839; "Lynn Female A.S. Society," *Liberator*, Apr. 12, 1839; "The Intermarriage Law," *National Anti-Slavery Standard*, Mar. 16, 1843; "Petitions-Petitions-Petitions!" *Liberator*, Nov. 29, 1839.

16. Massachusetts Legislature, *House Reports, 1839. No. 28*, 8; "Amalgamation," *Liberator*, Feb. 8, 1839; "Massachusetts Legislature," *Liberator*, Feb. 12, 1841; "Mass. Legislative," *Newburyport Herald*, Feb. 18, 1842; "Massachusetts Legislature," *Liberator*, Feb. 25, 1842; "The Marriage of Whites With Blacks," *Boston Weekly Messenger*, Mar. 2, 1842.

17. "An Unjust Law," *Liberator*, Jan. 29, 1831. See *The Quock Walker Cases* (1781, 1783), in *Proceedings of the Massachusetts Historical Society*, vol. 13, 1873–1875, 294; Arthur Zilversmit, "Quok Walker, Mumbet, and the Abolition of Slavery in Massachusetts," *William and Mary Quarterly* 25 (1968), 614–624.

18. "Petitions-Petitions-Petitions!" *Liberator*, Nov. 29, 1839; "Debate on the Bill repealing the Law forbidding the Intermarriage of Persons of different Races," *Liberator*, Apr. 17, 1840. "The Marriage Law," *Liberator*, Apr. 30, 1831; "Substance of Rev. Charles T. Torrey's Argument," *Massachusetts Abolitionist*, Feb. 27, 1840; "Legislative," *Liberator*, Jan. 29, 1841.

19. Massachusetts Legislature, *House Reports, 1840. No. 46*, 3; "Massachusetts," *The Emancipator*, Apr. 9, 1840; "Massachusetts Legislature," *Colored American*, Apr. 25, 1840; "To the Editor of the Daily Advertiser and Patriot," *Boston Advertiser*, Jan. 3, 1843.

20. "The Law Prohibiting Intermarriages Between the White and Colored Races," *Liberator*, Feb. 19, 1841; Child, *An Appeal*, 196–197; "White and Black," *Brooklyn Eagle*, Feb. 22, 1842. Abolitionists' focus on "taste" might also have been an appeal to a cultural shift that gave increased leeway in marital choice to the two parties involved. See Elise Lemire, *"Miscegenation": Making Race in America* (Philadelphia, 2002), 56–57, 160–161.

21. Massachusetts Legislature, *House Reports, 1840, No. 46* (1840), 2–3; "Massachusetts," *The Emancipator*, Apr. 9, 1840; "Massachusetts Legislature," *Colored American*, Apr. 25, 1840.

22. "Caste in the United States: A Review," *Quarterly Anti-Slavery Magazine* 2 (Jan. 1837), 196; Child, *An Appeal*, 74; Rael, *Black Identity and Black Protest*, 177.

23. "Election Sermon," *Liberator*, Feb. 5, 1841; "The American Union," *Liberator*, Jan. 10, 1845; Aileen S. Kraditor, *Means and Ends in American Abolitionism: Garrison and His Critics on Strategy and Tactics, 1834–1850* (Chicago, 1967), 25–26; Lewis Perry, *Radical Abolitionism: Anarchy and the Government of God in Antislavery Thought* (Ithaca, NY, 1973). On the divisions within abolitionism, see Richard H. Sewell, *Ballots for Freedom: Antislavery Politics in the United States, 1837–1860* (New York, 1976), 24–42. For more on leading Garrisonians' thinking about majoritarian democracy, see W. Caleb McDaniel, *The Problem of Democracy in the Age of Slavery: Garrisonian Abolitionists and Transatlantic Reform* (Baton Rouge, 2013).

24. "Political Action," *Massachusetts Abolitionist*, May 9, 1839; "'A Right Minded Minority,'" *Massachusetts Abolitionist*, Nov. 19, 1840; Sewell, *Ballots For Freedom*, 43–79.

25. "Dr. James McCune Smith," *Frederick Douglass' Paper*, Jan. 28, 1859; James McCune Smith, *The Destiny of the People of Color: A Lecture Delivered before the Philomathean Society and Hamilton Lyceum in January, 1841* (New York, 1843), in *The Works of James McCune Smith: Black Intellectual and Abolitionist*, ed. John Stauffer (New York, 2006), 48–60. For the key public statement of local black citizens against the marriage law, see "Meeting of the Colored Citizens of

Boston," *Liberator*, Feb. 10, 1843. The New York–based *Colored American* took an active interest in the debates in Massachusetts. See "From a Leading Editorial Article," *Colored American*, Mar. 3, 1838; "Unequal Laws—The Lynn Petition," *Colored American*, Feb. 23, 1839; "Massachusetts Legislature," *Colored American*, Apr. 25, 1840.

26. "The Marriage Law," *Liberator*, Feb. 5, 1841; "Legislation in Massachusetts," *Law Reporter* 3 (May 1840), 29–30; Bruce Laurie, *Beyond Garrison: Antislavery and Social Reform* (New York, 2005), 108–113.

27. "Encouragement to Amalgamationists," *Barre* (MA) *Gazette*, Jun. 9, 1843; "The legislature of Massachusetts…," *Racine* (WI) *Advocate*, Feb. 22, 1843; "Correspondence of the Richmond Whig," *Liberator*, Mar. 3, 1843; "A Virginian's Idea of Boston," *Signal of Liberty* (Ann Arbor, MI), Mar. 20, 1843.

28. "Amalgamation," *Boston Weekly Messenger*, Feb. 8, 1843; "Acts for Encouraging the Increase of the Colored Population," *Boston Weekly Messenger*, Feb. 1, 1843; "The locofoco papers in Massachusetts…," *New York Morning Courier and New York Enquirer*, Feb. 11, 1843; "Massachusetts," *Cattaraugus* (NY) *Republican*, Feb. 13, 1843.

29. "Essex Country Anti-Slavery Meeting," *Liberator*, Mar. 31, 1843; "Massachusetts," *Signal of Liberty* (Ann Arbor, MI), Apr. 24, 1843; "The Intermarriage Law," *National Anti-Slavery Examiner*, Mar. 16, 1843; J. F. Johnson, *Proceedings of the General Anti-Slavery Convention Called by the Committee of the British and Foreign Anti-Slavery Society and Held in London from Tuesday, June 13th to Tuesday, June 20th, 1843* (London, 1844), 273; "From Our Eastern Correspondent," *Philanthropist* (Cincinnati), Apr. 19, 1843.

30. "We need not…," *Liberator*, Aug. 28, 1846. For useful overviews of these conflicts see Arthur O. White, "Salem's Antebellum Black Community: Seedbed of the School Integration Movement," *Essex Institute Historical Collections* 108 (1972), 99–118; Barbara Linebaugh [White], *The African School and the Integration of Nantucket Public Schools* (MA thesis, Boston University, 1978); Barbara White, "The Integration of Nantucket Public Schools," *Historic Nantucket* 40 (Fall 1992), 59–62; Levesque, *Black Boston*, 165–229; James Oliver Horton and Lois E. Horton, *Black Bostonians: Family Life and Community Struggle in the Antebellum North*, 2nd ed. (New York, 1999), 76–86; Stephen Kendrick and Paul Kendrick, *Sarah's Long Walk: The Free Blacks of Boston and How Their Struggle for Equality Changed America* (Boston, 2004). For overviews of the common school movement and black education in the antebellum period, see Carl F. Kaestle, *Pillars of the Republic: Common Schools and American Society, 1780–1860* (New York, 1983); Davison M. Douglas, *Jim Crow Moves North: The Battle over Northern School Segregation, 1865–1954* (New York, 2005), 12–60; Hilary J. Moss, *Schooling Citizens: The Struggle for African American Education in Antebellum America* (Chicago, 2009).

31. Petition of Eunice F. Ross in aid of E. J. Pompey presented Feb. 26, 1845, Massachusetts State Archives; "Meeting of Colored Citizens," *Liberator*, Dec. 28, 1855; Goodman, *Of One Blood*, 45–53; Douglas, *Jim Crow Moves North*, 41–44; Moss, *Schooling Citizens*, 1–3; Rael, *Black Identity and Black Protest*, 98; Litwack, *North of Slavery*, 123–131; Stewart, *Holy Warriors*, 65; Susan Strane, *"A Whole-Souled Woman": Prudence Crandall and the Education of Black Women* (New York, 1990); *The Boston Mob of "Gentlemen of Property and Standing": Proceedings of the Anti-Slavery Meeting held in Stacy Hall, Boston, on the Twentieth Anniversary of the mob of October 21, 1835* (Boston, 1855), 11–12.

32. "We need not...," *Liberator*, Aug. 28, 1846; *Report of the Minority of the Committee of the Primary School Board on the Caste Schools of the City of Boston; with some Remarks on the City Solicitor's Opinion* (Boston, 1846), 12–13.

33. "Boston Olive Branch," *Liberator*, Aug. 8, 1845. See also *Report of the Primary School Committee, June 15, 1846, on the Petition of Sundry Colored Persons, for the Abolition of the Schools for Colored Children with the City Solicitor's Opinion* (Boston, 1846), 7–8, 13 (emphasis in originals).

34. "Public Schools—The Last Town-Meeting," *Nantucket Inquirer*, Apr. 1, 1843; "Schools and Colors," *Nantucket Inquirer*, May 20, 1843.

35. "Schools and Colors," *Nantucket Inquirer*, Apr. 15, 1843; *Report of the Primary School Committee, June 15, 1846*, 29; "The Smith School," *Liberator*, Nov. 9, 1849; "Schools and Colours," *Nantucket Inquirer*, Jul. 1, 1843; "Letter from Nantucket," *National Anti-Slavery Standard*, May 4, 1843; "School Committee's Report," *The Warder* (Nantucket), Feb. 14, 1846.

36. "Public Meeting," *Nantucket Morning Telegraph*, Feb. 28, 1844; "Public Meeting," *Liberator*, Mar. 15, 1844; "Meeting in Nantucket," *National Anti-Slavery Standard*, Mar. 14, 1844; *Report of the Minority of the Committee of the Primary School Board*, 4; "Copy of a Letter to a Member of the Boston School Committee," *Liberator*, Nov. 9, 1849; "Copy of a letter to a member of the Boston School Committee," *North Star*, Nov. 16, 1849.

37. "The Smith School," *National Anti-Slavery Standard*, Jul. 11, 1844; "Schools and Scholars," *Nantucket Inquirer*, Apr. 22, 1843; "No Title," *Nantucket Morning Telegraph*, Jun. 28, 1844; "Rights of Colored Citizens," *Liberator*, Jul. 12, 1844; "Resolutions of the Salem School Committee," *Common School Journal* 6 (Oct. 1844), 328.

38. "Schools and Scholars," *Nantucket Inquirer*, Apr. 22, 1843; *Commonwealth v. Dedham*, 16 Mass. 141 (1819).

39. "For the Morning Telegraph," *Nantucket Morning Telegraph*, Jun. 28, 1844; "Rights of Colored Citizens," *Liberator*, Jul. 12, 1844; "Resolutions of the Salem School Committee," *Common School Journal* 6 (Oct 1844), 328; "Separate Schools for Colored Children," *Emancipator and Weekly Chronicle*, Jun. 25, 1845.

40. "At a public meeting...," *Nantucket Inquirer*, Mar. 12, 1842; "Selections," *Liberator*, Mar. 18, 1842; "Several town meetings," *Nantucket Islander*, Mar. 18 1843.

41. White, "Salem's Antebellum Black Community," 111–114.

42. "Petition of Edward J. Pompey and 104 others of Nantucket for amendment of the Common School Law," Vault: Acts 1845, Chapter 214, Act Concerning Public Schools, March 25, 1845, Massachusetts Archives, Boston. See also "A Good Movement," *Liberator*, Feb. 14, 1845. For the support of the island's white abolitionists see "Petition of Peter Macy & 235 others in aid of E.J. Pompey & others," Vault: Acts 1845, Chapter 214, Act Concerning Public Schools, March 25, 1845, Massachusetts Archives, Boston. See also "Petition of Joseph Hunt & Thomas Macy & others requesting such alteration in the school law as shall extend to all children the same educational rights," Vault: Acts 1845, Chapter 214, Act Concerning Public Schools, March 25, 1845, Massachusetts Archives, Boston; "Public Schools," *National Anti-Slavery Standard*, Feb. 20, 1845.

43. "Public Schools in Massachusetts," *National Anti-Slavery Standard*, Apr. 24, 1845; "Speech of Hon. Mr. Wilson," *Liberator*, Mar. 7, 1845; Elias Nason, *The Life and Public Services of Henry Wilson* (Boston, 1881), 49–50.

44. *Roberts v. Boston*, 59 Mass. 198 (1849); "Public Schools in Massachusetts," *National Anti-Slavery Standard*, Apr. 24, 1845; "Horace Mann and Colored Schools," *Liberator*, Dec. 24, 1847.

45. "Interesting Suit," *Liberator*, Sep. 26, 1845; "Novel Suit," *Niles' National Register*, Sep. 20, 1845; "Admission of Colored Children in Common Schools," *New York Tribune*, Feb. 17, 1846; "Triumph of the Right," *Liberator*, Feb. 20, 1846. See also "Another Glorious Day," *New York Herald*, Feb. 15, 1846; "The town of Nantucket...," *Emancipator*, Feb. 18, 1846; "Three Cheers for Nantucket," *Liberator*, Feb. 20, 1846; "Colored People at Nantucket," *Cincinnati Daily Times*, Feb. 27, 1846; "Admission of Colored Children in Common Schools," *Friends' Weekly Intelligencer*, Mar. 7, 1846.

46. *Argument of Charles Sumner, Esq. Against the Constitutionality of Separate Colored Schools, in the Case of Sarah C. Roberts* v. *the City of Boston* (Boston, 1849), 13; "Equal School Rights," *Liberator*, Dec. 7, 1849; "The *Liberator*," *Boston Semi-Weekly Republican*, Dec. 8, 1849; "B.F. Roberts has published...," *Boston Semi-Weekly Republican*, Dec. 19, 1849; "Argument of Charles Sumner, Esq.," *Western Law Journal* 2 (May 1850), 353–365. On the boycott, see Carleton Mabee, "A Negro Boycott to Integrate Boston Schools," *New England Quarterly* 41 (1968), 341–361.

47. *Roberts v. City of Boston*, 59 Mass. 198, 206–209 (1849); *Plessy v. Ferguson*, 163 U.S. 537, 544 (1896). For examples of scholarship exploring the legal legacy of *Roberts*, see Leonard W. Levy and Harlan B. Phillips, "The Roberts Case: Source of the 'Separate but Equal' Doctrine," *American Historical Review* 56 (1951), 510–518; Roderick T. Baltimore and Robert F. Williams, "The State Constitutional Roots of the 'Separate but Equal' Doctrine: *Roberts v. City of Boston*," *Rutgers Law Journal* 17 (1985–1986), 537–552; Douglas J. Ficker, "From Roberts to Plessy: Educational Segregation and the 'Separate but Equal' Doctrine," *Journal of Negro History* 84 (Autumn, 1999), 301–314.

48. "From the Boston Post—Report on the Smith School," *Liberator*, Nov. 16, 1849; "Equal School Rights," *Frederick Douglass' Paper*, Apr. 13, 1855.

49. "Equal School Rights," *Liberator*, Oct. 5, 1849; "Meeting of the Friends of Equal School Rights," *Liberator*, Nov. 9, 1849; Let the Hall Be Crowded," *Liberator*, Nov. 23, 1849; "Continuation of Equal School Rights Meetings," *Liberator*, Dec. 14, 1849; "Equal School Rights Meeting," *Liberator*, Apr. 16, 1850; "Equal School Rights," *Liberator*, Jun. 21, 1850; "Equal School Rights," *Liberator*, Aug. 2, 1850; "Equal School Privileges," *Liberator*, Apr. 4, 1851; "New England Anti-Slavery Convention," *Liberator*, Jun. 6, 1851; "The National Convention of Colored People," *National Era*, Aug. 7, 1851.

50. "Equal School Rights—The Smith School," *Liberator*, Aug. 18, 1854; "Equal School Rights," *Frederick Douglass' Paper*, Aug. 25, 1854; "Equal School Rights in Boston," *Liberator*, Nov. 10, 1854; "Equal School Rights in Boston," *Anti-Slavery Bugle*, Nov. 25, 1854; "Freedom in Massachusetts," *Liberator*, Jan. 12, 1855; "Petitions for Equal School Rights," *Liberator*, Feb. 9, 1855; "Petitions for Equal School Rights," *Liberator*, Feb. 23, 1855; "Commonwealth of Massachusetts," *Liberator*, Mar. 30, 1855. On the Fugitive Slave Law in Boston, see especially Albert J. Von Frank, *The Trials of Anthony Burns: Freedom and Slavery in Emerson's Boston* (Cambridge, MA, 1998). On the conflict within the black community, see Arthur O. White, "Antebellum School Reform in Boston: Integrationists and Separatists," *Phylon* 34 (1973), 203–217; Hilary J. Moss, "The Tarring and Feathering of Thomas Paul Smith: Common Schools, Revolutionary Memory, and the Crisis of Black Citizenship in Antebellum Boston," *New England Quarterly* 80 (June 2007), 218–241.

51. "Equal School Rights," *Frederick Douglass' Paper*, Apr. 13, 1855; David Martin Ment, "Racial Segregation in the Public Schools of New England and New York, 1840–1940" (Ph.D. diss., Columbia University, 1975), 57–75; Laurie, *Beyond Garrison*, 280–282; Douglas, *Jim Crow Moves North*, 57.

52. "The School Question in Massachusetts—No Objection on Account of Color," *New York Herald*, Apr. 8, 1855; "Black Laws in Massachusetts," *New York Herald*, Apr. 20, 1855; "Black Laws in Massachusetts," *Boston Daily Courier*, Apr. 21, 1855; "Black Laws in Massachusetts," *Liberator*, May 4, 1855; "Colored National Council," *Liberator*, Jul. 27, 1855; "The Colored People and the School Law of Ohio," *Anti-Slavery Bugle* (Salem, OH), Jun. 6, 1855; "Equal School Rights," *Anti-Slavery Bugle*, Jan. 12, 1856.

53. George T. Downing et al., *To the Friends of Equal Rights in Rhode Island* (Providence, RI, 1859), 5, 7. On the Rhode Island conflicts, see Litwack, *North of Slavery*, 150–151; Lawrence Grossman, "George T. Downing and Segregation of Rhode Island Public Schools, 1855–1866," *Rhode Island History* 36 (1977), 99–105.

54. "The colored people…," *Nantucket Islander*, Mar. 18, 1843.

CHAPTER 5

1. William Wells Brown, *The American Fugitive in Europe: Sketches of Place and People Abroad* (Boston, 1855), 40, 312–315.
2. "New York Legal Rights Association," *New York Tribune*, Dec. 3, 1856.
3. Daniel Walker Howe, *What Hath God Wrought: The Transformation of America, 1815–1848* (New York, 2007), 211–242, 562–569; Patricia Cline Cohen, "Safety and Danger: Women on American Public Transport, 1750–1850," in *Gendered Domains: Rethinking Public and Private in Women's History*, ed. Dorothy O Helley and Susan M. Reverby (Ithaca, NY, 1992), 109–122; Barbara Y. Welke, "When All the Women Were White, and All the Blacks Were Men: Gender, Class, Race, and the Road to Plessy, 1855–1914," *Law and History Review* 13 (Autumn 1995), 268–270.
4. Brown, *American Fugitive*, 40; "Prejudice Against Color," *Emancipator and Free American*, Aug. 3, 1843; "From Our Eastern Correspondent," *Philanthropist*, Apr. 19, 1843; "For the Colored American," *Colored American*, Sep. 22, 1838. For foundational work on the discriminatory conditions of northern travel, see Leon Litwack, *North of Slavery: The Negro in the Free States, 1790–1860* (Chicago, 1961); 106–109; Carleton Mabee, *Black Freedom: The Nonviolent Abolitionists from 1830 through the Civil War* (New York, 1970), 112–126.
5. "Prejudice—An Incident," *Liberator*, Aug. 21, 1840; "Letter from Mr. Johnson," *Colored American*, Jan. 30, 1841; Louis Ruchames, "Jim Crow Railroads in Massachusetts," *American Quarterly* 8 (1956), 61–62.
6. "Colored People Allowed in This Car," *Frederick Douglass' Paper*, Dec. 8, 1854; "Communications," *Christian Inquirer*, Mar. 24, 1855; "Our New York Letter," *St. Paul Daily Pioneer*, Jan. 3, 1857; "A City Grievance," *New York Times*, Oct. 18, 1851; Clay McShande and Joel A. Tarr, *The Horse in the City: Living Machines in the Nineteenth Century* (Baltimore, 2007), 57–83.
7. "Correspondence," *Colored American*, Jun. 16, 1838; "A Trip to the East," *Colored American*, Aug. 25, 1838.
8. "Police Office," *Liberator*, Jan. 15, 1841; "Editorial Correspondence," *Colored American*, Jul. 20, 1839; "The Colored People of This City," *Friends' Intelligencer*, Sep. 15, 1860; James O. Horton and Lois E. Horton, *In the Hope of Liberty: Culture, Community, and Protest among Northern Free Blacks, 1700–1860* (New York, 1998), 171–172.
9. "Eastern Rail-Road Outrage," *Liberator*, Nov. 5, 1841; Thomas C. Holt, "Marking: Race, Race-making, and the Writing of History," *American Historical Review* 100 (1995), 1–20. In these ways, public transit joined the much-studied minstrel shows as another important site where knowledge about racial identity was conveyed in the antebellum North. See especially David Roediger, *The Wages of Whiteness: Race and the Making of the American Working Class* (New York, 1991); Eric Lott, *Love and Theft: Blackface Minstrelsy and the American Working Class* (New York, 1995).

10. "What Colored People Have Suffered," *Colored American*, Oct. 6, 1838; "Prejudice Against Color," *Colored American*, Dec. 22, 1838; "Railroad Distinctions of Color Arbitrary and Unlawful," *Friend of Man* (Utica, NY), Sep. 14, 1841.

11. "Have They Got a 'Jim Crow Car'?," *Liberator*, Aug. 1, 1845; "Modern 'Democracy' Illustrated," *National Anti-Slavery Standard*, Nov. 10, 1860; "Mr. Pennington and the Great Western," *Signal of Liberty* (Ann Arbor, MI), Oct. 2, 1843; "Outrage to Passengers Travelling in the Long Island Railroad Cars," *Liberator*, Mar. 27, 1846; "'The Color-Phobia As It Is,'" *Liberator*, Oct. 11, 1839; "Rebuke of Eastern Railroad Company," *Liberator*, Mar. 19, 1841.

12. "A Christian Example," *National Anti-Slavery Standard*, May 19, 1842; "Shame!," *New York Evangelist*, May 31, 1855; "Prejudice Against Color," *Liberator*, Jan. 13, 1843; Harriet Jacobs, *Incidents in the Life of a Slave Girl* [1861] (Mineola, NY, 2001), 135; Frederick Douglass, *My Bondage and My Freedom* [1855] (New York, 2005), 290. On slaves' locomotion, see especially Stephanie M. H. Camp, *Closer to Freedom: Enslaved Women and Everyday Resistance in the Plantation South* (Chapel Hill, 2004).

13. "Rebuke of the Eastern Railroad Company," *Liberator*, Mar. 19, 1841; "Prejudice Against Color," *Emancipator and Free American*, Aug. 3, 1843; "Shame!," *New York Evangelist*, May 31, 1855; "New-Bedford and Taunton Rail-Road," *Liberator*, Oct. 7, 1842; "A Wholesome Verdict," *New York Tribune*, Feb. 23, 1855; "Legal Rights Vindicated," *Frederick Douglass' Paper*, Mar. 2, 1855.

14. "To the Public," *Colored American*, Jan. 12, 1839; "M. George," *Emancipator and Free American*, Oct. 6, 1842; "Disabilities of Colored People," *Colored American*, Sep. 30, 1837.

15. "Shameful Treatment of David Ruggles," *Friend of Man* (Utica, NY), Aug. 3, 1841; Douglass, *My Bondage and My Freedom*, 296. For overviews, see Ruchames, "Jim Crow Railroads," 61–75; Mabee, *Black Freedom*, 112–126; Bruce Laurie, *Beyond Garrison: Antislavery and Social Reform* (New York, 2005), 113–116.

16. "More Ruffianism," *Liberator*, Oct. 8, 1841; "Case of David Ruggles," *Liberator*, Aug. 6, 1841. On the boycotts, see Mabee, *Black Freedom*, 121–124.

17. "Essex County Anti-Slavery Society," *Liberator*, Jul. 2, 1841; Welke, "When All the Women Were White," 273–274; Welke, *Recasting American Liberty: Gender, Race, and the Railroad Revolution, 1865–1920* (New York, 2001); A. K. Sandoval-Strausz, "Travelers, Strangers, and Jim Crow: Law, Public Accommodations, and Civil Rights in America," *Law and History Review* 23 (Feb. 2005), 53–94.

18. "Rights of Rail Road Corporations," *Boston Weekly Messenger*, Jul. 28, 1841; "The Disturbance on the Eastern Rail-Road," *Liberator*, Nov. 5, 1841; "Public opinion versus Justice," *Monthly Offering* (Nov. 1841), 168; "The Marriage Law," *Liberator*, Mar. 25, 1842.

19. "Legislative Items," *Boston Courier*, Jan. 30, 1843; "Case of Mr. Jinnings," *Liberator*, Jul. 2, 1841; Massachusetts Anti-Slavery Society, *Tenth Annual Report*

of the Board of Managers of the Massachusetts Anti-Slavery Society (Boston, 1842), 75–76; "Eastern Rail-Road Company," *Liberator*, Aug. 13, 1841; "Public Meeting," *Liberator*, Oct. 15, 1841; "To the Public," *Liberator*, Nov. 12, 1841; "Another Disgraceful Rail Road Outrage," *Liberator*, Nov. 12, 1841; "To the Public," *Liberator*, Nov. 22, 1841; "The Eastern Rail-Road Affair," *Liberator*, Nov. 5, 1841.

20. "Corporations," *Liberator*, Oct. 1, 1841; Massachusetts Anti-Slavery Society, *Tenth Annual Report*, 76; "Public opinion versus Justice," *Monthly Offering* (Nov. 1841), 166.

21. "Equal Rights *of all citizens in the cars*," *Bay State Democrat* (Boston), Feb. 18, 1842; "Legislative," *Liberator*, Mar. 4, 1842; "Remarks of Charles Lenox Remond," *Liberator*, Feb. 25, 1842; "Lions Painting Their Own Pictures," *National Anti-Slavery Standard*, Mar. 10 1842; Ruchames, "Jim Crow Railroads," 69–73; "Remarks of Ellis Gray Loring," *Liberator*, Mar. 4, 1842.

22. "Remarks of Ellis Gray Loring," *Liberator*, Mar. 4, 1842; Edward J. Balleisen, *Navigating Failure: Bankruptcy and Commercial Society in Antebellum America* (Chapel Hill, 2001); George M. Dennison, *The Dorr War: Republicanism on Trial, 1831–1861* (Lexington, KY, 1976); Reeve Huston, *Land and Freedom: Rural Society, Popular Protest, and Party Politics in Antebellum New York* (New York, 2000).

23. "Letter From Gerrit Smith," *Liberator*, Jul. 5, 1850. On Smith, see especially John Stauffer, *The Black Hearts of Men: Radical Abolitionists and the Transformation of Race* (Cambridge, MA, 2001).

24. "Commonwealth of Massachusetts," *Monthly Offering* (Mar. 1842), 44, 40–42; "Report of the Joint Special Committee, No. 63," *Massachusetts Legislative Documents—Senate* (Boston, 1842), 1–8; "Rights of Colored Persons," *National Anti-Slavery Standard*, Mar. 10, 1842; "Amalgamation," *Macon* (GA) *Weekly Telegraph*, Apr. 12, 1842.

25. "Massachusetts Legislature," *Boston Daily Mail*, Feb. 7, 1843; "Massachusetts Legislature," *Boston Courier*, Feb. 7, 1843; "Legislature of Massachusetts," *Liberator*, Feb. 17, 1843; "Convention at Southboro," *Liberator*, Mar. 17, 1843; Ruchames, "Jim Crow Railroads," 74–75; Laurie, *Beyond Garrison*, 116; "Massachusetts Legislature," *Boston Courier*, Feb. 7, 1843; Douglass, *My Bondage and My Freedom*, 297.

26. "Colored People Excluded from Public Vehicles," *Liberator*, Feb. 26, 1841; "Outrage," *Liberator*, Jan. 15, 1841; "The abuse of Downing…," *Colored American*, Jan. 16, 1841. On Downing, see John Hewitt, "Mr. Downing and His Oyster House: The Life and Good Works of an African-American Entrepreneur," *New York History* 74 (July 1993), 229–252; Hewitt, *Protest and Progress: New York's First Black Episcopal Church Fights Racism* (New York, 2000), 79–92.

27. "The Case of Mr. Downing," *Colored American*, Feb. 20, 1841.

28. "Outrage Upon Coloured Persons," *New York Tribune*, Jul. 19, 1854; "Outrage Upon Coloured Persons," *Frederick Douglass' Paper*, Jul. 28, 1854. For useful overviews of this incident, see John H. Hewitt, "The Search for Elizabeth

Jennings, Heroine of a Sunday Afternoon in New York City," *New York History* 62 (1990), 387–415; Leslie M. Alexander, *African or American? Black Identity and Political Activism in New York City, 1784–1861* (Chicago, 2008), 125–130.

29. "Thomas L. Jennings," *Frederick Douglass' Paper*, Feb. 18, 1859; "Thomas L. Jennings," *Anglo-African Magazine* 1 (Apr. 1859), 126–128; "Legal Rights Vindicated," *Frederick Douglass' Paper*, Mar. 2, 1855; "Another Disgraceful Rail Road Outrage," *Liberator*, Nov. 12, 1841. Thomas Jennings Jr. was trained by dentist Daniel Mann, who had initiated one of the key legal challenges to rail car segregation in Massachusetts. See "Improvements on a Valuable and Important Discovery," *Liberator*, Apr. 22, 1842.

30. "Outrage Upon Colored Persons," *New York Tribune*, Jul. 19, 1854; "Outrage Upon Colored Persons," *Frederick Douglass' Paper*, Jul. 28, 1854; "Outrage," *National Anti-Slavery Standard*, Jul. 29, 1854; "For Frederick Douglass' Paper," *Frederick Douglass' Paper*, Sep. 22, 1854.

31. "Appeal to the Citizens of Color," later published in "The Right of Colored Persons to Ride in the Railway Cars," *Pacific Appeal*, May 16, 1863.

32. "Court Record," *Brooklyn Eagle*, Feb. 23, 1855; "Rights of Colored People Vindicated," *Anti-Slavery Bugle* (Salem, OH), Mar. 10, 1855; "A Wholesome Verdict," *New York Tribune*, Feb. 23, 1855; "The rights of Colored Persons in Railway Cars," *Weekly Wisconsin* (Milwaukee), Mar. 7, 1855; "Rights of Coloured People Vindicated," *National Anti-Slavery Standard*, Mar. 3, 1855; "A Wholesome Verdict," *Cayuga Chief* (Auburn, NY), Mar. 6, 1855; "A New York exchange…," *Provincial Freeman*, Mar. 10, 1855; "Communications," *Christian Inquirer*, Mar. 24, 1855; "Coloured Woman," *Chamber's Journal of Popular Literature*, Apr. 28, 1855. For the later memory of Arthur's participation, see "Gen. Chester A. Arthur," *New York Times*, Jun. 9, 1880; "The New President," *New York Herald*, Sep. 20, 1881.

33. "Legal Rights Vindicated," *Frederick Douglass' Paper*, Mar. 2, 1855; James McCune Smith to Gerrit Smith, March 31, 1855 in *The Works of James McCune Smith: Black Intellectual and Abolitionist*, ed. John Stauffer (New York, 2006), 317.

34. James McCune Smith, *The Destiny of the People of Color* [1843], in *Works of James McCune Smith*, 48–60.

35. "Unity of Action," *Frederick Douglass' Paper*, May 12, 1854, in *Works of James McCune Smith*, 98–102.

36. "Prejudice," *National Enquirer and Constitutional Advocate of Universal Liberty* (Philadelphia), Sep. 14, 1837; "A Hard Case," *New York Evangelist*, Sep. 23, 1852. On Pennington, see especially R. J. M. Blackett, *Beating against the Barriers: Biographical Essays in Nineteenth-Century Afro-American History* (Baton Rouge, 1986); David E. Swift, *Black Prophets of Justice: Activist Clergy before the Civil War* (Baton Rouge, 1989).

37. On these other contemporary movements, see Howard C. Perkins, "A Neglected Phase of the Movement for Southern Unity, 1847–1852," *Journal of*

Southern History 12 (May 1946), 153–203; Nancy Isenberg, *Sex and Citizenship in Antebellum America* (Chapel Hill, 1998). On the liquor dealers, see Chapter 6.

38. "The First Colored Convention," *Weekly Anglo-African*, Oct. 15, 1859. Perhaps not surprisingly, Grice in 1859 was lodging with "the widow of his old friend and coadjutor Thomas L. J[e]nnings," who had died earlier that year. On the black convention movement, see Patrick Rael, *Black Identity and Black Protest in the Antebellum North* (Chapel Hill, 2002); Dana Weiner, *Race and Rights: Fighting Slavery and Prejudice in the Old Northwest, 1830–1870* (DeKalb, IL, 2013).

39. "Rights of Coloured People Vindicated," *National Anti-Slavery Standard*, Mar. 3, 1855; "Rights of Colored Citizens in Public Conveyances," *Christian Inquirer*, Mar. 31, 1855; "A New York exchange…," *Provincial Freeman*, Mar. 10, 1855; "Rights of Colored People," *Frederick Douglass' Paper*, May 18, 1855; "Rights of Colored People," *Anti-Slavery Bugle* (Salem, OH), May 19, 1855; "Anniversary Week in New York," *National Anti-Slavery Standard*, Apr. 28, 1855; "Anniversary of the American Anti-Slavery Society," *National Anti-Slavery Standard*, May 19, 1855; "Notice," *Frederick Douglass' Paper*, May 11, 1855.

40. "The Sixth-avenue Railroad vs. Colored Passengers," *New York Times*, May 12, 1855; "Police Intelligence," *New York Herald*, May 10, 1855; "Case of Rev. Mr. Pennington and the Sixth Avenue Railroad," *Liberator*, Jun. 8, 1855; "From Our New York Correspondent," *Daily National Intelligencer*, May 28, 1855; "Outrage upon a Doctor of Divinity," *New York Times*, May 25, 1855; "The Rev. Dr. Pennington," *New Albany* (IN) *Daily Ledger*, Jun. 2, 1855. For commentary, see "City Railroads and Colored Passengers," *Boston Traveller*, May 30, 1855; "A Colored D.D. in Trouble," *Pittsburgh Daily Morning Post*, May 28, 1855; "Colorphobia," *Syracuse Evening Chronicle*, Jun. 1, 1855.

41. "Colored People in City Cars," *New York Times*, May 29, 1855; "The Case of Rev. Dr. Pennington," *Frederick Douglass' Paper*, Jun. 8, 1855. Douglass here describes Tocqueville's *Democracy in America* as a "masterly treatise upon our *democratic* institutions." In 1837 abolitionist editor Elizur Wright Jr. provided a review of Beaumont, with translated passages, including those Douglass reprinted. See "Caste in the United States: A Review," *Quarterly Anti-Slavery Magazine* 2 (Jan. 1837), 175–199.

42. "The Legal Rights Association," *New York Tribune*, Aug. 25, 1855; "Legal Rights Association," *New York Times*, Aug. 27, 1855; "Meeting of Colored People," *Liberator*, Aug. 31, 1855; "Meeting of Colored People," *Christian Inquirer*, Sep. 1, 1855; "The Legal Rights Association," *Frederick Douglass' Paper*, Sep. 7, 1855; "The Colored People and Their Rights," *New York Tribune*, Sep. 24, 1855; "New-York Legal Rights Association," *New York Tribune*, Dec. 3, 1856; "Legal Rights Association," *New York Tribune*, Nov. 2, 1855; "Legal Rights Association," *New York Tribune*, Dec. 21, 1855; "New-York Legal Rights Association," *New York Tribune*, Dec. 16, 1856; "The New-York Society…," *New York Times*, May 11, 1858; "Dr. Pennington to the Stockholders of the Sixth-avenue Railroad," *New York Times*, Oct. 16, 1855.

43. "Legal Rights Association," *New York Tribune*, Sep. 27, 1855; "The Rights of Colored People in Cars—Meeting of Legal Rights Association," *New York Post*, Nov. 1, 1855; "Legal Rights Association," *New York Tribune*, Nov. 2, 1855; "The Rights of Colored People in Public Conveyances," *Oneida* (NY) *Sachem*, Nov. 10, 1855.

44. "Legal Rights Association," *New York Times*, Aug. 27, 1855; "The Rights of Colored People in Cars—Meeting of Legal Rights Association," *New York Post*, Nov. 1, 1855; "New-York Legal Rights Association," *New York Tribune*, Dec. 16, 1856; "Equal Rights Festival," *New York Tribune*, Feb. 23, 1856; "Anniversary," *New York Tribune*, Feb. 20, 1857; "A Colored Anniversary," *New York Evening Express*, Feb. 24, 1858; "The Legal Rights Association," *New York Tribune*, Feb. 25, 1858; "The Legal Rights Association Supper," *New York Tribune*, Feb. 27, 1863.

45. "The Legal Rights Association," *New York Tribune*, Feb. 25, 1858; Leslie M. Harris, *In the Shadow of Slavery: African Americans in New York City, 1626–1863* (Chicago, 2003), 275; "The African Race in the United States—A Colored Man on the Disabilities of Color," *New York Post*, Oct. 31, 1855; "Colored Consistency?," *New York Times*, Oct. 31, 1855; "Legal Rights Association," *New York Tribune*, Nov. 2, 1855.

46. "The War of Colors," *New York Times*, Oct. 5, 1855.

47. Martin Delany, "Political Destiny of the Colored Race on the American Continent," in *Pamphlets of Protest*, ed. Richard Newman, Patrick Rael, and Philip Lapansky (New York, 2001), 233, 230.

48. "New-York Legal Rights Association," *New York Tribune*, Dec. 3, 1856; "The colored people…," *New York Times*, Dec. 17, 1856; "Equal Rights Claimed," *Lowell Daily Citizen*, Dec. 22, 1856; "Important and Interesting Trial," *New York Times*, Dec. 18, 1856; "Superior Court," *New York Tribune*, Dec. 18, 1856; "Conclusion of the Pennington Case," *New York Times*, Dec. 20, 1856; "Right of Colored Persons to Ride in Cars," *New York Sun*, Dec. 19, 1856; "The Sixth-Avenue Railroad Case," *New York Times*, Dec. 19, 1856.

49. "The Sixth-Avenue Railroad Case," *New York Times*, Dec. 19, 1856; "Superior Court," *New York Tribune*, Dec. 18, 1856.

50. "Superior Court," *New York Herald*, Dec. 20, 1856; "Superior Court," *New York Herald*, Dec. 20, 1856; "Conclusion of the Pennington Case," *New York Times*, Dec. 20, 1856; "The Rights of Colored Persons," *Buffalo Courier*, Dec. 24, 1856. On Slosson, see "The Election," *New York Times*, Nov. 7, 1853; "Secession and the Laws—Note from Judge Slosson," *New York Times*, Dec. 22, 1860.

51. "The Pennington Case—Negro Drawbacks, North and South," *New York Herald*, Dec. 23, 1856; "Eastern Correspondence," *Presbyterian Banner and Advocate* (Pittsburgh), Jan. 3, 1857; "Negroes in the North and South," *Cincinnati Daily Enquirer*, Jan. 1, 1857.

52. James W. C. Pennington to Gerrit Smith, December 15, 1856, Gerrit Smith Papers, Syracuse University; "The Rights of Colored People in City Cars," *New York Times*, Mar. 22, 1858.

53. William Howard Day to Gerrit Smith, Mar. 27, 1856, Gerrit Smith Papers, Syracuse University. It seems likely that Gerrit Smith either loaned or gave Day some money to support his case. Two years later, Day wrote again to Smith asking him to support "another new project"—"a small self-sustaining Weekly Paper for the Colored People of Canada and the United States." William Howard Day to Gerrit Smith, Jun. 21, 1858, Gerrit Smith Papers, Syracuse University.

54. Day to Smith, Mar. 27, 1856; *Day v. Owen*, 5 Mich. 520 (1858); Blackett, *Beating against the Barriers*, 287–386; David M. Katzman, *Before the Ghetto: Black Detroit in the Nineteenth Century* (Urbana, IL, 1973), 40; Ronald P. Formisano, "The Edge of Caste: Colored Suffrage in Michigan, 1827–1861," *Michigan History* 56 (Spring 1972), 38; Roy E. Finkenbine, "A Beacon of Liberty on the Great Lakes: Race, Slavery, and the Law in Antebellum Michigan," in *The History of Michigan Law*, ed. Paul Finkelman and Martin J. Hershock (Athens, OH, 2006), 83–107.

55. Day to Smith, Mar. 27, 1856; "How It Is Treated," *Detroit Free Press*, Oct. 22, 1858.

56. 5 Mich. 520, 526–527.

57. "The Social Position of Negroes in Michigan," *Detroit Free Press*, Oct. 23, 1858. For notice of the decision, see "The Rights of Colored Passengers," *Baltimore Sun*, Oct. 25, 1858; "Varieties," *Philadelphia Public Ledger*, Oct. 26, 1858; "In the case...," *National Era*, Oct. 28, 1858; "The Rights of Colored Passengers," *National Anti-Slavery Standard*, Oct. 30, 1858; "Negro Contest for Social Equality," *Daily National Intelligencer*, Nov. 5, 1858; "Negro Contest for Social Equality," *New York Herald*, Nov. 14, 1858; "Negro Contest for Social Equality," *Lowell Daily Citizen and News*, Nov. 16, 1858; "Negro Contest for Social Equality," *Annapolis Gazette*, Nov. 18, 1858; "Negro Contest for Social Equality," *Weekly Wisconsin Patriot* (Madison), Nov. 20, 1858.

58. In *Plessy v. Ferguson*, Justice Henry Brown improperly cited *Day v. Owen* in support of this claim: "Similar statutes for the separation of the two races upon public conveyances were held to be constitutional." *Day v. Owen* involved no statute; the case broached no constitutional issues. *Plessy v. Ferguson*, 163 U.S. 537, 548 (1896). The Michigan legislature passed a Civil Rights Act in 1885 that prohibited racial discrimination aboard public conveyances and in public accommodations and public amusements. In *Ferguson v. Gies*, the Michigan Supreme Court used the measure to condemn racial discrimination in a restaurant. Speaking for the Court, Justice Morse discussed *Day v. Owen* and observed that "it must be remembered that the decision, as in the case of *Roberts v. Boston*, 59 Mass. 198, 5 Cush. 198, was made in the *ante bellum* days, before the colored man was a citizen, and when, in nearly one-half of the Union, he was but a chattel. It cannot now serve as a precedent." *Ferguson v. Gies*, 82 Mich. 358, 363–364 (1890).

59. *Scott v. Sandford*, 60 U.S. 393, 407 (1857). See especially Don Fehrenbacher, *The Dred Scott Case: Its Significance in American Law and Politics* (New York, 1978);

Austin Allen, *Origins of the Dred Scott Case: Jacksonian Jurisprudence and the Supreme Court, 1837–1857* (Athens, GA, 2006).

60. "What next is to be Done with Free Negroes," *Anti-Slavery Bugle* (Salem, OH), Apr. 4, 1857; "Marine Court," *New York Herald*, Apr. 20, 1858; "Law Intelligence," *New York Tribune*, Apr. 22, 1858.

61. "How It Is Treated," *Detroit Free Press*, Oct. 22, 1858; "The Supreme Court of the State of Michigan on the Social Status of Negroes," *Detroit Free Press*, Oct. 20, 1858.

62. "Black Republican Theory and Practice," *Cleveland Plain Dealer*, Oct. 27, 1858; "Status of the Negro in the Free States," *Civilian and Gazette Weekly* (Galveston, TX), Nov. 23, 1858; "Black Republicanism Balking," *Macon* (GA) *Weekly Telegraph*, Nov. 2, 1858. See also "A Black Republican Supreme Court sustaining the Dred Scott Decision," *Daily Missouri Republican* (St. Louis), Oct. 29, 1858; "A Black 'Republican' Supreme Court Sustaining the Dred Scott Decision," *Waukesha County* (WI) *Democrat*, Nov. 2, 1858; "A 'Republican' Supreme Court Sustaining the Dred Scott Decision!," *Madison Observer* (Morrisville, NY), Nov. 4, 1858; "A Black 'Republican' Supreme Court sustaining the Dred Scot decision!," *Dover* (NH) *Gazette and Strafford Advertiser*, Nov. 6, 1858; "The Dred Scott Decision Reaffirmed by a Black Republican Supreme Court," *Defiance* (OH) *Democrat*, Nov. 13, 1858; "The Supreme Court of Michigan," *New Hampshire Patriot*, Nov. 17, 1858; "The Boot on the Other Leg," *Gettysburg* (PA) *Compiler*, Nov. 22, 1858; "The Dred Scott Decision Reaffirmed by a Republican Supreme Court," *Newark* (OH) *Advocate*, Nov. 24, 1858; "The Decision of the Supreme Court in Day vs. Owen," *Jackson* (MI) *Citizen*, Mar. 3, 1859.

63. "Outrage Upon a Colored Gentleman," *New York Tribune*, Aug. 11, 1859; "Rights of Negroes in Sleeping-Cars," *Cincinnati Daily Enquirer*, Mar. 3, 1860; *State v. Kimber*, 30 Ohio Dec. 197 (Hamilton C. P. Ct. 1859); "Miscellaneous," *Chicago Tribune*, Feb. 8, 1860; *Goines v. M'Candless*, 4 Phil. Rep. 255, 256–257 (Dist. Ct. 1861).

64. "The Rights of Colored People," *Christian Recorder*, Jan. 26, 1861.

65. "The Rights of Colored People," *Christian Recorder*, Jan. 26, 1861. On these struggles, see James McPherson, *The Struggle for Equality: Abolitionists and the Negro in the Civil War and Reconstruction* (Princeton, NJ, 1964), 234–236; Philip S. Foner, "The Battle to End Discrimination against Negroes on Philadelphia Streetcars, Part I and Part II," *Pennsylvania History* 40 (Jul. 1973), 261–290; 40 (Oct. 1973), 355–379; Andrew Diemer, "Reconstructing Philadelphia: African Americans and Politics in the Post–Civil War North," *Pennsylvania Magazine of History and Biography* 133 (Jan. 2009), 29–58; Judith Giesberg, *Army at Home: Women and the Civil War on the Northern Home Front* (Chapel Hill, 2009), 92–118; Kate Masur, *An Example for All the Land: Emancipation and the Struggle over Equality in Washington, D.C.* (Chapel Hill, 2010), 100–112.

66. "Legal Rights' Association," *Daily Evening Bulletin* (San Francisco), May 31, 1862; "Our correspondent," *Pacific Appeal*, May 31, 1862; "What is Doing to Secure Our Right of Oath?," *Pacific Appeal*, Jul. 5, 1862; Rudolph M. Lapp, *Blacks in Gold Rush California* (New Haven, CT, 1977), 210–230.

67. "Rights of Colored Persons," *Albany Evening Journal*, Oct. 1, 1856; "Rights of Coloured Persons," *National Anti-Slavery Standard*, Oct. 11, 1856; "Law Intelligence," *New York Times*, Jan. 18, 1858; "Another Outrage Upon the Eighth-Avenue Railroad," *New York Tribune*, Dec. 17, 1856; "Outrage Upon a Colored Gentleman," *New York Tribune*, Aug. 11, 1859.

68. "Legal Rights Association Anniversary," *National Anti-Slavery Standard*, Mar. 12, 1859; "Legal Rights Association Anniversary," *Frederick Douglass' Paper*, Mar. 18, 1859; "Franchises and Duties," *New York Tribune*, Aug. 3, 1863; Sinclair Tousey, *A Business Man's Views of Public Matters* (New York, 1865), 57; "The Eighth Avenue Railroad," *New York Tribune*, Sep. 15, 1863.

69. "Colored Citizens and Our City Railroad Cars," *Daily National Intelligencer*, Feb. 12, 1864; "Colored People Admitted to the Fourth Avenue Cars," *New York Tribune*, Feb. 27, 1864; "Concentrated News," *Wisconsin* (Madison) *Daily Patriot*, Apr. 2, 1864.

70. "Riding in City Cars," *New Orleans Tribune*, Jul. 26, 1864; "Trials at Police Headquarters," *New York Herald*, Jul. 1, 1864; "The policeman…," *New York Times*, Jun. 24, 1864; "The policeman…," *New York Tribune*, Jun. 24, 1864.

71. "Thomas C. Action is Dead," *New York Times*, May 2, 1898; "Right of Colored People to Ride in the Street Cars—Important Case," *New York Tribune*, Jun. 30, 1864; "General News," *New York Times*, Jun. 30, 1864; "A policeman was tried," *New York Tribune*, Jun. 30, 1864; "General News," *New York Tribune*, Jul. 9, 1864.

72. "Justice Restored," *Christian Recorder*, Jul. 9, 1864; "An interesting case," *Chicago Tribune*, Jul. 3, 1864; "Our readers," *Milwaukee Daily Sentinel*, Jul. 7, 1864; "Our New York Correspondence," *Philadelphia Inquirer*, Jul. 8, 1864; "Letter from New York," *Sacramento Daily Union*, Jul. 27, 1864; "Colored People in Railroad Cars," *Brooklyn Eagle*, Jun. 30, 1864.

73. "Letters from New York," *Liberator*, Jul. 22, 1864.

CHAPTER 6

1. "Anti-Liquor Law Demonstration!!" *Chicago Tribune*, Jun. 28, 1855; "The Anti-Prohibition Demonstration," *Chicago Times*, Jul. 5, 1855; "Great Anti-Fanatic Demonstration!," *Chicago Times*, Jul. 5, 1855.

2. "Submission to the Will of the Majority," *Boston Investigator*, Jun. 27, 1855; "The Sunday Law and the German Press," *New York Times*, May 28, 1860.

3. Thomas R. Pegram, *Battling Demon Rum: The Struggle for a Dry America, 1800–1933* (Chicago, 1998), 39–40; Frank L. Byrne, *Prophet of Prohibition: Neal Dow and His Crusade* (Madison, WI, 1961), 42–47; Ian R. Tyrrell, *Sobering Up: From*

Temperance to Prohibition in Antebellum America, 1800–1860 (Westport, CT, 1979), 252–263.

4. Alfred Gale, *The Present License System, an Appeal to the People* (n.p., 1852), 11; N. A. Keyes, *A Temperance Sermon* (Lancaster, PA, 1852), 16; Lemuel Grosvenor, *The Maine Law No Vanity, but a sure Ground of Confidence* (Alton, IL, 1854), 21.

5. "The Maine Temperance Law," *New Englander* 10 (Feb. 1852), 63–64; "The Maine Liquor Law," *Christian Secretary*, Feb. 13, 1852; Samuel H. Hall, *The Prohibitory Law: A Sermon for the Times* (Marshall, MI, 1853), 13–14; "Temperance and Prayer," *New York Evangelist*, Mar. 25, 1852; Pegram, *Battling Demon Rum*, 40; Tyrrell, *Sobering Up*, 254–256.

6. "Temperance in Iowa," *The Lily*, Feb. 1, 1855; "The Maine Liquor Law," *Christian Secretary*, Feb. 13, 1852; *Proceedings of the Pennsylvania State Temperance Convention, held at Harrisburg, January 26th and 27th, 1854, with the Report of the State Central Committee, for 1853* (Philadelphia, 1854), 29; "State Temperance Convention," *New York Times*, Jan. 19, 1853; "Temperance Jubilee [sic]," *New York Evangelist*, Dec. 28, 1854; "Temperance and Prayer," *New York Evangelist*, Mar. 25, 1852; "Prohibition in California," *Boston Weekly Telegraph*, Aug. 3, 1855. On prohibitionists' antipartyism, see Mark Voss-Hubbard, *Beyond Party: Cultures of Antipartisanship in Northern Politics before the Civil War* (Baltimore, 2002), 71–74. On women in the Maine Law crusade, see Ian R. Tyrrell, "Women and Temperance in Antebellum America, 1830–1860," *Civil War History* 28 (1982), 128–152; Scott C. Martin, *Devil of the Domestic Sphere: Temperance, Gender, and Middle-Class Ideology, 1800–1860* (DeKalb, IL, 2008), 124–149.

7. "Prohibitory Liquor Laws," *Boston Traveller*, Feb. 3, 1855; Pegram, *Battling Demon Rum*, 40–41; Kevin Sweeney, "Rum, Romanism, Representation, and Reform: Coalition Politics in Massachusetts, 1847–1853," *Civil War History* 22 (1976), 116–137; Michael F. Holt, *Political Crisis of the 1850s* (New York, 1978); William E. Gienapp, *The Origins of the Republican Party, 1852–1856* (New York, 1987); Tyler Anbinder, *Nativism and Slavery: The Northern Know Nothings and the Politics of the 1850s* (New York, 1992).

8. "The Maine Law in New-York," *New York Evangelist*, Apr. 19, 1855; "Circular, of State Central Temperance Committee," *Weekly Reveille* (Vevay, IN), May 2, 1855; "The Prohibitory Liquor Law," *New York Herald*, Jun. 22, 1855; Tyrrell, *Sobering Up*, 293–294.

9. "Liquor Law Items," *Boston Daily Atlas*, Aug. 7, 1852; "The Maine Liquor Law," *Farmers' Cabinet*, Feb. 11, 1852; "Maine Law Items," *Syracuse Daily Standard*, Jul. 13, 1855; "Anti-Maine Law Speculation," *New York Weekly Herald*, Jul. 1, 1854.

10. "We did Governor Boutwell…," *New London Daily Chronicle*, May 31, 1852; Suzanne Thurman, "Cultural Politics on the Indiana Frontier: The American Home Missionary Society and Temperance Reform," *Indiana Magazine of History* 94 (1998), 300; "Anti-Maine Law Outrage," *New York Times*, Sep. 27, 1852; "Anti-Maine Law Outrage," *Albany Evening Journal*, Sep. 27, 1852; "More

Anti-Maine Law Incendiaries—Important Liquor Case," *Albany Evening Journal*,
Sep. 28, 1852; "Contemptible," *Geneseo* (NY) *Democrat*, Aug. 1, 1855; "The
Outrage at North Reading," *Boston Traveller*, Jan. 22, 1855; "Law and Order in
Massachusetts," *New York Post*, Jan. 31, 1855; "The Conspiracy at Chester, Mass,"
New York Evangelist, Feb. 8, 1855; "Letter From Michigan," *Puritan Recorder*, Feb.
15, 1855; "Opinion on the Portland 'Terrorism,'" *Boston Daily Times*, Jun. 12, 1855;
Byrne, *Prophet of Prohibition*, 60–69; Tyrrell, *Sobering Up*, 295–296.

11. "Anti-Maine Law Meeting," *Kalamazoo* (MI) *Gazette*, Feb. 17, 1854; Stephen D.
Bingham, *Early History of Michigan* (Lansing, 1888), 282, 318–319; "Anti-Liquor
Law Demonstration!!" *Chicago Tribune*, Jun. 28, 1855; A. T. Andreas, *History
of Chicago* (Chicago, 1884), 564; Arthur Charles Cole, *The Centennial History
of Illinois*, vol. 3 (Chicago, 1922), 453–454; "Anti-Maine Liquor Law Meeting,"
Milwaukee Sentinel, Feb. 14, 1852; "Anti-Maine Liquor Law Meeting," *Milwaukee
Sentinel*, Feb. 18, 1852; "Obituary—Col. Richard French," *New York Tribune*, Jul.
18, 1872; "A Rum Business," *New York Tribune*, Mar. 1, 1852.

12. "The Anti-Prohibitionists in the Park," *New York Herald*, Jul. 3, 1855. This com-
posite picture of anti-Maine Law events is drawn from numerous newspaper
reports. For examples, see "Anti-Maine Law Meeting," *New York Observer and
Chronicle*, Mar. 4, 1852; "Meeting in Opposition to the Maine Liquor Law,"
Brooklyn Daily Eagle, Mar. 2, 1852; "Anti-Prohibitory Law Demonstration,"
Wisconsin (Milwaukee) *Daily Free Democrat*, Mar. 28, 1855; "Trenton Anti-Maine
Law Convention," *Albany Evening Journal*, Oct. 15, 1852; "Anti-Maine Law
Demonstration," *Sandusky* (OH) *Register*, Apr. 6, 1854; "The Maine Law,"
Syracuse Daily Republican, Apr. 1, 1854; "Anti-Prohibition Meeting in Lancaster,"
Public Ledger (Philadelphia), Jun. 11, 1855; "Opposition to the Liquor Law," *Boston
Daily Times*, May 22, 1855; "The Liquor Question—Indiana," *New York Herald*,
May 13, 1855; "Anti-Liquor Law Demonstration!!," *Chicago Tribune*, Jun. 28, 1855;
Dan E. Clark, "The History of Liquor Legislation in Iowa, 1846–1861," *Iowa
Journal of History and Politics* 6 (Jan. 1908), 77. For more on antiprohibitionism's
social composition, see Tyrrell, *Sobering Up*, 297–305.

13. "The Anti-Prohibitionists in the Park," *New York Herald*, Jul. 3, 1855; "The Liquor
Law Veto in Wisconsin," *Milwaukee Daily Sentinel*, Mar. 30, 1855; "Infidelity in
the United States," *The National Magazine* 5 (Nov. 1854), 411; "Defeat of the
Prohibitory Law," *New York Evangelist*, Nov. 30, 1854; "Liquor Law Items," *Boston
Daily Atlas*, Aug. 7, 1852; "Lager Beer," *The Independent*, Oct. 12, 1854.

14. "The Anti-Maine-Law Paper," *Daily Ohio State Journal*, Aug. 1, 1853; "The
Anti-Maine law paper...," *Gallipolis* (OH) *Journal*, Aug. 11, 1853. The Ohio
anti-Maine Law paper was published in both English and German.

15. "Banner of Liberty," *Putnam* (NY) *County Courier*, Feb. 11, 1854; "Our Tour
through Indiana," *Banner of Liberty* (Middletown, NY), Oct. 1, 1854; G. J.
Beebe, *A Sure Cure for the Tetotal Mania, and a Quietus for the Maine Liquor
Law* (Middletown, NY, 1852), 1; "Anti-Maine Law Mass Meeting," *Trenton State*

Gazette, Sep. 25, 1852; "The Anti Maine Liquor Meeting...," *Trenton State Gazette*, Oct. 14, 1852; "News of the Morning," *New York Times*, Oct. 15, 1852; "Trenton Anti-Maine Law Convention," *New York Evening Post*, Oct. 15, 1852; "Temperance Movements," *Daily Scioto Gazette* (Chillicothe, OH), Aug. 16, 1853; "A Challenge—A Discussion," *Gallipolis* (OH) *Journal*, Aug. 11, 1853; "A Mr. G.J. Beebe...," *Wooster* (OH) *Republican*, Aug. 18, 1853; "The Great Discussion on the Maine Law," *Daily Ohio Statesman*, Aug. 22, 1853; "Mr. Beebe—The Temperance Discussion," *Daily Ohio Statesman*, Aug. 23, 1853; "Discussion of the Maine Law," *Daily Ohio Statesman*, Aug. 24, 1853; "Maine Law Discussion in Columbus," *New York Herald*, Aug. 27, 1853; "The Great Debate on the Maine Law," *Ohio State Journal*, Aug. 30, 1853; "Our Tour through Indiana," *Banner of Liberty* (Middletown, NY), Oct. 1, 1854.

16. "Remonstrance Against the 'Maine Liquor Law,' " *New York Tribune*, Feb. 10, 1852; "The New Prohibitory Liquor Law," *Boston Traveller*, May 22, 1855; "Important Meeting in the Park," *New York Herald*, Apr. 7, 1855; "The Prohibitory Law," *New York Herald*, Apr. 8, 1855; "The Effects and Defects of the Prohibitory Law," *New York Herald*, Apr. 16, 1855; "Fourth of July," *Irish American*, Jun. 16, 1855; "Liberty for the Rich, Prohibition for the Poor," *New York Herald*, Apr. 17, 1855.

17. "Anti-Maine Law Mass Meeting," *Trenton State Gazette*, Sep. 25, 1852; "The Maine Liquor Law," *New York Post*, Apr. 3, 1855; "Remonstrance Against the Maine Law," *Baltimore Sun*, Feb. 7, 1852; "The Maine Liquor Law," *Democratic Review* 30 (Mar. 1852), 273; "Announcements," *Gallipolis* (OH) *Journal*, Oct. 6, 1853; Edward Graf, *The Temperance Question, Answered on Principle of Morals and Religion* (Philadelphia, 1852), 13–14.

18. "The Temperance Law," *The Citizen* (New York), Apr. 1, 1854; " 'Tee-Total' Fanaticism," *Freeman's Journal and Catholic Register* (New York), Sep. 18, 1852; "Anti-Maine Law Meetings," *Kalamazoo* (MI) *Gazette*, Feb. 17, 1854; "The New Prohibitory Liquor Law," *Boston Traveller*, May 22, 1855; "A Rum Speech," *Brooklyn Eagle*, Oct. 11, 1852; "Meeting in Opposition to the Maine Liquor Law," *Brooklyn Eagle*, Mar. 2, 1852. On the longer history of sumptuary laws, see Alan Hunt, *Governance of the Consuming Passions: A History of Sumptuary Law* (New York, 1996).

19. A Primitive Washingtonian, *A Resurrection of the Blue-Laws; or Maine Reform in Temperate Doses* (Boston, 1852), 3; "Trenton Anti-Maine Law Convention," *Albany Evening Journal*, Oct. 15, 1852; "Anti-Maine Liquor Law Meeting," *Milwaukee Sentinel*, Feb. 14, 1852; "Anti-Liquor Law Meeting in the Park," *New York Herald*, Jul. 2, 1855; "Anti-Maine Law Mass Meeting," *Trenton State Gazette*, Sep. 25, 1852; "Liberty and Temperance vs. Tyranny and Fanaticism," *New York Herald*, Apr. 8, 1854; Jed Dannenbaum, *Drink and Disorder: Temperance Reform in Cincinnati from the Washingtonian Revival to the WCTU* (Chicago, 1984), 152; Graf, *The Temperance Question*, 3–4, 7–8.

20. A Primitive Washingtonian, *A Resurrection of the Blue-Laws*, 3; "The Anti-Prohibitionists in the Park," *New York Herald*, Jul. 3, 1855.

21. "Tyranny of the Majority," *Boston Weekly Messenger*, May 10, 1855; "Correspondence of the Courier," *Boston Courier*, Sep. 5, 1855.

22. "Prohibitory Liquor Laws," *Weekly Raleigh* (NC) *Register*, Jul. 26, 1854; "Why I Shall Vote Against the Maine Law," *Detroit Free Press*, Jun. 8, 1853;"Temperance Meetings and Their Resolutions," *The Anti-Prohibitionist* (Chicago), May 16, 1855; Carl Wittke, *Refugees of Revolution: The German Forty-Eighters in America* (Philadelphia, 1952), 141; Beebe, *A Sure Cure*, 11.

23. Beebe, *A Sure Cure*, 11.

24. "The Maine Liquor Law," *Democratic Review* 30 (Mar. 1852), 272; P. T. Barnum, "Appeal to the Democratic Voters of Connecticut," *New Haven Advocate*, Mar. 26, 1852; A. H. Saxon, *P.T. Barnum: The Legend and the Man* (New York, 1989), 386; "Necessity of Parties—American Democracy," *Democratic Review* 30 (Mar. 1852), 274.

25. *Rational Appeal to American Citizens*, 3–4 (emphasis in original).

26. Alexis de Tocqueville, *Democracy in America* [1835], ed. J. P. Mayer, George Lawrence, translation (New York, 1969), 183, 191–192.

27. "At a Meeting of the Liquor Dealers...," *New York Herald*, Jul. 2, 1855; "The Anti Maine Liquor Law Club," *Daily Alta California*, Aug. 29, 1855; Gilman M. Ostrander, *The Prohibition Movement in California, 1848–1933* (Berkeley, CA, 1957), 16–20; Asa Earl Martin, "The Temperance Movement in Pennsylvania Prior to the Civil War," *Pennsylvania Magazine of History and Biography* 49 (1925), 224–225; Dannenbaum, *Drink and Disorder*, 85; "The principal liquor dealers...," *Boston Daily Atlas*, Jan. 20, 1855; "The Constitution!," *Delaware State Reporter* (Dover), Nov. 30, 1855; "The Liquor Excitement...," *The Patriot* (London), May 21, 1855.

28. "Won't Give In," *Chicago Times*, May 17, 1855; Edwin G. Burrows and Mike Wallace, *Gotham: A History of New York City to 1898* (New York, 1999), 777; "Constitution of the Free Trade Society," *Milwaukee Daily Sentinel*, Jul. 13, 1853; "To Arms!," *Cayuga Chief* (Auburn, NY), Feb. 17, 1852; "The Liquor Dealers Moving," *Chicago Tribune*, Mar. 23, 1855.

29. "New York Affairs," *Atlanta Weekly Intelligencer*, Apr. 26, 1855; "To Arms!," *Cayuga Chief* (Auburn, NY), Feb. 17, 1852; "Constitution of the Free Trade Society," *Milwaukee Daily Sentinel*, Jul. 13, 1853; "Anti-Maine Law—Mass Meeting," *Daily Cleveland Herald*, Sep. 21, 1853; "The Anti-Maine Law Meeting," *Daily Cleveland Herald*, Sep. 23, 1853; "German Meeting," *Daily Cleveland Herald*, Oct. 3, 1853; "Meeting of Liquor Dealers," *New York Herald*, Feb. 26, 1855; "Meeting of Liquor Dealers," *Trenton State Gazette*, Feb. 27, 1855; "Jersey City," *Trenton State Gazette*, Mar. 22, 1855; "Anti-Maine Law Everywhere," *Weekly Reveille* (Vevay, IN), Jul. 25, 1855.

30. "The Effects of the New Liquor Law in the Metropolis," *New York Herald*, Apr. 15, 1855; "New York Affairs," *Atlanta* (GA) *Weekly Intelligencer*, Apr. 26. 1855.

31. "Legal Opinions," *Milwaukee Daily Sentinel*, Apr. 24, 1855; Metropolitan Society for the Protection of Private and Constitutional Rights, *The Unconstitutionality of the Prohibitory Liquor Law Confirmed* (New York, 1855); "The Maine Law Again," *The Citizen*, Apr. 28, 1855; "Prohibitory Liquor Law," *National Anti-Slavery Standard*, May 5, 1855; "Rebellion Against the Liquor Law," *New York Evangelist*, Apr. 26, 1855; "The Prohibitory Law," *New York Times*, Apr. 28, 1855; "The News," *Boston Traveller*, Jun. 27, 1855. For examples of published opinions, see "The Prohibitory Law—Legal Opinion of Nicholas Hill, Jr.," *New York Times*, Apr. 28, 1855; "Liquor in Brooklyn—Another Opinion on the Prohibitory Liquor Law," *New York Times*, May 12, 1855; "Opinion on the New York Temperance Law," *New Yorker Staats Zeitung*, May 12, 1855; "Another Opinion," *New York Times*, Jun. 11, 1855.

32. "Fermentation Among the N.Y. Liquor Dealers," *Boston Traveller*, Apr. 16, 1855; "The Maine Liquor Law Meeting of Hotel Proprietors at the Astor House," *New York Times*, Apr. 16, 1855; "New York Affairs," *Atlanta Weekly Intelligencer*, Jun. 5, 1855; "Instructions to Liquor Dealers," *New York Times*, Jul. 4, 1855; "The Liquor Traffic in Brooklyn," *New York Times*, Jun. 27, 1855.

33. "The Maine Liquor Law Meeting of Hotel Proprietors at the Astor House," *New York Times*, Apr. 16, 1855; "Liquor Dealers," *New York Times*, May 8, 1855; "The Liquor Traffic in Brooklyn," *New York Times*, Jun. 27, 1855; "The Liquor Law in Buffalo," *Augusta* (GA) *Chronicle*, Jun. 20, 1855.

34. "Kings County Liquor Dealers' Association," *New York Times*, May 1, 1855. On the fate of Maine Laws before the several state high courts, see especially Tyrrell, *Sobering Up*, 290–293; William J. Novak, *The People's Welfare: Law and Regulation in Nineteenth-Century America* (Chapel Hill, 1996), 177–189, 326. Though Wynehamer's membership in the Buffalo Liquor Dealer Association is unclear, it seems unlikely that he would have avoided joining or could have afforded the costs of appealing his case to the Court of Appeals without assistance from the association. On organized resistance in Buffalo, see "Anti-Maine Law Meeting in Buffalo," *Albany Evening Journal*, Jun. 26, 1855; "Anti-Maine Law Meeting in Buffalo," *New York Evening Express*, Jun. 27, 1855; "The Liquor Dealers of Buffalo," *Jamestown* (NY) *Journal*, Jun. 29, 1855.

35. *Wynehamer v. The People*, 13 NY 378, 383–385, 406 (1856); Novak, *People's Welfare*, 186–187; Lex Renda, "Slavery, Law, Liquor, and Politics: The Case of *Wynehamer v. The People*," *Mid-America* 80 (Winter 1998), 35–53.

36. 13 NY 378, 386–387.

37. *Beebe v. State*, 6 Ind. 401, 416–417 (1855); "The liquor dealers…," *Weekly Reveille* (Vevay, IN), Jul. 4, 1855. See also *Herman v. State*, 8 Ind. 490, 506 (1855).

38. *Scott v. Sandford*, 60 U.S. 393; Don Ferenbacher, *The Dred Scott Case: Its Significance in American Law and Politics* (New York, 1978); Austin Allen, *Origins of the Dred Scott Case: Jacksonian Jurisprudence and the Supreme Court, 1837–1857* (Athens, GA, 2006). Scholars debate the legacy of *Wynehamer*'s enunciation of

"substantive due process" and its relationship to *Dred Scott*. See the contrasting positions of Edward S. Corwin, "The Doctrine of Due Process of Law before the Civil War," *Harvard Law Review* 24 (Apr., 1911), 460–479; James W. Ely Jr., "The Oxymoron Reconsidered: Myth and Reality in the Origins of Substantive Due Process," *Constitutional Commentary* 16 (Summer 1999), 315–346; Austin Allen, "An Exaggerated Legacy: Dred Scott and Substantive Due Process," in *The Dred Scott Case: Historical and Contemporary Perspectives on Race and Law*, ed. David Thomas Konig, Paul Finkelman, and Christopher Alan Bracey (Athens, OH, 2010), 83–99; Jed Shugerman, "Economic Crisis and the Rise of Judicial Elections and Judicial Review," *Harvard Law Review* 123 (March 2010), 1063–1150; Matthew J. Lindsay, "In Search of 'Laissez-Faire Constitutionalism,'" *Harvard Law Review Forum* 123 (March 2010), 55–78.

39. "The Great Municipal Question of the Day—The Rights of Minorities," *New York Herald*, Jul. 3, 1857; "Temperance Convention," *The Lily*, Jan. 15, 1856; "State Temperance Convention at Albany," *New York Times*, Dec. 20, 1856.

40. Gale, *The Present License System*, 11; "The New Liquor Law," *New York Herald*, Apr. 23, 1857; "Opposition to the Liquor Law in Buffalo," *New York Herald*, Apr. 27, 1857; "Various Items," *Chicago Tribune*, Jun. 13, 1857; "Liquor Dealers' Appeal," *Journal of the American Temperance Union and New York Prohibitionist* 22 (Dec. 1858), 181–182. See also "The License Law—The Liquor Dealers and the State Temperance Society," *New York Times*, Apr. 28, 1857; "Organized Opposition," *Chicago Tribune*, Apr. 29, 1857; "Affairs in Albany," *New York Herald*, Apr. 29, 1857; "The Liquor Dealers' Association," *New York Sun*, May 8, 1857.

41. *California Laws, 1858*, 124–125; *Ex Parte Newman*, 9 Cal. 502, 510, 513–514 (1858).

42. "The Sabbath," *Boston Investigator*, Aug. 4, 1858; "Sunday Laws," *Occident and American Jewish Advocate* 16 (Sep. 1858), 282; "The German Republican Club and the Sunday Law," *Utica Morning Herald*, Aug. 31, 1858; "The Sunday Law Decision," *Israelite* (Cincinnati), Aug. 6, 1858; "Sunday Law Decisions," *Israelite*, Sep. 24, 1858; "Sunday Law Decisions," *Israelite*, Oct. 1, 1858; "Sunday Laws Unconstitutional," *Brooklyn Eagle*, Aug. 7, 1858; "Religious Intelligence," *New York Herald*, Aug. 8, 1858.

43. "Anti-Sunday Law Jollification in Sacramento," *Daily Evening Bulletin* (San Francisco), Jun. 30, 1858; "Rejoicings," *San Joaquin Republican*, Jul. 3, 1858; "Future Enforcement of the Sunday Laws—A Warning," *Daily Evening Bulletin*, Jun. 4, 1858; "Observance of the Sunday Law," *Sacramento Daily Union*, Jun. 7, 1858; "Sunday Law," *Sacramento Daily Union*, Jun. 9, 1858; "Prosecutions," *San Joaquin Republican*, Jun. 12, 1858; "Violation of the Sunday Law," *Sacramento Daily Union*, Jun. 14, 1858; "Our San Francisco Correspondence," *New York Herald*, Jul. 28, 1858; "Sunday Law and the French," *Daily Evening Bulletin*, Jul. 10, 1858.

44. "The Liquor Dealers and the Sunday Law Again," *Daily Evening Bulletin*, Jun. 10, 1858; "Another Meeting of the Liquor Dealers," *Daily Evening Bulletin*, Jun.

11, 1858; "Resisting the Sunday Law," *San Joaquin Republican*, Jun. 12, 1858; "Resisting the Sunday Law," *San Joaquin Republican*, Jun. 12, 1858.

45. "The Topics of the Week," *Frank Leslie's Illustrated Newspaper*, Aug. 6, 1859; "The Sunday Question," *Quincy* (IL) *Daily Herald*, Jul. 30, 1859; "The Sunday Question," *New York Times*, Aug. 8, 1859.

46. "A Nation's Right to Worship God," *Biblical Repertory and Princeton Review* 31 (Oct. 1859), 697; "The Sunday Question," *New York Times*, Feb. 10, 1858; "Another Sabbath-Observance Meeting at Yonkers," *New York Tribune*, Nov. 9, 1858; "The Sabbath Meeting at Irving Hall," *New York Observer and Chronicle*, Feb. 21, 1861; New York Sabbath Committee, *The Sabbath as It Was and As It Is* (New York, 1858), 2–3; "Sabbath Laws in Newark," *New York Observer and Chronicle*, Jul. 22, 1858; "The Sunday Question," *Chicago Tribune*, Jul. 21, 1859; Alexis McCrossen, *Holy Day, Holiday: The American Sunday* (Ithaca, NY, 2000), 41–46.

47. "The Clergy Upon Sabbath Desecration," *Chicago Tribune*, Jul. 16, 1859; "The Sunday Question," *Chicago Tribune*, Jul. 30, 1859; "The Sabbath Question," *Chicago Tribune*, Dec. 31, 1859; "Sunday Legislation," *Boston Investigator*, Apr. 23, 1858; "An Anti-Sunday Car Meeting," *Sabbath Recorder*, Mar. 14, 1861; "Sunday or No Sunday," *Christian Observer*, Sep. 29, 1859.

48. *Twentieth Anniversary of the Philadelphia Sabbath Association* (Philadelphia, 1861), 5; "History of the Institution of the Sabbath Day," *Biblical Repertory and Princeton Review* 31 (Oct. 1859), 743.

49. *Sunday Legislation. Proceedings of a Public Meeting, held in the City of Buffalo, February 13, 1858, Against Closing the Canal Locks and Stopping the Mails on Sunday, and against Sunday Legislation Generally* (Buffalo, 1858), 8; "The Sunday Question in Philadelphia," *New York Herald*, Aug. 1, 1859; "Observance of the Sabbath," *New York Herald*, Aug. 7, 1859.

50. "Equal Laws—*For Sunday too*," *Baltimore Sun*, Aug. 2, 1859; "The Sunday Law," *Daily Ohio Statesman*, Nov. 11, 1858; "Sabbatarianism," *National Anti-Slavery Standard*, Jan. 30, 1858.

51. "A German View," *Chicago Tribune*, Aug. 4, 1859; "The Sunday Law—Meeting of the Germans," *Boston Investigator*, Feb. 16, 1859.

52. "Sunday Laws," *Davenport* (Iowa) *Daily Gazette*, Nov. 28, 1859.

53. New York Sabbath Committee, *Progress of the Sabbath Reform* (New York, 1860), 19; "The Sabbath Meeting at Irving Hall," *New York Observer and Chronicle*, Feb. 21, 1861; Erskine Norman White, *Norman White: His Ancestors and His Descendants* (New York, 1905), 56–57, 75–77; Philip L. White, *The Beekmans of New York in Politics and Commerce* (New York, 1956), 553–630; Sven Beckert, *The Monied Metropolis: New York City and the Consolidation of the American Bourgeoisie, 1850–1896* (New York, 2001), 28, 75. On the political climate surrounding the Metropolitan Police Act, see Burrows and Wallace, *Gotham*, 838–839; Mary Ryan, *Civic Wars: Democracy and Public Life in the American City during the Nineteenth Century* (Berkeley, CA, 1997), 151–157; Paul Weinbaum,

"Temperance, Politics, and the New York City Riots of 1857," *New York Historical Society Quarterly* 59 (1975), 246–270; Stanley Nadel, *Little Germany: Ethnicity, Religion, and Class in New York City, 1845–80* (Chicago, 1990), 132–133.

54. "Rev. J. L. Hatch," *The Congregationalist* (Boston), May 28, 1858; "The Rev. J. L. Hatch," *New York Times*, Jul. 1, 1858; "Letter from the Rev. J. L. Hatch, Concerning his Dismissal from a Pastoral Charge," *New York Times*, Jul. 3, 1858; "The Rev. J. L. Hatch and the Church of the Puritans," *New York Tribune*, Mar. 4, 1859; "More Trouble in Dr. Cheever's Church," *Boston Investigator*, Mar. 16, 1859.

55. "Church and State—A new Sunday Law called for," *Brooklyn Eagle*, Feb. 5, 1858; "Liberty versus Partisan Legislation," *New York Herald*, Feb. 27, 1858; "Religious Intelligence," *New York Times*, Jun. 26, 1858; "The Rev. J. L. Hatch and the Sabbath," *New York Times*, Jun. 30, 1858; "The Question of the Day," *New York Herald*, Jul. 24, 1859; J. L. Hatch, *The Sabbath, A Festival: Appointed for Recreation and Enjoyment* (New York, 1858); "Observance of the Sabbath," *New York Herald*, Aug. 7, 1859; "Sunday Laws in New York," *New York Herald*, Aug. 14, 1859; "The Challenge not Accepted," *Boston Investigator*, Sep. 8, 1858; "Sunday Laws," *New York Herald*, Sep. 3, 1859; "The Sunday Relaxation Movement—Sunday Laws and their Effect," *New York Herald*, Jul. 3, 1859.

56. "Police Commissioners," *New York Times*, Jul. 2, 1859; "Anti-Sunday Law Remonstrance," *Boston Investigator*, Jul. 27, 1859.

57. "The Great Question of the Day—Organized Opposition to the Sunday Laws," *New York Herald*, Jul. 21, 1859; "German Association and the Sunday Laws," *New York Herald*, Jul. 21, 1859; "The German Republican Central Committee," *New York Times*, Dec. 14, 1861; "City Intelligence," *New York Herald*, Dec. 15, 1861; "The German Republican Central Committee," *New York Times*, Jan. 13, 1862. On New York City's German community, see especially Nadel, *Little Germany*.

58. "German Association and the Sunday Laws," *New York Herald*, Jul. 21, 1859; "Organized Opposition to Sunday Laws," *Sabbath Recorder*, Aug. 4, 1859. On New York's liquor dealer associations, see "The Liquor-dealers," *New York Times*, Nov. 2, 1858; "Liquor Dealers' Appeal," *Journal of the American Temperance Union* 22 (Dec. 1858), 181–182; "From the City of New York," *Daily National Intelligencer*, Aug. 5, 1859; "A Dwindling Giant," *New York Times*, Aug. 26, 1859; "The Liquor and Lager Dealers," *New York Times*, Oct. 6, 1859; "Liquor Dealers," *New York Times*, May 2, 1860.

59. "Anti-Sabbath Agitation," *New York Tribune*, Sep. 14, 1859; "The Anti-Sabbatarian Movement," *New York Herald*, Sep. 14, 1859; "Anti-Sabbatarian Meeting," *New York Times*, Sep. 14, 1859; "The Anti-Sunday-Law Movement," *Sabbath Recorder*, Sep. 22, 1859. On continued activism of these groups and the work of the committee, see "The Candidates Catechised," *New York Herald*, Dec. 6, 1859; "Wood's Election a Triumph over Sabbatarianism," *New York Herald*, Dec. 10, 1859; "New York Legislature," *New York Herald*, Dec. 31, 1860; "Sunday Laws in the Legislature," *Sabbath Recorder*, Jan. 17, 1861; "Mass Meeting," *New York*

Herald, Mar. 2, 1861; "Anti-Sunday Law Demonstration," *New York Times*, Mar. 4, 1861; "The Sunday Law," *New York Herald*, Mar. 18, 1861; "The Anti-Sunday Law Movement," *New York Herald*, Mar. 25, 1861.

60. New York Sabbath Committee, *Sunday Theatres, "Sacred Concerts" and Beer-Gardens* (New York, 1860); "The Second Sunday Amusement Law," *New York Herald*, Mar. 26, 1860; "Another Sunday Law," *New York Herald*, Mar. 26, 1860.

61. "A number of German…," *Brooklyn Eagle*, Mar 12, 1860; "Small Beer Instead of Lager," *New York Times*, Mar. 21, 1860; "A mass meeting…," *Brooklyn Eagle*, Apr. 26, 1860; "The German Innkeepers…," *New York Herald*, Apr. 27, 1860; "The Germans and the Sunday Law in New York," *Vermont* (Montpelier) *Patriot*, May 19, 1860; "The Sunday Law and the German Press," *New York Times*, May 28, 1860; "Thwarting the Police," *New York Times*, Jun. 1, 1860; "The Sunday Question," *New York Times*, Jun. 13, 1860; "The Anti-Sunday Law Movement," *Brooklyn Eagle*, Jun. 28, 1860; "The Sunday Law Indictments," *New York Herald*, Jun. 2, 1860; "The Violators of the Liquor Law," *New York Times*, Jun. 2, 1860; "General Sessions," *New York Times*, Jun. 6, 1860; "Court of General Sessions," *New York Herald*, Jun. 9, 1860; "The Sunday Liquor Cases…," *Brooklyn Eagle*, Jun. 13, 1860; "Law Reports," *New York Times*, Jun. 16, 1860; "The Sunday Law," *New York Times*, Jun. 20, 1860; "Law Reports," *New York Times*, Jun. 22, 1860; "The Sunday Law Question," *New York Times*, Jun. 26, 1860; "Law Reports," *New York Times*, Jun. 28, 1860; "A Sunday Law Laid on the Shelf," *New York Herald*, Jul. 22, 1860; "Common Sense in Brooklyn, N.Y.," *Boston Investigator*, Aug. 1, 1860.

62. "An Incident Illustrating the Enforcement of the Sunday Law," *New York Evening Express*, Apr. 24, 1860; "The German Theatrical Managers…," *New York Evening Express*, May 7, 1860; "Lager Bier, &c., on Sunday," *New York Tribune*, Aug. 6, 1860; "Court of Oyer and Terminer," *New York Times*, Nov. 19, 1860; "Arrests Under the New Sunday Law," *New York Tribune*, Apr. 26, 1860; "The Germans and the Sunday Law," *New York Times*, May 2, 1860; "How the Sunday Laws are Evaded," *Public Ledger* (Philadelphia), May 10, 1860; "Another Saloon Closed up," *New York Times*, Oct. 20, 1860; "The Sunday Theatre Law," *New York Times*, Nov. 19, 1860; "The German Shaker Association," *Philadelphia Inquirer*, Nov. 20, 1860; "The Sunday Theatre Case—A Conviction," *New York Herald*, Nov. 21, 1860; "The Lager Bier Dodge," *New York Evangelist*, Nov. 29, 1860; "As to the Constitutionality of the 'Sunday Law' in New York," *Daily Evening Bulletin*, Dec. 10, 1860; "A 'Lager Beer' Denomination," *Anti-Slavery Bugle* (Salem, OH), Jan. 12, 1861

63. "Court of Oyer and Terminer," *New York Times*, Nov. 19, 1860; "Court of Oyer and Terminer," *New York Tribune*, Nov. 20, 1860; "The Oyer and Terminer," *New York Evening Express*, Nov. 22, 1860; "Constitutionality of the Sunday Law—Opinion of the General Term," *New York Times*, Jun. 4, 1861; *Lindenmuller v. The*

People, 33 Barb. 548 (1861); "The Death of James T. Brady," *New York Times*, Feb. 10, 1869.

64. "The Constitutionality of the Sunday Laws," *American Theological Review* 12 (Oct. 1861), 693–710; "Legal Protection of the Sabbath," *Daily National Intelligencer* (Washington, DC), Nov. 2, 1861. For more on Lindenmuller, see Donald Erlenkotter, "Gustavus Lindenmueller: The Myth, the Man, the Mystery," *Civil War Token Society* (Feb. 2011), http://cwtsociety.com/AOTM/index.html, accessed Jun. 15, 2012.

65. "Sunday…," *Sabbath Recorder*, May 9, 1861; McCrossen, *Holy Day, Holiday*, 46–49; "Notice," *Daily Evening Bulletin*, Aug. 1, 1861; "Liquor Dealers," *Daily Evening Bulletin*, Aug. 6, 1861; "Association Against the Sunday Law," *Daily Evening Bulletin*, Aug. 9, 1861; *Ex Parte Andrews*, 18 Cal. 679 (1861); "Enthusiastic Sunday Law Meeting," *Daily Evening Bulletin*, Nov. 13, 1861; "The Sunday Law," *Daily Evening Bulletin*, Sep. 28, 1861.

66. "The Sunday Law," *Daily Alta California* (San Francisco), Oct. 4, 1861; John Stuart Mill, *On Liberty and Other Writings* [1859], ed. Stefan Collini (New York, 1989), 8, 88–91. See also "The Sunday Law," *Weekly Gleaner*, Oct. 11, 1861; "Sunday Laws in California," *Occident and American Jewish Advocate* (Jan. 1862), 454–457.

67. "Baltimore-Sunday Laws," *Israelite* (Cincinnati), Jun. 26, 1857; "The Sunday Law," *Daily Alta California*, Oct. 4, 1861.

68. "How the Sunday Law was Observed Yesterday," *Daily Evening Bulletin*, Sep. 30, 1861; "The Barbers and the Sunday Law," *Daily Evening Bulletin*, Oct. 12, 1861; "Cigar Dealers," *Daily Evening Bulletin*, Nov. 9, 1861; "Anti-Sunday-Law-League at Stockton," *Daily Evening Bulletin*, Dec. 16, 1861; "Liquor Dealers," *Sacramento Daily Union*, Sep. 3, 1861; "The San Francisco Sabbath Committee Moving," *Daily Evening Bulletin*, Dec. 19, 1861; "The Sunday Law Question," *Daily Evening Bulletin*, Oct. 6, 1862; *Proceedings of the National Sabbath Convention held at Saratoga Springs, Aug. 11–13, 1863* (New York, 1864), 3.

EPILOGUE

1. *United States v. Windsor*, 570 U.S. ___ (2013), 25–26; *Hollingsworth v. Perry*, 570 U.S. ___ (2013).

2. George Chauncey, "The Long Road to Marriage Equality," *New York Times*, Jun. 26, 2013.

3. *House of Representatives Report on Defense of Marriage Act* (Washington, DC, 1996), 15–16; *Romer v. Evans*, 517 U.S. 620, 653 (1996); Maggie Gallagher, "Above the Hate," Townhall.com, Nov. 25, 2008.

4. *Lawrence v. Texas*, 539 U.S. 558, 571 (2003); Martha T. Moore, "Gov. Chris Christie, a Catholic, Tiptoes on Gay Marriage," *Washington Post*, Jul. 17, 2013; "Gay Marriage: Civil Unions Aren't a Substitute," *Philadelphia Inquirer*, Jan. 30, 2012.

5. American Foundation for Equal Rights, "Sir Elton John to Join Prop. 8 Case with Private L.A. Benefit," Nov. 30, 2010; Moore, "Gov. Chris Christie," *Washington Post*, Jul. 17, 2013; Richard Kim, "Why Gay Marriage Is Winning," *The Nation*, Jul 2, 2013, www.thenation.com; Erik Eckholm, "Both Sides on Same-Sex Marriage Focus on Next Battlegrounds," *New York Times*, Jun. 27, 2013.

6. *Proceedings of the First Annual Meeting of the National Equal Rights League, held in Cleveland, Ohio* (Philadelphia, 1865), 38–44; Hugh Davis, *"We Will Be Satisfied With Nothing Less": The African American Struggle for Equal Rights in the North during Reconstruction* (Ithaca, NY, 2011). The NERL, of course, was only one important mode of black political activism in the aftermath of the Civil War. See Stephen Hahn, *A Nation under Our Feet: Black Political Struggles in the Rural South from Slavery to the Great Migration* (Cambridge, MA, 2003).

7. "The Washington Convention," *Christian Recorder*, Jan. 26, 1867; "Civil Rights—Call for a National Convention," *Chicago Tribune*, Nov. 6, 1873; "The National Equal Rights League," *Christian Recorder*, Feb. 2, 1867; "An Appeal," *Elevator*, Mar. 14, 1865; "Letter from Rev. Benjamin Lynch," *Christian Recorder*, Sep. 23, 1865; "Communications," *Elevator*, Jun. 30, 1865; "Letter from Harrisburg," *Christian Recorder*, Oct. 7, 1865; "Proceedings of the Annual Meeting of the Pennsylvania Equal Rights' League," *Christian Recorder*, Nov. 18, 1865; "The Equal Rights' Leagues," *Christian Recorder*, Feb. 17, 1866; "The National Equal Rights League," *Christian Recorder*, Feb. 2, 1867; "School Privileges for Colored Children," *Christian Recorder*, Jul. 21, 1866; "Things About Cincinnati, Long live the Equal Rights League," *Anglo-African*, Dec. 23, 1865; "Indianapolis Correspondence," *Christian Recorder*, Nov. 17, 1867; Davis, *We Will Be Satisfied*; Roger A. Fischer, "A Pioneer Protest: The New Orleans Street-Car Controversy of 1867," *Journal of Negro History* 53 (Jul. 1968), 219–233. For court action, see J. Morgan Kousser, *Dead End: The Development of Nineteenth-Century Litigation on Racial Discrimination* (New York, 1986); Barbara Young Welke, *Recasting American Liberty: Gender, Race, Law, and the Railroad Revolution, 1865–1920* (New York, 2001); Davison M. Douglas, *Jim Crow Moves North: The Battle over Northern School Segregation, 1865–1954* (New York, 2005); Davis, *We Will Be Satisfied*.

8. "New York's Lack of Public Spirit," *New York Age*, Sep. 20, 1890; *Eighteenth Annual Report of the National Association for the Advancement of Colored People* (New York, 1928), 5; "The Legal Rights Association," *The Crisis* 75 (June–July 1968), 197–199. On black rights activism in the late nineteenth century, see Leslie A. Schwalm, *Emancipation's Diaspora: Race and Reconstruction in the Upper Midwest* (Chapel Hill, 2009); Shawn Leigh Alexander, *An Army of Lions: The Civil Rights Struggle before the NAACP* (Philadelphia, 2012); Susan D. Carle, *Defining the Struggle: National Organizing for Racial Justice, 1880–1915* (New York, 2013). On the NAACP and the continuing struggles for civil rights in the twentieth century, see Mark V. Tushnet, *The NAACP's Legal Strategy against*

Segregated Education, 1925–1950 (Chapel Hill, 1987); Patricia Sullivan, *Lift Every Voice: The NAACP and the Making of the Civil Rights Movement* (New York, 2009); Michael J. Klarman, *From Jim Crow to Civil Rights: The Supreme Court and the Struggle for Racial Equality* (New York, 2004); Thomas J. Sugrue, *Sweet Land of Liberty: The Forgotten Struggle for Civil Rights in the North* (New York, 2008); Glenda Gilmore, *Defying Dixie: The Radical Roots of Civil Rights, 1919–1950* (New York, 2008).

9. "Sunday Liquor Traffic a Disgrace," *New York Tribune*, Jun. 3, 1876; "Newark's Quiet Sunday," *New York Sun*, Apr. 29, 1879; "Shut up the Saloons," *Rocky Mountain News*, Feb. 11, 1889; "By Sunday Laws," *Milwaukee Sentinel*, Jun. 24, 1889; "Lager is King," *Cincinnati Enquirer*, Mar. 16, 1866; "From Indianapolis," *Cincinnati Enquirer*, Apr. 10, 1866; "The New Liquor Law in New York," *Cincinnati Enquirer*, May 4, 1866; "Interrupted by a Dog," *Washington Post*, Jan. 13, 1890. On Sunday laws in nineteenth-century courts, see Andrew J. King, "Sunday Law in the Nineteenth Century," *Albany Law Review* 64 (2000), 675–772; Steven K. Green, *The Second Disestablishment: Church and State in Nineteenth-Century America* (New York, 2010), 345–351.

10. *Equal Rights in Religion. Report of the Centennial Congress of Liberals, and Organization of the National Liberal League, at Philadelphia, on the Fourth of July, 1876* (Boston, 1876), 5, 75–83; Steven K. Green, *The Bible, the School, and the Constitution: The Clash That Shaped Modern Church-State Doctrine* (New York, 2012), 138–175; Green, *Second Disestablishment*, 334–339. On the Christian amendment, see Gaines M. Foster, *Moral Reconstruction: Christian Lobbyists and the Federal Legislation for Morality, 1865–1920* (Chapel Hill, 2002). On Kilgore, see Elizabeth K. Maurer, "The Sphere of Carrie Burnham Kilgore," *Temple Law Review* 65 (1992), 827–854.

11. "Against Prohibition," *Morning Oregonian* (Portland), Nov. 1, 1887; "The 'Personal Liberty League'…," *North American* (Philadelphia), Oct. 26, 1882; *Minutes of the Twentieth Annual Convention of the Connecticut Temperance Union* (Hartford, CT, 1886), 15; *The Sixteenth Annual Report of the Connecticut Temperance Union* (Hartford, 1882), 15; K. Austin Kerr, *Organized for Prohibition: A New History of the Anti-Saloon League* (New Haven, CT, 1985), 27–31; Amy Mittelman, *Brewing Battles: A History of American Beer* (New York, 2008); Richard F. Hamm, *Shaping the 18th Amendment: Temperance Reform, Legal Culture, and the Polity, 1880–1920* (Chapel Hill, 1995), 48–91.

12. "Wheeler Clashes with Darrow Here in Dry Law Debate," *New York Times*, Apr. 24, 1927. Darrow himself was a part of that continued activism, serving on the NAACP's legal committee in the late 1920s. See *Seventeenth Annual Report of the National Association for the Advancement of Colored People* (New York, 1927), iv.

13. *United States v. Carolene Products*, 304 U.S. 144 (1938); James T. Patterson, "The Rise of Rights and Rights Consciousness in American Politics, 1930s–1970s," in *Contesting Democracy: Substance and Structure in American Political History,*

1775–2000, ed. Byron E. Shafer and Anthony J. Badger (Lawrence, KS, 2001), 201–223; Mark Tushnet, "The Rights Revolution in the Twentieth Century," in *The Cambridge History of Law in America*, vol. 3, ed. Michael Grossberg and Christopher Tomlins (New York, 2008), 377–402; John D. Skrentny, *The Minority Rights Revolution* (Cambridge, MA, 2002).

14. "India's Historic Ruling on Gay Rights," *Time*, Jul. 2, 2009; Vanessa Gera, "Lech Walesa Shocks Poland with Anti-gay Words," *Yahoo! News*, Mar. 3, 2013; Albert Che Suh-Nwji, "Role of Diaspora in Post–Arab Spring Reconstruction—Analysis," *Eurasia Review*, Jul. 21, 2013; "Former Anglican Bishop Warns of 'Tyranny of the Majority' in Mideast Region," *Christian Post*, Aug. 5, 2013.

Index

ne lovejoy (?)